Shaw

SHAW

An Autobiography

1856–1898

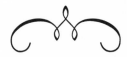

Selected from his writings by
STANLEY WEINTRAUB

Weybright and Talley
NEW YORK

The editor is grateful to the Academic Center Library,
University of Texas at Austin, for permission to publish extracts
from manuscript material as identified in the end-notes.

First printing, August, 1969
Second printing, January, 1970

Published in the United States by
WEYBRIGHT AND TALLEY, INC.,
3 East 54th Street,
New York, New York 10022.

Published simultaneously in Canada by
CLARKE, IRWIN & COMPANY LIMITED,
Toronto and Vancouver.

Library of Congress Catalog Card Number: 74-84621

PRINTED IN THE UNITED STATES OF AMERICA

Contents

G.B.S.: SKETCHES FOR A SELF-PORTRAIT, vii

Illustrations appear after page 48

G.B.S.

Sketches for a Self-Portrait

WHEN BERNARD SHAW was a young man, he observed from the safety of an anonymous book review that an autobiography was "usually begun with interest by reader and writer alike, and seldom finished by either. Few men care enough about their past to take the trouble of writing its history. Braggarts like Benvenuto Cellini, and morbidly introspective individuals like Rousseau, are the exceptions that prove the rule." A generation later—although he was guilty himself by then of perpetrating scattered pieces of memoir—he had not changed his mind. "The autobiographer," he gibed to compulsive autobiographer Frank Harris, "is the dog returning to his vomit." Serious memoirists, he thought, proved the weakness of the form by avoiding themselves in their histories. Goethe, for example, found it necessary to retreat from the subject of himself to write about uninteresting and otherwise-forgotten friends of his youth, while Wagner wrote more vividly about his musical associates than himself, and even Rousseau faded out of his own confessions as his favorite subject became an adult. He understood the reaction, Shaw told Harris. "I find I can't go over my autobiographical stuff again, not only from lack of time, but from loathing."

Whatever the reasons, G.B.S. resisted the urge to fashion a formal autobiography, and waited until his nineties to piece together a scrappy substitute, out of his own confessions. Building upon *Shaw Gives Himself Away,* a thin volume of essays and extracts privately printed (in 300 copies) in 1939, he produced a trade-edition parallel, *Sixteen Self Sketches* (1949). Few of the sketches were new, while some of the sixteen were no more than unannounced revisions of essays published as much as fifty years before. Obviously Shaw, over the years, had had much more to say about himself, and had done so elsewhere and at great length, but even with a curious concluding section of padding labeled "Biographers' Blunders Corrected," the *Sketches* ran to only 134 pages. Why the passed-over pieces escaped inclusion he failed to explain, but why all of them were originally written was made carefully clear: "Only when I can make a case of myself, economic, artistic, sociologic, or what not, can I make literary use of myself. . . ." Shaw made literary use of himself—and wrote his autobiography—all his life.

Always a believer in the utilitarian function of the writer's art, he saw no valid aesthetic or psychological excuse for memoir-production and condemned as misguided any reader interest in the private life of an author—"because the actual facts of an author's life are for the most part mere accidents, and have no more to do with his genius than the shape of his nose; less, in fact." It was the reason why, he said, when people asked him why he did not write his own life he would reply, "I am not at all interesting biographically. . . . Nothing very unusual has happened to me." Amid the protestations, Shaw nevertheless continued to write several very different kinds of self-portraits, identifying the most public of himself as the subtle and not always subconscious autobiography one can read between the lines of his novels and plays. "Things have not happened to me: on the contrary, it is I who have happened to them," he explained, underplaying himself, "and all my happenings have taken the form of books and plays. Read them, or spectate them; and you have my whole story: the rest is only breakfast, lunch, dinner, sleeping, wakening and washing. . . ."

Elsewhere, too, Shaw confessed as much. To Frank Harris he had pointed out that he never would have thought of the idea of Joey Percival, the boy with three fathers in *Misalliance* (1909), had he not had three fathers himself. The three of them, we learn in the play, "took charge of Joey's conscience. He used to hear them arguing like mad about everything. . . . Between the lot of them Joey got cultivated no end." In Dublin, Shaw had his legal father, his medical Uncle Walter and his unofficial musical mentor "Professor" Lee. Lee even lived in the Shaw house in Hatch Street, and when Uncle Walter came to visit, the three men gossiped and argued into the morning—and young G.B.S. listened. There is even a naive young clerk in the play, employed, like the teenage Shaw in Dublin, as a cashier proud of never being a farthing wrong in his accounts.

Shaw's clerkship was first fictionalized in his first novel, *Immaturity* (1879), in which there is little unsupported by early Shavian experience—his hero's encounters with employers, preachers, artists, romantic and rationalistic women, with the Chelsea and South Kensington locales in which he prowled, solitarily, full of extravagant thoughts about his future. Both "Smith" and Shaw perform the barren drudgery of their clerkships conscientiously, despise their employers, loathe their servility, and retain so much of the vocation after their resignations that each writes in the best commercial style, painstakingly perfected in large canvas-covered ledgers.

The young genius in London, frustrated by the rejection of his early fiction by every publisher to which he took his manuscripts, and defensively cultivating within himself a defiant self-sufficiency, is magnified by Shaw in his third novel into a turbulent British Beethoven. Unwilling to bow to popular taste for cheap success Owen Jack, of *Love Among the Artists* (1881), insists, "I must make my own music, such as it is or such as I am. . . ." So with Shaw, although he narrowly missed popular success with *Cashel Byron's Profession* (1882), a novel of ideas based broadly upon his own experiences as amateur boxer and reader of *Bell's Life*. Shaw's last completed novel, *An Unsocial Socialist* (1883), was another self-portrait, this time of the young Marxist missionary who, like his hero Sidney Trefusis, was beginning to discover that while he ran from women who had designs upon him, he was still fascinatedly drawn to them. "Poverty and fastidiousness" kept him from "a concrete love affair" until he was twenty-nine, he wrote Frank Harris, but "the five novels I wrote before that . . . show much more knowledge of sex than most people seem to acquire after bringing up a family of fifteen."

Covert confessions and sly self-portraits turn up in many of his plays. The No. 1 Hatch Street *ménage à trois* of George Carr Shaw, Lucinda Shaw and George John Lee is suggested in the 1908 comedy *Getting Married*. G.B.S.'s philanderings with widow Jenny Patterson and actress Florence Farr, which led to a hair-pulling match over him, become the basis for an altercation between the two female leads in *The Philanderer* (1893), while Charteris, the hero, is a variation upon the author. Shaw's infatuation with phonetic language is translated into Professor Higgins of *Pygmalion* (1913), while his infatuation with the play's first Eliza, Mrs.

Patrick Campbell (which led to her once trying to physically restrain him from leaving her to meet his wife) is translated into the closely parallel amatory interlude in *The Apple Cart* (1929). Even his prosaically happy marriage with Charlotte has its parallels in the dowdy but devoted and practical queens of *The Apple Cart* and *In Good King Charles's Golden Days* (1939), while additional Shavian self-portraits appear in the articulate young revolutionary John Tanner of *Man and Superman* (1903) and in Captain Shotover, the ageing postwar prophet of *Heartbreak House* (1920). "The best autobiographies are confessions," he observed in his last years; "but if a man is a deep writer, all his works are confessions."

Shaw's earliest confessional work was his diary, at first an irregular scrappy collection of jottings begun in a tuppence notebook in 1872, when he was a teenage clerk in the Dublin office of Charles Uniacke Townshend. But for some cryptic personal references, such as to youthful infatuations, it was a careful record of expenditures and encounters, suggesting erroneously that the young man was temperamentally well-suited to the ledger and the cashier's stool. As his life became more complex, so did some of the entries, which recorded—in the London continuation of his notes—beginnings of fads, friendships, and attempts at fiction-writing, experiences with vegetarianism, smallpox, speechmaking, French verbs and German economics. The journal faded out in 1884, and in the following year Shaw began a different kind of diary—more informative, because it detailed not only his multifarious professional and social activities but what he ate and how he slept, yet paradoxically less informative than before, because he kept the diary in his own idiosyncratic version of Pitman shorthand, an appropriate medium for an eccentric life of erratic hours, irregular food, occasional income and unusual friends. Enthusiasm for the journal often flagged, but Shaw persisted with it, sometimes catching up omissions with extended *ex post facto* entries. But by 1894 it had become more engagement book than diary, and by the end of 1897 his diary was blank, a victim of his increasingly complicated juxtaposition of careers.

Although the diaries were personal rather than public documents, meant for an audience of one, Shaw later returned to the journal form as a deliberately autobiographical method, meant for publication, noting on the third day of the new venture, "I am going to try to keep [the diary] for a year, as a sample slice of my life." But the notes, begun with gusto on January 1, 1917, faltered to nothing in a fortnight. With the experiment abandoned, there was always other personal writing he could turn to, especially his private letters, although there too he appeared to be writing for the small audience of the recipient and himself. Still, when Shaw, in mid-career, recorded portions of his outer and his inner life in the many thousands of his letters, he had long since reached certainty that his letters—even the most terse of his postcards—would be preserved by his friends, treasured by his admirers, hoarded by library archivists and sold and re-sold by manuscript dealers. Once he had become a public figure, his private letters, whether or not he desired it so, were largely destined for posterity. He could not help but write for it.

Some of Shaw's letters were deliberately and calculatedly confessional— the hundreds of them he wrote to interviewers and biographers, in a generally successful effort to satisfy them beyond their desire to search further than he cared to have them probe, to throw them off—if necessary —troublesome scents, to establish a persona consistent with his public image. Yet at the same time, the writing of them was often a considerable and a considerate effort to provide facts. In many cases, grateful biographers used Shaw's words verbatim and at great length. One of his many long letters to his first biographer Archibald Henderson—then a young mathematics professor in North Carolina—ran to fifty-four pages. (Frugally, Shaw later cribbed heavily from his copy of the letter when writing the autobiographical preface to *London Music*.) Shaw not only came close to writing the first Henderson biography (of three) himself; he offered suggestions for its construction and even for its promotion. Keep on the lines, he recommended, "of Boswell's Johnson and Lockhart's Scott, not to mention Plutarch. . . . If you really want an introduction, better let *me* write it." Shaw was more serious than Henderson could have imagined, for when Frank Harris and Hesketh Pearson began their Shavian biographies, their subject not only provided much of the information in interviews and letters, but then rewrote large sections of the text himself— assistance far more elaborate than the furnishing of an introduction.

G.B.S. would have done the same in other cases, if given the opportunity, but usually was sufficiently generous by mail. One scholar even more obscure than was Henderson at the time Shaw authorized his biographical researches—Henderson had a recent doctorate from Chicago, albeit in mathematics—was Thomas Denis O'Bolger, whose queries elicited eager offerings of autobiography from Shaw, in letters primarily about the Dublin years. O'Bolger was an Irishman resident in Philadelphia, writing a doctoral dissertation on the most famous living Irishman, and Shaw found it difficult to refuse a fellow émigré. Letter after letter crossed the Atlantic, with details about Shaw's Dublin relatives and about the curious *ménage à trois* in Hatch Street, where young George had two fathers in residence, a phlegmatic, alcoholic legitimate one, and a fascinating, musical surrogate one. But when O'Bolger drew disturbing inferences from the household arrangements, G.B.S. prevented O'Bolger's biography from being published. Eventually Shaw published some of the letters mildly altered. But even earlier he had drawn upon the material himself, for the autobiographical preface to the belated first publication of his first novel. He had kept, he confided to Frank Harris in 1918, copies of many of the autobiographical letters ("notes" he called them) he had sent to Henderson and O'Bolger, and it had occurred to him to look up the file "and publish a recast of it as my own, on a plan of my own." The fact that he had carefully retained copies and drafts of the lengthy confessional correspondence may only have been Shaw's usual business-like behavior, but it may also be a clue as to how long the writing of his own autobiography (in a substantial manner) had been in the back of his mind.

Although Shaw was just as calculatedly helpful to Frank Harris, he had more logical reasons to help him than he had to provide an unknown young mathematics professor or an even more obscure doctoral candidate in literature with the crucial original materials likely to create an academic or authorial reputation for the recipient. He felt twinges of old journalistic loyalties toward the disreputable Harris, who had made for himself a shaky new career as a memoirist, not only with the censorable *My Life and Loves,* but more legitimately by way of a series of biographical magazine pieces he labeled "Contemporary Portraits." Near the end of his financial rope as well as the end of his life, Harris had seized desperately upon a commission from an American publisher to do a biography of Shaw. Knowing Harris's penchant for scandal, G.B.S. reluctantly agreed to supply material to the down-and-out ex-editor for whose magazine a generation before he had written his famous theater columns. Even that failed, for Harris completed only sixty-five faltering pages before his health cracked altogether and ghost writer Frank Scully took over, completing the job by the use of paid researchers and Shaw's letters. Harris saw the proofs before he died, but never saw Shaw's later corrections and additions. As far as Shaw was concerned, it was mostly his book, although Scully had told him after examining the printed version that the text was really seventy-two percent Scully (often through rewriting Shaw's letters), twenty-two percent Shaw and two percent Harris. In any case, Harris's widow got the royalties, and Shaw had his autobiographical way with another biography.

Earlier, in 1919, Shaw had already practiced the Harris style. His "How Frank Would Have Done It" was a self-portrait in the third person which parodied Harris's biographical method. Its purpose may have been sheer spoofery, yet its effect was to reduce to absurdity some of the tales about his life Shaw did not want taken seriously. Harris, grateful for something saleable in his drab, declining years, published it in an otherwise lame volume of his *Contemporary Portraits,* but—Shaw thought— "I cannot believe he ever read it." No praise of Shaw was ever more fulsome—or more obviously ironic.* No disparaging anecdote then printable was left out. "Dramatizing myself from an objective point of view," Shaw observed, was a "method [which] came natural to me. . . ." (Pursuing the illusion of objectivity, he later used third-person headings for all the pieces he included in *Shaw Gives Himself Away,* suggesting that an editor, rather than the subject, had chosen and arranged the selections; but afterwards, in a belated burst of honesty, he pencilled into the printer's proofs a *me* or an *I* to replace each *Shaw.*)

Since Harris relished. writing about his subjects' sex lives, Shaw furnished what Harris might have discovered—or invented, concluding with a tale involving Beerbohm Tree and Mrs. Patrick Campbell:

> Shaw's gallantries are for the most part non-existent. He says, with some truth, that no man who has any real work in the world has time or money for a pursuit so long and expensive as the pursuit of women. . . . Nobody knows the history in this respect, as he is far too correct a person to kiss and tell. To all appearances he is a model husband; and in the various political movements in which his youth was passed there was no scandal about him. Yet a popular anecdote describes a well known actor manager as saying one day at rehearsal to an actress of distinguished beauty, "Let us give Shaw a beefsteak and put some red blood into him." "For heaven's sake don't!" exclaimed the actress: "he is bad enough as it is; but if you give him meat, no woman in London will be safe."

* Oscar Wilde said of him, Shaw wrote (as "Harris"), "He has not an enemy in the world; and none of his friends like him." As "Harris" he added, "If I cannot say that Shaw touches nothing that he does not adorn, I can at least testify that he touches nothing that he does not dust and polish and put back in its place much more carefully than the last man who handled it."

"How Frank Would Have Done It" was one of many autobiographical effusions Shaw produced in the third person, most of them taking the less formal form of self-interviews purporting to be live and spontaneous give-and-take. But there were also elaborate third-person attempts, some serious efforts to control his history, others only private jokes, such as the elaborate one he created for Cyril Maude. In November, 1902, Shaw wrote —for Maude's *History of the Haymarket Theatre*—a good humored chapter (XXVII) describing the disastrous rehearsals there for a production of *You Never Can Tell*. The comedy had never come off, because of differences between the author and the management as to how it was to be handled. As Shaw had the exaggeratedly dour actor-manager tell the story, the crisis became inevitable when the playwright turned up at rehearsals in his curious limp one-piece health-suit manufactured by Dr. Jaeger. "Nobody," the author chronicled, "who had not seen Mr. Shaw sitting there day after day in a costume which the least self-respecting carpenter would have discarded months before, could possibly have understood the devastating effect of the new suit on our minds. . . ." The clash of personalities ended, "Maude" explained, when it was agreed to withdraw the play; but he had, nevertheless, retained great admiration for Shaw's talents in other fields than the theatrical. "In any other walk of life than that of a dramatic author, I should expect him to achieve a high measure of success. I understand that he has made considerable mark as a vestryman (for the London borough of St. Pancras) collecting dust with punctuality, and supervising drainage with public-spirited keenness. . . ."

Forty years later Shaw spent months rewriting and adding to Hesketh Pearson's biography, first making pencilled corrections and interpolations Pearson could rewrite and rub out, and red-inked comments meant for background rather than for publication. Pearson, who had received fifteen times his usual publisher's advance on the strength of Shaw's consent to let the book be done, tried to hurry the elaborate corrections and amplifications, but Shaw shrugged off the importunities with "You don't know how long this takes." Turning over the last installment he assured Pearson that he could have written three plays in the time that it took him to revise and emend the information based on the so-called authorities Pearson had consulted. "Posterity," Pearson replied with as much sarcasm as he felt he could get away with, "will be grateful to me." The wit was not lost on Shaw, whose reaction, Pearson afterwards thought, "lacked restraint."

The problem for the biographer was that he had been saddled, both for better and for worse, with the autobiographer as collaborator. Thinking of ways to emphasize as an attractive feature of the book what Shaw had referred to as the "unique private history" he had contributed to it, Pearson came up with the suggestion that all the Shavian additions and revisions to be shown in the text between square brackets or by indentation in the usual manner. "Not on your life, Hesketh!" Shaw exploded. "What I have written I have written in your character, not in my own. As an autobiographer I would have written quite differently. There are things that you may properly say which would come less gracefully from me." Pearson could, Shaw conceded, acknowledge personal help from his subject, including consultation on points of fact. "But if a word is said to connect me with the authorship of the book . . . I shall be driven to the most desperate steps to disclaim it. If you are not prepared to father my stuff, you can rewrite it; but you must not publish it as mine. . . ." Pearson took the hint and sent the copy to the printer unchanged. But Shaw had more to say, sending on several additional pages with recommendation that they not be de-Shavianized out of concern that "readers—least of all the critics—will spot any difference between your stuff and mine. They won't. In the Harris book they didn't. If the story carries them along they won't start detective work; and, anyhow, my style won't disgrace you."

The press of potential Boswells compelled Shaw to tell more than one prospective chronicler that he had exhausted himself as a subject for books: "Everything about me that is of the smallest public interest has been told, and very well told by myself. . . ." Much of potential public interest he found useful to evade, disguise or ignore, but such prefaces as those to *Plays Pleasant and Unpleasant* (1898), *Immaturity* (1930) and *London Music* (1937) he had written substantially as memoirs. Less noticeable autobiography was written into his drama and music criticism: a leaflet entitled *Trade Unionism for Clerks;* introductions or afterwords to books by or about such political or theatrical colleagues as Sydney Olivier, Lillah MacCarthy, William Archer, Ellen Terry and Henry Salt; BBC talks; Fabian essays and lectures; City Temple sermons; periodical and newspaper journalism—even to letters-to-the-editor—and other publications which lent themselves to personal statements and asides. This overt telling of his own story, of memoirs written as such, in prefaces and articles and reviews, in political tracts, pamphlets and polemical essays, in sermons, self-interviews and speeches, was his fourth variety of autobiography, and the only one written in the spirit of true autobiography. It had been a task often urged upon Shaw, but not in the piecemeal, occasional way he supplied it. "What one really wishes," J.C. Squire had appealed in 1915, "is that Mr. Shaw would write his own biography. The numerous small portions of it which he has produced have given us a great thirst for the whole. If he cannot find time to write it, let him hire a corps of typists and dictate it."

In time Shaw largely fulfilled Squire's hopes, for however much he was an ascetic in other ways, he was seldom guilty of self-denial as an auto-biographer; and in his own defense he had provided justification for this side of his writing early in his career. "It is quite true," he wrote Henderson in 1904, "that the best authority on Shaw is Shaw. My activities have lain in so many watertight compartments that nobody has yet given anything but a sectional and inaccurate account of me except when they have tried to piece me out of my own confessions." Accordingly, for forty-six more years—the second half of his long life—he continued to produce pages of additional "confessions," the raw material for what is very likely one of the great biographies in the English language.

This edition reconciles and integrates some of the "numerous small portions" of raw material into autobiographical continuity with the larger, more formal segments of memoir. But for an occasional bridging work (in editor's square brackets) the prose is Shaw's own, unaltered except by omission; for G.B.S. produced many more words, even of confessions, than would be viable in a volume or two devoted to piecing them to-gether. Here is Shaw as he wanted the world to remember him—not the only G.B.S., but perhaps the most likeable and entertaining G.B.S., and close enough to the real thing, that, like Hamlet with Yorick's skull, Shaw could look on the result and own that he knew the subject well.

Stanley Weintraub

Preface

ALL AUTOBIOGRAPHIES are lies. I do not mean unconscious, unintentional lies: I mean deliberate lies. No man is bad enough to tell the truth about himself during his lifetime, involving, as it must, the truth about his family and his friends and colleagues. And no man is good enough to tell the truth to posterity in a document which he suppresses until there is nobody left alive to contradict him.

People keep asking me why I do not write my own biography. I reply that I am not at all interesting biographically. I have never killed anybody. Nothing very unusual has happened to me. The first time I had my hands examined by a palmist he amazed me by telling me the history of my life, or as much of it as he had time for. Apparently he knew about things I had never told to anyone. A few days later I mentioned in conversation with a friend (William Archer) that I had been dabbling in palmistry. He immediately put out his hand and challenged me to tell him anything in his life that I did not know from my acquaintance with him. I told him about himself exactly what the palmist had told me about myself.

He too was amazed, just as I had been. We had believed our experiences to be unique, whereas they were ninetynine-point-nine per cent. the same; and of the point-one per cent. the palmist had said nothing.

It was as if a couple of monkeys had believed their skeletons to be unique. To the extent of a bone or two they would have been right; for anatomists tell us that no two skeletons are exactly alike. Consequently a monkey is fully entitled to exhibit his unique bone or two as curiosities; but the rest of his skeleton he must reject as totally uninteresting. He must keep it to himself on pain of boring people with it intolerably.

And here comes my difficulty as an autobiographer. How am I to pick out and describe that point-five per cent. of myself that distinguishes me from other men more or less fortunate than I? What earthly interest is there in a detailed account of how the illustrious Smith was born at Number Six High Street, and grew taller and taller until he was twenty, when the obscure Brown, Jones, and Robinson, born at Number Seven, Eight, and Nine, went through exactly the same routine of growing, feeding, excreting, dressing and undressing, lodging and moving? To justify a biography Smith must have had adventures. Exceptional things must have happened to him.

Now I have had no heroic adventures. Things have not happened to me: on the contrary it is I who have happened to them; and all my happenings have taken the form of books and plays. Read them, or spectate them; and you have my whole story: the rest is only breakfast, lunch, dinner, sleeping, wakening, and washing, my routine being just the same as everybody's routine. Voltaire tells you in two pages all you need know about Moliere's private life. A hundred thousand words about it would be unbearable.

Then there is the difficulty that when an adventure does come, somebody else is usually mixed up in it. Now your right to tell your own story does not include the right to tell anyone else's. If you violate this right, and the other party still lives, you are sure to be indignantly contradicted; for no two people recollect the same incident in the same way; and very few people know what has actually happened to them, or could describe it artistically. And biographies must be artistic if they are to be readable.

The best autobiographies are confessions; but if a man is a deep writer all his works are confessions. One of the greatest men who ever attempted an autobiography was Goethe. After his childhood, which is the readablest part of even the worst autobiography, his attempts to escape from his subject are pitiable. He takes refuge in sketches of all the Toms, Dicks, and Harrys he knew in his youth, persons utterly unmemorable, until the book drops from your hand and is not picked up again. I am one of the very few people who have read Rousseau's confessions through to the end, and can certify that from the moment when he ceases to be a rather rascally young adventurer, and becomes the great Rousseau, he might as well be anybody else for all one can grasp or remember of his everyday life.

Of Madame de Warens when he was sixteen I have a lively recollection. Of Madame d'Houdetot when he was fortyfive I have not the faintest impression, and remember only the name. In short, the confessions tell us next to nothing of any importance about the adult Rousseau. His works tell us everything we need to know. If Shakespear's everyday life from his birth to his death were to come to light, and Hamlet and Mercutio to be simultaneously lost, the effect would be to substitute a perfectly commonplace man for a very interesting one. In the case of Dickens so much is known about him that might have happened to Wickens or Pickens or Stickens that his biographers have obliterated him for those who do not read his books, and for those who do, spoilt his portrait very painfully.

Therefore the autobiographical fragments which pad this volume do not present me from my own point of view, of which I am necessarily as unconscious as I am of the taste of water because it is always in my mouth. They tell you mostly what has been overlooked or misunderstood. I have pointed out, for instance, that a boy who knows the masterpieces of modern music is actually more highly educated than one who knows only the masterpieces of ancient Greek and Latin literature. I have illustrated the wretched lot in our society of the Downstart, as I call the boy-gentleman descended through younger sons from the plutocracy, for whom a university education is beyond his father's income, leaving him by family tradition a gentleman without a gentleman's means or education, and so only a penniless snob. I have thought it well to warn the young that it is as dangerous to know too much as to know too little, to be too good as to be too bad, and how Safety First lies in knowing and believing and doing what everyone knows and believes and does.

These things are mentioned not because I have been unbearably persecuted nor as yet assassinated, but because they concern my whole Downstart class, and, when intelligibly stated and understood, may help to make it class conscious and better behaved. Thus, being incorrigibly didactic, I violate the biographical laws I began this apology with by telling you little about myself that might not have happened to a thousand Shaws, and a million Smiths. Perhaps our psycho-analysts may find in such dull stuff clues that have escaped me.

To relieve the dulness there are tales of my relatives which must be read as ordinary fiction, the Irish Family Shaw having been occasionally funnier than the Swiss Family Robinson, and perhaps not less instructive to those who are capable of such instruction. As to myself, my goods are all in the bookshop window and on the stage: what is communicable has been already communicated in a long life of which, though I cannot say that no day of it has been left without a written line, yet I have perhaps brought it as near to that Roman ideal as is healthily and humanly possible.

G.B S

1

My First Biographer

HE WAS my father, George Carr Shaw, writing from his office at 67 Jervis Street in the City of Dublin, where the firm of Clibborn & Shaw operated as corn merchants, not very efficiently, as Clibborn had been trained to the cloth trade, and my father to no trade at all, having been an ex-civil servant whose department in the Four Courts had been abolished and its staff pensioned. He had sold his pension, and with the capital thus procured, joined Clibborn in the business which neither of them understood, but which with offices and a warehouse in Jervis Street and a water mill in Rutland Avenue, a romantic looking village suburb of Dolphin's Barn, itself a suburb, seemed to them a promising investment. On the strength of it my father married in his middle age; and the union produced three children: the eldest Lucinda Frances (Lucy), Elinor Agnes (Aggie or Yuppy), and finally a son George (Sonny): in short, myself.

In July 1857, when I was a year old, my mother left our home in Synge Street on a visit to her father Walter Bagenal Gurly, a country gentleman of Carlow family but resident at Oughterard in Galway though for the moment his address was Kinlough in Leitrim. My mother, christened Lucinda Elizabeth Gurly (Bessie), took Lucy with her to Kinlough, leaving me and Yuppy in charge of our father.

Their correspondence begins my biography. I cannot verify it, having not the faintest recollection of learning to walk and being called Bob. However, here it is.

17 July 1857
Poor whiggedie whellow was very sick in his stomach about 1 o'clock

in the night, but he is all right and as brisk as ever this morning. Nurse attributes it to some currants he ate.

20.7.

The young beggar is getting quite outrageous. I left him this morning roaring and heaving like a bull. I expect he will be able to run down the street to meet you when you are returning.

22.7.

Nurse is in great blood about having the young chap able to walk when you come back, besides I am sure she thinks it will be a great relief to herself. He made a famous attempt this morning. They were all to have gone up to your Aunt's to-day [Aunt Ellen Whitcroft].

24.7.

Bob flitterd his hat to pieces yesterday and Nurse says I must give him a new one. I told her to do so herself and I will pay her, so I suppose I will be stuck. . . . Nurse says that Bob walked in great style for your Aunt.

27.7

Nurse and Sarah [housemaid] and the two little people came over after Church and had a Royal feast in the garden. . . . Nurse got a new hat for Bob and nothing short of a Tuscan would do her so I had to hand over 10/-. However it was his birthday and so I will say nothing.[1] . . . Yup and Bob both fell out of bed yesterday morning on the tops of their heads; neither appears to have been hurt, but they might have been.

28.7.

Bobza honors me with his company and we have walking matches together. His exploits in that way have not yet extended beyond a couple of yards which he performs in a plunge from Nurse to me and back again to Nurse or Caroline Brabazon [G.B.S.'s godmother], whoever happens to be in possession at the time being. His hat is very grand but I think Nurse will be walking into you for feathers for it when you come home.

[Undated] Sunday morning. ½ past 11 as usual.

Bob spent some time in bed with me this morning as did also breakfast etc., . . . He just got a toss but after a few roars is now laughing.

[6]

30.7.

I brought the two youngsters out yesterday morning and gave them a drive in the perambulator which they, indeed I too, enjoyed greatly. Bob is growing very unruly. The *threshing season* is approaching and he had better look out or I'll flail him.

3.8.

I will feel disappointed every morning that Bob does not stagger into me with a letter from you—and desperate fighting there is to get it from him. The young ruffian tore the newspaper this morning. Nurse and her two charges left home yesterday with the intention of spending the day at Kingstown but she happened to look in at the shop in King St and found that Miss Malone was in town which to her great disappointment put a stop to the expedition. Monday next has now been fixed for the Excursion.

6.8.

I was home in the middle of the day and had a good ½ hour's fun with Yup and Bob. . . . Cecilia [his sister, G. B. S.'s Aunt Ciss] has called to see the children.

7.8.

Nurse said to me this morning that Bob has her nearly broken down! And indeed he must be a very tiresome youngster to mind altogether without any help.

8.8.

I delivered your kisses to Yup and Bob but contrary to your instructions I fobbed a few for myself—you know how sweet a stolen kiss is!

11.8.

Poor Bob had a narrow escape on Tuesday morning. He was sitting on the kitchen table in charge of Nurse, who merely, she says, stooped down to pick up something off the floor, when he suddenly fell back and his head went slap through a pane of glass and against the iron bar outside; miraculous to say he was not even scratched; had he fallen with his face against the glass he would have been ruined. I was in my dressing room at the time, and when I heard the crash I ran down and found Nurse so paralysed with terror that she could hardly lift the poor fellow up. I do not know how the poor fellow escaped; but it does not appear to have given him even a pane in his head.

15.8.

Poor Bob is annoyed with his teeth, and is consequently very uneasy both day and night.

2

A Boy in Dublin

THE SCENE of one of Mr. Arnold Bennett's novels is laid in a certain *cul de sac* off the Brompton Road, nearly opposite the West Brompton District Post Office. He calls it Alexandra Grove; but its actual name is Victoria Grove. As he describes it, the houses now contrive a double rent to pay, as the gardens have been fitted up with studios, thus quietly modernizing London by the back-to-back housing so vehemently denounced as a relic of barbarism in Leeds. When I arrived there as an Irish emigrant of 20, this intensification of population had not occurred. The houses were semi-detached villas with plenty of air space round them (you could call it garden). On the other side of the back wall were orchards; for the huge Poor Law Infirmary which now occupies this space, with its tower on the Fulham Road, was not yet built. The land between West Brompton and Fulham and Putney, now closely packed with streets and suburban roads, had still plenty of orchard and market garden to give it a countrified air and to make it possible to live there, as I did for years, without feeling that one must flee to the country or wither in the smoke. All the parallel Groves connected the Fulham Road with King's Road, Chelsea, where Cremorne Gardens, an unlaid ghost from the eighteenth century, was desperately fighting off its final exorcism as a rendezvous of the half world. Hence these now blameless thoroughfares were then reputed Bohemian, whilst Victoria Grove, as a blind alley, remained as respectable as Clapham.

I came to London from Dublin in the spring of 1876, and found my mother and my one surviving sister[1] (I had no brothers) established in No. 13 Victoria Grove, trying to turn their musical accomplishments to account: my mother by teaching, my sister by singing. My father, left in Dublin, spared us a pound a week from his slender resources; and by getting into debt and occasionally extracting ourselves by drawing on a maternal inheritance of £4000 over which my mother had a power of appointment, and which therefore could be realized bit by bit as her three children came of age, we managed to keep going somehow.

Impecuniosity was necessarily chronic in the household. And here let me distinguish between this sort of poverty and that which furnishes an element of romance in the early lives of many famous men. I am almost tempted to say that it is the only sort of poverty that counts, short of the privations that make success impossible. We all know the man whose mother brought him up with nineteen brothers and sisters on an income of eighteen shillings a week earned by her own labor. The road from the log cabin to the White House, from the bench in the factory to the Treasury Bench, from the hovel to the mansion in Park Lane, if not exactly a crowded road, always has a few well fed figures at the end of it to tell us all about it. I always assure these gentlemen that they do not know what poverty and failure is. Beginning with as much as they expected or were accustomed to, they have known nothing but promotion. At each step they have had the income of the society in which they moved, and been able to afford its clothes, its food, its habits, its rents and rates. What more has any prince? If you would know what real poverty is, ask the younger son of a younger son of a younger son. To understand his plight you must start at the top without the income of the top, and curse your stars that you were not lucky enough to start at the bottom.

Our institution of primogeniture may have been a feudal necessity. It kept the baronies together; and the barons and their retainers kept the king and the country supplied with an army, a magistracy, and a network of local governments. But it took no account of the younger sons. These unhappy ones were brought up in the baronial castle. Let us represent the income of the barony by the figure 1000. Both sons and daughters were brought up to know no other mode of life than life at this figure. When the eldest took all, what was there left for the girls' dowries and the boys' allowances? Only the scrapings and leavings of the mother's dowry, and such charity as the new baron might choose (if he could afford it) to bestow on his poor relations. A younger son's figure, especially if he had many brothers, might easily be 20 or less, even to zero. What was the poor wretch to do, knowing no other way of living but the way that cost 1000? Easy to tell him that he must cut his coat according to his cloth. Impossible to do it without being trained to that measure from childhood. Impossible anyhow without dropping every relative and friend in the world, and stepping down, a mistrusted, ridiculous, incongruous stranger, into the social circle of his mother's maid and his brother's butler. Impossible often even to go into the army, where an officer cannot live on his pay unless he is a promoted ranker in a line regiment, and not even then with any ease. There is nothing for it but to live beyond one's income, to spunge, to beg, to take credit at the shops without means, to borrow without the prospect of being able to repay, and to blackmail the baron by presenting him with a choice between paying up and having his brother haled before the criminal courts for swindling. The alternative (to marry the daughter of a rich *parvenu,* American or British) is not always available. Who would be an Honorable on such terms if he could help it?

But think of his son, and of his son's son: the undisguised commoner, for whom, because it costs too much, there is not even the public school and university education of the baron's cadet, and who cannot avail himself of the public elementary and secondary schools because such a step would disclass the man of family! Think of the attempt to go into business with some pitiful little capital! think of the struggle to make the loathed occupation yield a living! think of the son for whom there is nothing but a clerkship in the office of some goodnatured business acquaintance! and bear in mind that the descent implies that every generation is, like the original younger son, brought up to a mode of life more expensive than its income can compass; so that it is condemned to pull the devil by the tail from its adolescence to its grave!

. . . My father was second cousin to a baronet, and my mother the daughter of a country gentleman whose rule was, when in difficulties, mortgage. That was my sort of poverty. The Shaws were younger sons from the beginning, as I shall shew when I reveal my full pedigree. Even the baronetcy was founded on the fortunes of a fifth son who came to Dublin and made that city his oyster. Let who will preen himself on his Mother Hubbard's bare cupboard, and play for sympathy as an upstart: I was a downstart and the son of a downstart.

. . . One of my grandfathers was clever with his hands. His "study" was fitted like a carpenter's shop. He built his own boats, and would have been a valuable member of society as a craftsman living by his talent. Unfortunately his station was that of a country gentleman, forbidden to make money by his gift of manual dexterity. For the management of his landed estate he had not the smallest aptitude. He did not even live on it: as sport was not good there he moved to another and wilder county, where he hunted and shot and fished (in the boat he built for himself) consummately; for he could ride any horse, however unmanageable, and was a dead shot with any sort of firearm. Meanwhile all he did as a landlord was to leave his estate in charge of an agent, and mortgage it until it was completely insolvent. He was not naturally incompetent or inactive, very much the reverse: he was a square peg in a round hole. In a sensibly organized society he would have had a useful and prosperous career as a craftsman. As a member of the landed gentry he was—what he was.

One of my greatgrandfathers did much better by practising an extraordinary social imposture. To all appearances he was a country gentleman intermarrying with the best county blood in Ireland. Yet all the time he was amassing riches by secretly carrying on the business of a pawnbroker in one of the poorest quarters in Dublin. His life should have been chronicled by Samuel Smiles as an example of Self Help. How he contrived to have a greatgrandson so utterly destitute of his qualities as I am remains a biological mystery. I should hardly have weathered my early years of rejection by the publishers but for what was left of the profits of his pawnbroking.

This social *degringolade* never stops in these islands. It produces a class which deserves a history all to itself. Do not talk of the middle class: the expression is meaningless except when it is used by an economist to denote the man of business who stands in the middle between land and capital on the one hand, and labor on the other, and organizes business for both. I sing my own class: the Shabby Genteel, the Poor Relations, the Gentlemen who are No Gentlemen. If you want to know exactly where I came in, you will get at such facts as that of my many uncles only one, the eldest, contrived to snatch a university education. The rest shifted as best they could without it (rather better than he, mostly). One distinguished himself as a civil servant. He had a gun, and went shooting. One made a fortune in business, and attained to carriage horses; but he lost the fortune in a premature attempt to develop the mineral resources of Ireland without waiting for the new railways produced by the late war. Two emigrated to Tasmania, and, like Mr. Micawber, made history there. One was blind and dependent on his brothers: another became blind later, but remained independent and capable. One aunt married the rector of St Bride's (now demolished) in Dublin. The others married quite prosperously, except the eldest, whose conception of the family dignity was so prodigious (the family snobbery being unmitigated in her case by the family sense of humor) that she would have refused an earl because he was not a duke, and so died a very ancient virgin. Dead or alive, there were fourteen of them; and they all, except perhaps the eldest, must have had a very straitened time of it in their childhood after their father died, leaving my grandmother to bring up an unconscionable lot of children on very inadequate means. The baronet came to the rescue by giving her a quaint cottage, with Gothically pointed windows, to live in at Terenure (we called the place Round-town). It stands in, or rather creeps picturesquely along, its little walled garden near the tram terminus to this day, though my grandfather's brass helmet and sword (he was in the Yeomanry or Militia as a gentleman amateur soldier) no longer hang in the hall. Professionally, he was some sort of combination of solicitor, notary public, and stockbroker that pre-vailed at that time. I suspect that his orphans did not always get enough to eat; for the younger ones, though invincibly healthy and long lived, were not athletic, and exhibited such a remarkable collection of squints (my father had a stupendous squint) that to this day a squint is so familiar to me that I notice it no more than a pair of spectacles or even a pair of boots.

On the whole, they held their cherished respectability in the world in spite of their lack of opportunity. They owed something perhaps, to the confidence given them by their sense of family. In Irish fashion they talked of themselves as the Shaws, as who should say the Valois, the Bourbons, the Hohenzollerns, the Hapsburgs, or the Romanoffs; and their world conceded the point to them. I had an enormous contempt for this family snobbery, as I called it, until I was completely reconciled to it by a certain Mr Alexander Mackintosh Shaw, a clansman who, instead of taking his pedigree for granted in the usual Shaw manner, hunted it up, and published 100 copies privately in 1877. Somebody sent me a copy; and my gratification was unbounded when I read the first sentence of the first chapter, which ran: "It is the general tradition, says the Rev. Lachlan Shaw [bless him!], that the Shaws are descended of McDuff, Earl of Fife." I hastily skipped to the chapter about the Irish Shaws to make sure that they were my people; and there they were, baronet and all, duly traced to the third son of that immortalized yet unborn Thane of Fife who, invulnerable to normally accouched swordsmen, laid on and slew Macbeth. It was as good as being descended from Shakespear, whom I had been unconsciously resolved to reincarnate from my cradle.[2]

Years after this discovery I was staying on the shores of Loch Fyne, and being cooked for and housekept by a lady named McFarlane, who treated me with a consideration which I at first supposed to be due to my eminence as an author. But she undeceived me one day by telling me that the McFarlanes and the Shaws were descended from the Thanes of Fife, and that I must not make myself too cheap. She added that the McFarlanes were the elder branch.

I was born in Dublin in 1856, which may be taken as 1756 by London reckoning. I was contemporary with Swift and Johnson, and even with Samuel Pepys; for the smoke of battle from the Boyne had not cleared away from my landscape, nor the glorious pious and immortal memory of Dutch William faded from my consciousness, when my sense of history was formed. . . . The fact that I am an Irish Protestant, and that I published a volume called Three Plays for Puritans, has created a legend about the gloomy, sour, Sabbath-ridden, Ulster-Covenanting home in which I was brought up, and in which my remarkable resemblance to St. Paul, St. Anthony, and John Knox was stamped on me. . . . (As a matter of fact I was brought up in an atmosphere in which two of the main constituents were Italian opera and complete freedom of thought; and my attitude to[ward] conventional British life ever since has been that of a missionary striving to understand the superstitions of the natives in order to make himself intelligible to them.)

I believe Ireland, as far as the Protestant gentry is concerned, to be the most irreligious country in the world. I was christened by my uncle; and as my godfather was intoxicated and did not turn up, the sexton was ordered to promise and vow in his place, precisely as my uncle might have ordered him to put more coals on the vestry fire. I was never confirmed; and I believe my parents never were either. Of the seriousness with which English families took this rite I had no conception; for Irish Protestantism was not then a religion: it was a side in political faction, a class prejudice, a conviction that Roman Catholics are socially inferior persons who will go to Hell when they die and leave Heaven in the exclusive possession of Protestant ladies and gentlemen. In my childhood I was sent every Sunday to a Sunday-school where genteel little children repeated texts, and were rewarded with cards inscribed with them. After an hour of this we were marched into the adjoining church (the Moly-neux in Upper Leeson Street), to sit round the altar rails and fidget there until our neighbors must have wished the service over as heartily as we did.

. . . To sit motionless and speechless in your best suit in a dark stuffy church on a morning that is fine outside the building, with your young limbs aching with unnatural quiet, your restless imagination tired of speculating about the same grown-up people in the same pews every Sunday, your conscience heavy with the illusion that you are the only reprobate present sufficiently wicked to long for the benediction, and to wish that they would sing something out of an opera instead of Jackson in F, not to mention hating the clergyman as a sanctimonious bore, and dreading the sexton as a man likely to turn bad boys out and possibly to know them at sight by official inspiration: all this is enough to lead any sensitive youth to resolve that when he grows up and can do as he likes, the first use he will make of his liberty will be to stay away from church. . . . I suffered this, not for my salvation, but because my father's respect-ability demanded it. When we went to live in Dalkey we broke with the observance and never resumed it.

My uncles did not trouble about Macduff: it was enough for them that they were Shaws. They had an impression that the Government should give them employment, preferably sinecure, if nothing else could be found; and I suppose this was why my father, after essaying a clerkship or two (one of them in an ironworks), at last had his position recognized by a post in the Four Courts, perhaps because his sister had married the brother of a law baron. Anyhow the office he held was so undeniably superfluous that it actually got abolished before I was born; and my father naturally demanded a pension as compensation for the outrage. Having got it, he promptly sold it, and set up in business as a merchant dealing wholesale (the family dignity made retail business impossible) in flour and its cereal concomitants. He had an office and warehouse in Jervis Street in the city; and he had a mill in Dolphin's Barn on the country side of the canal, at the end of a rather pretty little village street called Rutland Avenue. The mill has now fallen to pieces; but some relics of it are still to be seen from the field with the millpond behind Rutland House at the end of the avenue, with its two stone eagles on the gate-posts. My father used to take me sometimes to this mill before breakfast (a long walk for a child); and I used to like playing about it. I do not

ing mountain, a sort of Primrose Hill. On the peak there was perched a small, pinched, upper part, and on top of that a human head. That, to me, at the period of life when one is young and receiving indelible impressions, was a woman. One day, when I was perhaps five years of age, a lady paid us a visit, a very handsome lady who was always in advance of the fashion. Crinolines were going out; and she had discarded hers. I, an innocent unprepared child, walked bang into the room and suddenly saw, for the first time, a woman not shaped like Primrose Hill, but with a narrow skirt which evidently wrapped a pair of human legs. I have never recovered from the shock, and never shall.

After that, there was a certain reaction. Primrose Hill began to be reproduced again in various shapes, with bustles at the back and things of that sort. You see them in the old numbers of Punch, in pictures by Leech and others. But, generally speaking, the reduction of women to vulgar flesh and blood continued to be prevented by a system of dressing not at all like what we now know as dressing a woman. In fact, woman was not dressed in the sense we are familiar with. She was upholstered. She was dressed in upholstering fabrics called reps; and if she was not studded with buttons all over her tempting contours like a sort of super-sofa, she was pinched in and padded out so as to produce as much of that effect as possible. You do not remember that. I do. The last woman who bravely kept up the upholstered appearance to the end was my late friend Marie Corelli. She being gone, I look round the world, and I do not see any woman now who is upholstered.

I lived on to an advanced age, and received another shock. I received a visit at Adelphi-terrace from a foreign princess, a very charming woman bearing the name of one of Napoleon's marshals. She sat down on the sofa, and I talked to her; and as she had a very pretty face I was principally occupied by that. But after we had been conversing—though I do not know that she had much chance in the conversation; so let us say when I had been shewing off for a quarter of an hour—I paused for breath, and in the course of my pausing I happened to look down. To my utter amazement I discovered that her skirt came only to her knees. I had never before seen such a spectacle except on the stage. I thought, "Great Heavens! the princess has forgotten her skirt!"; and I almost lost my presence of mind. Well, now all that is gone; I can stand any amount of ladies with their skirts to their knees without turning a hair.

I am telling you all this with a serious purpose. The dress has changed, but the morality has not. People are still full of the old idea that woman is a special creation. I am bound to say that of late years she has been working extremely hard to eradicate that impression.

. . . If my father had been able to turn his social opportunities to account, I might have had a quite respectable and normal social training. My mother, socially very eligible, was made welcome in all directions. She sang very well; and the Shaws were naturally a musical family. All the women could "pick out tunes" on the piano, and support them with the chords of the tonic, subdominant, dominant, and tonic again. Even a Neapolitan sixth was not beyond them. My father played the trombone, and could vamp a bass on it to any tune that did not modulate too distractingly. My eldest uncle (Barney: I suppose I was called Bernard after him; but he himself was Uncle William) played the ophicleide, a giant keyed brass bugle, now superseded by the tuba. Berlioz has described it as a chromatic bullock; but my uncle could make it moo and bellow very melodiously. My aunt Emily played the violoncello. Aunt Shah (Charlotte), having beautiful hands, and refinements of person and character to match them, used the harp and tambourine to display them. Modern readers will laugh at the picture of an evening at Bushy Park, with the bachelor Sir Robert and his clan seated round an ottoman on which my uncle Barney stood, solemnly playing Annie Laurie on the ophicleide. The present distinguished inheritor of the title may well find it incredible. But in those days it was the fashion for guests to provide their own music and gentlemen to play wind instruments as a social accomplishment: indeed that age of brass is still remembered and regretted by the few makers of musical instruments whose traditions go back far enough.

And now you will ask why, with such unexceptional antecedents and social openings, was I not respectably brought up? Unfortunately or fortunately (it all depends on how you look at it) my father had a habit which eventually closed all doors to him, and consequently to my mother, who could not very well be invited without him. If you asked him to dinner or to a party, he was not always quite sober when he arrived; and he was invariably scandalously drunk when he left. Now a convivial drunkard may be exhilarating in convivial company. Even a quarrelsome or boastful drunkard may be found entertaining by people who are not particular. But a miserable drunkard—and my father, in theory a teetotaller, was racked with shame and remorse even in his cups—is unbearable. We were finally dropped socially. After my early childhood I cannot remember ever paying a visit at a relative's house. If my mother and father had dined out, or gone to a party, their children would have been much more astonished than if the house had caught fire.

My mother was the daughter of a country gentleman, and was brought up with ruthless strictness to be a paragon of all ladylike virtues and accomplishments by her grand aunt, whom I remember from my very early childhood as a humpbacked old lady with a pretty face, whose deformity seemed to me quaintly proper to her as a beneficent fairy. Had she known the magically favorable impression she made on me, she would perhaps have left me her property; and I now believe I was brought to her in the hope that I should attract her to this extent. But I was a failure. She had brought my mother up to make such a distinguished marriage as would finally wipe out an unmentionable stain on her pedigree; for though on her parents' side her extraction was everything that could be desired, her grandfather was a mysterious master spirit whose birth was so obscure that there was some doubt as to whether he ever had any legal parents at all. Under cover of the name of an employee named Cullen, he had made a fortune by keeping a pawnshop in one of the poorest quarters of Dublin. Meanwhile, by assuming the rank of country gentleman at a "seat" in the County Dublin, he married into a genuine county family.

But still he kept the pawnshop and the pawnshop kept him; consequently my fairy great grand aunt Ellen was resolute that the daughter of her dead sister-in-law should be brought up in an unquestionably ladylike manner. So my mother had a Spartan childhood, and carried the straightbacked stamp of it to her grave. Misfortunes that would have crushed ten untrained women broke on her like waves on granite.

Nature, expelled with a fork, came back again and wrecked the life plans of her fairy aunt. When my mother grew up, she knew thoroughbass as taught by her musicmaster Johann Bernhard Logier (famous in Dublin as the inventor of the chiroplast, a mechanical finger exerciser which set his piano pupils all wrong); she could repeat two of La Fontaine's fables in French with perfect pronunciation; she could carry herself with complete dignity; and she could have worked as a ragpicker without losing her entire conviction that she was a lady, of a species apart from servants and common persons. But she could not housekeep on a small income; she had no notion of the value of money; she detested her grand aunt and regarded all that had been taught her as religion and discipline as tyranny and slavery. Consequently, as she was naturally very humane, she abandoned her own children to the most complete anarchy. Both my parents, as it happened, were utterly uncoercive.

In due time she was floated in Dublin society to get married. Among other persons with whom she came in contact was George Carr Shaw, an apparently harmless gentleman of forty, with a squint and a vein of humor which delighted in anti-climax, and would have made him an appreciative listener for Charles Lamb. He was a member of a large family which spoke of itself as "the Shaws," and got invited, on the strength of a second cousinship, to Bushy Park, the seat of the bachelor Sir Robert Shaw, Bart., as to whom see Burke's Landed Gentry. George Carr Shaw seemed very safe company for my carefully guarded mother, because nobody could conceive his having the audacity, the enterprise, nor the means, to marry anybody, even if it could be supposed that his years or his squint could appeal to so well brought-up a female as Miss Lucinda Elizabeth Gurly. He was therefore well spoken of to her by her relatives as a quite eligible person to know in a general social way. They forgot that, having never been taught what marriage really means, nor experienced impecuniosity, she might marry any adventurer without knowing how much she was doing.

Her tragedy came about by external pressure of a sort that nobody could have foreseen.

Her widowed father most unexpectedly married again: this time the penniless daughter of an old friend of his whose bills he had backed with ruinous consequences. The alliance did not please the family of his first wife, especially his brother-in-law, a Kilkenny squire, to whom he owed money, and from whom he concealed his intention to marry again.

Unfortunately my mother innocently let out the secret to her uncle. The consequence was that my grandfather, going out on his wedding morning to buy a pair of gloves for the ceremony, was arrested for debt at the suit of his brother-in-law. One can hardly blame him for being furious. But his fury carried him beyond all reason. He believed that my mother had betrayed him deliberately so as to stop the marriage by his arrest. My mother, who was on a visit to some relatives in Dublin at the time, had to choose between two homes to return to. One was the house of a stepmother and an enraged father. The other was the house of her aunt, which meant the old domestic slavery and tyranny.

It was at this moment that some devil, perhaps commissioned by the Life Force to bring me into the world, prompted my father to propose marriage to Miss Bessie Gurly. She caught at the straw. She had heard

[21]

that he had a pension of £60 a year; and to her, who had never been allowed to have more than pocket money nor to housekeep, £60 seemed an enormous and inexhaustible sum. She calmly announced her engagement, dropping the bombshell as unconcernedly as if it were a colored glass ball from her solitaire board. People played solitaire in those days.

Finding it impossible to make her see the gravity of the pecuniary situation, or to induce her to cancel her engagement on such a ground, her people played another card. They told her that George Carr Shaw was a drunkard. She indignantly refused to believe them, reminding them that they had never objected to him before. When they persisted, she went to him straightforwardly and asked him was it true. He assured her most solemnly that he was a convinced and lifelong teetotaller. And she believed him and married him. But it was true. He drank.

Without attempting to defend my father for telling this whopper, I must explain that he really was in principle a convinced teetotaller. Unfortunately it was the horror of his own experience as an occasional dipsomaniac that gave him this conviction, which he was miserably unable to carry into practice.

I can only imagine the hell into which my mother descended when she found out what shabby-genteel poverty with a drunken husband is like. She told me once that when they were honeymooning in Liverpool (of all places) she opened her bridegroom's wardrobe and found it full of empty bottles. In the first shock of the discovery she ran away to the docks to get employed as a stewardess and be taken out of the country. But on the way she was molested by some rough docklanders and had to run back again.

I have elsewhere recorded how, when my father, taking me for a walk, pretended in play to throw me into the canal, he very nearly did it. When we got home I said to my mother as an awful and hardly credible discovery "Mamma: I think Papa is drunk." This was too much for her. She replied "When is he anything else?"

It is a rhetorical exaggeration to say that I have never since believed in anything or anybody; but the wrench from my childish faith in my father as perfect and omniscient to the discovery that he was a hypocrite and a dipsomaniac was so sudden and violent that it must have left its mark on me.

Her aunt cut her off ruthlessly in spite of my infant charms. All my mother had from her was an earlier gift of a bundle of I.O.U.s signed by my grandfather. She was innocent enough to let him see them and ask what she should do with them. He promptly put them into the fire. This did not matter, as he would not have paid them anyhow; but he also tried to use a power of appointment under her grandfather's (the pawnbroker's) will to deprive her of any share of his bequests to his grandchildren; and though the Gurly family solicitor rescued some £40 a year for her by absolutely refusing to allow him to do his worst, it left my mother convinced that her father was a vindictive parent, not too scrupulously conscientious in money matters.

Then there was her brother, my maternal Uncle Walter. But he was dissolute, and had offended her once by being savagely violent to her in a fit of temper. He went their father's feckless way as to the property. Everybody had disappointed her, or betrayed her, or tyrannized over her.

She was not at all soured by all this. She never made scenes, never complained, never nagged, never punished nor retaliated nor lost her superiority to spites and tantrums and tempers. She was neither weak nor submissive; but as she never revenged, so also she never forgave. There were no quarrels and consequently no reconciliations. You did a wrong; and you were classed by her as a person who did such wrongs, and tolerated indulgently up to a point. But if at last you drove her to break with you, the breach was permanent: you did not get back again. Among my Maxims for Revolutionists[3] there is "Beware of the man who does not return your blow." From my mother I had learned that the wrath on which the sun goes down is negligible compared to the clear vision and criticism that is neither created by anger nor ended with it.

Under all the circumstances it says a great deal for my mother's humanity that she did not hate her children. She did not hate anybody, nor love anybody. The specific maternal passion awoke in her a little for my younger sister, who died at 20; but it did not move her until she lost her, nor then noticeably. She did not concern herself much about us; for she had never been taught that mothering is a science, nor that it matters in the least what children eat or drink: she left all that to servants whose wage was £8 a year and could neither write nor read. She had no sense of the value of her own training, and gave it no credit for its results, which she may have regarded as gifts of nature; but she had a deep sense of its cruelties. As we grew up and had to take care of ourselves unguided, we met life's difficulties by breaking our shins over them, gaining such wisdom as was inevitable by making fools of ourselves. On the whole it was easier for my mother than her aunt's plan; and it was certainly meant to be kinder: in fact it was very much kinder, but not so much so as she thought. Letting a calf stray into every china shop is not the only alternative to goading it along the street. In short, my mother was, from the technical point of view of a modern welfare worker, neither a mother nor a wife, and could be classed only as a Bohemian anarchist with ladylike habits.

My father was impecunious and unsuccessful: he could do nothing that interested her; and he did not shake off his miserable and disgraceful tippling (he did eventually) until it was too late to make any difference in their relations. Had there not been imagination, idealization, the charm of music, the charm of lovely seas and sunsets, and our natural kindliness and gentleness, it is impossible to say what cynical barbarism we might not have grown into.

My mother's salvation came through music. She had a mezzo-soprano voice of extraordinary purity of tone; and to cultivate it she took lessons from George John Vandeleur Lee, already well established in Dublin as an orchestral conductor, an organizer of concerts, and a teacher of singing so heterodox and original that he depended for his performances on amateurs trained by himself, and was detested by his professional rivals, whom he disparaged as voice wreckers, as indeed they mostly were. He extended this criticism to doctors, and amazed us by eating brown bread instead of white, and sleeping with the window open, both of which habits I acquired and have practised ever since. His influence in our household, of which he at last became a member, accustomed me to the scepticism as to academic authority which still persists in me.

He not only made my mother sing by a method that preserved her voice perfectly until her death at over eighty but gave her a Cause and a Creed to live for.

Those who know my play Misalliance, in which the lover has three fathers, will note that I also had a natural father and two supplementaries, making three varieties for me to study. This widened my outlook very considerably. Natural parents should bear in mind that the more supplementaries their children find, at school or elsewhere, the better they will know that it takes all sorts to make a world. Also that though there is always the risk of being corrupted by bad parents, the natural ones may be—probably ten per cent. of them actually are—the worst of the lot.

My parents took no moral responsibility for me. I was just something that happened to them and had to be put up with and supported. I never suffered the meddlesomeness of those morbidly conscientious parents who are so busy with their children's characters that they have no time to look after their own. I cannot remember having ever heard a single sentence uttered by my mother in the nature of moral or religious instruction. My father made an effort or two. When he caught me imitating him by pretending to smoke a toy pipe he advised me very earnestly never to follow his example in any way; and his sincerity so impressed me that to this day I have never smoked, never shaved,[4] and never used alcoholic stimulants. He taught me to regard him as an unsuccessful man with many undesirable habits, as a warning and not as a model. In fact he did himself some injustice lest I should grow up like him; and I now see that this anxiety on his part was admirable and lovable; and that he was really just what he so carefully strove not to be: that is, a model father. . . .

. . . Let me tell you a story of my father. When I was a child, he gave me my first dip in the sea in Killiney Bay. He prefaced it by a very serious exhortation on the importance of learning to swim, culminating in these words "When I was a boy of only fourteen, my knowledge of swimming enabled me to save your Uncle Robert's life." Then, seeing that I was deeply impressed, he stooped, and added confidentially in my ear "and, to tell you the truth, I never was so sorry for anything in my life afterwards." He then plunged into the ocean, enjoyed a thoroughly refreshing swim, and chuckled all the way home.

Now I have never aimed consciously at anti-climax: it occurs naturally in my work. But there is no doubt some connection between my father's chuckling and the enjoyment produced in the theatre by my comedic methods.

Then there was my maternal Uncle Walter. During my boyhood he was a ship's surgeon on the Inman line . . . visiting us between voyages. He had been educated at Kilkenny College, in his time the Eton of Ireland. When he was the smallest boy there, and the only one who could squeeze himself out under the locked college gates, he was sent by the elder boys at night into the town to make assignations for them with ladies of the street, his reward being whisky enough to make him insensibly drunk. (He was, by the way, astonished and horrified by the homosexualities of English public schools, and maintained that schools should always be, like Kilkenny College, within reach of women.) From Trinity College in Dublin, his university, he had had to retire to recuperate after excessive dissipation. Then, as his father, always short of money through backing bills for his friends and recklessly mortgaging, could not support him, he qualified as a surgeon and took the Inman job. He could learn subjects for examination and pass them easily enough, and was apparently an efficient medical officer under discipline.

He was a most exhilarating person, because he had, like my mother, though without her dignity, a youthfulness that no dissipation could exhaust, and was robust and fullblooded. His profanity and obscenity in conversation were of Rabelaisian exuberance; and as to the *maxima reverentia* due to my tender years, he had rather less of it, if possible, than Falstaff had for Prince Hal. To the half dozen childish rhymes taught me by my mother he added a stock of unprintable limericks that constituted almost an education in geography. He was always in high spirits, and full of a humor that, though barbarous in its blasphemous indecency, was Scriptural and Shakespearean in the elaboration and fantasy of its literary expression. Being full of the Bible, he quoted the sayings of Jesus as models of facetious repartee. He considered Anthony Trollope's novels the only ones worth reading (in those days they were regarded as daring exposures of the Church!); and his favorite opera was Auber's Fra Diavolo. Possibly if he had been cultivated artistically in his childhood, he would have been a man of refined pleasures, and might have done something in literature. As it was, he was a scoffer and a rake, because no better pleasures had ever been either revealed or denied to him. In spite of his excesses, which were not continuous, being the intermittent debauches of a seafarer on shore, he was an upstanding healthy man until he married an English widow in America and settled as a general practitioner in Leyton, Essex, then a country district on the borders of Epping Forest. His wife tried to make him behave himself according to English lights: to go to church; to consult the feelings and prejudices of his patients; to refrain from the amusement of scandalizing their respectability; or at least to stint himself in the item of uproarious blasphemy. It was quite useless: her protests only added to the zest of his profanities. Nevertheless, he held his own in Leyton county society because he was very amusing, and was perceptibly a gentleman who drove his own horse and had bought his select practice.

Soon, however, east London spread and swallowed up Leyton. The country houses of his patients were demolished and replaced by rows of little brick boxes inhabited by clerks in tall hats supporting families on fifteen shillings a week. . . .

When I was a young man in Dublin several of my intimate friends were doctors; and they were rash enough to talk shop with freedom before me. Among other things, they used to discuss their fees; and it always came to the same thing—none of them would take less than a guinea; none would tolerate a man that took less than a guinea, or consider him a gentleman, or a man that they ought to go into consultation with. Of course, they had to make concessions in a poor country like Ireland: they would give you four visits for the guinea; but they would not go beyond that: they would not take five shillings for one visit. My uncle had these ideas when he bought his practice. It was one of those nice practices where your patients live mostly in country houses, with parks, carriages, and horses. My uncle had a horse and trap, and maintained his position of an Irish gentleman, and had a great contempt for poor doctors. One rival came and settled in the district—a disgraceful person who took half-crown fees: my uncle's contempt for him was beyond expression. He would not meet him in consultation, and considered that such a person should be wiped off the face of the earth. . . .

The change occurred before he had been more than three or four years in practice. I saw the whole process going on, and after it had completed itself I used occasionally to go down and stay with my uncle. My uncle's clothes at that time had become very shabby, and the horse and trap had been sold. I slept in the next room to him and occasionally heard the night bell; and this is the sort of thing I used to hear: "Who is that?" "Who did you say?" "What road?" "Oh; have you got the money?"— "Rattle it at the tube then." . . . If you were a doctor practising at Leyton you would not think that funny. It may appear to you to be one of my jokes, but it is—like most of my jokes— an exceedingly serious matter. I took occasion after one of these experiences to say to my uncle: "You used to be very indignant with So-and-so because he took a half-crown fee; would you take a half-crown fee?" "Yes," he said, "and be very glad to get it." I said, "What is the smallest fee you would take now?" He replied, "The Royal Mint has not yet coined so small a coin but that I would take it."

. . . The change ruined my uncle. His wife died of disgust and despair, leaving everything she possessed to the relatives of her former husband. . . . When he died, and I inherited his estate, . . . I discovered . . . that my estate did not belong to me at all, and that I had no power to control it or direct its management. Instead of the title deeds I received a bundle of mortgages and a packet of pawn tickets.

I was not greatly surprised: for my uncle, from whom I inherited, had died shabby and almost indigent. . . . The wages of his one faithful servant were seventeen years in arrear; and his gold watch had been pawned, leaving him to count pulses by a silver one which he had presented me with many years before, and was afterwards obliged to borrow from me. I had been with him when he bought the gold watch for £30. He had pawned it for £3-10-0, and for years clung to the right to redeem it by borrowing the interest on that sum from my mother.

Inheriting this right, I took the ticket to the pawnbroker and redeemed the watch. I then took it to a place in London where I handed it in for sale by auction. It sold for £3-10-0, which I duly got back less the auctioneer's commission. Having made no profit on the transaction, and lost the commission, I accepted this result as typical and dropped all the other pawn tickets into the waste-paper basket. His father had long before mortgaged the estate up to the hilt; and I should have had to repudiate my inheritance of it had it come to me a few years earlier. As it was, I was able to pay off the mortgages, rebuild the wrecked houses, support the poor relations, and restore the estate to solvency. Finally I municipalized it, having to procure an Act of the Dail (the parliament of Eire) to enable me to do so, or anyone else to follow my example.

How my mother rescued herself . . . by her musical talent I will tell elsewhere. My father reduced his teetotalism from theory to practice when a mild fit, which felled him on our doorstep one Sunday afternoon, convinced him that he must stop drinking or perish. It had no worse effect; but his reform, though complete and permanent, came too late to save the social situation; and I, cut off from the social drill which puts one at one's ease in private society, grew up frightfully shy and utterly ignorant of social routine. My mother, who had been as carefully brought up as Queen Victoria, was too humane to inflict what she had suffered on any child; besides, I think she imagined that correct behavior is inborn, and that much of what she had been taught was natural to her. Anyhow, she never taught it to us, leaving us wholly to the promptings of our blood's blueness, with results which may be imagined.

In England, if people are reasonably goodnatured and amiable, they are forgiven any sort of eccentricity of behavior if only they are unaffected and all of one piece. If when I came to London I had been merely shy provincially, with incorrect table manners and wrong clothes; if I had eaten peas with a knife and worn a red tie with an evening suit, kind people would have taken me in hand and drilled me in spite of the infernal and very silly Irish pride which will never admit the need of such tuition. But my difficulties were not of that easily remediable kind. I was sensible enough to inform myself so exactly as to what I should do with a finger bowl when it was placed before me on a dessert plate, that I could give a lead in such matters to other novices who were hopelessly floored by that staggering problem. Clever sympathetic women might divine at a glance that I was mortally shy; but people who could not see through my skin, and who were accustomed to respect, and even veneration, from the young, may well have found me insufferable, aggressive, and impudent. When a young man has achieved nothing and is doing nothing, and when he is obviously so poor that he ought to be doing something very energetically, it is rather trying to find him assuming an authority in conversation, and an equality in terms, which only conspicuous success and distinguished ability could make becoming. . . .

Not that my opinions were conventional. . . . I had been accustomed to regard myself as a sceptic outside institutional religion, and therefore one to whom the conventional religious observances were fair game for scoffing. In this my manners were no better and no worse than those of my class generally. It never occurred to pious ladies and gentlemen to respect a sceptic; and it never occurred to a sceptic to respect a believer: reprobation and ostracism were considered natural and even obligatory on the one side, like derision, even to blasphemy, on the other. In Ireland Protestants and Catholics despised, insulted, and ostracized one another as a matter of course. In England Church people persecuted Dissenters; and Dissenters hated the Church with a bitterness incredible to anyone who has never known what it is to be a little village Dissenter in a Church school. I am not sure that controversial manners are any better now; but they certainly were odious then: you thought it your right and your duty to sneer at the man who was a heretic to your faith if you could not positively injure him in some way. As my manners in this respect were no better than other people's, and my satirical powers much more formidable, I can only hope that my natural civility, which led me to draw back when I found I was hurting people's feelings, may have mitigated my offensiveness in those early days when I still regarded controversy as admitting of no quarter. I lacked both cruelty and will-to-victory.

It may be asked here how I came by my heterodox opinions, seeing that my father's alcoholic neurosis, though it accounts for my not going into society, does not account for my not going to church. My reply,

[29]

if put in the conventional terms of that day, would be that I was badly brought up because my mother was so well brought up. Her character reacted so strongly against her strict and loveless training that church-going was completely dropped in our family before I was ten years old.

The first book I ever possessed was a Bible bound in black leather with gilt metal rims and a clasp, slightly larger than my sisters' Bibles because I was a boy, and was therefore fitted with a bigger Bible, precisely as I was fitted with bigger boots. In spite of the trouble taken to impress me with the duty of reading it (with the natural result of filling me with a conviction that such an occupation must be almost as disagreeable as going to church), I acquired a considerable familiarity with it, and indeed once read the Old Testament and the four Gospels straight through, from a vainglorious desire to do what nobody else had done.

. . . In my childhood I exercised my literary genius by composing my own prayers. I cannot recall the words of the final form I adopted; but I remember that it was in three movements, like a sonata, and in the best Church of Ireland style. It ended with the Lord's Prayer; and I repeated it every night in bed. I had been warned by my nurse that warm prayers were no use, and that only by kneeling by my bedside in the cold could I hope for a hearing; but I criticised this admonition unfavorably on various grounds, the real one being my preference for warmth and comfort. I did not disparage my nurse's authority in these matters because she was a Roman Catholic: I even tolerated her practice of sprinkling me with holy water occasionally.* But her asceticism did not fit the essentially artistic and luxurious character of my devotional exploits. Besides, the penalty did not apply to my prayer; for it was not a petition. I had too much sense to risk my faith by begging for things I knew very well I should not get; so I did not care whether my prayers were answered or not: they were a literary performance for the entertainment and propitiation of the Almighty; and though I should not have dreamt of daring to say that if He did not like them He might lump them (perhaps I was too confident of their quality to apprehend such a rebuff), I certainly behaved as if my comfort were an indispensable condition of the performance taking place at all.

The Lord's Prayer I used once or twice as a protective spell. Thunderstorms are much less common in Ireland than in England; and the first

* My own nursemaid kept me in order by threatening that if I persisted in disobeying her "the cock would come down the chimney." To me the cock was an avenging deity.

two I remember frightened me horribly. During the second I bethought me of the Lord's Prayer, and steadied myself by repeating it. . . . In my infancy I was told that if I was a bad child I should spend eternity after my death burning in a brimstone hell in an agony of thirst, tortured by a magical combustion that would never consume me. This fable served its turn while I was young enough to believe it; but when I was old enough to laugh at it I was left without any credible reason for behaving honorably, and with a habit of deriding all religious teaching as fraudulent, ridiculous, and characteristic of superstitious fools and humbugs. Fortunately by that time I had also evolved a sense of honor which inhibited my worst impulses and dictated my best ones; and I took to pointing out, in my capacity as a boy atheist, that this natural sense of honor, nowhere mentioned in The Bible, was the real source of honorable behavior and was quite independent of religious instruction. I ranked it, and still do, as a passion.

When I was a little boy, I was compelled to go to church on Sunday; and though I escaped from that intolerable bondage before I was ten, it prejudiced me so violently against churchgoing that twenty years elapsed before, in foreign lands and in pursuit of works of art, I became once more a churchgoer. To this day, my flesh creeps when I recall that genteel suburban Irish Protestant church, built by Roman Catholic workmen who would have considered themselves damned had they crossed its threshold afterwards. Every separate stone, every pane of glass, every fillet of ornamental ironwork—half-dog-collar, half-coronet—in that building must have sowed a separate evil passion in my young heart. Yes; all the vulgarity, savagery, and bad blood which has marred my literary work, was certainly laid upon me in that house of Satan! The mere nullity of the building could make no positive impression on me; but what could, and did, were the unnaturally motionless figures of the congregation in their Sunday clothes and bonnets, and their set faces, pale with the malignant rigidity produced by the suppression of all expression. And yet these people were always moving and watching one another by stealth, as convicts communicate with one another. So was I. I had been told to keep my restless little limbs still all through those interminable hours; not to talk; and, above all, to be happy and holy there and glad that I was not a wicked little boy playing in the fields instead of worshipping God. I hypocritically acquiesced; but the state of my conscience may be imagined, especially as I implicitly believed that all the rest of the congregation were perfectly sincere and good. I remember at that time dreaming one night that I was dead and had gone to heaven. The picture of heaven which the efforts of the then Established Church of Ireland had conveyed to my childish imagination was a waiting room with walls of pale sky-coloured tabbinet, and a pew-like bench running all around, except at one corner, where there was a door. I was, somehow, aware that God was in the next room, accessible through that door. I was seated on the bench with my ankles tightly interlaced to prevent my legs dangling, behaving myself with all my might before the grown-up people, who all belonged to the Sunday congregation, and were either sitting on the bench as if at church or else moving solemnly in and out as if there were a dead person in the house. A grimly-handsome lady who usually sat in a corner seat near me in church, and whom I believed to be thoroughly conversant with the arrangements of the Almighty, was to introduce me presently into the next room—a moment which I was supposed to await with joy and enthusiasm. Really, of course, my heart sank like lead within me at the thought; for I felt that my feeble affectation of piety could not impose on Omniscience, and that one glance of that all-searching eye would discover that I had been allowed to come to heaven by mistake. Unfortunately for the interest of this narrative, I awoke, or wandered off into another dream, before the critical moment arrived. But it goes far enough to show that I was by no means an insusceptible subject: indeed, I am sure, from other early experiences of mine, that if I had been turned loose in a real church, and allowed to wander and stare about, or hear noble music there instead of that most accursed Te Deum of Jackson's and a senseless droning of the Old Hundredth, I should never have seized the opportunity of a great evangelical revival, which occurred when I was still in my teens, to begin my literary career with a letter to the Press (which was duly printed), announcing with inflexible materialistic logic, and to the extreme horror of my respectable connections, that I was an atheist. When, later on, I was led to the study of the economic basis of the respectability of that and similar congregations, I was inexpressibly relieved to find that it represented a mere passing phase of industrial confusion, and could never have substantiated its claims to my respect if, as a child, I had been able to bring it to book. To this very day, whenever there is the slightest danger of my being mistaken for votary of the blue tabbinet waiting-room or a supporter of that morality in which wrong and right, base and noble, evil and good, really mean nothing more than the kitchen and the drawing-room, I hasten to claim honourable exemption, as atheist and socialist, from any such complicity.

When I at last took to church-going again, a kindred difficulty beset me, especially in Roman Catholic countries. In Italy, for instance, churches are used in such a way that priceless pictures become smeared with filthy tallow-soot, and have sometimes to be rescued by the temporal power and placed in national galleries. But worse than this are the innumerable daily services which disturb the truly religious visitor. If these were decently and intelligently conducted by genuine mystics to whom the Mass was no mere rite or miracle, but a real communion, the celebrants might reasonably claim a place in the church as their share of the common human right to its use. But the average Italian priest, personally uncleanly, and with chronic catarrh of the nose and throat, produced and maintained by sleeping and living in frowsy, ill-ventilated rooms, punctuating his gabbled Latin only by expectorative hawking, and making the decent guest sicken and shiver every time the horrible splash of spitten mucus echoes along the vaulting from the marble steps of the altar: this unseemly wretch should be seized and put out, bell, book, candle and all, until he learns to behave himself. The English tourist is often lectured for his inconsiderate behaviour in Italian churches, for walking about during service, talking loudly, thrusting himself rudely between a worshipper and an altar to examine a painting, even for stealing chips of stone and scrawling his name on statues. But as far as the mere disturbance of the services is concerned, and the often very evident disposition of the tourist—especially the experienced tourist—to regard the priest and his congregation as troublesome intruders, a week spent in Italy will convince any unprejudiced person that this is a perfectly reasonable attitude. . . . That right should be unflinchingly asserted on all proper occasion. I know no contrary right by which the great Catholic churches made for the world by the great church-builders should be monopolised by any sect as against any man who desires to use them. My own faith is clear: I am a resolute Protestant; I believe in the Holy Catholic Church; in the Holy Trinity of Father, Son (or Mother, Daughter) and Spirit; in the Communion of Saints, the Life to Come, the Immaculate Conception, and the everyday reality of Godhead and the Kingdom of Heaven. Also, I believe that salvation depends on redemption from belief in miracles; and I regard St. Athanasius as an irreligious fool—that is, in the only serious sense of the word, a damned fool. I pity the poor neurotic who can say, "Man that is born of a woman hath but a short time to live, and is full of misery," as I pity a maudlin drunkard; and I know that the real religion of to-day was made possible only by the materialistic-physicists and atheist-critics who performed for us the indispensable preliminary operation of purging us thoroughly of the ignorant and vicious superstitions which were thrust down our throats as religion in our helpless childhood. How those who assume that our churches are the private property of their sect would think of this profession of faith of mine I need not describe. But am I, therefore, to be denied access to the place of spiritual recreation which is my inheritance as much as theirs? If, for example, I desire to follow a good old custom by pledging my love to my wife in the church of our parish, why should I be denied due record in the registers unless she submits to have a moment of deep feeling made ridiculous by the reading aloud of the *naive* impertinences of St. Peter, who, on the subject of Woman, was neither Catholic nor Christian, but a boorish Syrian fisherman. If I want to name a child in the church, the prescribed service may be more touched with the religious spirit—once or twice beautifully touched—but, on the whole, it is time to dismiss our prayerbook as quite rotten with the pessimism of the age which prescribed it. In spite of the stolen jewels with which it is studded, an age of strength and faith and noble activity can have nothing to do with it: Caliban might have constructed such a ritual out of his own terror of the supernatural, and such fragments of the words of the saints as he could dimly feel some sort of glory in.

My demand will not be understood without any ceremonious formulation of it. No nation, working at the strain we face, can live cleanly without public-houses in which to seek refreshment and recreation. To supply that vital want we have the drinking-shop with its narcotic, stimulant poisons, the conventicle with its brimstone-flavoured hot gospel, and the church. In the church alone can our need be truly met, nor even there save when we leave outside the door the materialisms that help us to think the unthinkable, completing the refuse-heap of "isms" and creeds with our vain lust for truth and happiness, and going in without thought or belief or prayer or any other vanity, so that the soul, freed from all that crushing lumber, may open all its avenues of life to the holy air of the true Catholic Church.

I continued . . . pious habits long after the conventional compulsion to attend church and Sunday School had ceased, and I no longer regarded such customs as having anything to do with an emancipated spirit like mine. But one evening, as I was wandering through the furze bushes on Torca Hill in the dusk, I suddenly asked myself why I went on repeating my prayer every night when, as I put it, I did not believe in it. Being thus brought to book by my intellectual conscience I felt obliged in common honesty to refrain from superstitious practices; and that night, for the first time since I could speak, I did not say my prayers. I missed them so much that I asked myself another question. Why am I so uncomfortable about it? Can this be conscience? But next night the discomfort wore off so much that I hardly noticed it; and the night after I had forgotten all about my prayers as completely as if I had been born a heathen. It is worth adding that this sacrifice of the grace of God, as I had been taught it, to intellectual integrity synchronized with that dawning of moral passion in me which I have described in the first act of Man and Superman. Up to that time I had not experienced the slightest remorse in telling lies whenever they seemed likely to help me out of a difficulty: rather did I revel in the exercise of dramatic invention involved. Even when I was a good boy I was so only theatrically, because, as actors say, I saw myself in the character; and this occurred very seldom, my taste running so strongly on stage villains and stage demons (I painted the whitewashed wall in my bedroom in Dalkey with water-color frescoes of Mephistopheles) that I must have actually bewitched myself; for, when Nature completed my countenance in 1880 or thereabouts (I had only the tenderest sprouting of hair on my face until I was 24), I found myself equipped with the upgrowing moustaches and eyebrows, and the sarcastic nostrils of the operatic fiend whose airs (by Gounod) I had sung as a child, and whose attitudes I had affected in my boyhood.

When I was a fastidious youth, my elders, ever eager to confer bad advice on me and to word it with disgusting homeliness, used to tell me never to throw away dirty water until I got it clean. To which I would reply that as I had only one bucket, the thing was impossible. So until I grew middle-aged and sordid, I acted on the philosophy of Bunyan's couplet:

> A man there was, tho' some did count him mad,
> The more he cast away, the more he had.

Indeed, in the matter of ideals, faiths, convictions and the like, I was of opinion that Nature abhorred a vacuum, and that you might empty your bucket boldly with the fullest assurance that you would find it fuller than ever before you had time to set it down again. But herein I youthfully deceived myself. I grew up to find the genteel world full of persons with empty buckets.

My father disapproved of the detachment of his family from the conventional observances that were associated with the standing of the Shaw family. But he was in the grip of a humorous sense of anticlimax which I inherited from him and used with much effect when I became a writer of comedy. The more sacred an idea or a situation was by convention, the more irresistible was it to him as the jumping-off place for a plunge into laughter. Thus, when I scoffed at the Bible he would instantly and quite sincerely rebuke me, telling me, with what little sternness was in his nature, that I should not speak so; that no educated man would make such a display of ignorance; that the Bible was universally recognized as a literary and historical masterpiece; and as much more to the same effect as he could muster. But when he had reached the point of feeling really impressive, a convulsion of internal chuckling would wrinkle up his eyes; and (I knowing all the time quite well what was coming) would cap his eulogy by assuring me, with an air of perfect fairness, that even the worst enemy of religion could say no worse of the Bible than that it was the damndest parcel of lies even written. He would then rub his eyes and chuckle for quite a long time. It became an unacknowledged game between us that I should provoke him to exhibitions of this kind. . . .

I know how long such things stick. When I was a child I was told that a gentleman who had paid us a visit was a Unitarian. I asked my father what a Unitarian was; and he, being the victim of a sense of humor and a taste for anticlimax . . . thoughtlessly replied that the Unitarians are people who believe that our Lord was not really crucified at all, but was seen "running away down the other side of the Hill of Calvary." Childlike, I accepted this statement *au pied de la lettre,* and believed it devoutly until I was thirty-five or thereabouts, when, having occasion one day to make some reference to Unitarianism in print, and being led thereby to consider it more closely, I perceived that my father's account of the matter would not stand the fire of the Higher Criticism. . . .

With such a father my condition was clearly hopeless as far as the conventions of religion were concerned. In essential matters his influence was as good as his culture permitted. One of my very earliest recollections is reading The Pilgrim's Progress to him, and being corrected by him for saying grievious instead of grievous. I never saw him, as far as I can remember, reading anything but the newspaper; but he had read Sir Walter Scott and other popular classics; and he always encouraged me to do the same, and to frequent the National Gallery, and to go to the theatre and the opera when I could afford it. His anticlimaxes depended for their effect on our sense of the sacredness he was reacting against: there would have been no fun whatever in saying that the Adventures of Munchausen (known to us as Baron Mun Chawzon) were a parcel of lies. If my mother's pastors and masters had had a little of his humor, she would not simply have dropped the subject of religion with her children in silent but implacable dislike of what had helped to make her childhood miserable, and resolved that it should not do the same to them. The vacuum she left by this policy had, I think, serious disadvantages for my two sisters (the younger of whom died just before I came to London); but in my case it only made a clear space for positive beliefs later on.

My mother, I may say here, had no comedic impulses, and never uttered an epigram in her life: all my comedy is a Shavian inheritance. She had plenty of imagination, and really lived in it and on it. Her brother, my uncle Walter, who stayed with us from time to time in the intervals of his trips across the Atlantic as a surgeon on the Inman Liners, had an extraordinary command of picturesque language, partly derived by memory from the Bible and Prayer Book, and partly natural. The conversation of the navigating staffs and pursers of our ocean services was at that time (whatever it may be today) extremely Rabelaisian and profane. Falstaff himself could not have held his own with my uncle in obscene anecdotes, unprintable limericks, and fantastic profanity; and it mattered nothing to him whether his audience consisted of his messmates on board ship or his schoolboy nephew: he performed before each with equal gusto. To do him justice, he was always an artist in his obscenity and blasphemy, and therefore never sank to the level of incontinent blackguardism. His efforts were controlled, deliberate, fastidiously chosen and worded. But they were all the more effective in destroying all my inculcated childish reverence for the verbiage of religion, for its legends and personifications and parables. In view of my subsequent work in the world it seems providential that I was driven to the essentials of religion by the reduction of every factitious or fictious element in it to the most irreverent absurdity. . . .

. . . Try to imagine me, a very small boy, with my ears very wide open, in what Mr. Gilbert K. Chesterton calls my "narrow, Puritan home." Well, on the occasion which I am going to recall, there were in that narrow, Puritan home three gentlemen who were having what they believed to be a very heated discussion about religion. One was my father, another my maternal uncle, and the third a visitor of ours. The subject of the dispute was the raising of Lazarus. Only one of the parties took what would then, I think, have been called the Christian view. I shall call it the evangelical view, a less compromising term. That view was that the raising of Lazarus occurred exactly as it is described in the Gospels. I shouldn't object to call that the Christian view if it had not involved the opinion, very popular among religious people at that time, that the reason why you admired Jesus and followed Jesus was that he was able to raise people from the dead. Perhaps the reason why some of them always spoke very respectfully of him was a sort of feeling in their mind that a man who could raise people from the dead might possibly on sufficient provocation reverse the operation. However, one of the parties took this view. Another, the visitor, took the absolutely sceptical view; he said that such a thing had never happened—that such stories were told of all great teachers of mankind—that it was more probable that a storyteller was a liar than that a man could be raised from the dead. But the third person, my maternal uncle, took another view; he said that the miracle was what would be called in these days a put-up job, by which he meant that Jesus had made a confederate of Lazarus—had made it worth his while, or had asked him for friendship's sake, to pretend he was dead and at the proper moment to pretend to come to life. . . . I listened with very great interest, and I confess to you that the view which recommended itself most to me was that of my maternal uncle. I think, on reflection, . . . that was the natural and healthy side for a growing boy to take, because my maternal uncle's view appealed to the sense of humor, which is a very good thing and a very human thing, whereas the other two views—one appealing to our mere credulity and the other to mere scepticism—really did not appeal to anything at all that had any genuine religious value. . . .

It would be the greatest mistake to conclude that this shocking state of affairs was bad for my soul. In so far as the process of destroying reverence for the inessential trappings of religion was indecent, it was deplorable; and I wish my first steps to grace had been lighted by my uncle's wit and style without his obscenity. My father's comedy was entirely decent. But that the process was necessary to my salvation I have no doubt whatever. A popular book in my youth was Mark Twain's New Pilgrim's Progress, which horrified the thoughtlessly pious by making fun of what they called sacred things. . . .

I remember when I was young I had it pushed into me that everything that was pious was old; even when I read the Pilgrim's Progress, which I did when a very small child, when I came to the second part even Mr. Valiant-for-Truth I conceived as an old man, at any rate a grownup person. I remember my surprise afterwards when arriving at years of discretion to discover by carefully reading the introduction in verse, which a child always skips, that Bunyan had conceived Valiant-for-Truth as being a young man in all the glory of youth. But in those days the ruler of the universe was an elderly gentleman . . . .

. . . Yet Mark Twain was really a religious force in the world: his Yankee at the Court of King Arthur was his nearest approach to genuine blasphemy; and that came from want of culture, not from perversity of soul. His training as a Mississippi pilot must have been, as to religion, very like my training as the nephew of a Transatlantic surgeon.

Later on, I discovered that in the Ages of Faith the sport of making fun of the accessories and legends of religion was organized and practised by the Church to such an extent that it was almost part of its ritual. The people were instructed in spiritual history and hagiology by stage plays full of comic passages which might have been written by my uncle. For instance, my uncle taught me an elaborate conversation supposed to have passed between Daniel in the lion's den and King Darius, in which each strove to outdo the other in Rabelaisian repartee. The medieval playwright, more daring than my uncle, put on the stage comical conversations between Cain and his Creator, in which Cain's language was no more respectful than that of Fielding's Squire Western, and similarly indecent. In all Catholic countries there is a hagiology that is fit for publication and a hagiology that is not. In the Middle Ages they may have condemned a story as lewd or blasphemous; but it did not occur to them that God or His Church could be shaken by it. No man with any faith worth respecting in any religion worth holding ever dreams that it can be shaken by a joke, least of all by an obscene joke. It is Messieurs

Formalist and Hypocrisy who feel that religion is crumbling when the forms are not observed. The truth is, humor is one of the great purifiers of religion, even when it is itself anything but pure.

The institution of the family, which is the centre of reverence for carefully brought-up children, was just the opposite for me. In a large family there are always a few skeletons in the cupboard; and in my father's clan there were many uncles and aunts and cousins, consequently many cupboards, consequently some skeletons. Our own particular skeleton was my father's drunkenness. It was combined with a harmlessness and humaneness which made him the least formidable of men; so that it was impossible for him to impress his children in the manner that makes awe and dread almost an instinct with some children. It is much to his credit that he was incapable of deliberately practising any such impressiveness, drunk or sober; but unfortunately the drunkenness was so humiliating that it would have been unendurable if we had not taken refuge in laughter. It had to be either a family tragedy or a family joke; and it was on the whole a healthy instinct that decided us to get what ribald fun was possible out of it, which, however, was very little indeed. If Noah had made a habit of drinking, his sons would soon have worn out the pious solicitude which they displayed on the occasion of his single lapse from sobriety. A boy who has seen "the governor," with an imperfectly wrapped-up goose under one arm and a ham in the same condition under the other (both purchased under heaven knows what delusion of festivity), butting at the garden wall in the belief that he was pushing open the gate, and transforming his tall hat to a concertina in the process, and who, instead of being overwhelmed with shame and anxiety at the spectacle, has been so disabled by merriment (uproariously shared by the maternal uncle) that he has hardly been able to rush to the rescue of the hat and pilot its wearer to safety, is clearly not a boy who will make tragedies of trifles instead of making trifles of tragedies. If you cannot get rid of the family skeleton, you may as well make it dance.

Then there was my Uncle William, a most amiable man, with great natural dignity. In early manhood he was not only an inveterate smoker, but so insistent a toper that a man who made a bet that he would produce Barney Shaw sober, and knocked him up at six in the morning with that object, lost his bet. But this might have happened to any common drunkard. What gave the peculiar Shaw finish and humor to the case was that my uncle suddenly and instantly gave up smoking and drinking at one blow, and devoted himself to his accomplishment of playing the ophicleide. In this harmless and gentle pursuit he continued, a blameless old bachelor, for many years, and then, to the amazement of Dublin, renounced the ophicleide and all its works, and married a lady of distinguished social position and great piety. She declined, naturally, to have anything to do with us; and, as far as I know, treated the rest of the family in the same way. Anyhow, I never saw her, and only saw my uncle furtively by the roadside after his marriage, when he would make hopeless attempts to save me, in the pious sense of the word, not perhaps without some secret Shavian enjoyment of the irreverent pleasantries with which I scattered my path to perdition. He was reputed to sit with a Bible on his knees, and an opera glass to his eyes, watching the ladies' bathing place in Dalkey; and my sister, who was a swimmer, confirmed this gossip as far as the opera glass was concerned.

But this was only the prelude to a very singular conclusion, or rather catastrophe. The fantastic imagery of the Bible so gained on my uncle that he took off his boots, explaining that he expected to be taken up to heaven at any moment like Elijah, and that he felt that his boots would impede his celestial flight. He then went a step further, and hung his room with all the white fabrics he could lay hands on, alleging that he was the Holy Ghost. At last he became silent, and remained so to the end. His wife, warned that his harmless fancies might change into dangerous ones, had him removed to an asylum in the north of Dublin. My father thought that a musical appeal might prevail with him, and went in search of the ophicleide. But it was nowhere to be found. He took a flute to the asylum instead; for every Shaw of that generation seemed able to play any wind instrument at sight. My uncle, still obstinately mute, contemplated the flute for a while, and then played Home Sweet Home on it. My father had to be content with this small success, as nothing more could be got out of his brother. A day or two later my uncle, impatient for heaven, resolved to expedite his arrival there. Every possible weapon had been carefully removed from his reach; but his custodians reckoned without the Shavian originality. They had left him somehow within reach of a carpet bag. He put his head into it, and in a strenuous effort to decapitate or strangle himself by closing it on his neck, perished of heart failure. I should be glad to believe that, like

Elijah, he got the heavenly reward he sought; for he was a fine upstanding man and a gentle creature, nobody's enemy but his own, as the saying is.

Still, what sort of gravity could a boy maintain with a family history of this kind? However, I must not imply that all my uncles were like that. They were mostly respectable normal people. I can recall only two other exceptions to this rule. One of my uncles married an elegant and brilliant lady, from whom he separated after scandalizing the family by beating her; but as Job himself would have beaten her when she lost her very unstable temper, nobody who knew her intimately ever blamed him. Though the neurosis which produced my father's joyless craving for alcohol had the same effect, with the same curious recalcitrance and final impermanence, in one or two other cases, and was perhaps connected with occasional family paroxysms of Evangelical piety, and some share of my father's comedic love of anticlimax, yet on the whole our collection of skeletons was not exceptionally large. But as, compared with similar English families, we had a power of derisive dramatization that made the bones of the Shavian skeletons rattle more loudly; and as I possessed this power in an abnormal degree, and frequently entertained my friends with stories of my uncles (so effectively, by the way, that nobody ever believed them), the family, far from being a school of reverence for me, was rather a mine from which I could dig highly amusing material without the trouble of inventing a single incident. What idle fancy of mine could have improved on the hard facts of the Life and Death of Uncle William?

Thus the immediate result of my family training in my Victoria Grove days was that I presented myself to the unprepared stranger as a most irreverent young man. My Mephistophelean moustache and eyebrows had not yet grown; and there was nothing in my aspect to break the shock of my diabolical opinions. Later on, when I had made a public reputation as an iconoclast, people who met me in private were surprised at my mildness and sociability. But I had no public reputation then: consequently expectation in my regard was normal. And I was not at all reticent of the diabolical opinions. I felt them to be advantageous, just as I felt that I was in a superior position as an Irishman, without a shadow of any justification for that patriotic arrogance. As it never occurred to me to conceal my opinions any more than my nationality, and as I had, besides, an unpleasant trick of contradicting everyone from whom I thought I could learn anything in order to draw him out and enable me to pick his brains, I think I must have impressed many amiable persons as an extremely disagreeable and undesirable young man.

And yet I was painfully shy, and was simply afraid to accept invitations, with the result that I very soon ceased to get any. I was told that if I wanted to get on, I must not flatly refuse invitations—actually dinner invitations—which were meant to help me, and the refusal of which was nothing short of a social outrage. But I knew very well that introductions could be of no use to one who had no profession and could do nothing except what any clerk could do. I knew I was useless, worthless, penniless, and that until I had qualified myself to do something, and proved it by doing it, all this business of calling on people who might perhaps do something for me, and dining out without money to pay for a cab, was silly. Fortunately for me, the realism that made me face my own position so ruthlessly also kept before me the fact that if I borrowed money I could not pay it back, and therefore might more candidly beg or steal it. I knew quite well that if I borrowed £5 from a friend and could not pay it back, I was selling a friend for £5, and that this was a foolish bargain. So I did not borrow, and therefore did not lose any friends; though some of them, who could have had no illusions about my financial capacity, hinted that they were quite willing, and indeed anxious, to call a gift a loan.

I feel bound to confess here, in reference to my neglect of the few invitations and offers of introductions that reached me, that behind the conviction that they could lead to nothing that I wanted lay the unspoken fear that they might lead to something I did not want: that is, commercial employment. I had had enough of that. No doubt it would have been a great relief to my mother if I could have earned something. No doubt I could have earned something if I had really meant to. No doubt if my father had died, and my mother been struck dumb and blind, I should have had to go back to the office desk (the doom of shabby gentility) and give up all hope of acquiring a profession; for even the literary profession, though it exacts no academic course and costly equipment, does exact all one's time and the best of one's brains. As it was, I dodged every opening instinctively. With an excellent testimonial and an unexceptionable character, I was an incorrigible Unemployable. I kept up pretenses (to myself as much as to others) for some time. I answered advertisements, not too offensively.[5] I actually took a berth in a telephone company (then a sensational novelty) and had some difficulty in extricating myself from the Company which bought it up. I can remember an interview with a bank manager in Onslow Gardens (procured for me, to my dismay, by an officious friend with whom I *had* dined) with a view to employment in the bank. I entertained him so brilliantly (if I may use an adverb with which in later years I was much plagued by friendly critics) that we parted on the best of terms, he declaring that, though I certainly ought to get something to do without the least difficulty, he did not feel that a bank clerkship was the right job for me.

I have said that I had an excellent testimonial as an employee in a business office. I had, as a matter of fact, spent four and a half years at a desk in Dublin before I emigrated. I have already given the economic reasons why boys of my class have to do without university education, just as they have to do without horses and guns. And yet I cannot deny that clergymen no better off than my father do manage somehow to start their sons in life with a university degree. They regard it as an absolute necessity, and therefore do not consider whether they can afford it or not. They must afford it. The need for it may be an illusion; but we are subject to such illusions: one man cannot live without a grand piano, another without a boat, another without a butler, another without a horse, and so on through a whole range of psychological imperatives. . . . To say that my father could not afford to give me a university education is like saying that he could not afford to drink, or that I could not afford to become an author. Both statements are true; but he drank and I became an author all the same. I must therefore explain, just as seriously as if my father had had fifty thousand a year, why I did not graduate at Trinity College, Dublin.

Becoming Halfeducated

May I, as a conspicuous specimen of the halfeducated, say a word about my own schooling?

My parents fed me and schooled me and lodged me as well as they could afford to. They paid a governess to teach me to read and write and do a few sums in simple arithmetic. The arithmetic did not get above simple addition and subtraction, because the poor old lady was incapable of explaining the nature of division; . . . because she kept saying two into four, three into six, and so forth without ever explaining what the word "into" meant in this connection. This was explained to me on my first day at school; and I solemnly declare that it was the only thing I ever learnt at school. . . . My own incapacity for numerical calculation . . . is so marked that I reached my fourteenth year before I solved the problem of how many herrings one could buy for elevenpence in a market where a herring and a half fetched three halfpence. . . .

She tried to give me and my two sisters a taste for poetry by reciting "Stop; for thy tread is on an empire's dust" [1] at us, and only succeeded, poor lady, in awakening our sense of derisive humor . . . and as to the reading, I could never understand why she kept bothering me with a spelling and reading book; for I must have been born able to read—or else I acquired the power along with my first set of teeth: at all events I can remember no time at which a printed page was not as intelligible to me as it is to-day; and I could not understand why I should be made to draw pothooks and hangers when I knew perfectly well how to write. To her dying day this old lady no doubt believed that she had taught the most famous of her pupils to read and write; but she only confronted me with the problem of what the spelling book meant by the word *ab-ba, abba.* I wondered what it meant, and I am still wondering.

. . . She punished me by little strokes with her fingers that would not have discomposed a fly, and even persuaded me that I ought to cry and feel disgraced on such occasions. She gave us judgment books and taught us to feel jubilant when after her departure we could rush to the kitchen crying "No marks today" and to hang back ashamed when this claim could not be substantiated. . . . I believe she regarded this as a triumph of moral training; but if so she was completely mistaken; for the truth is that I was such a ridiculously sensitive child that almost any sort of rebuff that did not enrage me hurt my feelings and made me cry; and I was also so imaginative that I boasted not only of the childish things I had actually done but of impossible fictitious adventures and exploits which were all the more heroic because I was in fact a most disgraceful little coward. Poor Miss Hill—that was the lady's name: why should she not have it inscribed on the roll of fame with my own?—had no suspicion that she should have been knocking both the excessive sensitiveness and the silly boastfulness out of me instead of practising on the one and encouraging the other. She was terribly poor; and as she had been brought up as a lady and was therefore helpless without an independent income, she had to earn her scanty shillings by teaching genteel infants her ladylike accomplishments and her appalling limitations. The Miss Hills are supposed to be an extinct species nowadays; but it is surprising what a lot of people you meet still who seem to have been educated by them, even at the universities.

I have no more recollection of my first book than of my first meal. I cannot recollect any time when I could not and did not read everything that came in my way. . . . When I was a small boy there was in the house a book on entomology, with colored plates. The beetles depicted in them were so gorgeous and fantastic that it was delightful to turn over ten plates or so. After that they palled, rapid and easy as the turning over of a bookleaf is; for the mind thirsted for a new idea. . . .

The two literary sensations of my childhood were undoubtedly The Pilgrim's Progress and The Arabian Nights. This shows that I was as good a critic in my infancy as I am now, though I could not then give such clever reasons for my opinion.

I seem to have been born with a knowledge of The Ancient Mariner and John Gilpin. Also with an unaccountable recollection of Baron Trenck and his escapes from prison.

I had to be encouraged by my mother to persevere at Robinson Crusoe until he reached the desert island, after which he carried me with him unaided. . . . Children's books, from the accursed Swiss Family Robinson onwards, I always loathed and despised for their dishonesty, their hypocrisy, their sickly immorality, and their damnable dulness. . . .

I acquired a very boyish (not childish) taste for Shakespear from the snippets printed beneath Selous' illustrations to Cassell's Family Shakespear. . . . I pity the man who cannot enjoy Shakespear. He has outlasted thousands of abler thinkers, and will outlast a thousand more. His gift of telling a story (provided some one else told it to him first); his enormous power over language, as conspicuous in his senseless and silly abuse of it as in his miracles of expression; his humor; his sense of idiosyncratic character; and his prodigious fund of that vital energy which is, it seems, the true differentiating property behind the faculties, good, bad, or indifferent, of the man of genius, enable him to entertain us so effectively that the imaginary scenes and people he has created become more real to us than our actual life—at least, until our knowledge and grip of actual life begins to deepen and glow beyond the common. When I was twenty I knew everybody in Shakespear, from Hamlet to Abhorson, much more intimately than I knew my living contemporaries; and to this day, if the name of Pistol or Polonius catches my eye in a newspaper, I turn to the passage with more curiosity than if the name were that of—but perhaps I had better not mention any one in particular.

A musician only has the right to criticize works like Shakespear's earlier histories and tragedies. The two Richards, King John, and the last act of Romeo and Juliet, depend wholly on the beauty of their music. There is no deep significance, no great subtlety and variety in their numbers; but for splendor of sound, magic of romantic illusion, majesty of emphasis, ardor, elation, reverberation of haunting echoes, and every poetic quality that can waken the heart-stir and the imaginative fire of early manhood, they stand above all recorded music. These things cannot be spectated . . . they must be heard. It is not enough to see Richard III: you should be able to *whistle* it.

My first lessons in Latin in the interval between being taught to read and write by a governess (and taught very well) and my going to school, took place privately in the house of my clerical uncle-in-law . . . William George (surnamed Carroll) who, being married to one of my many maternal aunts (my father had no end of brothers and sisters), had two boys of his own to educate, and took me on with them for awhile in the early mornings to such purpose that when his lessons were ended by my being sent to school, . . . at what is now Wesley College, and was then the Wesleyan Connexional School, I at once rose to the head of the First Latin Junior.

At School I learnt nothing from the curriculum, and at last forgot a good deal of what my uncle had taught me, although the school, snobbishly preparatory for the university, took no subjects seriously except Latin and Greek, . . . if asking a boy once a day in an overcrowded class the Latin for a man or a horse or what not, can be called teaching him Latin, . . . with a pretence of mathematics (Euclidean), of English history (mostly false and scurrilous), and some nominal geography of which I have no recollection. The classes were too large, and the teachers untrained in pedagogy, mostly picking up a living on their way to becoming Wesleyan ministers.

When the time came to teach me mathematics I was taught simply nothing: I was set to explain Euclid's diagrams and theorems without a word as to their use or history or nature. I found it so easy to pick this up in class that at the end of the half year I was expected to come out well in the examinations. I entirely disgraced myself because the questions did not pose the propositions but gave only their . . . numbers in the book, . . . of which I could recollect only the first five and the one about the square of the hypothenuse.

The next step was algebra, again without a word of definition or explanation. I was simply expected to do the sums in Colenso's schoolbook. . . in a, b, and x instead of in pence and shillings. . . .

Now an uninstructed child does not dissociate numbers or their symbols from the material objects it knows quite well how to count. To me a and b, when they meant numbers, were senseless unless they meant butter and eggs and a pound of cheese. I had enough mathematical faculty to infer that if $a = b$ and $b = c$, a must equal c. But I had wit enough to infer that if a quart of brandy equals three Bibles, and three Bibles the Apostles' Creed, the Creed is worth a quart of brandy, manifestly a *reductio ad absurdum*.

My schoolmaster was only the common enemy of me and my school-

The *ménage à trois*—Lucinda Elizabeth Shaw (left), George Carr Shaw (right) and G. J. Vandeleur Lee (lower center).

TOP: G.B.S. at eighteen (seated) with his closest boyhood friend, Edward McNulty (1874). BOTTOM: Shaw at twenty-three, his beard beginning to emerge (portrait taken July 4, 1879).

TOP: Shaw in his late twenties. BOTTOM: Shaw at age 30 (1886). *Photo copyright British Museum.*

OPPOSITE, TOP LEFT: Shaw's "Rabelaisian uncle," Dr. Walter John Gurly. TOP RIGHT: Sydney Olivier, Colonial Office civil servant and early Fabian. BOTTOM: Sidney Webb, Shaw's closest Fabian associate and closest friend all their lives. ABOVE: William Morris, Shavian mentor and elderly literary lion of the English Socialist movement.

ABOVE: May Morris, William Morris's daughter and unwitting partner with G.B.S. in what he called a "mystic betrothal." OPPOSITE, TOP LEFT: Eleanor Marx, youngest daughter of the author of *Capital,* and friend of G.B.S. TOP RIGHT: William Archer, the drama critic who introduced Shaw into London journalism and collaborated with him on the first false start of *Widowers' Houses.* BOTTOM: Annie Besant, freethinker, Fabian, feminist and friend of G.B.S.

TOP: Florence Farr, the first Louka in *Arms and the Man,* and one of Shaw's earliest loves. BOTTOM: Ellen Terry, Henry Irving's leading lady and G.B.S.'s correspondent in his most enduring "paper passion." OPPOSITE: Henry Irving, leading Shakespearean actor of his time.

BELOW: Fabian Society program, 1887. OPPOSITE, LEFT: Oscar Wilde, already in 1890 a London personality but not yet a London playwright. RIGHT: Frank Harris, Shaw's editor at *The Saturday Review*. BOTTOM: Shaw drawn for *The Sketch* in 1894, rehearsing his play *Arms and the Man* at the Avenue Theatre.

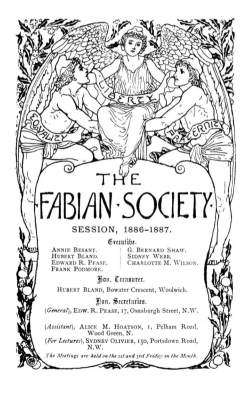

THE
FABIAN·SOCIETY

SESSION, 1886–1887.

Executive.

ANNIE BESANT.   G. BERNARD SHAW.
HUBERT BLAND.   SIDNEY WEBB.
EDWARD R. PEASE.   CHARLOTTE M. WILSON.
FRANK PODMORE.

Hon. Treasurer.

HUBERT BLAND, Bowater Crescent, Woolwich.

Hon. Secretaries.

(*General*), EDW. R. PEASE, 17, Osnaburgh Street, N.W.

(*Assistant*), ALICE M. HOATSON, 1, Pelham Road,
          Wood Green, N.
(*For Lectures*), SYDNEY OLIVIER, 150, Portsdown Road,
          N.W.

The Meetings are held on the 1st and 3rd Friday in the Month.

Meetings.

Sept. 16th ··· ··· **Willis' Rooms,**
(Ordinary)   King Street, St. James' Sq., S.W.
          HUBERT BLAND,
              "The Need for a New Departure."

Oct. 7th ··· ··· **Eleusis Club,**
(Public)   180, King's Road. Chelsea, S.W.
          ANNIE BESANT,
              "Why we work for Socialism."

Oct. 21st ··· ··· **Willis' Rooms.**
(Ordinary)
          WILLIAM SAUNDERS,
                      "Ground Rents."

Nov. 4th ··· ··· **Hampstead,**
(Public)   Vestry Hall. Haverstock Hill.
          GEORGE BERNARD SHAW,
              "Some Illusions of Individualism."

Nov. 25th ··· ··· **Willis' Rooms.**
(Ordinary)
          H. H. CHAMPION,
                      "How to make Converts."

Dec. 2nd ··· ··· **Hatcham Liberal Club,**
(Public)   Portland House, New Cross Road, S.E.
          SIDNEY WEBB,
                      "Socialism and Coöperation."

Dec. 16th ··· ··· **Willis' Rooms.**
(Ordinary)
          CHARLES BRADLAUGH, M.P.
              "The Limits of Legislative Duty."

Janet Achurch and her husband Charles Charrington in *A Doll's House* (1889).

A. E. Drinkwater (father of the playwright John Drinkwater) as Bluntschli in the first touring company of *Arms and the Man* (1895).

LEFT: Charlotte Payne-Townshend in the year of her marriage to G.B.S. (1897). BELOW: Mr. and Mrs. G.B.S. shortly after their marriage.

LEFT: G.B.S. at William Morris's London home at Hammersmith Terrace (1891).

ABOVE, RIGHT: G.B.S. on the beach at the Isle of Wight (1898). ABOVE: "Young Fabians"—Shaw, Olivier, and Beatrice and Sidney Webb—painted by Bertha Newcombe for *The Sketch* (July, 1895).

The Frederick H. Evans frontispiece portrait (1897) for *Plays Unpleasant* (published 1898).

fellows. In his presence I was forbidden to move, or to speak except in answer to his questions. Only by stealth could I relieve the torture of immobility by stealthily exchanging punches (called "the coward's blow") with the boy next me. Had my so-called teacher been my father, and I a child under six, I could have asked him questions, and had the matter explained to me. As it was, I did exactly what the Vatican felt everybody would do if Galileo picked a hole in the Bible. I concluded that mathematics are blazing nonsense, and thereafter made a fool of myself even in my twenties when I made the acquaintance of the editor of Biometrika, Karl Pearson, who maintained that no theory could be valid until it was proved mathematically. I threw in his teeth my conviction that his specialty was an absurdity. Instead of enlightening me he laughed (he had an engaging smile and was a most attractive man) and left me encouraged in my ignorance by my observation that though he was scrupulous and sceptical when counting and correlating, he was as credulous and careless as any ordinary mortal in selecting the facts to be counted. Not until Graham Wallas, a born teacher, enlightened me, did I understand mathematics and realize their enormous importance.

Only in literature did the school establish a claim to have foreseen my future celebrity. We were set to write essays; and I got a first class for a very florid description of the Liffey pool below bridges; but no prize nor serious importance was attached to this or to any subject but Latin.

. . . It would be useless for me to attempt to conceal my hopeless deficiencies as a linguist. I am very sorry; but I cannot learn languages. I have tried hard, only to find that men of ordinary capacity can learn Sanscrit in less time than it takes me to buy a German dictionary. The worst of it is that this disability of mine seems to be most humiliatingly exceptional. My colleagues sit at French plays, German plays, and Italian plays, laughing at all the jokes, thrilling with all the fine sentiments, and obviously seizing the finest shades of the language; whilst I, unless I have read the play beforehand, or asked someone during the interval what it is about, must either struggle with a sixpenny "synopsis" which invariably misses the real point of the drama, or else sit with a guilty conscience and a blank countenance, drawing the most extravagantly wrong inferences from the dumb show of the piece. The torture of this can only be adequately apprehended when it is considered that in ordinary novels, or plays, or conversations, the majority of sentences have no definite meaning at all; and that an energetic intellectual effort to grapple with them, such as one makes in trying to understand a foreign language, would at once discover their inconclusiveness, inaccuracy, and emptiness. When I listen to an English play I am not troubled by not understanding when there is nothing to understand, because I understand, at once that there is nothing to understand. But at a foreign play I do not understand this; and every sentence that means nothing in particular—say five out of six in the slacker moments of the action—seems to me to be a sentence of which I have missed the meaning through my unhappy and disgraceful ignorance of the language. Hence torments of shame and inefficiency, the betrayal of which would destroy my reputation as a critic at one blow. Of course I have a phrase or two ready at the end of my tongue to conceal my ignorance. My command of operatic Italian is almost copious, as might be expected from my experience as a musical critic. I can make love in Italian; I could challenge a foe to a duel in Italian if I were not afraid of him; and if I swallowed some agonizing mineral poison, I could describe my sensations very eloquently. And I could manage a prayer pretty well. But these accomplishments are too special for modern comedy and ordinary conversation. As to French, I can neither speak it nor understand it when spoken without an impracticably long interval for reflection; and I am, besides, subject to a curious propensity, when addressed by Italian or French people, to reply in fluent German, though on all other occasions that language utterly baffles me.

My school was conducted on the assumption that knowledge of Latin is still the be-all and the end-all of education. This was a matter of course: I was given no reason why I should learn Latin instead of some living language. There was, in fact, no reason, as there were plenty of translations of all the classics that have any survival value. The method of teaching was barbarous: I was ordered to learn the declensions and conjugations and instalments of the vocabulary by rote on pain of being caned or "kept in" after school hours if I failed to reel off my paradigms without prompting. When I could do this, which was easy enough to a child accustomed to pick up new words and memorize them, Caesar's commentaries and Virgil's famous epic were thrust into my hands, and without a word of explanation as to what these old commentaries had to do with me, or why I should concern myself laboriously about an ancient Trojan called Eneas, I was ordered to enter the lists against Dryden and extemporize translations of these works, failing in which I should, as before, be caned or kept in. And all the time, even when I was not *being* punished, I was suffering imprisonment, the worst of punishments, for half the day, condemned to sit still, silent and attentive all the time, except for half an hour of relaxation. . . .

There was only one method of teaching. Instead of the pupil asking, and the teacher answering and explaining, the teacher asked the questions. If the pupil could not give the book answer, he received a bad mark, and at the end of the week expiated it by suffering not more than six "tips" (slaps across the palm with a cane) which did not hurt sufficiently to do more than convince me that corporal punishment, to be effective, must be cruel.

After some years of this imprisonment, which though educationally null, at least took me for half the day off the hands of my parents at home, my clerical uncle examined me, and found that I was learning nothing, and forgetting what he had taught me. I was taken away from the Wesleyan, and sent to a very private school in Glasthule, between Kingstown and Dalkey, kept by a family named Halpin. There was an end of this when we presently moved back from our villeggiatura in Dalkey (pronounced Dawky) to Dublin.

I must add that as I was a day boy and never a boarder, and under no sort of control from my amiable and most uncoercive parents in my free time, which included some long intervals between one school and another, my relations with other boys were those of gangsters, rather worse in fact, because gangsters presumably work for plunder, whereas we made mischief for its own sake in mere bravado. Just as we had been in a conspiracy against our school-masters we were in a conspiracy against the police, into whose hands I should probably have fallen had I been in the streets instead of, as it happened, mostly a solitary wanderer in enchanting scenery to the magic of which I was very susceptible. All the same, when I visited a Russian penal settlement in 1931, and was asked to address some edifying remarks to a crowd of juvenile delinquents (boy thieves mostly), I felt obliged to tell them that though I was a very distinguished and "successful" person, I should have been taken up by the police in my boyhood but that by chance I had not been found out.

. . . The day boys, being more numerous, despised the boarders and spoke of them as the skinnies. The boarders were equally contemptuous and opprobrious. Now in Ireland a day boy was really only a half-day boy: he did not return to school in the afternoon. The school was not inspected nor kept up to the mark in any way by the education authorities: in fact there was no mark to be kept up to. Lessons were set me which I had to learn on pain of punishment not cruel enough to effect its purpose with boys who like me were free enough at home to have something more interesting to do than poring over unreadable schoolbooks; but I was not taught manners nor loyalties, nor held to any standards of dress or care of my person. Discipline was confined to silence and sitting still, which did not prevent me from carrying on furtive conversations or fights with the boy sitting next, who might be a friend or a foe. I hated school, and learnt there nothing of what it professed to teach. When I escaped from it, and at the age of fifteen was condemned to five years penal servitude in another sort of prison called an office, I knew at the end of my sentence much more of the world than a university graduate from Eton plus Oxford or Harrow plus Cambridge; but I was frightfully undertrained civically and socially. Even my table manners and company manners I got from a most useful volume called The Manners and Tone of Good Society, an admirable textbook which is, I hope, still current and up to date. With this equipment I was able to hold my own to the extent of my parents' straitened means (I had no means of my own, as I preferred penniless unemployability to any more prison); but all the work of educating, disciplining and forming myself, which should have been done for me when I was a child I had to do for myself as an adult.

Then came my snob tragedy. I have elsewhere described how our household was shared by George John Vandeleur Lee, mesmeric conductor and daringly original teacher of singing, who was my mother's musical tutor and colleague. My parents seem hardly to have considered whether I was educated or not, provided I went to school according to custom. But Lee, though almost wholly preoccupied with music, thought that something ought to be done about it; for I was clearly learning nothing except what I had better not have learnt. It happened that just then he made the acquaintance of a certain Mr Peach, who was drawing master at the Central Model Boys' School in Marlborough Street, undenominational and classless in theory but in fact Roman Catholic, where the boys whose parents could afford it brought five shillings to school periodically, and were caned in the Wesleyan manner if they failed. It was an enormous place, with huge unscaleable railings and gates on which for me might well have been inscribed "All hope abandon, ye who enter here"; for that the son of a Protestant merchant-gentleman and feudal downstart should pass those bars or associate in any way with its hosts of lower middle class Catholic children, sons of petty shopkeepers and tradesmen, was inconceivable from the Shaw point of view.

But Peach had impressed on Lee that the teaching, as far as it went, was skilled and genuine, and that the cheaper genteel private schools were worse than useless. So I was sent to Marlborough Street, and at once lost caste outside it and became a boy with whom no Protestant young gentleman would speak or play.

Not so within the railings. There I was a superior being, and in play hour did not play, but walked up and down with the teachers in their reserved promenade.

It did not last long. I was in my thirteenth year (1869) and endured it from February to September. I for the first time set myself against my fate, and flatly refused to go back to the Model School on any terms. My father, as much ashamed of it as I was, and much less resolute, let me have my way; and I was duly restored to genteel Protestantism in a day school of the Incorporated Society For Promoting Protestant Schools in Ireland. It was in Aungier Street (pronounced Ainjer) and labelled Dublin English Scientific and Commercial Day School. It was closed in 1878. This was my last school prison. I left it in 1871 to become, in my fifteenth year, junior clerk in a highly exclusive gentlemanly estate office crowded with premium paying apprentices who, being mostly university graduates, were fully up to Shaw standards of gentility, and were addressed as Mister whilst I was plain Shaw.

My school bill in Aungier Street was £4 a quarter, plus four shillings for drawing, which was an extra, and was the only extra my parents ever thought of paying for. The drawing master made no pretence of teaching or keeping order. Once a week a clergyman held a bible class, at which we played all sorts of tricks on him and never dreamt of taking religion seriously.

I am not sure that if Marlborough Street had been explained to me as an experimental model school for pupils, not of the laboring "common people" but for the children of persons of modest means engaged in retail instead of wholesale trade, Catholic or Protestant, I might have been spared all my shame; for I was already in revolt against the Shaw snobbery, and observant of the fact that my father's tailor had a country house in Dalkey, a yacht in Dalkey Sound, and could afford to send his sons, much better dressed and equipped than I, to expensive preparatory schools and to college. To rank him as socially inferior to my impecunious father, whose bills were never paid punctually, was as patently absurd to me at 12½ years of age as it is now in my nineties. Far from being a Protestant bigot I was a Boy Atheist, and proud of it, having quite deliberately given up praying as an irrational practice. And my mother's musical activities had cured me of social prejudice against Roman Catholics as well as of my inculcated belief that they all went to hell when they died. My political leanings were flatly Fenian. I was not unreasonable: quite the contrary. I was too open to reason.

All the same, the facts were too stubborn. The classes would not mix. Only sufficient equality of income to make classes intermarriageable will break down class segregation; and in my boyhood it had not yet done so. It has done so since only where the incomes are big. Many years after I shook the dust of the Model School from my feet I lunched one day, an honored guest, at the house of Viscount Powerscourt, an aristocrat among Irish aristocrats. When his daughter left the party early to go up to Dublin it was apologetically explained to me that she had to do so because she was going that evening to a ball at the house of Sir John Arnot, a mammoth Dublin shopkeeper.

I was amazed. In my time she could not have spoken to a shopkeeper, except across the counter, without being ostracized as completely as I was when I was planted out at the Model School, not knowing that it was a model school, and taking it for a common "National School" for the poorest and lowest. But this was never explained to me. Nothing was explained to me. I have been finding out for myself ever since.

I remember thinking when I was a boy how silly it was that my father, whose business was wholesale business, should consider himself socially superior to his tailor, who had the best means of knowing how much poorer than himself my father was, and who had a handsome residence, with ornamental grounds and sailing-boats, at the seaside place where we spent the summer in a six-roomed cottage-villa with a small garden. The great Grafton Street shopkeepers of Dublin outshone the tailor with their palaces and yachts; and their children had luxuries that I never dreamt of as possible for me, besides being far more expensively educated. My father's conviction that they were too lowly to associate with me, when it was so clear that I was too poor to associate with them, may have had some sort of imaginary validity for him; but for me it was snobbish nonsense. I lived to see those children entertaining the Irish peerage and the Viceroy without a thought of the old social barriers; and very glad the Irish peers were to be entertained by them. I lived to see those shops become multiple shops managed by salaried employees who have less chance of entertaining the peerage than a baked-potato man of entertaining the King.

My father was an employer whose whole capital added to that of his partner would not have kept a big modern company in postage stamps for a fortnight. . . . My father's tailor . . . treated him as his social superior because both of them held that a shopkeeper is socially inferior to a merchant; and my father, when he went into business, did so as a merchant selling his goods wholesale. When I was a small boy, and wore out my clothes, my father bought a few yards of cloth and took them to a poorer tailor who sat crosslegged on his board in his tiny shop and was quite obviously no gentleman. And this ancient practice had established the notion that a gentleman could not associate in private with the man who stitched his coat and trousers. It persisted long after leading tailors in Savile Row in London and Dawson Street in Dublin had become commercial princes and their names household words in the most fashionable circles. The great-grandson of a duke might be an impoverished commoner, unable to pay his opulent cheesemonger; but the cheesemonger, however rich, did not presume to dispute his social precedence.

I can remember the time when the standard wage of a clerk in London was fifteen shillings a week whilst that of a skilled mechanic was two pounds; yet people brought up their sons to be clerks instead of masons, carpenters, or fitters, because the black coat, the starched collar, and the pen, were more respectable than the fustian jacket, the corduroy trousers, the chisel, the saw, and the hammer. The clerk, pitiably poorer than the mechanic, was at least richer than the ploughman with his thirteen shillings, or the farmer's "boy" in Oxfordshire with eight shillings and two or three children. I recall these now incredible British figures for the instruction of those who dismiss all changes as Utopian on the general ground that human nature (meaning human conduct, which is infinitely changeable) cannot be changed.

I look back on the oddest class conventions. Sixty years ago, before knockers disappeared from house doors, and wrenching them off at night was a sport of young bloods, I, ranking myself as a gentleman, demanded admission with a volley of raps in a pattern that I could design for myself. It resembled a burst of machine gun fire. But a common person was permitted a single knock only, unless he were a postman, in which case he gave two knocks, peremptory and violent in virtue of his office. As pre-electric bells could not be manipulated in this way, a gentleman's house had two bell pulls, one for visitors and one for tradesmen. To give a knock or ring a bell improper to one's rank was unthinkable. Inevitably we began by associating a single knock with poverty, quite reasonably, and ended, quite unreasonably, by respecting the person who knocked like a machine gun, and despising the single knockist even when the latter was the richer of the two.

These conditioned reflexes, as our scientists now call them, are harder to get rid of than class distinctions due solely to the incompatibility of the rich man's way of living with the poor man's. They will disappear when the basic share of the national income which we call the minimum wage rises to the point at which an extra ten thousand a year can add nothing to the food, dress, lodging, and education of its possessor that is not equally within the reach of Mr Everyman, nor exempt him from doing his daily share of the nation's work any more than it does at present from military service.

Why did the Model School afflict me with a shame which was more or less a psychosis? I have told elsewhere that my esthetic hatred of poverty and squalor, and of the species of human animal they produce, was acquired not at the Model School, where the boys were not worse clad and fed than I, but in the slums into which my nursemaid took me on her visits to her friends when she was supposed to be exercising me in the parks. I hated these experiences intensely. My artist nature, to which beauty and refinement were necessities, would not accept poor people as fellowcreatures, nor slum tenements as fit for human habitation. To me they were places where I could not possibly live. The mental process thus set up culminated some fifty years later in my play Major Barbara, in which the millionaire saint, Andrew Undershaft, thunders his doctrine that poverty is not the natural and proper punishment of vice, but a social crime compared to which our sporadic murders and thefts are negligible. . . .

Now that so many Cabinet Ministers and Secretaries of State come from ungentlemanly proletarian schools it may not be easy for English, Scottish and American readers to understand why I should have made a guilty secret of the Model School. But where there is poverty there is still no change. Manual laborers and gentlemen remain distinct species. It was far worse in Ireland when I was born. Railway carriages were first, second, and third class; and ladies and gentlemen could not travel third class. There were no cushions in the third class. Male passengers smoked shag, and expectorated in all directions. They wore corduroys tied at the knee, collarless shirts which had been left so long unwashed that they offended the second class nose. None of them could read or write: to them the Model School was an aristocratic middle class university beyond their utmost social aspirations. In town they lived in slum tenements: in the country they shared mud-floored cabins with their livestock, or rented dilapidated cowhouses. Their schools, when they had any, were called Ragged Schools; and their women wore shoes and socks only on great occasions when they attended a fair or a religious service. Nevertheless they were human, sometimes to a saintly degree, and just as much divided into categories of Nature's gentry and Nature's cads as the House of Lords. They were full of their own class snobberies, as those of us know who have tried to establish Women's Institutes in English villages and found that none of the women would meet oneanother as social equals.

But, I must repeat, such common humanities did not make the classes associable. In any house large enough to have a kitchen and a drawing-room the pet dog was as much at home with the servants as with their employers; but the human animals were immovably segregate. I was born in a house where there was a kitchen and a drawing-room, and always at least one "thorough-servant," paid £8 a year in cash, and lodged in the basement. . . .

The Incorporated Society's School, though cheap and Protestant and genteel like the Wesleyan, did not pretend to be preparatory for university graduation, and frankly excluded classics from its curriculum. It was for pupils whose fathers, like my own, could not afford to send them to Trinity College, and aimed no higher than to have them trained not for scholarship but for business. Two or three older boys who had a special aptitude for higher mathematics sat apart, not in class, and taught themselves; for nobody else even pretended to teach them. The headmaster sat in his study and had no contact with the boys except when they were sent there to be caned. He was hastily preparing himself for ordination in the then Established Protestant Episcopal Church of Ireland so that he might be qualified for "commutation" when Gladstone disestablished it. The teaching method was the Wesleyan all over again.

I, however, was not the same person I had been at the Wesleyan. . . . At the Wesleyan I had never dreamt of learning my lessons, nor of telling the truth to that common enemy and executioner, the schoolmaster. My scruples began in the Model School; and in Aungier Street, lying was beneath my new moral dignity as a head boy, a position which I shared with a schoolfellow named Dunne who had been with me at the Wesleyan, and had developed a precocity so extraordinary that at sixteen or thereabouts he had the bearing and moral weight of a bishop. So I had to keep up my credit by doing my class work (very trifling) conscientiously. I had only one conflict with the school discipline. Some offence was committed; and the master, to discover whom to punish, asked each boy in succession whether he was the culprit. I refused to answer on the ground that no boy was legally bound to criminate himself, and that the interrogation was a temptation to boys to lie. A day or two passed during which I was supposed to be doomed to some appalling punishment; but I heard no more of it: the situation was new to the teaching staff. When authorities do not know what to do, they can only do what was done last time. As I had created an unprecedented situation, they did nothing; but there were no more such interrogatories. It was my first reform.

At the Model School I had already asserted myself in another direction. The reading lessons in history ignored Ireland and glorified England. I always substituted Ireland for England in such dithyrambs. The boys wondered what would happen to me. But the teacher smiled and said nothing. I was, in fact, a young Fenian in my political sympathies, such as they were. . . .

I am no doubt biased in this matter; for I attribute my own eminence, such as it is, to the fact that I am much better educated than the public school and university products, by whose reckoning I am wholly uneducated. By this is meant that though I began with an extensive knowledge of music, English, German, and Italian, from the sixteenth century to the nineteenth, not by reading books about it but by listening to it and singing it; though I knew the nine symphonies of Beethoven and the three greatest of Mozart's as well as I knew Pop Goes The Weazel; though I had looked at pictures and engravings of pictures until I could recognize the handiwork of the greatest painters at a glance, yet I could not read the Satires of Juvenal in the original Latin, my imprisonment for years in a school where nothing was counted as educational except Latin and Greek having left me unable to read the most conventional Latin epitaph without guessing, or to write a single Ciceronian sentence. I possess Dryden's translation of the Satires and have dipped into them enough to know that it is impossible to read more than a page or two of such a mass of ignorance, vulgarity, bad manners, and filth; and though, thanks mainly to Gilbert Murray, I know as much as anyone need know of the ancient Greek drama, and have learnt all that is now to be learnt from Homer and Virgil from Lord Derby, Morris, Dryden, and Salt, yet I consider myself lucky in having had my mind first well stocked in my nonage by Michael Angelo and Handel, Beethoven and Mozart, Shakespear and Dickens and their like, and not by Latin verse-mongers and cricketers.

Take the case of history as an indispensable part of the education of a citizen. Have you ever reflected on the impossibility of learning history from a collection of its bare facts in the order in which they actually occurred? You might as well try to gather a knowledge of London from the pages of the telephone directory. French history was not one of my school subjects; but by reading with great entertainment the historical novels of Dumas *père* I had a vivid conspectus of France from the six-teenth to the eighteenth century, from Chicot to Cagliostro, from the conquest of the nobility by the monarchy under Richelieu to the French Revolution. Like Marlborough, I had already learnt all I knew of Eng-lish history, from King John to the final suicide of the English feudal aristocracy and its supersession by the capitalists on Bosworth Field, from the chronicle plays of Shakespear. Adding to these congenial authorities the Waverley novels of Walter Scott I came out with a taste for history and an acquaintance with its personages and events which made the philosophy of history real for me when I was fully grown. Macaulay did not repel me as a historian (of sorts) nor Hegel and Marx bore and be-wilder me. At last I became a historian myself. I wrote a play entitled In Good King Charles' Golden Days. For the actual occurrence of the incidents in it I cannot produce a scrap of evidence, being quite con-vinced that they never occurred; yet anyone reading this play or witness-ing a performance of it will not only be pleasantly amused, but will come out with a knowledge of the dynamics of Charles' reign: that is, of the political and personal forces at work in it, that ten years of digging up mere facts in the British Museum or the Record Office could not give. And whereas most of us leave school resolved never to open a school-book again or even think of these instruments of torture, I should starve if the effect of my books and plays were not to make the sort of people I write for buy another of them and yet another until there are no more to read.

That I can write as I do without having to think about my style is due to my having been as a child steeped in the Bible, The Pilgrim's Progress, and Cassell's Illustrated Shakespear. I was taught to hold the Bible in such reverence that when one day, as I was buying a pennyworth of sweets in a little shop in Dublin, the shopkeeper tore a leaf out of a dismembered Bible to wrap them in, I was horrified, and half expected to see him struck by lightning. All the same I took the sweets and ate them; for to my Protestant mind the shopkeeper, as a Roman Catholic, would go to hell as such Bible or no Bible, and was no gentleman anyhow. Besides, I liked eating sweets. I was too infantile then to reach my more mature conclusion that the reason I could read and remember the Bible stories and not read school books was that the Bible stories were translated when English literary art was at the summit of its majesty, the translators having believed that they were Englishing the very words of God himself.

. . . I can remember sitting in a row of about fifty boys in alphabetical order called a history class. Each day we were set a chapter in The Students' Hume. The teacher would go through the chapter and through the alphabet, asking questions about the facts and dates mentioned in it. As my name began with the letter S, I could calculate within ten lines or so what question would fall to me. I can still remember that in the chapter about the Peninsular War the answer to the question that always came was "The retreat from Burgos." From the ten lines hastily read on my way to the classroom I was even able to afford a prompt to the boy next to me if he had not been equally studious.

Now though I cannot deny that on these occasions I not only gave my enemy the teacher an excuse for pretending to believe that I had exhumed the whole history of the Peninsular War, but learnt that there had been a retreat from Burgos, it can hardly be claimed that I was learning history, whereas when I was at home reading Quentin Durward, A Tale of Two Cities, or the Three Musketeers, I was learning it very agreeably. And inasmuch as attendance at school kept me away from such books for half the day, I must affirm that my schooling not only failed to teach me what it professed to be teaching, but prevented me from being educated to an extent which infuriates me when I think of all I might have learnt at home by myself.

It is evident that my schooling was a complete failure, and that the aesthetic education I received out of school was my salvation. My excuse for describing it here as a matter of public importance is . . . an unpatriotic habit into which many of my critics have fallen. Whenever my view strikes them as being at all outside the range of, say, an ordinary suburban churchwarden, they conclude that I am echoing Schopenhauer, Nietzsche, Ibsen, Strindberg, Tolstoy, or some other heresiarch in northern or eastern Europe.

I confess there is something flattering in this simple faith in my accomplishment as a linguist and my erudition as a philosopher. But I cannot countenance the assumption that life and literature are so poor in these islands that we must go abroad for all dramatic material that is not common and all ideas that are not superficial. I therefore venture to put my critics in possession of certain facts concerning my contact with modern ideas.

About half a century ago, an Irish novelist, Charles Lever, wrote a story entitled A Day's Ride: A Life's Romance. It was published by Charles Dickens in Household Words, and proved so strange to the public taste that Dickens pressed Lever to make short work of it. I read scraps of this novel when I was a child; and it made an enduring impression on me. The hero was a very romantic hero, trying to live bravely, chivalrously, and powerfully by dint of mere romance-fed imagination, without courage, without means, without knowledge, without skill, without anything real except his bodily appetites. Even in my childhood I found in this poor devil's unsuccessful encounters with the facts of life, a poignant quality that romantic fiction lacked. The book, in spite of its first failure, is not dead: I saw its title the other day in the catalogue of Tauchnitz.

Now why is it that when I also deal in the tragi-comic irony of the conflict between real life and the romantic imagination, critics never affiliate me to my countryman and immediate forerunner, Charles Lever, whilst they confidently derive me from a Norwegian author of whose language I do not know three words, and of whom I knew nothing until years after the Shavian *Anschauung* was already unequivocally declared in books full of what came, ten years later, to be perfunctorily labelled Ibsenism? I was not Ibsenist even at second hand; for Lever, though he may have read Henri Beyle, *alias* Stendhal, certainly never read Ibsen. Of the books that made Lever popular, such as Charles O'Malley and Harry Lorrequer, I know nothing but the names and some of the illustrations. But the story of the day's ride and life's romance of Potts (claiming alliance with Pozzo di Borgo) caught me and fascinated me as something strange and significant, though I already knew all about Alnaschar and Don Quixote and Simon Tappertit and many another romantic hero mocked by reality. From the plays of Aristophanes to the tales of Stevenson that mockery has been made familiar to all who are properly saturated with letters.

Where, then, was the novelty in Lever's tale? Partly, I think, in a new seriousness in dealing with Potts's disease. Formerly, the contrast between madness and sanity was deemed comic: Hogarth shews us how fashionable people went in parties to Bedlam to laugh at the lunatics. I myself have had a village idiot exhibited to me as something irresistibly funny. On the stage the madman was once a regular comic figure: that was how Hamlet got his opportunity before Shakespear touched him. The originality of Shakespear's version lay in his taking the lunatic sympathetically and seriously, and thereby making an advance towards the eastern consciousness of the fact that lunacy may be inspiration in disguise, since a man who has more brains than his fellows necessarily appears as mad to them as one who has less. But Shakespear did not do for Pistol and Parolles what he did for Hamlet. The particular sort of madman they represented, the romantic make-believer lay outside the pale of sympathy in literature: he was pitilessly despised and ridiculed here as he was in the east under the name of Alnaschar, and was doomed to be, centuries later, under the name of Simon Tappertit. When Cervantes relented over Don Quixote, and Dickens relented over Pickwick, they did not become impartial: they simply changed sides, and became friends and apologists where they had formerly been mockers.

In Lever's story there is a real change of attitude. There is no relenting towards Potts: he never gains our affections like Don Quixote and Pickwick: he has not even the infatuate courage of Tappertit. But we dare not laugh at him, because, somehow, we recognize ourselves in Potts. We may, some of us, have enough nerve, enough muscle, enough luck, enough tact or skill or address or knowledge to carry things off better than he did; to impose on the people who saw through him; to fascinate Katinka (who cut Potts so ruthlessly at the end of the story); but for all that, we know that Potts plays an enormous part in ourselves and in the world, and that the social problem is not a problem of story-book heroes of the older pattern, but a problem of Pottses, and of how to make men of them. To fall back on my old phrase, we have the feeling—one that Alnaschar, Pistol, Parolles, and Tappertit never gave us—that Potts is a piece of really scientific natural history as distinguished from funny story telling. His author is not throwing a stone at a creature of another and inferior order, but making a confession, with the effect that the stone hits each of us full in the conscience and causes our self-esteem to smart very sorely. Hence the failure of Lever's book to please the readers of Household Words. That pain in the self-esteem nowadays causes critics to raise a cry of Ibsenism. I therefore assure them that the sensation first came to me from Lever and may have come to him from Beyle, or at least out of the Stendhalian atmosphere.

. . . I was in school a shamelessly unscrupulous liar in my excuses for neglecting my school lessons and leaving my exercises unwritten, the true reason being that I was too busy reading readable books (the school books were utterly unreadable), listening to music, looking at pictures, and roaming over Dalkey Hill: that is, doing the things that really educated me and made me loathe my school prison, where art and beauty had no place. . . .

. . . There is in Dublin a modest National Gallery, with the usual collection of casts from the antique. Here boys are permitted to prowl. I prowled. . . . Let me add a word of gratitude to that cherished asylum of my boyhood, the National Gallery of Ireland. I believe I am the only Irishman who has ever been in it, except the officials. But I know that it did much more for me than the two confiscated medieval Cathedrals so magnificently "restored" out of the profits of the drink trade.[2]

. . . A well-known Dublin musician, Joseph Robinson, allowed me to call on him periodically and borrow a volume of Duchesne's outlines of the old masters—20 volumes of them, I think. When I had any money —which hardly ever happened—I bought volumes of the Bohn translation of Vasari and read them with immense interest. Result, at fifteen, I knew enough about a considerable number of Italian & Flemish painters to recognize their work at sight. . . . On the whole, I got some education, thanks to Communism in pictures.

Again, we had, for our summer residence, a cottage high up on a hill commanding the northern bight of Dublin Bay, from Howth to Dalkey Sound on one side, and the southern bight, from Dalkey Island to Bray Head, on the other. There is not two penn'orth of really grand mountain or tree in that landscape, but I have never seen more beautiful skies, even in Italy; and I always look at the sky.

Consequently my university has three colleges—the musical society, the National Gallery, and Dalkey Hill.

What was the Romantic movement? I don't know, though I was under its spell in my youth. All I can say is that it was a freak of the human imagination, which created an imaginary past, an imaginary heroism, an imaginary poetry out of what appears to those of us who are no longer in the vein for it as the show in a theatrical costumier's shop window. Everybody tells you that it began with somebody and ended with somebody else; but all its beginners were anticipated; and it is going on still. Byron's Laras and Corsairs look like the beginning of it to an elderly reader until he recollects The Castle of Otranto; yet The Castle of Otranto is not so romantic as Otway's Venice Preserved, which, again, is no more romantic than the tales of the knights errant beloved in Don Quixote. Romance is always, I think, a product of *ennui,* an attempt to escape from a condition in which real life appears empty, prosaic, and boresome—therefore essentially a gentlemanly product. The man who has grappled with real life, flesh to flesh and spirit to spirit, has little patience with fools' paradises. When Carlyle said to the emigrants, "Here and now is your America," he spoke as a realist to romanticists; and Ibsen was of the same mind when he finally decided that there is more tragedy in the next suburban villa than in a whole imaginary Italy of unauthentic Borgias.

For all that, the land of dreams is a wonderful place; and the great Romancers who found the key of its gates were no Alnaschars. These artists, inspired neither by faith and beatitude, nor by strife and realization, were neither saints nor crusaders, but pure enchanters, who conjured up a region where existence touches you delicately to the very heart, and where mysteriously thrilling people, secretly known to you in dreams of your childhood, enact a life in which terrors are as fascinating as delights; so that ghosts and death, agony and sin, become, like love and victory, phases of an unaccountable ecstasy. Goethe bathed by moonlight in the Rhine to learn this white magic, and saturated even the criticism and didacticism of Faust with the strangest charm by means of it. Mozart was a most wonderful enchanter of this kind: he drove very clever men—Oublicheff, for example—clean out of their wits by his airs from heaven and blasts from hell in Le Nozze di Figaro and Don Giovanni. From the middle of the eighteenth to the middle of the nineteenth century Art went crazy in its search for spells and dreams; and many artists who, being neither Mozarts nor Goethes, had their minds burnt up instead of cleansed by "the sacred fire," yet could make that fire cast shadows that gave unreal figures a strange majesty, and phantom landscapes a "light that never was on sea or land." These phrases which I quote were then the commonplaces of critics' rhapsodies.

. . . We have been led forth from the desert in which these mirages were always on the horizon to a land overflowing with reality and earnestness. But if I were to be stoned for it this afternoon by fervent Wagnerites and Ibsenites, I must declare that the mirages were once dear and beautiful, and that the whole Wagnerian criticism of them, however salutary (I have been myself one of its most ruthless practitioners), has all along been a pious dialectical fraud, because it applies the tests of realism and revelation to the arts of illusion and transfiguration.

I somehow knew this when I began, as a boy entering on my teens, to think about such things. I remember saying, in some discussion that arose on the subject of my education, that T.C.D.[3] men were all alike (by which I meant all wrong), and that I did not want to go through college. I was entirely untouched by university idealism. When it reached me later on, I recognized how ignorantly I had spoken in my boyhood; but when I went still further and learnt that this idealism is never realized in our schools and universities, and operates only as a mask and a decoy for our system of impressing and enslaving children and stultifying adults, I concluded that my ignorance had been inspired, and had served me very well. I have not since changed my mind.

However that may be, I decided, at thirteen or thereabouts, that for the moment I must go into business and earn some money and begin to be a grown-up man.

A Genteel Profession

. . . THERE WAS at that time, on one of the quays in Dublin, a firm of cloth merchants, by name Scott, Spain, and Rooney. A friend of ours knew Scott, and asked him to give me a start in life with some employment. I called on this gentleman by appointment. I had the vaguest notion of what would happen: all I knew was that I was "going into an office." I thought I should have preferred to interview Spain, as the name was more romantic. Scott turned out to be a smart handsome man, with moustachios; and I suppose a boy more or less in his warehouse did not matter to him when there was a friend to be obliged: at all events, he said only a few perfunctory things and was settling my employment, when, as my stars would have it, Rooney appeared. Mr Rooney was much older, not at all smart, but long, lean, grave and respectable.

The last time I saw the late Sir George Alexander (the actor) he described to me his own boyhood, spent in a cloth warehouse in Cheapside, where they loaded him with bales, and praised him highly for his excellent conduct, even rewarding him after some years to the extent of sixteen shillings a week. Rooney saved me from the bales. He talked to me a little, and then said quite decisively that I was too young, and that the work was not suitable to me. He evidently considered that my introducer, my parents, and his young partner, had been inconsiderate; and I presently descended the stairs, reprieved and unemployed. . . . I have not forgotten his sympathy.

A year later, or thereabouts, my uncle Frederick, an important official in the Valuation Office, whom no land agent or family solicitor in Dublin could afford to disoblige, asked a leading and terribly respectable firm of land agents, carrying on business at 15 Molesworth Street, to find a berth for me. They did so; and I became their office boy (junior clerk I called myself) at eighteen shillings a month. It was a very good opening for anyone with a future as a land agent, which in Ireland at that time was a business of professional rank. It was utterly thrown away on me. However, as the office was overstaffed with gentlemen apprentices, who had paid large fees for the privilege of singing operatic selections with me when the principals were out, there was nothing to complain of socially, even for a Shaw; and the atmosphere was as uncommercial as that of an office can be. Thus I learnt business habits without being infected with the business spirit.

In a Gilbert and Sullivan opera a promoted British office boy tells us how he cleaned the windows and swept the floor and polished up the handle of the big front door. I did nothing so ungentlemanly. . . . For £18 a year I filed the incoming letters and found them when required. Of the outgoing letters I took impressions in a copying press before posting them. The only account I kept was the postage account. I was Errand Boy to the extent of taking leases to the Custom House to be stamped, and so experienced the Circumlocution Office incivility I had read about in Little Dorrit. My lunch was a penny roll; and as I had to go out to buy this, I bought for the rest of the staff as well. At that time luncheon was not a serious meal: at most it was only a snack. Later in life I came up against old actors who knew nothing of it and could not understand why rehearsals should be interrupted for it or young players knock off work for it.

No more than at school was anything explained to me. If some odd job puzzled me I was told to "see what was done last time"; and to this I owe my knowledge of how necessary political Constitutions are in the long intervals between able monarchs, leaders, or dictators, when the authorities can think of nothing except continuing an established routine. I had the rare faculty for learning and generalizing from experience, though I did not then know that it was rare, and attached no importance to it. I took not the slightest interest in land agency; but I laid up a large stock of observations which became useful when Henry George explained their political significance to me. At the time I simply disliked business, and did not think politically about it.

At the end of about a year, a sudden vacancy occurred in the most active post in the office: that of head cashier. As this involved banking business for the clients, and the daily receipt and payment of cheques and all sorts of rents, interests, insurances, and private allowances, it was a bustling post, and a position of trust as well. The vacancy occurred so suddenly that I had to stop the gap pending the engagement of a new cashier of mature age and high character. But as I found no difficulty in doing the work, and succeeded in changing my sloped, straggly, boyish handwriting for a very fair imitation of the compact script of my predecessor; and as, furthermore, the doubling of my salary (now £24) to £48 was a considerable step ahead, the engagement of a mature cashier was first delayed, and then dropped. I proved a conscientiously correct cashier and accountant. Though I never knew how much money I had in the pocket I reserved for my own private cash, I was never a farthing out in my office accounts. And so I was no longer an office boy. I was chief cashier, head cashier, sole cashier, equal to any of the staff, and the most active and responsible member of it.

But my heart was not in the business. I never made a payment without a hope that I should never have to make it again. Yet I was so wanting in enterprise, and shy and helpless in worldly matters (though I believe I had the air of being rather the reverse) that every six months I found myself making the payment again.

On the other hand, the office secured for me the society of a set of gentlemen apprentices, who had paid big premiums to be taught a genteel profession. They learnt little for their money except the scraps of operas I taught them. I recall one occasion when an apprentice, perched on the washstand with his face shewing above the screen that decently concealed it and stood for Manrico's tower dungeon, sang *Ah, che la morte*[1] so passionately that he was unconscious of the sudden entry of the senior partner, Charles Uniacke Townshend, who stared stupended at the bleating countenance above the screen, and finally fled upstairs, completely beaten by the situation.

Thus I had in the office some fun and the society of university men; but I hated my position and my work; and in 1876, I walked out and threw myself recklessly into London, joining my mother there immediately after the death of my sister Agnes in the Isle of Wight.

One or two other things I may as well mention. A little time after I entered the office the appalling discovery was made that instead of being a Protestant church-goer, as became a youth introduced by a high official in the Valuation Office, I was actually what used to be called in those days an Infidel. Arguments arose in which I, being young and untrained in dialectic, got severely battered. "What is the use," said Humphrey Lloyd (an apprentice), "of arguing when you dont know what a syllogism is?" I went to the dictionary and found out what it was, learning, like Molière's bourgeois hero, that I had been syllogizing all my life without knowing it. On the matter coming to the ears of my senior employer Charles Uniacke Townshend, a pillar of the Church, of the Royal Dublin Society, and of everything else pillarable in Dublin, he respected my freedom of conscience so far as to make no attempt to reason with me nor interfere with my religion or irreligion; but he demanded a promise not to discuss the subject in his office. Against my conscience I gave him my word, and kept it, not because my living was at stake (I have never hesitated to burn my boats) but because I did not intend to live under such limitations permanently. The incident put land-agency and office life out of the question for me as a serious career. I remained ashamed of my promise; and when my employers after I left gave me a handsome testimonial at my father's request I was unreasonably furious that such a demand should have been made. I am now (1947) rather proud of the document.

Nevertheless I was by no means clearly conscious of my own value and destiny. But one day the apprentice who sang *Ah, che la morte* so passionately happened to remark that every boy thinks he is going to be a great man. The shock that this gave me made me suddenly aware that this was my own predicament, though I could do nothing that gave me the smallest ground for classing myself as born to the hierarchy of Shakespear, Shelley, Mozart, Praxiteles, and Michael Angelo. Such a pretence in a promoted office boy seemed monstrous: my youthful diffidence and cowardice told me I was only an ignorant duffer. But my desk and cash-box gave me the habit of daily work, and taught me that I must learn to do something instead of daydreaming, and that nothing but technical skill, practice, efficiency: in short, mastery, could be of any use to me. The sort of *aplomb* my cousins seemed to derive from the consciousness that their great-great-grandfathers had also been the great-great-grandfathers of Sir Robert Shaw of Bushy Park was denied to me. You cannot be imposed on by baronets as such if you belong to the republic of art. I was chronically ashamed and unhappy because I could not do anything I wanted to do. I could keep Uniacke Townshend's cash and never dream of stealing it (riper years have made me aware that many of my artistic feats may be less highly estimated in the books of the Recording Angel);

but at the time it counted for less than nothing. It was a qualification for what I hated.

My literary activity during this time, though I did not count it as such, had begun. An old schoolfellow of mine, Matthew Edward McNulty, later the author of three novels of Irish life, was an official in the Bank of Ireland, and had been drafted to the Newry branch of that institution. We had struck up a friendship, being both imaginative geniuses, although circumstances separated us so effectually that after our schooldays we saw no more of one another. But during these boyish years we kept up a correspondence by return of post, writing immense letters to one another illustrated with crude drawings and enlivened by burlesque dramas. It was understood that the letters were to be destroyed as soon as answered, as we did not like the possibility of our unreserved soul histories falling into strange hands.

I vaguely remember that when I was a boy I concocted a short story and sent it to some boys' journal. It was about a man with a gun attacking another man in the Glen of the Downs. The gun was the centre of interest to me. My correspondence with Edward McNulty worked off my incipient literary energy.

I also made a most valuable acquaintance through the accident of coming to lodge in the same house with him. This was Chichester Bell, a cousin of Graham Bell, the inventor of the telephone, consequently a nephew of Melville Bell the inventor of the phonetic script known as Visible speech. His father was Alexander Bell, author of the Standard Elocutionist, and by far the most majestic and imposing man that ever lived on this or any other planet. He had been elocution professor in my old school, the Wesleyan Connexional, now Wesley College. Chichester Bell was a qualified physician who had gone to Germany and devoted himself to chemistry and physics in the school of Helmholtz. My intercourse with him was of great use to me. We studied Italian together; and though I did not learn Italian I learned a good deal else, mostly about physics and pathology. I read Tyndall and Trousseau's Clinical Lectures. And it was Bell who made me take Wagner seriously. I had heard nothing of his except the Tannhäuser march played by a second-rate military band; and my only comment was that the second theme was a weak imitation of the famous air, made up of a chain of turns, in Weber's Freischütz overture. When I found that Bell regarded Wagner as a great

[71]

composer, I bought a vocal score of Lohengrin: the only sample to be had at the Dublin music shops. The first few bars completely converted me.

I sometimes dream that I am back in that office again, bothered by a consciousness that a long period has elapsed during which I have neglected my most important duties. I have drawn no money at the bank in the mornings, nor lodged any in the afternoons. I have paid no insurance premiums, nor head-rents, nor mortgage interests. Whole estates must have been sold up, widows and orphans left to starve, mortgages foreclosed, and the landed gentry of Ireland abandoned to general ruin, confusion, and anarchy, all through my unaccountable omission of my daily duties for years and years, during which, equally unaccountably, neither I nor anyone else in the office has aged by a single day. I generally wake in the act of asking my principals, with the authority which belongs to my later years, whether they realize what has happened, and whether they propose to leave so disgracefully untrustworthy a person as myself in a position of such responsibility.

In some ways I had a better time of it than most clerks. My associates in the office were apprentices of good social standing, mostly University men. I was not precluded from giving myself certain airs of being in the same position; and when, making a journey on the firm's business, I travelled first-class, my expenses were not challenged. But as it was assumed that I was a youth in training to be a man of business, I never got a living wage, though during most of that four and a half years I occupied a post of considerable responsibility.

. . . When, later in life, and active in the Socialist movement, I was posed with the usual assumption that inequality of work requires inequality of pay, I could answer from experience that, other things being equal, the higher the work the less people would do it for. If my employers had asked me to do the job of a charwoman they would have had to overcome my repugnance to it by a salary at least twenty times as large as they actually paid me after my promotion.

As my father had to make up the difference between what my employer paid me and what my subsistence cost, my employer was really sweating my father. He managed the estates of Irish landlords for them: a business in which agents got shot occasionally. Thus the industry which was feeding the country was exploited by the industry which was bleeding it to death. I speak without malice; for in the course of time I inherited an estate myself, and became an absentee Irish landlord, agent and all. Accordingly I now maintain that landlordism is not always and necessarily bad: there were landlords even in Ireland who did more for their estates than their estates did for them. My wife's Irish estate cost her £600 a year until I induced her to sell it.

Forty years after I had shaken the dust of that office from my feet I found myself one morning standing in the street outside it, having in the meantime pulled off the Great Man Stunt, and been recently held up to an admiring Europe as "the Molière of the Twentieth Century." I was looking for a Commissioner of Oaths to witness some legal profanity or other; and it suddenly struck me that there was one on the first floor of the building where I had slaved as a clerk. It was a good excuse for going in and peeping through the glass door of my old prison as I passed. I was disgusted to find that they had built a pártition which shut off the view of my part of the formerly spacious room, and, as we would have said in my time, "made the place look like a pawnbroker's."

I went upstairs. The Commissioner of Oaths was out. His clerk was no common clerk: he was every inch a churchwarden, frock coated, large, dignified, prosperous, and, I could swear, a Master Mason in the Lodge next door. Still, only a clerk, legally unable to make anyone swear but his employer. I am by profession a communicative person; and as it was a fine morning, and we were not yet pressed for time, we chatted for a moment. I mentioned that I had been a clerk myself in that building forty years before. Instantly the distinguished consideration he had been beguiled into treating me with by my air of being somebody in particular changed into undisguised contempt, barbed by incredulity. He expressed the contempt in his tone, and the incredulity, in these staggering words:

"I don't remember you."

He had been there when I was there. He had been there for forty years. All that time, whilst I was making six or seven reputations, touching nothing that I did not adorn, being abused by all the papers as only the famous are abused, and surveying mankind, if not from China to Peru, at least from Stamboul to Jamaica, he had kept on coming at ten every morning and going home at five every evening, and was good for another ten years of it. And that is what would have happened to me but for the pure accident of my turning out to be the one man in every million or so who happens to have the knack of telling lies so attractively that people go to the theatre to see actors pretending they are true. Granted that he was nothing like so worn out as I, and was obviously on better terms with himself. Granted that he was none of your English Newman Noggses,[2] but an Irish metropolitan solicitor's right hand man. Granted that he had never entered a third class carriage in his life; that he despised shorthand as the craft of a common reporter; that he did not know at sight a typewriter from a cash register. Still, I cannot believe that when he and I were youths together in the eighteenseventies he intended to be a clerk all his life any more than I did.

I fled from his majestic presence recalling many memories. I remembered the old bookkeeper whom I had asked whether his son was a clerk, and who had said, with a ferocity that amazed me, that he would rather see him dead, and told me how he had struggled to save him from that fate by apprenticing him to a pharmaceutical chemist. I remembered how I had been offered his post, and had flatly refused it, to the astonishment of my employer. I remembered how my father, who had managed to obtain a sinecure in the law courts, and had on its abolition received some hundreds of pounds compensation, had thereupon set up in a business he knew nothing about in partnership with a gentleman who had been apprenticed to another and quite different business; so that the two had become employers with clerks of their own; and I reflected on how utterly impossible such an absurdity would be now, although then it happened every day. . . .

I did not set foot in Ireland again until 1905, and not then on my own initiative. I went back to please my wife; and a curious reluctance to retrace my steps made me land in the south and enter Dublin through the backdoor from Meath rather than return as I came, through the front door on the sea. In 1876 I had had enough of Dublin. James Joyce in his Ulysses has described, with a fidelity so ruthless that the book is hardly bearable, the life that Dublin offers to its young men, or, if you prefer to put it the other way, that its young men offer to Dublin. No doubt it is much like the life of young men everywhere in modern urban civilization. A certain flippant futile derision and belittlement that confuses the noble and serious with the base and ludicrous seems to me peculiar to Dublin; but I suppose that is because my only personal experience of that phase of youth was a Dublin experience; for when I left my native city I left that phase behind me, and associated no more with men of my age until, after about eight years of solitude in this respect, I was drawn into the Socialist revival of the early eighties, among Englishmen intensely serious and burning with indignation at very real and very fundamental evils that affected all the world; so that the reaction against them bound the finer spirits of all the nations together instead of making them cherish hatred of one another as a national virtue. Thus, when I left Dublin I left (a few private friendships apart) no society that did not disgust me. To this day my sentimental regard for Ireland does not include the capital. I am not enamored of failure, of poverty, of obscurity, and of the ostracism and contempt which these imply; and these were all that Dublin offered to the enormity of my unconscious ambition. The cities a man likes are the cities he has conquered. Napoleon did not turn from Paris to sentimentalize over Ajaccio, nor Catherine from St Petersburg to Stettin as the centre of her universe.

. . . I never thought of myself as destined to become what is called a great man: indeed I was diffident to the most distressing degree; and I was ridiculously credulous as to the claims of others to superior knowledge and authority. But one day in the office I had a shock. One of the apprentices, by name C. J. Smyth, older than I and more a man of the world, remarked that every young chap thought he was going to be a great man. On a really modest youth this commonplace would have had no effect. It gave me so perceptible a jar that I suddenly became aware that I had never thought I was to be a great man simply because I had always taken it as a matter of course. The incident passed without leaving any preoccupation with it to hamper me; and I remained as diffident as ever because I was still as incompetent as ever. But I doubt whether I ever recovered my former complete innocence of subconscious intention to devote myself to the class of work that only a few men excel in, and to accept the responsibilities that attach to its dignity.

Now this bore directly on my abandonment of Dublin, for which many young Irishmen of today find it impossible to forgive me. My business in life could not be transacted in Dublin out of an experience confined to Ireland. I had to go to London just as my father had to go to the Corn Exchange. London was the literary centre for the English language, and for such artistic culture as the realm of the English language (in which I proposed to be king) could afford. There was no Gaelic League in those days, nor any sense that Ireland had in herself the seed of culture. Every Irishman who felt that his business in life was on the higher planes of the cultural professions felt that he must have a metropolitan domicile and an international culture: that is, he felt that his first business was to get out of Ireland. I had the same feeling. For London as London, or England as England, I cared nothing. . . .

Behold me therefore in my twentieth year, with a business training, in an occupation which I detested as cordially as any sane person lets himself detest anything he cannot escape from. In March 1876 I broke loose. I gave a month's notice. My employers naturally thought I was discontented with my salary (£84, I think, by that time), and explained to me quietly that they hoped to make my position more eligible. My only fear was that they should make it so eligible that all excuse for throwing it up would be taken from me. I thanked them and said I was resolved to go; and I had, of course, no reason in the world to give them for my resolution.[3] They were a little hurt, and explained to my uncle that they had done their best, but that I seemed to have made up my mind. I had. After enjoying for a few days the luxury of not having to go to the office, and being, if not my own master, at least not anyone else's slave, I packed a carpet bag; boarded the North Wall boat; and left the train next morning at Euston, where, on hearing a porter cry, in an accent quite strange to me (I had hardly ever heard an h dropped before) "Ensm' faw weel?" which I rightly interpreted as "Hansom or four wheel?" I was afraid to say hansom, because I had never been in one and was not sure that I should know how to get in. So I solemnly drove in a growler through streets whose names Dickens had made familiar to me, London being at its spring best, which is its very best, to Victoria Grove, where the driver accepted four shillings as a reasonable fare for the journey.

Escape from Becoming a
Successful Novelist

I was driven to write because I could do nothing else. In an old novel of mine—"Cashel Byron's Profession"—the hero, a prizefighter, remarks that it's not what a man would like to do, but what he *can* do, that he must work at in this world. I wanted to be another Michael Angelo, but found that I could not draw. I wanted to be a musician, but found I could not play—to be a dramatic singer, but had no voice. I did not want to write: that came as a matter of course without any wanting. . . .

At 20, I . . . blindly plunged into London. My published works at this time consisted of a letter written when I was 16 or 17 to "Public Opinion" in which I sought to stem the force of the first great Moody & Sankey revival by the announcement that I, personally, had renounced religion as a delusion.[1] London was not ripe for me. . . . My first appearance in print was in a boys' paper: two lines in the correspondence column. But it was in "Public Opinion" that I made my *debut* as a critic and controversialist. The only result was an emergency meeting of my uncles to discuss the horrifying news that the Shaw family had produced an Atheist. I still hold that thinkers who are not militant atheists in their teens will have no religion at all when they are 40. I was already a Creative Evolutionist in the bud. . . .

One evening in 1878 or thereabouts, I, being then in my earliest twenties, was at a bachelor party of young men of the professional class in the house of a doctor in the Kensingtonian quarter of London.[2] They fell to talking about religious revivals; and an anecdote was related of a man who, having incautiously scoffed at the mission of Messrs Moody and Sankey, a then famous firm of American evangelists, was subsequently carried home on a shutter, slain by divine vengeance as a blasphemer. A timid minority, without quite venturing to question the truth of the incident—for they naturally did not care to run the risk of going home on shutters themselves—nevertheless shewed a certain disposition to cavil at those who exulted in it; and something approaching to an argument began. At last it was alleged by the most evangelical of the disputants that Charles Bradlaugh, the most formidable atheist on the Secularist platform, had taken out his watch publicly and challenged the Almighty to strike him dead in five minutes if he really existed and disapproved of atheism. The leader of the cavillers, with great heat, repudiated this as a gross calumny, declaring that Bradlaugh had repeatedly and indignantly contradicted it, and implying that the atheist champion was far too pious a man to commit such a blasphemy.

The gentleman who made the accusation took the old-fashioned view; it had prevailed in this country for about three hundred years, that very dark period in which Christians, instead of being Christians in any reasonable sense, worshiped the Bible as a talisman. For instance, in tract shops you saw copies of the Bible exhibited with the dent of a bullet in them, and you were given to understand that the soldier who had in his pocket a testament given him by his mother had been saved from death because the book had stopped the enemy's bullet. The gentleman who told the story about Mr. Bradlaugh was a Bible worshiper, and believed, among other things, the story in the Bible that when Elisha the prophet was mocked because of his bald head by some young children, God sent a couple of bears out of a wood to eat those children.

. . . This exquisite confusion of ideas roused my sense of comedy. It was clear to me that the challenge attributed to Charles Bradlaugh was a scientific experiment of a quite simple, straightforward, and proper kind to ascertain whether the expression of atheistic opinions really did involve any personal risk. It was certainly the method taught in the Bible, Elijah having confuted the prophets of Baal in precisely that way, with every circumstance of bitter mockery of their god when he failed to send down fire from heaven. Accordingly I said that if the question at issue were whether the penalty of questioning the theology of Messrs Moody and Sankey was to be struck dead on the spot by an incensed deity, nothing could effect a more convincing settlement of it than the very obvious experiment attributed to Mr Bradlaugh, and that consequently if he had not tried it, he ought to have tried it. The omission, I added, was one which could easily be remedied there and then, as I happened to share Mr Bradlaugh's views as to the absurdity of the belief in these violent interferences with the order of nature by a short-tempered and thin-skinned supernatural deity. . . . I said, "Look here; after all, if people do believe this crude thing, that the world is regulated by a very touchy deity who strikes people dead, is not that a very practical way of testing it?" And with that I took my watch out of my pocket. . . .[3]

The effect was electrical. Neither sceptics nor devotees were prepared to abide the result of the experiment. In vain did I urge the pious to trust in the accuracy of their deity's aim with a thunderbolt, and the justice of his discrimination between the innocent and the guilty. In vain did I appeal to the sceptics to accept the logical outcome of their scepticism: it soon appeared that when thunderbolts were in question there were no sceptics. . . . One of the party appealed to us to turn the conversation to a more lively channel, and a gentleman present who had a talent for singing comic songs sat down at the piano and sang the most melancholic song I ever heard in my life.

. . . Our host, seeing that his guests would vanish precipitately if the impious challenge were uttered, leaving him alone with a solitary infidel under sentence of extermination in five minutes, interposed and forbade the experiment, pleading at the same time for a change of subject. I of course complied, but could not refrain from remarking that though the dreadful words had not been uttered, yet, as the thought had been formulated in my mind it was very doubtful whether the consequences could be averted by sealing my lips. However, the rest appeared to feel that the game would be played according to the rules, and that it mattered very little what I thought so long as I said nothing. Only the leader of the evangelical party, I thought, was a little preoccupied until five minutes had elapsed and the weather was still calm.

. . . In those days we thought in terms of time and space, of cause and effect, as we still do; but we do not now demand from a religion that it shall explain the universe completely in terms of cause and effect, and present the world to us as a manufactured article and as the private property of its Manufacturer. We did then. We were invited to pity the delusion of certain heathens who held that the world is supported by an elephant who is supported by a tortoise. Mahomet decided that the mountains are great weights to keep the world from being blown away into space. But we refuted these orientals by asking triumphantly what the tortoise stands on? Freethinkers asked which came first: the owl or the egg. Nobody thought of saying that the ultimate problem of existence, being clearly insoluble and even unthinkable on causation lines, could not be a causation problem. To pious people this would have been flat atheism, because they assumed that God must be a Cause, and sometimes called him The Great First Cause, or, in still choicer language, The Primal Cause. To the Rationalists it would have been a renunciation of reason. Here and there a man would confess that he stood as with a dim lantern in a dense fog, and could see but a little way in any direction into infinity. But he did not really believe that infinity was infinite or that the eternal was also sempiternal: he assumed that all things, known and unknown, were caused.

Hence it was that I found myself one day towards the end of the eighteen-seventies in a cell in the old Brompton Oratory arguing with Father Addis,[4] who had been called by one of his flock to attempt my conversion to Roman Catholicism.[5] The universe exists, said the father: somebody must have made it. If that somebody exists, said I, somebody must have made him. I grant that for the sake of argument, said the Oratorian. I grant you a maker of God. I grant you a maker of the maker of God. I grant you as long a line of makers as you please; but an infinity of makers is unthinkable and extravagant: it is no harder to believe in number one than in number fifty thousand or fifty million; so why not accept number one and stop there, since no attempt to get behind him will remove your logical difficulty? By your leave, said I, it is as easy for me to believe that the universe made itself as that a maker of the universe made himself: in fact much easier; for the universe visibly exists and makes itself as it goes along, whereas a maker for it is a hypothesis. Of course we could get no further on these lines. He rose and said that we were like two men working a saw, he pushing it forward and I pushing it back, and cutting nothing; but when we had dropped the subject and were walking through the refectory, he returned to it for a moment to say that he should go mad if he lost his belief. I, glorying in the robust callousness of youth and the comedic spirit, felt comfortable and said so; though I was touched, too, by his evident sincerity.

. . . One hardly knows which is the more appalling: the abjectness of the credulity or the flippancy of the scepticism. The result was inevitable. All who were strong-minded enough not to be terrified by the bogey were left stranded in empty contemptuous negation, and argued, when they argued at all, as I argued with Father Addis. But their person was not intellectually comfortable. A member of parliament expressed their discomfort when, objecting to the admission of Charles Bradlaugh into parliament, he said "Hang it all, a man should believe in something or somebody." It was easy to throw the bogey into the dustbin; but none the less the world, our corner of the universe, did not look like a pure accident: it presented evidences of design in every direction. There was mind and purpose behind it. As the anti-Bradlaugh member would have put it, there must be somebody behind the something: no atheist could get over that.[6]

For the first couple of years of my life in London I did nothing decisive. I acted as ghost for a musician who had accepted a berth as musical critic;[7] and as such ghosts must not appear, and I was therefore cut off from the paper and could not correct proofs, my criticisms, mostly very ruthless ones, appeared with such misprints, such mutilations and venal interpolations by other hands, so inextricably mixed up with other criticisms most offensive to my artistic sense, that I have ever since hidden this activity of mine as a guilty secret, lest someone should dig out these old notices and imagine that I was responsible for everything in them and with them. . . . I wrote the criticisms; and he handed the emoluments over to me without deduction, contenting himself with the consciousness of doing generously by a young and forlorn literary adventurer, and with the honor and glory accruing from the reputed authorship of my articles. To them I owe all my knowledge of the characteristics of bad criticism. I cannot here convey an adequate impression of their demerits without overstepping the bounds of decorum. They made me miserable at the time; but I did not know even enough to understand that what was torturing me was the guilt and shame which attend ignorance and incompetence. The paper, with my assistance, died, and my sins are buried with it; but I still keep, in a safe hiding place, a set of the critical crimes I contributed to it, much as a murderer keeps the bloodstained knife under which his victim fell. Whenever I feel that I am getting too conceited, or am conscious of crediting myself with a natural superiority to some younger brother of the craft, I take myself down by reading some of that old stuff—though indeed the bare thought of it is generally sufficient. And yet neither in literary ability nor musical knowledge was I unpardonably deficient at that time. I should have been a very decent critic for my age, if only I had known how to criticize. . . . Even now I can hardly bring myself to reveal that the name of the paper was The Hornet, and that it had passed then into the hands of a certain Captain Donald Shaw, who was not related to me, and whom I never met. It died on his hands, and partly, perhaps, at mine.[8]

I began a profane Passion Play, with the mother of the hero represented as a termagant, but never carried it through.[9] I was always, fortunately for me, a failure as a trifler. All my attempts at Art for Art's Sake broke down: it was like hammering nails into sheets of notepaper. . . .

I had one article accepted—by G. R. Sims, who had just started a short-lived weekly paper of his own. It brought me fifteen shillings. Full of hope & gratitude I wrote a really brilliant contribution. That finished me at once.[10] On another occasion a publisher showed me some old blocks which he had bought up with the intention of having verses fitted to them & using them as a school prize book. I wrote a parody of the sort of thing he wanted, and sent it to him as a friendly joke. To my stupefaction he thanked me seriously and paid me five shillings. I was touched, and wrote him a serious verse for another picture. He took it as a joke in questionable taste, and my career as a versifier ended. Once I got a £5 job; but as it was not from a publisher or editor, but from a lawyer who wanted a medical essay—evidently for use as an advertisement for some patent medicine—I was unable to follow up this success. Total, £6 in nine years.

Then my cousin, Mrs Cashel Hoey, a woman of letters, daughter of the aunt who played the tambourine with her beautiful hands, gave me an introduction to Arnold White, then secretary to the Edison Telephone Company. He found a berth for me in the Way Leave Department of that shortlived company; and I presently found myself studying the topography of the east end of London, and trying to persuade all sorts of people to allow the Company to put insulators and poles and derricks and the like on their roofs to carry the telephone lines. I liked the exploration involved; but my shyness made the business of calling on strangers frightfully uncongenial; and my sensitiveness, which was extreme, in spite of the brazen fortitude which I simulated, made the impatient rebuffs I had to endure occasionally, especially from much worried women who mistook me for an advertisement canvasser, ridiculously painful to me. But I escaped these trials presently; for I soon had to take charge of the department, and organize the work of more thick-skinned adventurers instead of doing it myself. . . . The Edison Telephone Company was presently swallowed up by the Bell Telephone Company; and I seized the opportunity to recover my destitute freedom by refusing

to apply for the employment promised by the amalgamation to the dis-
banded staff. This was the end of my career as a commercial employee.
I soon dropped even the pretence of seeking any renewal of it. . . .

The telephone episode occurred in 1879; [11] and in that year I had done
what every literary adventurer did in those days, and many do still. I
had written a novel. My office training had left me with a habit of doing
something regularly every day as a fundamental condition of industry as
distinguished from idleness. I knew I was making no headway unless
I was doing this, and that I should never produce a book in any other
fashion. I bought supplies of white paper, demy size, by sixpennorths at
a time; folded it in quarto; and condemned myself to fill five pages of it
a day, rain or shine, dull or inspired. I had so much of the schoolboy
and the clerk still in me that if my five pages ended in the middle of a
sentence I did not finish it until next day. On the other hand, if I missed
a day, I made up for it by doing a double task on the morrow. On this
plan I produced five novels in five years. It was my professional apprenticeship, doggedly suffered with all the diffidence and dissatisfaction
of a learner with a very critical master, myself to wit, whom there was
no pleasing and no evading, and persevered in to save my self-respect
in a condition of impecuniosity which, for two acute moments (I still
recall them with a wry face), added broken boots and carefully hidden
raggedness to cuffs whose edges were trimmed by the scissors, and a tall
hat so limp with age that I had to wear it back-to-front to enable me
to take it off without doubling up the brim.

I had no success as a novelist. I sent the five novels to all the publishers
in London and some in America. None would venture on them. Fifty
or sixty refusals without a single acceptance forced me into a fierce self-
sufficiency. I became undiscourageable, acquiring a superhuman insensi-
tiveness to praise or blame which has been useful to me at times since,
though at other times it has retarded my business affairs by making me
indifferent to the publication and performance of my works, and even
impatient of them as an unwelcome interruption to the labor of writing
their successors.

Four of the five novels of my nonage, as I call them, at last got into
print. . . . But the first of them never got published at all. Opening the
old parcel, . . . (it is like opening a grave that has been closed for . . .
years), I find a pile of cahiers of twenty pages each, and realize with
some dismay that I am face-to-face with a novel containing nearly

200,000 words. The title is Immaturity. The handwriting, which slopes slightly backwards, has all the regularity and legibility of my old cash book. Unfortunately, the mice have eaten so much of two of the cahiers that the ends of the lines are missing. This is awkward . . . .

. . . Though my early style now makes me laugh at its pedantry, yet I have a great respect for the priggish conscientiousness of my first efforts. They prove too that, like Goethe, I knew all along, and have added more to my power of handling, illustrating, and addressing my material than to the material itself. Anyhow, . . . there must be a certain quality of youth in it which I could not now recapture, and which may even have charm as well as weakness and absurdity. . . .

. . . I can guarantee the propriety of my early style. It was the last thing in correctness. I have never aimed at style in my life: style is a sort of melody that comes into my sentences by itself. If a writer says what he has to say as accurately and effectively as he can, his style will take care of itself, if he has a style. But I did set up one condition in my early days. I resolved that I would write nothing that should not be intelligible to a foreigner with a dictionary, like the French of Voltaire; and I therefore avoided idiom. (Later on I came to seek idiom as being the most highly vitalized form of language) . . . . Also, there will be nothing of the voice of the public speaker in it: the voice that rings through so much of my later work. Not until Immaturity was finished, late in 1879, did I for the first time rise to my feet in a little debating club called The Zetetical Society, to make, in a condition of heartbreaking nervousness, my first assault on an audience.

. . . Many of the characters in this first novel of mine owed something to persons I had met, including members of my family (not to mention myself); but none of them are portraits; and with one exception the models are unknown to the public. That exception was Cecil Lawson, whose early death lost us the only landscape painter who ever reminded me of the spacious and fascinating experiments of Rubens in that branch of painting. When I lived at Victoria Grove the Lawsons: father, mother, Malcolm, and two sisters, lived in one of the handsome old houses in Cheyne Walk, Chelsea. Cecil and another brother, being married, boarded out. Malcolm was a musician; and the sisters sang. One, a soprano, dark, quick, plump and bright, sang joyously. The other, a contralto, sang with heartbreaking intensity of expression, which she deepened by dressing esthetically, as it was called then, meaning in the Rossettian taste. Miss Lawson produced this effect, not by the ugly extravagances which made the fashionable milliners' version of the esthetic mode ridiculous, but by very simple grey and brown gowns which somehow harmonized with her habitual expression of sadness and even suffering; so that when she sang "Oh, don't deceive me: oh, never leave me," she produced a picture as well as a tone poem. Cecil, who had just acquired a position by the few masterpieces which remain to us, was very much "in the movement" at the old Grosvenor Gallery (now the Aeolian Hall), then new, and passing through the sensational vogue achieved by its revelations of Burne Jones and Whistler.

Malcolm was conducting a Gluck Society, at which I had discovered Gluck through a recital of Alceste, in which Theo Marzials, who had a charming baritone voice, sang the part of Hercules. My mother had met Marzials in the course of her musical activities: he introduced her to Malcolm Lawson: she lent him a hand in the chorus of the Gluck Society; and the result was that I found myself invited to visit the Lawsons, who were at home in Cheyne Walk every Sunday evening. I suffered such agonies of shyness that I sometimes walked up and down the Embankment for twenty minutes or more before venturing to knock at the door: indeed I should have funked it altogether, and hurried home asking myself what was the use of torturing myself when it was so easy to run away, if I had not been instinctively aware that I must never let myself off in this manner if I meant ever to do anything in the world. Few men can have suffered more than I did in my youth from simple cowardice or been more horribly ashamed of it. I shirked and hid when the peril, real or imaginary, was of the sort I had no vital interest in facing; but when such an interest was at stake, I went ahead and suffered accordingly. The worst of it was that when I appeared in the Lawsons' drawingroom I did not appeal to the goodnature of the company as a pardonably and even becomingly bashful novice. I had not then tuned the Shavian note to any sort of harmony; and I have no doubt the Lawsons found me discordant, crudely self-assertive, and insufferable. I hope they, and all the others on whom I jarred at this time, forgave me in later years, when it turned out that I really had something to assert after all. The house and its artistic atmosphere were most congenial to me; and I liked all the Lawsons; but I had not mastered the art of society at that time, and could not bear making an inartistic exhibition of myself; so I soon ceased to plague them, and, except for an occasional chance meeting with Malcolm, passed out of their lives after touching them very lightly in passing.

Cecil Lawson was the spoilt child of that household. He pontificated on art in a wayward grumbling incoherent musing fashion of his own. When, following my youthful and very irritating system of contradicting everyone from whom I thought I could learn anything, I suggested that Whistler was something short of the greatest artist of all time, he could not form a sentence to crush me with, but groaned inarticulately for a moment, like a clock about to strike, and then uttered the words Titian Turner Rembrandt Velasquez Whistler. He was goodlooking, not a big man, but trimly built, with just enough crisply curled hair to proclaim the artist without compromising the man. I had seen his work in the public exhibitions (never in private); and, thanks to my boyish prowlings in the Dublin National Gallery (as a boy I wanted to be a painter, never a writer), I knew its value. His untimely death, which occurred soon after my visits, must have broken up the Sunday evenings at Cheyne Walk very badly. I did not venture to intrude after it.

I used him in Immaturity as a model for the artist Cyril Scott, an invented name which has since been made famous by a British composer. I chose it because Cyril resembled Cecil metrically, and because I thought Lawson was a Scot (he was, I learn, born in Shropshire). But I must again warn the reader against taking the man in the book as an authentic portrait of the great painter, or inferring that his courtship and marriage or any of the circumstances I have invented for him, represent facts in Lawson's life. I knew nothing whatever about him except what I saw of him during my few visits to Cheyne Walk; and I have learnt nothing since. He set my imagination to work: that was all.

I have now told as much as seems to me necessary of the circumstances and relevant antecedents of my first book. It is the book of a raw youth, still quite out of touch with the country to which he had transported himself; and if I am to be entirely communicative on this subject, I must add that the mere rawness which so soon rubs off was complicated by a deeper strangeness which has made me all my life a sojourner on this planet rather than a native of it. Whether it be that I was born mad or a little too sane, my kingdom was not of this world: I was at home only in the realm of my imagination, and at my ease only with the mighty dead. Therefore I had to become an actor, and create for myself a fantastic personality fit and apt for dealing with men, and adaptable to the various parts I had to play as author, journalist, orator, politician, committee man, man of the world, and so forth. In this I succeeded later on only too well. In my boyhood I saw Charles Mathews act in a farce called Cool as a Cucumber. The hero was a young man just returned from a tour of the world, upon which he had been sent to cure him of an apparently hopeless bashfulness; and the fun lay in the cure having overshot the mark and transformed him into a monster of outrageous impudence. I am not sure that something of the kind did not happen to me; for when my imposture was at last accomplished, and I daily pulled the threads of the puppet who represented me in the public press, the applause that greeted it was not unlike that which Mathews drew in Cool as a Cucumber. Certainly the growls of resentful disgust with which my advances were resisted closely resembled those of the unfortunate old gentleman in the farce whose pictures and furniture the young man so coolly rearranged to his own taste. At the time of which I am writing, however, I had not yet learnt to act, nor come to understand that my natural character was impossible on the great stage of London. When I had to come out of the realm of imagination into that of actuality I was still uncomfortable. I was outside society, outside politics, outside sport, outside the Church. If the term had been invented then I should have been called The Complete Outsider. But the epithet would have been appropriate only within the limits of British barbarism. The moment music, painting, literature, or science came into question the positions were reversed: it was I who was the Insider. I had the intellectual habit; and my natural combination of critical faculty with literary resource needed only a clear comprehension of life in the light of an intelligible theory: in short, a religion, to set it in triumphant operation. It was the lack of this last qualification that lamed me in those early days in Victoria Grove, and that set limits to this ungainly first novel of mine. . . .

. . . There is nothing one gets so tired of in fiction as what is called "flesh and blood." The business of a novelist is largely to provide working models of improved types of humanity. . . . My first working model of this kind was the hero of my second novel . . . a huge work called The Irrational Knot. This was really an extraordinary book for a youth of twenty-four to write; but, from the point of view of the people who think that an author has nothing better to do with his genius than to amuse them, it was a failure, because the characters, though life-like, were a dreary company, all undesirable as personal acquaintances; whilst the scenes and incidents were of the most commonplace and sordid kind. My model man, named Conolly, was a skilled workman who became rich and famous by inventing an electro-motor. He married a woman whom I took no end of trouble to make as "nice" as the very nicest woman can be according to conventional ideas. The point of the story was that though Conolly was a model of sound sense, intelligence, reasonableness, good temper, and everything that a thoroughly nice woman could desire and deserve, the most hopeless incompatibility developed itself between them; and finally she ran away with a man whose deficiency in every desirable quality made him as unlike her husband as it is possible for one man to be unlike another. Eventually she got rid of her lover, and met her husband again; but after a survey of the situation, Conolly decided, like Nora in A Doll's House, that the matrimonial relation between them had no prospect of success under the circumstances, and walked out of the house, his exit ending the book.

. . . Of course, I am not the author of The Irrational Knot. Physiologists inform us that the substance of our bodies (and consequently of our souls) is shed and renewed at such a rate that no part of us lasts longer than eight years: I am therefore not now in any atom of me the person who wrote The Irrational Knot in 1880. The last of that author perished in 1888; and . . . I cannot be expected to take any very lively interest in the novels of my literary great-grandfather. Even my personal recollections of him are becoming vague and overlaid with those most misleading of all traditions, the traditions founded on the lies a man tells, and at last comes to believe, about himself *to* himself. Certain things, however, I remember very well. For instance, I am significantly clear as to the price of the paper on which I wrote The Irrational Knot. It was cheap—a white demy of unpretentious quality—so that sixpennorth lasted a long time. . . . I remember also that Bizet's Carmen being then new in London, I used it as a safety-valve for my romantic impulses. When I was tired of the sordid realism of Whatshisname (I have sent my only copy of The Irrational Knot to the printers, and cannot remember the name of my hero) I went to the piano and forgot him in the glamorous society of Carmen and her crimson toreador and yellow dragoon. . . .

When I say that *I* did and felt these things, I mean, of course, that the predecessor whose name I bear did and felt them. The I of to-day is (? am) cool towards Carmen; and Carmen, I regret to say, does not take the slightest interest in him (? me). And now enough of this juggling with past and present Shaws. The grammatical complications of being a first person and several extinct third persons at the same moment are so frightful that I must return to the ordinary misusage, and ask the reader to make the necessary corrections in his or her own mind.

This book is not wholly a compound of intuition and ignorance. Take for example the profession of my hero, an Irish-American electrical engineer. That was by no means a flight of fancy. For you must not suppose, because I am a man of letters, that I never tried to earn an honest living. I began trying to commit that sin against my nature when I was fifteen, and persevered, from youthful timidity and diffidence, until I was twenty-three. My last attempt was in 1879, when a company was formed in London to exploit an ingenious invention by Mr. Thomas Alva Edison—a much too ingenious invention as it proved, being nothing less than a telephone of such stentorian efficiency that it bellowed your most private communications all over the house instead of whispering them with some sort of discretion. This was not what the British stockbroker wanted; so the company was soon merged in the National Telephone Company, after making a place for itself in the history of literature, quite unintentionally, by providing me with a job. Whilst the Edison Telephone Company lasted, it crowded the basement of a huge pile of offices in Queen Victoria Street with American artificers. These deluded and romantic men gave me a glimpse of the skilled proletariat of the United States. They sang obsolete sentimental songs with genuine emotion; and their language was frightful even to an Irishman. They worked with a ferocious energy which was out of all proportion to the actual result achieved. Indomitably resolved to assert their republican manhood by taking no orders from a tall-hatted Englishman whose stiff politeness covered his conviction that they were, relatively to himself, inferior and common persons, they insisted on being slave-driven with genuine American oaths by a genuine free and equal American foreman. They utterly despised the artfully slow British workman who did as little for his wages as he possibly could; never hurried himself; and had a deep reverence for anyone whose pocket could be tapped by respectful behavior. Need I add that they were contemptuously wondered at by this same British workman as a parcel of outlandish adult boys, who sweated themselves for their employer's benefit instead of looking after their own interests? They adored Mr. Edison as the greatest man of all time in every possible department of science, art and philosophy, and execrated Mr. Graham Bell, the inventor of the rival telephone, as his Satanic adversary; but each of them had (or pretended to have) on the brink of completion, an improvement on the telephone, usually a new transmitter. They were free-souled creatures, excellent company: sensitive, cheerful, and profane; liars, braggarts, and hustlers; with an air of making slow old England hum which never left them even when, as often happened, they were wrestling with difficulties of their own making, or struggling in no-thoroughfares from which they had to be retrieved like strayed sheep by Englishmen without imagination enough to go wrong.

In this environment I remained for some months. As I was interested in physics and had read Tyndall and Helmholtz, besides having learnt something in Ireland through a fortunate friendship with a cousin of Mr. Graham Bell who was also a chemist and physicist, I was, I believe, the only person in the entire establishment who knew the current scientific explanation of telephony; and as I soon struck up a friendship with our official lecturer, a Colchester man whose strong point was pre-scientific agriculture, I often discharged his duties for him in a manner which, I am persuaded, laid the foundation of Mr. Edison's London reputation: my sole reward being my boyish delight in the half-concealed incredulity of our visitors (who were convinced by the hoarsely startling utterances of the telephone that the speaker, alleged by me to be twenty miles away, was really using a speaking-trumpet in the next room), and their obvious uncertainty, when the demonstration was over, as to whether they ought to tip me or not: a question they either decided in the negative or never decided at all; for I never got anything.

So much for my electrical engineer! To get him into contact with fashionable society before he became famous was also a problem easily solved. I knew of three English peers who actually preferred physical laboratories to stables, and scientific experts to gamekeepers: in fact, one of the experts was a friend of mine. And I knew from personal experience that if science brings men of all ranks into contact, art, especially music, does the same for men and women. An electrician who can play an accompaniment can go anywhere and know anybody. As far as mere access and acquaintance go there are no class barriers for him. My difficulty was not to get my hero into society, but to give any sort of plausibility to my picture of society when I got him into it. I lacked the touch of literary diner-out; and I had, as the reader will probably find to his cost, the classical tradition which makes all the persons in a novel, except the comically vernacular ones, or the speakers of phonetically spelt dialect, utter themselves in the formal phrases and studied syntax of eighteenth century rhetoric. In short, I wrote in the style of Scott and Dickens; and as fashionable society then spoke and behaved as it still does, in no style at all, my transcriptions of Oxford and Mayfair may nowadays suggest an unaccountable and ludicrous ignorance of a very superficial and accessible code of manners. I was not, however, so ignorant as might have been inferred at that time from my somewhat desperate financial condition.

I had, to begin with, a sort of backstairs knowledge; for in my teens I struggled for life in the office of an Irish gentleman who acted as land agent and private banker for many persons of distinction. Now it is possible for a London author to dine out in the highest circles for twenty years without learning as much about the human frailties of his hosts as the family solicitor or (in Ireland) the family land agent learns in twenty days: and some of this knowledge inevitably reaches his clerks, especially the clerk who keeps the cash, which was my particular department. He learns, if capable of the lesson, that the aristocratic profession has as few geniuses as any other profession; so that if you want a peerage of more than, say, half a dozen members, you must fill it up with many common persons, and even with some deplorably mean ones. For "service is no inheritance" either in the kitchen or the House of Lords; and the case presented by Mr. Barrie in his play of The Admirable Crichton, where the butler is the man of quality, and his master, the Earl, the man of rank, is no fantasy, but a quite common occurrence, and indeed to some extent an inevitable one, because the English are extremely particular in selecting their butlers, whilst they do not select their barons at all, taking them as the accident of birth sends them. The consequences include much ironic comedy. For instance, we have in England a curious belief in first rate people, meaning all the people we do not know; and this consoles us for the undeniable secondrateness of the people we do know, besides saving the credit of aristocracy as an institution. The unmet aristocrat is devoutly believed in; but he is always round the corner, never at hand. That *the* smart set exists; that there is above and beyond that smart set a class so blue of blood and exquisite in nature that it looks down even on the King with haughty condescension; that scepticism on these points is one of the stigmata of plebian baseness: all these imaginings are so common here that they constitute the real popular sociology of England. . . .

This I knew very well when I wrote my novels; and if, as I suspect, I failed to create a convincingly verisimilar atmosphere of aristocracy, it was not because I had any illusions or ignorances as to the common humanity of the peerage, and not because I gave literary style to its conversation, but because, as I had never had any money, I was foolishly indifferent to it, and so, having blinded myself to its enormous importance, necessarily missed the point of view, and with it the whole moral basis, of the class which rightly values money, and plenty of it, as the first condition of a bearable life.

Money is indeed the most important thing in the world; and all sound and successful personal and national morality should have this fact for its basis. Every teacher or twaddler who denies it or suppresses it, is an enemy of life. Money controls morality . . . .

This, as I have said, I did not then understand; for I knew money only by the want of it. . . . I remember once buying a book entitled How to Live on Sixpence a Day, a point on which at that time circumstances compelled me to be pressingly curious. I carried out its instructions faithfully for a whole afternoon; and if ever I have an official biography issued, I shall certainly have it stated therein, in illustration of my fortitude and self-denial, that I lived for some time on sixpence a day. . . .

. . . I remember one evening during the novel-writing period when nobody would pay a farthing for a stroke of my pen, walking along Sloane Street in that blessed shield of literary shabbiness, evening dress. A man accosted me with an eloquent appeal for help, ending with the assurance that he had not a penny in the world. I replied, with exact truth, "Neither have I." He thanked me civilly, and went away, apparently not in the least surprised, leaving me to ask myself why I did not turn beggar too, since I felt sure that a man who did it as well as he, must be in comfortable circumstances.

I became a vegetarian in 1880 or 81.[12] It was at that period that vegetarian restaurants began to crop up here and there, and to make vegetarianism practically possible for a man too poor to be specially catered for. My attention had been called to the subject, first by Shelley (I am an out-and-out Shelleyan), and later on by a lecturer. But of course the enormity of eating the scorched corpses of animals—cannibalism with its heroic dish omitted—becomes impossible the moment it becomes conscious instead of thoughtlessly habitual. I am also a teetotaller, my family having paid the Shaw debt to the distilling industry so munificently as to leave me no obligations in that direction. I flatly declare that a man fed on whiskey and dead bodies cannot do the finest work of which he is capable.

Another reminiscence. A little past midnight, in the same costume, I was turning from Piccadilly into Bond Street, when a lady of the pavement, out of luck that evening so far, confided to me that the last bus for Brompton had passed, and that she should be grateful to any gentleman who would give her a lift in a hansom. My old-fashioned Irish gallantry had not then been worn off by age and England: besides, as a novelist who could find no publisher, I was touched by the similarity of our trades and predicaments. I excused myself very politely on the ground that my wife (invented for the occasion) was waiting for me at home, and that I felt sure so attractive a lady would have no difficulty in finding another escort. Unfortunately this speech made so favorable an impression on her that she immediately took my arm and declared her willingness to go anywhere with me, on the flattering ground that I was a perfect gentleman. In vain did I try to persuade her that in coming up Bond Street and deserting Piccadilly, she was throwing away her last chance of a hansom: she attached herself so devotedly to me that I could not without actual violence shake her off. At last I made a stand at the end of Old Bond Street. I took out my purse; opened it; and held it upside down. Her countenance fell, poor girl! She turned on her heel with a melancholy flirt of her skirt, and vanished.

Now on both these occasions I had been in the company of people who spent at least as much in a week as I did in a year. Why was I, a penniless and unknown young man, admitted there? Simply because, though I was an execrable pianist, and never improved until the happy invention of the pianola made a Paderewski of me, I could play a simple accompaniment at sight more congenially to a singer than most amateurs . . . .

Conceive me then at the writing of The Irrational Knot as a person neither belonging to the world I describe nor wholly ignorant of it, and on certain points quite incapable of conceiving it intuitively . . . . I, always on the heroic plane imaginatively, had two disgusting faults which I did not recognize as faults because I could not help them. I was poor and (by day) shabby. I therefore tolerated the gross error that poverty, though an inconvenience and a trial, is not a sin and a disgrace; and I stood for my self-respect on the things I had: probity, ability, knowledge of art, laboriousness, and whatever else came cheaply to me.

Because I could walk into Hampton Court Palace and the National Gallery (on free days) and enjoy Mantegna and Michael Angelo whilst millionaires were yawning miserably over inept gluttonies; because I could suffer more by hearing a movement of Beethoven's Ninth Symphony taken at a wrong tempo than a duchess by losing a diamond necklace, I was indifferent to the repulsive fact that if I had fallen in love with the duchess I did not possess a morning suit in which I could reasonably have expected her to touch me with the furthest protended pair of tongs; and I did not see that to remedy this I should have been prepared to wade through seas of other people's blood. Indeed it is this perception which constitutes an aristocracy nowadays. It is the secret of all our governing classes, which consist finally of people who, though perfectly prepared to be generous, humane, cultured, philanthropic, public spirited and personally charming in the second instance, are unalterably resolved, in the first, to have money enough for a handsome and delicate life, and will, in pursuit of that money, batter in the doors of their fellow men, sell them up, sweat them in fetid dens, shoot, stab, hang, imprison, sink, burn and destroy them in the name of law and order. And this shews their fundamental sanity and rightmindedness; for a sufficient income is indispensable to the practice of virtue; and the man who will let any unselfish consideration stand between him and its attainment is a weakling, a dupe and predestined slave. If I could convince our impecunious mobs of this, the world would be reformed before the end of the week; for the sluggards who are content to be wealthy without working and the dastards who are content to work without being wealthy, together with all the pseudo-moralists and ethicists and cowardice mongers generally, would be exterminated without shrift, to the unutterable enlargement of life and ennoblement of humanity. We might even make some beginnings of civilization under such happy circumstances.

In the days of The Irrational Knot I had not learnt this lesson . . . . I was an ablebodied and ableminded young man in the strength of my youth; and my family, then heavily embarrassed, needed my help urgently. That I should have chosen to be a burden to them instead was, according to all the conventions of peasant lad fiction, monstrous. Well, without a blush I embraced the monstrosity.[13] I did not throw myself into the struggle for life: I threw my mother into it. I was not a staff to my father's old age: I hung on to his coat tails. His reward was to live just long enough to read a review of one of these silly novels written in an obscure journal by a personal friend of my own (. . . Mr. John Mackinnon Robertson) prefiguring me to some extent as a considerable author.[14] I think, myself, that this was a handsome reward, far better worth having than a nice pension from a dutiful son struggling slavishly for his parent's bread in some sordid trade. Handsome or not, it was the only return he ever had for the little pension he contrived to export from Ireland for his family. My mother reinforced it by drudging in her elder years at the art of music which she had followed in her prime freely for love. I only helped to spend it. People wondered at my heartlessness: one young and romantic lady had the courage to remonstrate openly and indignantly with me, "for the which" as Pepys said of the ship-wright's wife who refused his advances, "I did respect her."[15] Callous as Comus to moral babble, I steadily wrote my five pages a day . . . (at my mother's expense) . . . . And I protest that I will not suffer . . . any romanticist to pass me off as a peasant boy qualifying for a chapter in Smiles's Self Help, or a good son supporting a helpless mother, instead of a stupendously selfish artist leaning with the full weight of his hungry body on an energetic and capable woman. . . . My mother worked for my living instead of preaching that it was my duty to work for hers . . . .

On coming back to this Irrational Knot as a stranger . . . I am proud to find that its morality is not readymade. The drunken prima donna of a bygone type of musical burlesque is not depicted as an immoral person, but as a person with a morality of her own, no worse in its way than the morality of her highly respectable wine merchant in *its* way. The sociology of the successful inventor is his own sociology too; and it is by his originality in this respect that he passes irresistibly through all the readymade prejudices that are set up to bar his promotion. And the heroine, nice, amiable, benevolent, and anxious to please and behave well, but hopelessly secondhand in her morals and nicenesses, and consequently without any real moral force now that the threat of hell has lost its terrors for her, is left destitute among the failures which are so puzzling to thoughtless people. "I cannot understand why she is so unlucky: she is such a nice woman!": that is the formula. As if people with any force in them ever were altogether nice!

And so I claim the first order for this jejune exploit of mine, and . . . note that the final chapter, so remote from Scott and Dickens and so close to Ibsen, was written years before Ibsen came to my knowledge, thus proving that the revolt of the Life Force against readymade morality in the nineteenth century was not the work of a Norwegian microbe, but would have worked itself into expression in English literature had Norway never existed. In fact, when Miss Lord's translation of A Doll's House appeared in the eighteen-eighties, and so excited some of my Socialist friends that they got up a private reading of it in which I was cast for the part of Krogstad, its novelty as a morally original study of a marriage did not stagger me as it staggered Europe. I had made a morally original study of a marriage myself, and made it, too, without any melodramatic forgeries, spinal diseases, and suicides, though I had to confess to a study of dipsomania. At all events, I chattered and ate caramels in the back drawing-room (our green-room) whilst Eleanor Marx, as Nora, brought Helmer to book at the other side of the folding doors.[16] Indeed I concerned myself very little about Ibsen until, later on, William Archer translated Peer Gynt to me *viva voce*, when the magic of the great poet opened my eyes in a flash to the importance of the social philosopher.

I seriously suggest that The Irrational Knot may be regarded as an early attempt on the part of the Life Force to write A Doll's House in English by the instrumentality of a very immature writer aged 24. . . .

It is interesting to me as marking a crisis in my progress as a thinker. It carried me as far as I could go in Rationalism and Materialism; and when, having finished it, I was carried by my daily task of five pages into a third novel, entitled Love Among the Artists, I found that I had come to the end of my Rationalism and Materialism, and to get a step forward had to throw them both overboard and take as my hero a British Beethoven, utterly unreasonable and unaccountable, and even outrageous, but a vital genius, powerful in an art that is beyond logic and even beyond words.

The lot of such a genius is not an easy one in a commercialized middle-class which has nothing to live by but its wits. In 1881, to get bread, composers had to "give lessons" in five finger exercises while electrical engineers made fortunes. My composer was even less understood by the publisher's readers than my mechanic. He was, it seemed, simply no gentleman.

Love Among the Artists was unanimously rejected. The manuscript was scattered as waste paper on my absence during my mother's removal from 29 Fitzroy Square. It was retrieved by Mr. Dan Ryder; but he was obliged to sell it to finance his Rent Act campaign. After that it seems to have been dismembered into separate pages, of which there are six in the New York public library. The rest I have not traced.

I can recall a certain difficulty, experienced even whilst I was writing the book, in remembering what it was about. Twice I clean forgot the beginning, and had to read back, as I might have read any other man's novel, to learn the story. . . . I can guarantee you against any plot. . . . None of the characters will turn out to be somebody else in the last chapter: no violent accidents or strokes of pure luck will divert events from their normal course: forger, long lost heir, detective, nor any commonplace of the police court or of the realm of romance shall insult your understanding. . . . This book has no winding-up at the end. Mind: it is not, as in The Irrational Knot, a case of the upshot being unsatisfactory! There is absolutely no upshot at all. The parties are married in the middle of the book; and they do not elope with or divorce one another, or do anything unusual or improper. When as much is told concerning them as seemed to me at the time germane to my purpose, the novel breaks off.

. . . Love Among the Artists was written in 1881, and was interrupted by an attack of smallpox, my share of the epidemic of that year. Whether this enfeebled my intellectual convictions or not I cannot say; but it is a fact that the story exalts the wilful characters to the utter disparagement of the reasonable ones. As in most of my works, my aim throughout was to instruct rather than to entertain. I desired to shew our numerous amateurs of the fine arts, who would never have fallen in love with music or painting if they had not read books about them, the difference between their factitious enthusiasm and the creative energy of real genius. Some of the character studies are admirable, notably that of the musical composer Owen Jack, who is partly founded on Beethoven. I have a much higher opinion of this work than is as yet generally entertained; and, granting that it is perhaps hardly for an ordinary reader to persevere to the end without skipping, yet I think that he who reads as much of it as he finds he can bear, will be able to lay it down unfinished without any sense of having wasted his time provided always that it is worth his while to read fiction at all.

After Love among the Artists came Cashel Byron's Profession, which I confess I wrote mainly to amuse myself. . . .

An intimate acquaintance of mine in 1882 was Pakenham Beatty, a minor poet and amateur pugilist, both of which tastes an independent income enabled him to gratify to the utmost of his powers. He insisted on my accompanying him to all the boxing exhibitions, meeting his teachers, and finally putting on the gloves and acting as his sparring partner after studying an instruction book by Ned Donnelly, who is sketched in the resultant novel as Ned Skene.

In this way I became observant of professional boxing; but it attracted me first on its economic side by the comedy of the contrast between the visionary prizefighter as romantic warrior hero and the matter-of-fact trader in fisticuffs at certain weights and prices and odds. There are, besides, no sports which bring out difference of character more dramatically than boxing, wrestling, and fencing. I acquired a taste for them (as a spectator) that I retain to this day, and that enabled me to add a few articles on boxing to my more becoming and expected achievements in criticism, and to write the . . . novel. . . . I soon got an imaginary reputation in my little circle as a boxer; and as I looked credibly like a tall man with a straight left and had in fact picked up some notion of how to defend myself, I was never attacked with bodily violence nor troubled by any fear of it from political opponents. . . .

Cashel Byron's Profession was the nearest to a popular novel I had produced. It was so acceptable that it must have been refused on the forbidding reputation of the others. When it crept into print through the back door of a Socialist magazine, it was praised by Stevenson and Henley, whereupon Bentley, then a leading publisher, hastily wrote to me to let him consider it again, and was furious when I had to tell him that he had lost his chance, as it had just gone to a rival whom he regarded as an outsider.

I never think of Cashel Byron's Profession without a shudder at the narrowness of my escape from becoming a successful novelist at the age of twenty-six. At that moment an adventurous publisher might have ruined me. Fortunately for me, there were no adventurous publishers at that time; and I was forced to fight my way, instead of being ingloriously bought off at the first brush. Not that Cashel Byron's Profession was my very first novel. It was my fourth, and was followed by yet another. I recall these five remote products of my nonage as five heavy brown paper parcels which were always coming back to me from some publisher, and raising the very serious financial question of the sixpence to be paid to Messrs Carter, Paterson, and Co., the carriers, for passing them on to the next publisher. Eventually, Carter, Paterson, and Co. were the only gainers; for the publishers had to pay their readers' fees for nothing but a warning not to publish me; and I had to pay the sixpences for sending my parcels on a bootless errand. At last I grew out of novel-writing, and set to work to find out what the world was really like. The result of my investigations, so far, entirely confirms the observation of Goethe as to the amazement, the incredulity, the moral shock with which the poet discovers that what he supposed to be the real world does not exist, and that men and women are made by their own fancies in the image of the imaginary creatures in his youthful fictions, only much stupider.

Unfortunately for the immature poet, he has not in his nonage the satisfaction of knowing that his guesses at life are true. Bring a peasant into a drawing-room, and though his good sense may lead him to behave very properly, yet he will suffer torments of misgiving that everything he does must be a solecism. In my earlier excursions into literature I confess I felt like the peasant in the drawing-room. I was, on the whole, glad to get out of it. Looking back now with the eyes of experience, I find that I certainly did make blunders in matters outside the scope of poetic divination. To take a very mild example, I endowed the opulent heroine of this very book with a park of thirty acres in extent, being then fully persuaded that this was a reasonable estimate of the size of the Isle of Wight or thereabouts. But it is not by the solecisms of ignorance that the young man makes himself most ridiculous. Far more unnatural than these were my proprieties and accuracies and intelligences. I did not know my England then. I was young, raw from eighteenth century Ireland, modest, and anxious lest my poverty and provinciality should prevent me from correctly representing the intelligence, refinement, conscience, and good breeding which I supposed to be as natural and common in English society as in Scott's novels. I actually thought that educated people conscientiously learnt their manners and studied their opinions— were really educated, in short—instead of merely picking up the habits and prejudices of their set, and confidently presenting the resultant absurd equipment of class solecisms to the world as a perfect gentility. Consequently the only characters which were natural in my novels were the comic characters, because the island was (and is) populated exclusively by comic characters. Take them seriously in fiction, and the result is the Dickens heroine or the Sarah Grand hero: pathetically unattractive figments both of them. Thus my imaginary persons of quality became quite unlike any actual persons at large in England, being superior to them in a priggish manner which would nowadays rouse the humor of our younger publishers' readers very inopportunely. In 1882, however, the literary fashion which distinguished the virtuous and serious characters in a novel by a decorous stylishness and scrupulousness of composition, as if all their speeches had been corrected by their governesses and schoolmasters, had not yet been exploded by the "New Journalism" of 1888 and the advent of a host of authors, who had apparently never read anything, catering for a proletariat newly made literate by the Education Act. The distinction between the naturalness of Caleb Balderstone and the artificiality of Edgar and Lucy was still regarded as one of the social decencies by the seniors of literature; and this probably explains the fact that the only intimations I received that my work had made some impression, and had even been hesitatingly condemned, were from the older and more august houses whose readers were all grave elderly lovers of literature. And the more I progressed towards my own individual style and ventured upon the freer expression of my own ideas, the more I disappointed them. As to the regular novel-publishing houses, whose readers were merely on the scent of popularity, they gave me no quarter at all. And so between the old stool of my literary conscientiousness and the new stool of a view of life that did not reach publishing-point in England until about ten years later, when Ibsen drove it in, my novels fell to the ground. . . .

The Socialist revival of the eighties, into which I had plunged, produced the usual crop of propagandist magazines, in the conduct of which payment of the printer was the main problem, payment of contributors being quite out of the question. The editor of such a magazine can never count on a full supply of live matter to make up his tale of pages. But if he can collect a stock of unreadable novels, the refuse of the publishing trade, and a stock of minor poems (the world is full of such trash), an instalment of serial novel and a few verses will always make up the magazine to any required size. And this was how I found a use at last for my brown paper parcels. It seemed a matter of no more consequence than stuffing so many broken windowpanes with them; but it had momentous consequences; for in this way four of the five got printed and published in London, and thus incidentally became the common property of the citizens of the United States of America.[17] These pioneers did not at first appreciate their new acquisition; and nothing particular happened except that the first novel (No. 5; for I ladled them out to the Socialist magazine editors in inverse order of composition) made me acquainted with William Morris, who, to my surprise, had been reading the monthly instalments with a certain relish. But that only proved how much easier it is to please a great man than a little one, especially when you share his politics. No. 5, called An Unsocial Socialist, was followed by No. 4, Cashel Byron's Profession; and Cashel Byron would not lie quiet in his serial grave, but presently rose and walked as a book.

It happened in this way. The name of the magazine was To-Day, not the present paper of that name, but one of the many To-days which are now Yesterdays. It had several editors, among them Mr Belfort Bax and the late James Leigh Joynes; but all the editors were in partnership with Mr Henry Hyde Champion who printed the magazine, and consequently went on for ever, whilst the others came and went. It was a fantastic business, Joynes having thrown up an Eton mastership, and Champion a commission in the army, at the call of Socialism. But Champion's pugnacity survived his abdicated adjutancy: he had an unregenerate taste for pugilism, and liked Cashel Byron so much that he stereotyped the pages of To-Day which it occupied, and in spite of my friendly remonstrances, hurled on the market a misshapen shilling edition. My friend Mr William Archer reviewed it prominently; the Saturday Review, always susceptible in those days to the arts of self-defence, unexpectedly declared it the novel of the age; Mr W. E. Henley wanted to have it dramatized; Stevenson wrote a letter about it, of which more presently; the other papers hastily searched their waste-paper baskets for it and reviewed it, mostly rather disappointedly; and the public preserved its composure and did not seem to care.

That shilling edition began with a thousand copies; but it proved immortal. I never got anything out of it; and Mr Champion never got anything out of it; for he presently settled in Australia, and his printing presses and stereo plates were dispersed. But from that time forth the book was never really out of print; and though Messrs Walter Scott soon placed a revised shilling edition on the market, I suspect that still, in some obscure printing office, those old plates of Mr. Champion's from time to time produce a "remainder" of the original Modern Press edition, which is to the present what the Quarto Hamlet is to the Folio.

On the passing of To-Day, I became novelist in ordinary to a magazine called Our Corner, edited by Mrs. Annie Besant. It had the singular habit of paying for its contributions, and was, I am afraid, to some extent a device of Mrs. Besant's for relieving necessitous young propagandists without wounding their pride by open almsgiving. She was an incorrigible benefactress, and probably revenged herself for my freely expressed scorn for this weakness by drawing on her private account to pay me for my jejune novels. At last Our Corner went the way of all propagandist magazines, completing a second nonage novel and its own career at the same moment. This left me with only one unprinted masterpiece, my Opus I, which had cost me an unconscionable quantity of paper, and was called, with merciless fitness, Immaturity. Part of it had by this time been devoured by mice, though even they had not been able to finish it. . . .

. . . Cashel Byron's Profession, is, at bottom, a mere boy's romance. It has a sort of cleverness which has always been a cheap quality in me; and it is interesting, amusing, and at one point—unique in my works—actually exciting. The excitement is produced by the brutal expedient of describing a fight. It is not, as usual in novels, a case in which the hero fights a villain in defence of the heroine, or in the satisfaction of a righteous indignation. The two men are paid to fight for the amusement of the spectators. They set to for the sake of the money, and strive to beat each other out of pure ferocity. The success of this incident is a conclusive proof of the superfluity of the conventional hypocrisies of fiction. I guarantee to every purchaser of Cashel Byron's Profession, a first class fight for his money. At the same time he will not be depraved by any attempt to persuade him that his relish for blood and violence is the sympathy of a generous soul for virtue in its eternal struggle with vice. I claim that from the first upper cut with which Cashel Byron stops his opponent's lead-off and draws his cork (I here use the accredited terminology of pugilism) to the cross-buttock with which he finally disables him, there is not a single incident which can be enjoyed on any other ground than that upon which the admittedly brutalized frequenter of prize-fights enjoys his favourite sport. Out of the savagery of my imagination I wrote the scene; and out of the savagery of your tastes you delight in it. My other novels contain nothing of the kind. And none of them have succeeded as well as Cashel Byron's Profession.

The late James Runciman, himself, I understand, an amateur boxer of some distinction, wanted to dramatise Cashel Byron's Profession, an enterprise from which I strongly dissuaded him on the ground that the means by which I had individualised the characters in the novel would prove quite ineffective on the stage; so that all that could be done was, not to dramatise the novel, but to take the persons out of it, and use them over again on the stage in an otherwise original play. Lest there should be any heir to Runciman's design, I may as well point out that the two incidents in the story which have dramatic potency in them have already been used prominently on the stage. All the essentials of the glove fight in which the hero vanquishes an antagonist personally much less attractive than himself in the presence of a fashionable audience which includes the heroine, are to be found in a play of Shakespere's called As You Like It. Rosalind, Orlando, Charles the Wrestler, and Le Beau are sufficiently close copies of Lydia, Cashel, Paradise and Lord Worthington. The second instance is the episode of Bashville, the foot-man who loves his mistress. His place on the stage is already occupied by Victor Hugo's Ruy Blas, the valet who loves the Queen of Spain. And Bulwer Lytton disputed the novelty of Ruy Blas on the ground that the central idea was to be found in Claude Melnotte's passion for the Lady of Lyons. But as the only unusual feature in Victor Hugo's play springs from his perception that a domestic servant is a human being, Fielding's Joseph Andrews is more nearly related to Ruy Blas and Bashville than Claude, who was a gardener. If I had not seen quite clearly that the fact of my not being a footman myself was the merest accident (a proposition which most of our novelists would undoubtedly repudiate with the greatest indignation) I could not have created Bash-ville. Such romances, by the bye, are probably common enough in real life. One of my own relations, an elderly lady, was, in her teens, cau-tiously approached by her father's gardener with honorable overtures on the part of his son, who was enamoured of the young lady of the house. Unlike Lydia Carew, however, she did not take a democratic view of the offer: she regarded it rather as an act of insane presumption on the part of a being of another and inferior order. And though she has long since been to a great extent cured of this crude class feeling, and has even speculated once or twice as to whether she did not then throw away a more valuable opportunity than that of which she subsequently availed herself, she has not quite lost the old sense that the proposal was, relatively to the ideas of the current epoch, somewhat too Radical. Pauline Deschapelles, and not Lydia Carew, is still the representative of the com-mon feeling among the footman-keeping classes on the subject of matri-monial overtures from the kitchen to the drawing-room.

On a previous page I have alluded to a letter from Robert Louis Stevenson to Mr William Archer about Cashel Byron's Profession. Part of that letter has been given to the public in the second volume of Mr

Sidney Colvin's edition of Stevenson's letters. . . . The suppressed part
of Stevenson's verdict . . . is in the form of an analysis of the book's
composition.

> "Charles Reade   1   part
> Henry James or some kindred author, badly
>   assimilated   1   part
> Disraeli (perhaps unconscious)   .   .   ½ part
> Struggling, overlaid original talent   .   1½ part
> Blooming gaseous folly   1   part

"That is the equation as it stands. What it may become, I don't know,
nor any other man. *Vixere fortes*—O, let him remember that—let him
beware of his damned century: his gifts of insane chivalry and animated
narration are just those that might be slain and thrown out like an
untimely birth by the Dæmon of the Epoch.

"And if he only knew how I had enjoyed the chivalry! Bashville—O
Bashville! *j'en chortle!* (which is finely polygot)." [18]

. . . But long before this happened my self-respect took alarm at the
contemplation of the things I had made. I resolved to give up mere
character sketching and the construction of models for improved types
of individual, and at once to produce a novel which should be a gigantic
grapple with the whole social problem. But, alas! at twenty-seven one
does not know everything. When I had finished two chapters of this
enterprise—chapters of colossal length, but containing the merest preliminary matter—I broke down in sheer ignorance and incapacity. Few
novelists would have had their perseverance shaken by a consideration of
this nature; but it must be remembered that at this time all my works
were in manuscript: the complete unanimity of the publishers in their
conviction that there were more remunerative enterprises open to them
than the publication of my works, had saved me from becoming pe-
cuniarily dependent on fiction.

One day, as I was sitting in the reading room of the British Museum,
beginning my fifth and last novel, . . . I saw a young lady with an
attractive and arresting expression, bold, vivid, and very clever, working
at one of the desks. On that glimpse of a face I instantly conceived the
character and wrote the description of Agatha Wylie. I have never
exchanged a word with that lady; never made her acquaintance; saw
her again under the same circumstances but very few times; yet if I

mention her name, which became well known in literature (she too was writing a novel then, probably, and perhaps had the hero suggested to her by my profile), she will be set down as Agatha Wylie to her dying day, with heaven knows how much more scandalous invention added to account for my supposed intimate knowledge of her character. Before and since, I have used living models as freely as a painter does, and in much the same way: that is, I have sometimes made a fairly faithful portrait founded on intimate personal intercourse, and sometimes, as in Agatha's case, developed what a passing glance suggested to my imagination.

. . . I remember once, at a time when I made daily use of the reading-room of the British Museum—a magnificent communistic institution—I gave a £2 copying job to a man whose respectable poverty would have moved a heart of stone: an ex-schoolmaster, whose qualifications were out of date, and who, through no particular fault of his own, had drifted at last into the reading-room as less literate men drifted into Salvation Army Shelters. He was a sober, well-spoken, well-conducted, altogether unobjectionable man, really fond of reading, and eminently eligible for a good turn of the kind I did him. His first step in the matter was to obtain from me an advance of five shillings; his next, to sublet the commission to another person in similar circumstances for one pound fifteen, and so get it entirely off his mind and return to his favorite books. This second, or rather, third party, however, required an advance from my acquaintance of one-and-sixpence to buy paper, having obtained which, he handed over the contract to a fourth party, who was willing to do it for one pound thirteen and sixpence. Speculation raged for a day or two as the job was passed on; and it reached bottom at last in the hands of the least competent and least sober copyist in the room, who actually did the work for five shillings, and borrowed endless sixpences from me from that time to the day of her death, which each sixpence probably accelerated to the extent of fourpence, and staved off to the extent of twopence. She was not a deserving person: if she had been she would have come to no such extremity. Her claims to compassion were that she could not be depended upon, could not resist the temptation to drink, could not bring herself to do her work carefully, and was therefore at a miserable disadvantage in the world: a disadvantage exactly similar to that suffered by the blind, the deaf, the maimed, the mad, or any other victims of imperfect or injured faculty. I learnt from her that she had once been recommended to the officials of the Charity Organization

Society; but they, on inquiring into her case, had refused to help her because she was "undeserving," by which they meant that she was incapable of helping herself. Here was surely some confusion of ideas. She was very angry with the Society, and not unreasonably so; for she knew that their funds were largely subscribed by people who regarded them as ministers of pity to the poor and downcast. On the other hand, these people themselves had absurdly limited the application of their bounty to sober, honest, respectable persons: that is to say, to the persons least likely to want it, and alone able to be demoralized by it. . . .

Throughout the eighties at least, and probably for some years before, the British Museum reading room was used daily by a gentleman of such astonishing and crushing ugliness that no one who had once seen him could ever thereafter forget him. He was of fair complexion, rather golden red than sandy; aged between forty-five and sixty; and dressed in frock coat and tall hat of presentable but never new appearance. His figure was rectangular, waistless, neckless, ankleless, of middle height, looking shortish because, though he was not particularly stout, there was nothing slender about him. His ugliness was not unamiable; it was accidental, external, excrescential. Attached to his face from the left ear to the point of his chin was a monstrous goitre, which hung down to his collar bone, and was very inadequately balanced by a smaller one on his right eyelid. Nature's malice was so overdone in his case that it somehow failed to produce the effect of repulsion it seemed to have aimed at. When you first met Thomas Tyler you could think of nothing else but whether surgery could really do nothing for him. But after a very brief acquaintance you never thought of his disfigurements at all, and talked to him as you might to Romeo or Lovelace; only, so many people, especially women, would not risk the preliminary ordeal, that he remained a man apart and a bachelor all his days. I am not to be frightened or prejudiced by a tumor; and I struck up a cordial acquaintance with him, in the course of which he kept me pretty closely on the track of his work at the Museum, in which I was then, like himself, a daily reader.

He was by profession a man of letters of an uncommercial kind. He was a specialist in pessimism; had made a translation of Ecclesiastes of which eight copies a year were sold; and followed up the pessimism of Shakespear and Swift with keen interest. He delighted in a hideous conception which he called the theory of the cycles, according to which the history of mankind and the universe keeps eternally repeating itself without the slightest variation throughout all eternity; so that he had

lived and died and had his goitre before and would live and die and
have it again and again and again. He liked to believe that nothing that
happened to him was completely novel: he was persuaded that he often
had some recollection of its previous occurrence in the last cycle. He
hunted out allusions to this favorite theory in his three favorite pessimists.
He tried his hand occasionally at deciphering ancient inscriptions, reading them as people seem to read the stars, by discovering bears and bulls
and swords and goats where, as it seems to me, no sane human being
can see anything but stars higgledy-piggledy. Next to the translation of
Ecclesiastes, his *magnum opus* was his work on Shakespear's Sonnets, in
which he accepted a previous identification of Mr W. H., the "onlie
begetter" of the sonnets, with the Earl of Pembroke (William Herbert),
and promulgated his own identification of Mistress Mary Fitton with
the Dark Lady. Whether he was right or wrong about the Dark Lady
did not matter urgently to me: she might have been Maria Tompkins
for all I cared. But Tyler would have it that she was Mary Fitton; and
he tracked Mary down from the first of her marriages in her teens to her
tomb in Cheshire, whither he made a pilgrimage and whence returned in
triumph with a picture of her statue, and the news that he was convinced
she was a dark lady by traces of paint still discernible.

In due course he published his edition of the Sonnets, with the evidence
he had collected. He lent me a copy of the book, which I never returned.
But I reviewed it in the Pall Mall Gazette on the 7th of January 1886, and
thereby let loose the Fitton theory in a wider circle of readers than the
book could reach. Then Tyler died, sinking unnoted like a stone in the
sea.

. . . It may very well be that he got his knowledge of Hebrew in reading for the Church; and there was always something of the clergyman
or the schoolmaster in his dress and air. Possibly he may actually have
been ordained. But he never told me that or anything else about his
affairs; and his black pessimism would have shot him violently out of
any church at present established in the West. We never talked about
affairs: we talked about Shakespear, and the Dark Lady, and Swift, and
Koheleth, and the cycles, and the mysterious moments when a feeling
came over us that this had happened to us before, and about the forgeries
of the Pentateuch which were offered for sale to the British Museum,
and about literature and things of the spirit generally. He always came
to my desk at the Museum and spoke to me about something or other,
no doubt finding that people who were keen on this sort of conversation

were rather scarce. He remains a vivid spot of memory in the void of my forgetfulness, a quite considerable and dignified soul in a grotesquely disfigured body. . . . I, as a pious duty to Tyler's ghost, remind . . . the world that it was to Tyler we owed the Fitton theory . . . . I . . . have personal reasons for remembering Tyler, and for regarding myself as in some sort charged with the duty of reminding the world of his work.

[My last] novel finished me with the publishers. One of them refused even to read it. I had read the first volume of Karl Marx's Capital, and made my hero a Marxian Socialist. This was beyond endurance. A clerk for a hero (my first) was not a recommendation; but at least he accepted the world as it was and wore a white linen collar in its social eddies. I was perhaps to be encouraged. But my second, a working electrical engineer crashing through the castes and mastering them: that was distasteful and incorrect. I was going wrong. Then a British Beethoven, careless of his clothes, ungovernable, incomprehensible, poor, living in mean lodgings at an unfashionable address: this was absurd. The next, a prizefighter, wooing and marrying a priggishly refined lady of property, made a bit of a romance, without a dying child in it but with a fight or two. But a Socialist! A Red, an enemy of civilization, a universal thief, atheist, adulterer, anarchist, and apostle of the Satan he disbelieved in!! And presented as a rich young gentleman, eccentric but not socially unpresentable. Too bad.

Eventually the two prodigious chapters of my aborted *magnum opus* were published as a complete novel, in two "books," under the title, An Unsocial Socialist. Though to me they are a monument of my failure, I unhesitatingly challenge any living writer of fiction to produce anything comparable in vivacity and originality to the few early scenes in which the hero, Trefusis, introduces himself by masquerading as Jefferson Smilash at the girls' school. It is true that a moderately intelligent poodle, once started, could have done a good deal of the rest; but this is true of all works of art, more or less. The hero is remarkable because, without losing his pre-eminence as hero, he not only violates every canon of propriety, like Tom Jones or Des Grieux, but every canon of sentiment as well. In an age when the average man's character is rotted at the core by the lust to be a true gentleman, the moral value of such an example as Trefusis is incalculable.

. . . I recommend the works of my youth, in spite of their occasional vulgarity, puerility and folly. Indeed, to the vulgar my vulgarity, to the puerile my puerility, and to the foolish my folly will be a delight instead of a drawback. For the merely inane there is twaddle about Art and even a certain vein of philandering and flirtation. . . . An extraordinary increase in the popularity of An Unsocial Socialist is indicated by the fact that my royalties upon it in the year 1891 were 170 per cent. greater than those received in 1889. I doubt if any other living novelist can shew such a record. In fact 170 is an understatement; for the exact figures were two and tenpence for 1889 and seven and tenpence for the year 1891.

Of [*An Unfinished Novel,* written in 1887–88] I have not the faintest recollection. I should deny its existence if it were not before me as I write, all the more energetically as it is a complete throwback to the Victorian novel with its triangle of husband wife and lover, who reappear some ten years later in my play called Candida. But in the play marriage is triumphant, with the pair left in an exalted and unassailable union, whilst the lover vanishes into the night, having sanctified their household instead of desecrating it. In the . . . fragment the convention of George Eliot's supremely famous novel Middlemarch still prevails: the lover is the hero and the husband only the wife's mistake.

It is not surprising that I found nothing new for me to do in that direction, and abandoned my abortive attempt to return to it so soon and completely that I dropped it and forgot all about it when I had barely introduced the three leading characters in their three degrees of mental scope.

Let who will and can finish it to their taste if they can bear to give it another thought.[19]

Thus, after . . . years of novel writing, I was a complete professional failure. The more I wrote and the better I wrote the less I pleased the publishers. This first novel of mine, though rejected, at least elicited some expressions of willingness to read any future attempts. Blackwood actually accepted and then revoked. Sir George Macmillan, then a junior, not only sent me a longish and evidently considered report by the firm's reader, John (afterwards Lord) Morley, but suggested to him that I might be of some use to him in his capacity as editor of the Pall Mall Gazette.

All such responses ceased with my second novel; and I had no means of knowing, and was too young and inexperienced to guess, that what was the matter was not any lack of literary competence on my part, but the antagonism raised by my hostility to respectable Victorian thought and society. I was left without a ray of hope; yet I did not stop writing novels until, having planned my fifth effort on a colossal scale, I found at the end of what were to me only the first two sections of it, that I had no more to say and had better wait until I had educated myself much farther. And when, after an interval of critical journalism, I resumed the writing of fiction, I did so as a playwright and not as a novelist.

. . . Except for a day or two in 1881, when I earned a few pounds by counting the votes at an election in Leyton, I was an Unemployable, an ablebodied pauper in fact if not in law, until the year 1885, when for the first time I earned enough money directly by my pen to pay my way.

6

The Fabian Experience

In the winter of 1880,[1] James Lecky, exchequer clerk from Ireland, and privately interested in phonetics, keyboard temperament, and Gaelic, all of which subjects he imposed on me, dragged me to a meeting of a debating society called The Zetetical: a junior copy of the once well known Dialectical Society founded to discuss John Stuart Mill's Essay on Liberty when that was new. Both societies were strongly Millite. In both there was complete freedom of discussion, political, religious, and sexual. Women took an important part in the debates, a special feature of which was that each speaker, at the conclusion of his speech, could be cross-examined on it. The tone was strongly individualistic, atheistic, Malthusian, Ingersollian, Darwinian, and Herbert Spencerian. Huxley, Tyndall, and George Eliot were on the shelves of all the members. Championship of the Married Women's Property Act had hardly been silenced even by the Act itself. Indignation at prosecutions for blasphemous libel was *de rigueur*; and no words were too strong for invective against such leading cases as those of Annie Besant and Shelley, whose children were torn from them by the Lord Chancellor because, as professed atheists, they were presumed to be unfit for parentage. Socialism was regarded as an exploded fallacy of Robert Owen's; and nobody dreamt that within five years Marxist Socialism would snatch away all the younger generation, and sweep the Dialectical and Zetetical Societies into the blind cave of eternal night. Cobdenist individualism in industry was fundamental.

When I went with Lecky to the Zetetical meeting I had never spoken in public. I knew nothing about public meetings or their order. I had an air of impudence, but was really an arrant coward, nervous and self-conscious to a heartbreaking degree. Yet I could not hold my tongue. I started up and said something in the debate, and then, feeling that I had made a fool of myself, as in fact I had, I was so ashamed that I vowed I would join the Society; go every week; speak in every debate; and become a speaker or perish in the attempt. I carried out this resolution. I suffered agonies that no one suspected. During the speech of the debater I resolved to follow, my heart used to beat as painfully as a recruit's going under fire for the first time. I could not use notes: when I looked at the paper in my hand I could not collect myself enough to decipher a word. And of the four or five points that were my pretext for this ghastly practice I invariably forgot the best.

The Society must have hated me; for to it I seemed so uppish and self-possessed that at my third meeting I was asked to take the chair. I consented as offhandedly as if I were the Speaker of the House of Commons; and the secretary probably got his first inkling of my hidden terror by seeing that my hand shook so that I could hardly sign the minutes of the previous meeting. My speeches must have been little less dreaded by the Society than they were by myself; but I noticed that they were hardly ever ignored; for the speaker of the evening, in replying, usually addressed himself almost exclusively to my remarks, seldom in an appreciative vein. Besides, though ignorant of economics, I had read, in my boyhood, Mill on Liberty, on Representative Government, and on the Irish Land Question; and I was as full of Darwin, Tyndall, and George Eliot as most of my audience. Yet every subject struck my mind at an angle that produced reflections new to my audience. My first success was when the Society paid to Art, of which it was utterly ignorant, the tribute of setting aside an evening for a paper on it by a lady in the esthetic dress momentarily fashionable in Morrisan cliques just then. I wiped the floor with that meeting; and several members confessed to me afterwards that it was this performance that first made them reconsider their first impression of me as a bumptious discordant idiot.

I persevered doggedly. I haunted all the meetings in London where debates followed lectures. I spoke in the streets, in the parks, at demonstrations, anywhere and everywhere possible. In short, I infested public meetings like an officer afflicted with cowardice, who takes every opportunity of going under fire to get over it and learn his business.

I had quiet literary evenings in University College at the meetings of the New Shakespear Society under F. J. Furnivall, and breezier ones at his Browning Society, reputedly an assembly of longhaired esthetes, but really a conventicle where evangelistic elderly ladies discussed their religion with Furnivall, who, being what was called a Muscular Christian (slang for sporting parson), could not forgive Jesus for not putting up a fight in Gethsemane.

I was a leading feature at all Furnivall's societies—the New Shakespeare (or Old Spelling) Society, the Browning and the Shelley—because as I was an inveterate public speaker, and could always be depended on to enliven a discussion, Furnivall enlisted me without consulting me, and never troubled me for a subscription. I hope I had the decency to pay my way, as Furnivall always provided tea and cake as well as discussion. I had never read a line of Browning's when I was conscripted in this fashion; but I was full of Shakespeare and Shelley.

The oddity of these bodies was that Furnivall's crowd was a Browning crowd to whom Browning was a religious leader; and Furnivall openly scorned Jesus because, as he put it, "the fellow let himself be spat upon without at least giving the spitter a black eye." I and the late E. C. K. Gonner, still in our mischievous youth, used to egg him on to horrify the pious old ladies whose subscriptions kept the Societies going.[2]

They followed him into the Shelley Society in all innocence; and when I, at the first meeting in the lecture theatre of University College, announced that as a good Shelleyan I was a Socialist, an Atheist, and a vegetarian, two of them resigned on the spot.

I joined another very interesting debating society called the Bedford, founded by Stopford Brooke, who had not then given up his pastorate at Bedford Chapel to devote himself to literature.

At all these meetings I took part in the debates. My excessive nervousness soon wore off. One of the public meetings I haunted was at the Nonconformist Memorial Hall in Farringdon Street in 1882.[3] The speaker of the evening, very handsome and eloquent, was Henry George, American apostle of Land Nationalization and Single Tax. He struck me dumb and shunted me from barren agnostic controversy to economics. . . . I knew he was an American because he pronounced "necessarily"—a favorite word of his—with the accent on the third syllable instead of the first, because he was deliberately and intentionally oratorical, which is not customary among shy people like the English; because he spoke of Liberty, Justice, Truth, Natural Law, and other strange eighteenth century superstitions; and because he explained with great simplicity and sincerity the views of the Creator, who had gone completely out of fashion in London in the previous decade and had not been heard of since. I noticed also that he was a born orator, and that he had small, plump, pretty hands.

Now at that time I was a young man not much past 25, of a very revolutionary and contradictory temperament, full of Darwin and Tyndall, of Shelley and De Quincey, of Michael Angelo and Beethoven, and never having in my life studied social questions from the economic point of view, except that I had once, in my boyhood, read a pamphlet by John Stuart Mill on the Land Question. The result of my hearing that speech, and buying from one of the stewards of the meeting a copy of Progress and Poverty (Heaven only knows where I got that sixpence), was that I plunged into a course of economic study, and at a very early stage of it became a Socialist and spoke from that very platform on the same great subject, and from hundreds of others as well, sometimes addressing distinguished assemblies in a formal manner, sometimes standing on a borrowed chair at a street corner, or simply on a curbstone. And I, too, had my oratorical successes; for I can still recall with some vanity a wet afternoon (Sunday, of course) on Clapham Common, when I collected as much as sixteen and sixpence in my hat after my lecture, for the Cause.[4] And that the work was not all gas, let the tracts and pamphlets of the Fabian Society attest.

When I was thus swept into the Great Socialist Revival of 1883, I found that five-sixths of those who were swept in with me had been converted by Henry George. This fact would have been more widely acknowledged had it not been that it was not possible for us to stop where Henry George had stopped. America, in spite of all its horrors of rampant Capitalism and industrial oppression, was, nevertheless, still a place for the individualist and the hustler. Every American who came over to London was amazed at the apathy, the cynical acceptance of poverty and servitude as inevitable, the cunning shuffling along with as little work as possible, that seemed to the visitor to explain our poverty, and moved him to say, "Serve us right!"

. . . I am glad to say that I never denied or belittled our debt to Henry George. If we outgrew Progress and Poverty in many respects, so did he himself too; and it is, perhaps, just as well that he did not know too much when he made his great campaign here; for the complexity of the problem would have overwhelmed him if he had realized it, or, if it had not, it would have rendered him unintelligible. . . . Some of us regretted that he was an American and therefore necessarily about fifty years out of date in his economics and sociology from the viewpoint of the older country; but only an American could have seen in a single lifetime the growth of the whole tragedy of civilization from the primitive forest clearing. An Englishman grows up to think that the ugliness of Manchester and the slums of Liverpool have existed since the beginning of the world.

. . . I read his Progress and Poverty, and went to a meeting of Hyndman's Marxist Democratic Federation, where I rose and protested against its drawing a red herring across the trail blazed by George. I was contemptuously dismissed as a novice who had not read the great first volume of Marx's Capital.

I promptly read it, and returned to announce my complete conversion by it. Immediately contempt changed to awe; for Hyndman's disciples had not read the book themselves, it being then accessible only in Deville's French version in the British Museum reading room, my daily resort. From that hour I was a speaker with a gospel, no longer only an apprentice trying to master the art of public speaking.

I at once applied for membership of the Democratic Federation, but withdrew my application on discovering the newly founded Fabian Society, in which I recognized a more appropriate *milieu* as a body of educated middle-class intelligentsia: my own class in fact. Hyndman's congregation of manual-working pseudo-Marxists could for me be only hindrances.

After my conversion I soon became sufficiently known as a Socialist orator to have no further need to seek out public debates: I was myself sought after. This began when I accepted an invitation from a Radical Club at Woolwich to lecture to it. At first I thought of reading a written lecture; for it seemed hardly possible to speak for an hour without text when I had hitherto spoken for ten minutes or so only in debates. But if I were to lecture formally on Socialism for an hour, writing would be impossible for want of time: I must extemporize. The lecture was called Thieves, and was a demonstration that the proprietor of an unearned income inflicted on the community exactly the same injury as a burglar does. I spoke for an hour easily, and from that time always extemporized.[5]

Once you are at home on the platform the trick is easy enough. You start your address tentatively and go on until you say something that is applauded. Then you say it again and again. You challenge anyone to deny it: you declare that the fate of the human race depends upon it.

The oftener you say it the more the audience applauds. You end in a frenzy; and the audience, worked up to insanity, salutes you with thunders of applause. But that trick was no use to me. I did not want the audience to dictate my speech to me: I had to convince them against all their prejudices that they ought to change their minds and become Socialists. I had to start them thinking instead of fuddling them and muddling them. My tactics often had to be shock tactics. You can if you like give me what credit I can claim from the fact that I always held my audience, and that the people who had heard me once came again. I got the earnest and sober sort of applause, the half dumb-foundered sort, not the drunken sort.

This went on for about twelve years, during which I sermonized on Socialism at least three times a fortnight average. I preached whenever and wherever I was asked. It was first come first served with me: when I got an application for a lecture I gave the applicant the first date I had vacant, whether it was for a street corner, a public-house parlor, a market place, the economic section of the British Association, the City Temple, a cellar or a drawing room. My audiences varied from tens to thousands. I expected opposition but got hardly any. Twice, in difficulties raised by attempts of the police to stop Socialist street meetings (they always failed in the end because the religious sects, equally active in the open air, helped the Socialists to resist them), I was within an ace of going to prison. The first time was in Dod Street in dockland, where the police capitulated on the morning of the day when I volunteered to defy them. The second time, many years later at the World's End[6] in Chelsea, a member of a rival Socialist Society disputed the martyr's palm with me, and, on a division, defeated me by two votes, to my secret relief. My longest oration lasted four hours in the open air on a Sunday morning to crowds at Trafford Bridge in Manchester. One of my best speeches was delivered in Hyde Park in torrents of rain to six policemen sent to watch me, plus only the secretary of the Society that had asked me to speak, who held an umbrella over me. I made up my mind to interest those policemen, though as they were on duty to listen to me, their usual practice, after being convinced that I was harmless, was to pay no further attention. I entertained them for more than an hour. I can still see their waterproof capes shining in the rain when I shut my eyes.

. . . I spoke everywhere . . . from the British Association to the dock gates, the market places, and all the pitches in the country . . . . Henry James treated me with wondering awe because somebody told him that

I had stopped one day on the Embankment and harangued the passers-by until I had quite a decent crowd. He asked me whether it was really true; and when I said it was, he exclaimed: "I could not do it. I could not bring myself to do it." I have always maintained that the open air is the best school for a public speaker.

I suppose I have addressed as many hopeful progressive leagues as any man in London. I have sampled them nearly all . . . and it brings up in my mind . . . the meeting which I think was most unlike this of any I have ever attended in London. It was in a small and very shabby room in the neighborhood of Tottenham Court Road. I do not suppose there were more than twenty enthusiasts present; but they were very determined enthusiasts—so much so that they declined to elect a chairman, because that meant authority, and they were going to destroy authority. They were a very mild set of men, and therefore they called themselves Anarchists, as almost all very mild men do. The difficulty about them was that they were really not very dangerous men, except one. There was one man—a young man—there, a pioneer, a fragile and mild creature; and he really was dangerous, for he had provided himself with a dynamite bomb, on which he was sitting during the entire time I was addressing that meeting—a fact of which I was not aware at the time, or perhaps I should not have addressed them with so much self-possession as I did. Well, taking him as being the only dangerous man there, who was he dangerous to? Two days afterwards he took his bomb to Greenwich Park and blew himself into fragments with it—unintentionally. That is a thing that many progressive leagues do, though they may not blow themselves to pieces in such a very decisive way.[7]

I never took payment for speaking. It often happened that provincial Sunday Societies offered me the usual ten guinea fee to give the usual sort of lecture, avoiding controversial politics and religion. I always replied that I never lectured on anything but very controversial politics and religion, and that my fee was the price of my railway ticket third class if the place was further off than I could afford to go at my own expense. The Sunday Society would then assure me on these terms I might lecture on anything I liked and how I liked. Occasionally, to avoid embarrassing other lecturers who lived by lecturing, the account was settled by a debit and credit entry: that is, I was credited with the usual fee and expenses, and gave it back as a donation to the Society. In this way I secured perfect freedom of speech, and was armed against the accusation of being a professional agitator. For instance, at the election in 1892, I was making a speech in the Town Hall of Dover when a man rose and shouted to the audience not to let itself be talked to by a hired professional agitator from London. I immediately offered to sell him my emoluments for £5. He hesitated; and I came down to £4. I offered to make it five shillings—half-a-crown—a shilling—sixpence. When he would not deal even at a penny I claimed that he must know perfectly well that I was there at my own expense. If I had not been able to do this, the meeting, which was a difficult and hostile one (Dover being then a notoriously corrupt constituency), would probably have broken up.

How necessary was this entirely voluntary position I learnt from a professional speaker who was hired at £3 a week to follow me to all my meetings and confute me by the Duke of Argyll's Liberty & Property Defence League. Travelling together we soon became pleasant acquaintances. He always made the same speech and I always made the same smashing reply. When his League broke up he offered his services to the Fabian Society, and was amazed to learn that Fabian speakers were unpaid, and that I had actually been lecturing "for nothing."

Once, in St. James's Hall, London, at a meeting in favor of Women's Suffrage, I ventured on a curious trick with success. Just before I spoke, a hostile contingent entered the room; and I saw that we were outnumbered, and that an amendment would be carried against us. The intruders were all Socialists of the anti-Fabian persuasion, led by a man whom I knew very well, and who was at that time excitable almost to frenzy, worn out with public agitation and private worries. It occurred to me that if, instead of carrying an amendment, they could be goaded to break up the meeting and disgrace themselves, the honors would remain with us. I made a speech that would have made a bishop swear or a sheep fight. The leader, stung beyond endurance, dashed madly to the platform to answer me. His followers, thinking he was leading a charge, instantly stormed the platform; broke up the meeting; and reconstituted it with their leader as chairman. I then demanded a hearing, which was duly granted me as a matter of fair play; and I had another innings with great satisfaction to myself. No harm was done, nor any blow struck; but the papers next morning described a scene of violence and destruction that left nothing to be desired by the most sanguinary schoolboy.

I never challenged anyone to debate publicly with me. It seemed to me an unfair practice for a seasoned public speaker to challenge a comparative novice to a duel with tongues, of no more value than any other sort of duel. But I now regret that when I was myself still a novice, a debate between me and Charles Bradlaugh which the Socialist League (Morris's body) tried to arrange did not come off. Bradlaugh was a heroic fighting platform thunderer; and I should have been only a light weight trying to outbox a heavy one who had won in all his conflicts; but I could at least have said my say. The Socialist League challenged him to debate, and chose me as their champion, though I was not a member. I was frightened, but could not back out. Bradlaugh, however, made it a condition that I should be bound by all the pamphlets and utterances of the Social-Democratic Federation, a strongly anti-Fabian body. Of course I should have let him make what conditions he pleased, and paid no attention to them. But I was too green to see this. I proposed simply: "Will Socialism benefit the English people?" He would accept this only on condition that Socialism was to mean what Hyndman's Federation meant. I refused to be bound thus; and the debate—as I think he must have intended—did not come off, rather to my relief; for I was very doubtful of being able to make any show against him. I have never quite forgiven myself for this missed opportunity; but it was less cowardice than diffidence, with which in those early days I was still much afflicted. I was really a better speaker and a more formidable antagonist than I knew. I had already faced Bradlaugh on his own ground at the Hall of Science in the City Road. My seat was far back; and when I rose I had hardly uttered two sentences when Bradlaugh started up and said: "The gentleman is a speaker. Come to the platform," which I accordingly did through much curious staring. Bradlaugh devoted almost all his reply to my speech. He evidently thought more of me than I did of myself; and it pleases me to imagine that he refused a set debate with me much as Edmund Kean refused to act with Macready.

Later on he debated the Eight Hour Day with Hyndman, whom he was confident he could pulverize. Neither of them stuck to the subject; and the result was so inconclusive that both sides were dissatisfied; and it was arranged that the question should be re-debated by me with the late G. V. Foote, Bradlaugh's successor in the Presidency of the National Secular Society, and a firstrate speaker. In the Hall of Science we went at it hammer-and-tongs for two nights. Oratorically honors were even; but I was more at home in economics than Foote, and should, I believe, have won the verdict had a vote been taken. The debate was reported in a booklet published by George Standring.[8]

My public speaking brought me a very necessary qualification for political work: the committee habit. Whatever Society I joined I was immediately placed on the executive committee. At first I did what authors usually do in their Bohemian anarchism and individualism. When they are defeated on any issue they resign. I did this when the Land Restoration League refused to add Socialism to its program on my suggestion. I never did it again. I soon learnt the rule Never Resign. I learnt also that committees of agitators are always unanimous in the conviction that Something Must Be Done, but very vague as to what. They talk and talk and can come to no conclusion. The member who has something definite to propose, and who keeps it up his sleeve until the rest are completely bothered, is then master of the situation even when nobody quite agrees with him. It is that or nothing; and Something Must Be Done. This is how a man in a minority of one becomes a leader. I was often in a minority of one.

How lack of committee training and platform technique disables even the most gifted thinkers was illustrated by the case of H. G. Wells, with whom I had a famous debate when he tried to capture the Fabian Society at one blow. As a speaker and committee man I had the advantage of him by ten years, whilst he was a complete novice. To say that I annihilated him is nothing: he saved me the trouble by annihilating himself. He could only misbehave himself. Fortunately for him he did this so outrageously that the Society very sensibly saw through the situation, and, whilst dismissing him as tactically impossible, thought none the worse of him as a Socialist pioneer, and none the better of me for my superiority as a platform artist.[9]

I must not leave incipient orators to suppose that my technique as a speaker was acquired by practice alone. Practice only cured my nervousness, and accustomed me to speak to multitudes as well as to private persons. I have elsewhere described how I became acquainted with old Richard Deck, superannuated Alsatian *basso profundo* opera singer, who believed he had discovered a new method of *bel canto,* and imagined that he could not only renew his career as a singer when he had fully mastered it, but also regenerate civilization with it. He died destitute in University College Hospital. Meanwhile, however, being a pupil of Delsarte, he taught me that to be intelligible in public the speaker must relearn the alphabet with every consonant separately and explosively articulated, and foreign vowels distinguished from British diphthongs. Accordingly I practised the alphabet as a singer practises scales until I was in no danger of saying "Loheeryelentheethisharpointed sword" instead of "Lo here *I* lend *thee thiss sharp* pointed sword," nor imagine that when imitating the broadest dialects articulation is less to be studied than in classical declamation. Lessons in elocution should always be taken by public speakers when a phonetically competent teacher is available. But art must conceal its artificiality; and the old actor who professes to teach acting, and knows nothing of phonetic speech training, is to be avoided like the plague.

At last I could not deal with all the invitations I received. And the repetition of the same figures and arguments became tiresome: I was in danger of becoming a windbag with only one speech. I had seen too much of the fate of Trade Union organizers who, beginning as tee-totallers, were forced by the need for "stoking up" their fresh audiences with the same stale speech to stoke themselves up by drinking. By 1895 I was no longer in full blast; and a breakdown of my health, followed by my marriage in 1898, finished me as a Sunday platform star. Thenceforth I orated on special occasions only, or at Fabian public meetings and in the St Pancras Borough Council, to which I got elected while it was still a Vestry. But I did not forget my acquired technique as a platform artist. It lasted until my final retirement from personal performances in 1941: my eightyfifth year.

A few weeks after I joined the Zetetical Society I was much struck by a speaker who appeared once and took part in the debate. He was about 21, rather below middle height, with small hands and feet, and a profile that suggested an improvement on Napoleon the Third, his nose and imperial moustache being of that shape. He had a fine forehead, a long head, eyes that were built on top of two highly developed organs of speech (according to the phrenologists), and remarkably thick, strong, dark hair. He knew all about the subject of debate; knew more than the lecturer; knew more than anybody present; had read everything that had ever been written; and remembered all the facts that bore on the subject. He used notes, read them, ticked them off one by one, threw them away, and finished with a coolness and clearness that seemed to me miraculous.

This was the ablest man in England: Sidney Webb. Quite the wisest thing I ever did was to force my friendship on him and to keep it; for from that time I was not merely a futile Shaw but a committee of Webb and Shaw.

Webb, later Baron Passfield of Passfield Corner, now buried in Westminster Abbey at my urgent demand, proved one of the most extraordinary and capable of world-bettering administrators and historians. I somehow divined this whilst we were still both nobodies. As a disciple of John Stuart Mill he had grasped the economic certainty that private property in the sources of production plus freedom of contract must produce a plutocracy face to face with a proletariat, and substitute class war for genuine democracy. Adam Smith, Malthus and Ricardo, Austin and Macaulay, knew this, but saw no alternative. Webb, as a modern upper division civil servant, knew that there is a quite feasible corrective alternative in nationalization of the sources of production, and direct management of vital industries by the State, of the existence and success of which he had at his fingers' ends an overwhelming list of examples. On this basis he was a convinced Socialist. . . . When the Fabian Society was founded in 1884, I was attracted by its name and its tract called Why Are The Many Poor? I persuaded Webb to join, Marx having convinced me that what the movement needed was not Hegelian theorizing but an unveiling of the official facts of Capitalist civilization, which Webb had at his fingers' ends. His first contribution, a tract called Facts for Socialists, was the effective beginning of Fabianism.

The difference between Shaw with Webb's brains, knowledge, and official experience and Shaw by himself was enormous. But as I was and am an incorrigible histrionic mountebank, and Webb was the simplest of geniuses, I was often in the centre of the stage whilst he was invisible in the prompter's box.

My conversion to economics by Henry George brought me into contact with a Georgite body called The Land Reform Union, which survived for some years as The English Land Restoration League. Here I met James Leigh Joynes, an Eton master, Sydney Olivier, and Henry Hyde Champion, besides some Christian Socialist clergymen including Stewart Headlam, Symes of Nottingham, with Sarson and Shuttleworth, who were organized as The Guild of St Matthew. Symes, I remember, argued that Land Nationalization would settle everything, to which I replied that if capital were still privately appropriated, Symes would remain "the chaplain of a pirate ship." Sarson, on the strength of the First Article of the Church of England, held that Anglicanism was atheistic. He became known as Cecil Sharp's colleague in their collection of Somerset folk songs.

Now Joynes was a vegetarian, a humanitarian, a Shelleyan. He was deprived of his Eton post because he made a tour in Ireland with Henry George, and was arrested with him by the police, who supposed the two to be emissaries of the Clan na Gael. Joynes's sister was married to an Eton house master, Henry Salt. Salt was also a vegetarian, a humanitarian, a Shelleyan, a De Quinceyite. He loathed Eton housekeeping. As soon as he had saved enough to live in a laborer's cottage in the country (he had no children) he threw up his house; shook the dust of Eton from his feet; and founded a Humanitarian League. He and I and his wife, Kate Salt, with whom I used to play duets on the noisiest grand piano that ever descended from Eton to a Surrey cottage, became very close friends. My article headed A Sunday in the Surrey Hills in The Pall Mall Gazette describes my first visit to them in the country; and several scenes of my Plays Pleasant and Unpleasant were written in the heather during my visits to them.[10]

I remember basking in the heath outside his cottage and writing The Philanderer when I was staying with them. And it was Salt who, hearing me read Candida, exclaimed after the third act "Why, the man is a poet" meaning *me*.

Intimate in the Salt household was Edward Carpenter. We called him the Noble Savage. He also played duets with Kate, and induced me to wear sandals, which I discarded after my first long walk in them ended with bleeding feet.

I was always happy at the Salts. We never talked politics but gossiped endlessly about our friends and everything else. The bond between us was that we were Shelleyans and Humanitarians. He was also a keen Meredithian; but I disliked upper ten ladies and gentlemen so much (they bore me) that I could not read Meredith's novels (except the Tragic Comedians which was about Lassalle). . . .

As his last two books show Salt liked Cambridge. But he hated being Housemaster and kept saving enough to buy a pension of £800 a year which was then considered a minimum on which a Housemaster could retire. When he read a book in which Edward Carpenter advocated "the simple life," and said that it could be lived on £160 a year, which was just what Salt had by that time accumulated, he instantly shook the dust of Cambridge off his feet and took the Tilford cottage where I first met him. . . .

Kate (Mrs. Salt) loved me as far as she could love any male creature. Once, towards her end, when I had been absent for years and turned up unexpectedly after they had moved to Carpenter's neighbourhood in Yorkshire, she actually flung her arms round me. She was a queer hybrid. I never met anyone in the least like her, though another friend of mine, the Christian Socialist parson, Stewart Headlam, also had a wife who was a homo.

Salt's tragedy was that his wife (born Kate Joynes, and half German) would not consummate their marriage, calling herself an Urning. She got it from her close friend Edward Carpenter who taught Kate that Urnings are a chosen race. Carpenter and I used to meet at Salt's cottage at Tilford. We all called him "The Noble Savage," and wore the sandals he made. He and I played piano duets with Kate, making a fearful noise with Wagner's Kaisermarch and The Ring, and shared her friendship about equally. We were "Sunday husbands" to her. Salt was quite in the friendship.

Though Kate would not sleep with Salt she was always falling in love with some woman. . . . What she really needed was children; and I told her to get a job in a factory to bring her to her senses. To my surprise she actually did so, and became an employee in my friend Emery Walker's engraving works. But as she could not engrave she was set to work in the office. She soon left it and worked for me as unpaid typist secretary until my marriage. Finally she went back to Salt and lived with him until she faded out mentally and died. . . .

Salt, like Samuel Butler, was at war implacably with his father because he considered that his mother had been ill-treated by him and he represented me as saying something unfeeling about my mother to Robert Buchanan. He had mixed Buchanan up somehow with the scandal given by Cashel Byron's "I hate my mother" which so shocked Mrs. R. L. Stevenson that she shut the book with a bang and flung it away. All heroes in 1882 had to love their mothers and in due degree the rest of their relatives. I broke that convention partly because I knew H. W. Massingham, who hated his mother and was hated by her, but also because my father's relatives, though they quarrelled between themselves, combined against my mother, who one day, calling on one of my aunts, overheard her exclaiming to the servant who announced her "Oh, that bitch!" After that we all boycotted one another; and I came to regard all paternal relatives as obnoxious persons, and to make a joke of it. . . .

I never met the Reverend Joynes (Swinburne's tutor at Eton) and neither Butler nor Olivier ever met Salt or knew anything about him. It was J. L. Joynes, Junior, son of the Reverend, and brother-in-law to Salt, who introduced me to Salt. He also was an Eton master (not a Housemaster). He wore his red hair in long curls hanging round his neck and down his back and wrote some very good translations of the revolutionary poems of Freiligrath. He went to Ireland, spoke for the Land League there and was arrested, but released apologetically on pleading his Eton credentials. His heart failed; and he was murderd by the doctors, in whom his father believed fanatically. They immobilized him and fed him on whisky until he became a mere lump and died after writing some wretched verses in imitation of William Morris. This began my feud with the doctors, who are doing that still.

My visit to Swinburne at Putney was with Salt. It began with Salt and myself taking a walk over the common with Watts, who talked all the time about the great authors he had discovered and who were totally unknown to anyone else. The totally unknown were Meredith and Melville, about whom Salt had written a lot. . . .

I met him first at William Morris's Hammersmith house. J. L. Joynes was with him. He was smoking at the fireside of Morris's study when we came in. Morris was not there; so we went into the dining room to find him. Joynes said: "Who is the chap in the study?" Morris looked puzzled; and Joynes added explanatorily "Like a little infantry major."—"Do you mean Theodore WATTS?" said Morris, utterly astonished by this view of him.

Watts (I never picked up the Dunton) believed that his sonnets were the final perfection of poetry and his, gipsy novels immortal; but he was a friendly man and a serviceable friend. His advice was no use to me, as it was given when I was a journalist-critic; but it was good advice and meant as such. There was a ridiculous side to Theodore; but he was a . . . good man.

. . . Henry Salt and I once took a walk with Theodore round Putney Heath, and lunched at The Pines afterwards. Theodore treated Swinburne exactly like a tutor encouraging and patronizing a small boy. Also a little like the proprietor of a pet animal coaxing it to exhibit its tricks. Swinburne accepted these attitudes without protest but would not perform before me; and I had to talk all their heads off to prevent the luncheon being a dismal failure. Swinburne was then an old gentleman with the body of a boy, carrying a disproportionately large filbert shaped head. His eyes were like shirt buttons. I got nothing out of him; but Salt had some words alone with him and found him voluble enough. Apparently I terrified him—"banged him into dumbness" as Shakespear puts it.

As to Meredith, whom Salt admired, and who was a famous talker who never let anyone else get in a word edgewise, it was proposed by Salt and (I think) Clement Shorter that I should visit him and talk him off the stage. I had just spoken for four hours to a crowd in Salford. This plot did not come off; but years later when I [at] last visited Meredith at Box Hill he was shoved into a corner by his family, who wanted to hear *me* all the time. He was deaf and disabled by locomotor ataxy; but I had half an hour of private talk with him in his study before lunch. He had supported the reactionary candidate at a recent election, imagining that he represented the principles of the French Revolution, and Meredith was apologetic when I explained to him that my Fabianism was the latest thing. He was a relic of the Cosmopolitan Republican Gentleman of the previous generation, and must have contracted V.D. in his youth: hence the locomotor.

But he was still brightly blue eyed.

. . . Like Morris and Ruskin, Salt was a Humanitarian. The only author he celebrated and translated was Virgil, whom, like Ruskin, I could not read through, though I paid for the printing and publication of the translation on the understanding that I was to have half the profits until I was paid off. There were never any profits. I knew there would not be with Dryden and Morris in the field.

It was Salt who introduced William Archer to me. Both of them were Thoreau specialists: Salt wrote the life of Thoreau and William Archer called his cottage Walden. . . . In this circle there was no question of Henry George and Karl Marx, but a good deal of Walt Whitman and Thoreau.

I first met Sydney Olivier when we were both in our twenties, and had from different directions embraced Socialism as our creed. I had come by the way of Henry George and Karl Marx. He had begun with the Positivist philosophy of Auguste Comte, and was as far as I know, the only Fabian who came in through that gate.

He and Sidney Webb, Comtist at second-hand through John Stuart Mill, shared the duty of resident clerk at the Colonial Office. Both of them had passed into the upper division of the Civil Service, Olivier heading the competition list, apparently so easily that I never heard either of them speak of it, though to me it was a wonder, as the passing of even an elementary school examination has always been for me an impossible feat. There was no question then of peerages to come for either of them: by plunging into Socialism they were held to be burning their boats as far as any sort of official promotion was concerned, though as founders of Fabian Socialism they soon took The Cause off the barricades, and made it constitutional and respectable.

Olivier was an extraordinarily attractive figure, and in my experience unique; for I have never known anyone like him mentally or physically: he was distinguished enough to be unclassable. He was handsome and strongly sexed, looking like a Spanish grandee in any sort of clothes, however unconventional. . . .

Though Olivier came to positions of authority by sheer gravitation, he could never have become a popular idol, because his mental scope, like that of a champion chess player, enabled him to see the next five or six steps in an argument so clearly and effortlessly that he could not believe that anything so obvious need be stated. I found this out when I edited Fabian Essays in 1887. To that epoch-making volume, Olivier contributed the essay on the Moral Basis of Socialism. On reading his manuscript I found a hiatus in his argument which convinced me at first that a couple of pages must have dropped out. But as the hiatus occurred in the middle of a page I had to reconsider this. I had to think out the missing links for myself: and finally I wrote the page and a half needed to fill the gap in the argument, and brought it to Olivier to re-write in his own fashion. He said that my chain of reasoning was all right; but I could not persuade him that it was not too obvious to need mentioning, nor to take the trouble to translate my version into his own language. I could stick it in just as it was for the benefit of readers (if any) imbecile enough to be unable to follow the argument without it. Which I accordingly did.

This excess of mental and muscular power was accompanied by an excess of nervous power which hampered him as a public speaker. He spoke only on special provocation, and always had to wrestle with his speeches rather than deliver them comfortably. I once asked the chief of the Observatory on Mount Vesuvius why the energy wasted by the burning mountain was not utilized for industrial purposes. He replied that there was too much of it to be manageable. That was Olivier's case; but once I heard it serve him in good stead.

It was at the International Socialist Congress at Zurich, where he and I were the Fabian delegates. As usual, the Congress, instead of getting at once to real business, fell back on the old controversy between Marx and Bakunin, and began disputing whether anarchists should be expelled or not. Day after day was wasted in endless orations by the opposing windbags, followed by tedious translations into two languages, which, being made by amateur interpreters, who were also strong and eloquent partisans, either improved the originals recklessly or guyed them mercilessly. This went on and on, and was all the fun of the fair for most of the delegates; but to us Fabians, out for business, it became at last quite unbearable; and I was on the point of attempting some sort of protest when suddenly the silent Olivier shot up from his chair, and Vesuvius went into full eruption. In a voice like the roaring of a safety valve releasing a thousand horse-power, he discharged his impatience in a speech such as I had never heard before nor have heard since. It left me amazed, and the Congress stunned. When we recovered sufficiently to take action the Congress closed the discussion by throwing the Anarchists out. Once safely outside they produced credentials as trade unionists, and came back and resumed their seats unchallenged. That was what Socialist Congresses were like in those days.

... Olivier ... had made friends at Oxford with Graham Wallas, who afterwards joined us. For some years the leaders in the Politbureau or Thinking Cabinet of the Fabian policy were Webb, Olivier, Wallas, Shaw, and the Tory Democrat Hubert Bland.

As my colleagues were men of exceptional character and attainments, I was soon able to write with a Fabian purview and knowledge which made my feuilletons and other literary performances quite unlike anything that the ordinary literary hermit-crab could produce. Thus the reputedly brilliant extraordinary Shaw was in fact brilliant and extraordinary because he had in the Fabian Politbureau an incomparable critical threshing machine for his ideas. When I seemed most original and fantastic, I was often simply an amanuensis and a mouthpiece with a rather exceptional literary and dramatic knack, cultivated by dogged practice.

My colleagues knocked much nonsense, ignorance, and vulgar provinciality out of me; for we were on quite ruthless critical terms with oneanother.

In the Fabian Cabinet, however, there was considerable strife of temperaments; and in the other Socialist societies splits and schisms were frequent; for the English are very quarrelsome. I believe that some of my own usefulness lay in smoothing out these frictions by an Irish sort of tact which in England seemed the most outrageous want of it. Whenever there was a quarrel I betrayed everybody's confidence by analyzing it and stating it lucidly in the most exaggerated terms. Result: both sides agreed that it was all my fault. I was denounced on all hands as a reckless mischiefmaker, but forgiven as a privileged Irish lunatic.

I flatter myself that the unique survival of the Fabian Society among the forgotten wrecks of its rivals, all very contemptuous of it, was due not only to its policy, but in its early days to the one Irish element in its management.

If any[one] . . . thinks that the Fabian Society was wise from the hour of its birth, let him forthwith renounce that error. The Fabian wisdom, such as it is, has grown out of the Fabian experience; and our distinction, if we may claim any, lies more in our capacity for profiting by experience (a rarer faculty in politics than you might suppose) than in any natural superiority on our part to the follies of incipient Socialism. In 1883 we were content with nothing less than the prompt "reconstruction of society in accordance with the highest moral possibilities." In 1884 we were discussing whether money should be permitted under Socialism, or whether labor notes would not be a more becoming currency for us; and I myself actually debated the point with a Fabian who had elaborated a passbook system to supersede both methods. Then we were joined by Mrs Wilson, . . . one of the chief members of the Freedom Group of Kropotkinist Anarchists; and a sort of influenza of Anarchism soon spread through the society. When we issued our fortunately little-known Tract No. 4, What Socialism Is, we divided it into two sections, one answering the question from the Collectivist and the other from the Anarchist point of view. The answer did not amount to much either way; for the tract contains nothing that was not already to be found better stated in the famous Communist Manifesto of Marx and Engels.

The Fabian Society was warlike in its origin: it came into existence through a schism in an earlier society for the peaceful regeneration of the race by the cultivation of perfection of individual character. Certain members of that circle, modestly feeling that the revolution would have to wait an unreasonably long time if postponed until they personally had attained perfection, set up the banner of Socialism militant; seceded from the Regenerators; and established themselves independently as the Fabian Society. That was how the Fabian began; and although exactly the same practical vein which had led its founders to insist on an active policy afterwards made them the most resolute opponents of Insurrectionism, the Constitutionalism which now distinguishes us was as unheard of at the Fabian meetings in 1884 and 1885 as at the demonstrations of the Social Democratic Federation or the Socialist League. For example, in 1885, a conflict with the Government arose over the right of free speech at Dod Street*. . .

In short, we were for a year or two just as Anarchistic as the Socialist League and just as insurrectionary as the Federation. It will at once be asked why, in that case, we did not join them instead of forming a separate society. Well, the apparent reason was that we were then middle-class all through, rank and file as well as leaders, whereas the League and Federation were quite proletarian in their rank and file. But whatever weight this sort of consideration may have had with our members in general, it had none with our leaders, most of whom, indeed, were active members of the Federation as well. It undoubtedly prevented working men from joining the Fabian whilst we were holding our meetings in one another's drawing rooms; but it did not prevent any Fabian worth counting from joining the working-class organizations.

When Fabianism was born Socialism was a Red Spectre. Whenever a few Socialists set up little groups of mixed socialists and anarchists, and called themselves Federations, or Leagues, or Communist Internationals, Capitalism took fright, and estimated their numbers and revenues in thousands and tens of thousands, when the reality was less than forty inexperienced youth without a banking account. The First International, with Marx as its Head Centre, counted its office income in London in shillings. In France, where it could boast greater numbers, it was recruited by the police spies of Louis Napoleon. They must have been farcically disconcerted when they finally proceeded to arrest one another.

All these crude little combinations of beginners had the same policy and programme. They were to preach the Marxist description and explanation of the Capitalist system to popular audiences. These, on being convinced, would join the little society to which the preacher belonged, and subscribe a penny a week to it. They would abandon and abolish all rival proletarian combinations. When the pence and the membership had accumulated sufficiently, and recruited and united the "proletarians of all

---

* It may be useful to say here that "the way to do the Dod Street trick" is simply to find a dozen or more persons who are willing to get arrested at the rate of one per week by speaking in defiance of the police. In a month or two, the repeated arrests, the crowds which they attract, the scenes which they provoke, the sentences passed by the magistrates and at the sessions, and the consequent newspaper descriptions, rouse sufficient public feeling to force the Home Secretary to give way whenever the police are clearly in the wrong.

The method, however, is extremely hard on the martyrs, who suffer severely, and get no compensation, and but little thanks.

lands," Capitalism would be overwhelmed, and Communism established in its place within twenty-four hours or so. I well remember hearing Hyndman, the brilliant figurehead of the Social-Democratic Federation, declaring in reply to a heckler at an open-air meeting, "When we are twenty thousand strong we shall march." William Morris reset John Brown's Body to

> Lo the rolling of the thunder!
> Lo the sun! and lo thereunder
> Riseth wrath and hope and wonder
> And the host comes marching on.

As the host did not come marching on, the middle-class Fabian Society broke away from this policy by its characteristic practice of permeation. It asked nobody either to join it, or to boycott other associations. On the contrary it pressed its members to join every other association to which its members could gain admission, and infect it with constitutional Socialism. Membership of the Fabian Society was presented as a rare and difficult privilege of superior persons.

. . . Differences, which afterwards became explicit and definite, were latent from the first in the temperament and character of the Fabians. When I myself, on the point of joining the Social Democratic Federation, changed my mind and joined the Fabian instead, I was guided by no discoverable difference in program or principles, but solely by an instinctive feeling that the Fabian and not the Federation would attract the men of my own bias and intellectual habits who were then ripening for the work that lay before us.

Now the significant thing about the particular Socialist society which I joined was that the members all belonged to the middle class. Indeed its leaders and directors belonged to what is sometimes called the upper middle class: that is, they were either professional men like myself (I had escaped from clerkdom into literature) or members of the upper division of the civil service. Several of them have since had distinguished careers without changing their opinions or leaving the Society. To their Conservative and Liberal parents and aunts and uncles fifty years ago it seemed an amazing, shocking, unheard-of thing that they should become Socialists, and also a step bound to make an end of all their chances of success in life. Really it was quite natural and inevitable. Karl Marx was not a poor laborer: he was the highly educated son of a rich Jewish lawyer. His almost equally famous colleague, Friedrich Engels, was a well-to-do employer. It was precisely because they were liberally educated, and brought up to think about how things are done instead of merely drudging at the manual labor of doing them, that these two men, like my colleagues in The Fabian Society (note, please, that we gave our society a name that could have occurred only to classically educated men), were the first to see that Capitalism was reducing their own class to the condition of a proletariat.

I may mention, as illustrating the same point, that the Fabian Society, when I joined it immediately after its foundation in 1884, had only two rival Socialist Societies in London, both professing, unlike the Fabian, to be working-class societies. But one of them was dominated by the son of a very rich man who bequeathed large sums to religious institutions in addition to providing for his sons, to whom he had given a first-rate education. The other was entirely dependent on one of the most famous men of the nineteenth century, who was not only a successful employer and manufacturer in the business of furnishing and decorating palaces and churches, but an eminent artistic designer, a rediscoverer of lost arts, and one of the greatest of English poets and writers. These two men, Henry Mayers Hyndman and William Morris, left their mark on the working-class proletariat as preachers of Socialism, but failed in their attempts to organize a new working-class Socialist Party in their own upper middle class way under their own leadership and in their own dialect (for the language of ladies and gentlemen is only a dialect), because the working classes had already organized themselves in their own way, under their own leaders, and in their own dialect. The Fabian Society succeeded because it addressed itself to its own class in order that it might set about doing the necessary brain work of planning Socialist organization for all classes, meanwhile accepting, instead of trying to supersede, the existing political organizations which it intended to permeate with the Socialist conception of human society.

However, as I have said, in 1885 our differences were latent or instinctive; and we denounced the capitalists as thieves at the Industrial Remuneration Conference, and, among ourselves, talked revolution, anarchism, labor notes versus pass-books, and all the rest of it, on the tacit assumption that the object of our campaign, with its watchwords, "Educate, Agitate, Organize," was to bring about a tremendous smash-up of existing society, to be succeeded by complete Socialism. And this meant that we had no true practical understanding either of existing society or Socialism. Without being quite definitely aware of this, we yet felt it to a certain extent all along; for it was at this period that we contracted the invaluable habit of freely laughing at ourselves which has always distinguished us, and which has saved us from becoming hampered by the gushing enthusiasts who mistake their own emotions for public movements. From the first, such people fled after one glance at us, declaring that we were not serious. Our preference for practical suggestions and criticisms, and our impatience of all general expressions of sympathy with working-class aspirations, not to mention our way of chaffing our opponents in preference to denouncing them as enemies of the human race, repelled from us some warm-hearted and eloquent Socialists, to whom it seemed callous and cynical to be even commonly self-possessed in the presence of the sufferings upon which Socialists make war. But there was far too much equality and personal intimacy among the Fabians to allow of any member presuming to get up and preach at the rest in the fashion which the working classes still tolerate submissively from their leaders. We knew that a certain sort of oratory was useful for "stoking up" public meetings; but we needed no stoking up, and, when any orator tried the process on us, soon made him understand that he was wasting his time and ours. . . .

When I add that in 1885 we had only 40 members, you will be able to form a sufficient notion of the Fabian Society in its nonage. . . . We were overlooked in the excitements of the unemployed agitation, which had, moreover, caused the Tory money affair to be forgotten. The Fabians were disgracefully backward in open-air speaking. . . . Graham Wallas, myself, and Mrs Besant were the only representative open-air speakers in the Society, whereas the Federation speakers, Burns, Hyndman, Andrew Hall, Tom Mann, Champion, Burrows, with the Socialist Leaguers, were at it constantly. On the whole, the Church Parades and the rest were not in our line; and we were not wanted by the men who were organizing them. Our only contribution to the agitation was a report which we printed in 1886, which recommended experiments in tobacco culture, and even hinted at compulsory military service, as means of absorbing some of the unskilled unemployed, but which went carefully into the practical conditions of relief works. . . . It was drawn up by Bland, Hughes, Podmore, Stapelton, and Webb, and was the first of our publications that contained any solid information. Its tone, however, was moderate and its style somewhat conventional; and the Society was still in so hot a temper on the social question that we refused to adopt it as a regular Fabian tract, and only issued it as a report printed for the information of members. Nevertheless we were coming to our senses rapidly by this time. We signalized our repudiation of political sectarianism in June 1886, by inviting the Radicals, the Secularists, and anyone else who would come, to a great conference, modelled upon the Industrial Remuneration Conference, and dealing with the Nationalization of Land and Capital. It fully established the fact that we had nothing immediately practical to impart to the Radicals and that they had nothing to impart to us. The proceedings were fully reported for us; but we never had the courage even to read the shorthand writer's report, which still remains in MS. Before I refreshed my memory on the subject the other day, I had a vague notion that the Conference cost a great deal of money; that it did no good whatever; that Mr Bradlaugh made a speech; that Mrs Fenwick Miller, who had nothing on earth to do with us, was in the chair during part of the proceedings; and that the most successful paper was by a strange gentleman whom we had taken on trust as a Socialist, but who turned out to be an enthusiast on the subject of building more harbors. I find, however, on looking up the facts, that no less than fifty-three societies sent delegates; that the guarantee fund for expenses was £100; and that the discussions were kept going for three afternoons and three evenings. The Federation boycotted us; but The Times reported us. Eighteen papers were read, two of them by members of Parliament, and most of the rest by well-known people. William Morris and Dr Aveling read papers as delegates from the Socialist League; the National Secular Society sent Mr Foote and Mr Robertson, the latter contributing a Scheme of Taxation in which he anticipated much of what was subsequently adopted as the Fabian program; Wordsworth Donisthorpe took the field for Anarchism of the type advocated by the authors of A Plea for Liberty; Stewart Headlam spoke for Christian Socialism and the Guild of St Matthew; Dr Pankhurst dealt with the situation from the earlier Radical point of view; and various Socialist papers were read by Mrs Besant, Sidney Webb, and Edward Carpenter, besides one by Stuart-Glennie, who subsequently left us because we fought shy of the Marriage Question. . . .

. . . Yet all that can be said for it is that it made us known to the Radical clubs and proved that we were able to manage a conference in a businesslike way. It also, by the way, shewed off our pretty prospectus with the design by Crane at the top, our stylish-looking blood-red invitation cards, and the other little smartnesses on which we then prided ourselves. We used to be plentifully sneered at as fops and armchair So-

cialists for our attention to these details; but I think it was by no means
the least of our merits that we always, as far as our means permitted,
tried to make our printed documents as handsome as possible, and did
our best to destroy the association between revolutionary literature and
slovenly printing on paper that is nasty without being cheap. One effect
of this was that we were supposed to be much richer than we really were,
because we generally got better value and a finer show for our money
than the other Socialist societies.

The Conference was the last of our follies. We had now a very strong
Executive Committee, including Mrs Besant, who in June 1885 had
effected her public profession of Socialism by joining the Fabian. Five
out of the seven authors of Fabian Essays, which were of course still
unwritten, were at the helm by 1887. But by 1886 we had already found
that we were of one mind as to the advisability of setting to work by
the ordinary political methods and having done with Anarchism and
vague exhortations to Emancipate the Workers. We had several hot debates on the subject with a section of the Socialist League which called
itself Anti-State Communist, a name invented by Mr Joseph Lane of
that body. William Morris, who was really a free democrat of the
Kropotkin type, backed up Lane, and went for us tooth and nail. Records
of our warfare may be found in the volumes of the extinct magazine
called To-Day, which was then edited by Hubert Bland; and they are
by no means bad reading. We soon began to see that at the debates the
opposition to us came from members of the Socialist League, who were
present only as visitors. The question was, how many followers had our
one ascertained Anarchist, Mrs Wilson, among the silent Fabians. Bland
and Mrs Besant brought this question to an issue on the 17th September
1886, at a meeting in Anderton's Hotel, by respectively seconding and
moving the following resolution:

"That it is advisable that Socialists should organize themselves as a
political party for the purpose of transferring into the hands of the
whole working community full control over the soil and the means of
production, as well as over the production and distribution of wealth."

To this a rider was moved by William Morris as follows:

"But whereas the first duty of Socialists is to educate the people to
understand what their present position is, and what their future might
be, and to keep the principle of Socialism steadily before them; and
whereas no Parliamentary party can exist without compromise and con-
cession, which would hinder that education and obscure those principles,

it would be a false step for Socialists to attempt to take part in the Parliamentary contest."

I shall not attempt to describe the debate, in which Morris, Mrs Wilson, Davis, and Tochatti did battle with Burns, Mrs Besant, Bland, Shaw, Donald, and Rossiter: that is, with Fabian and S.D.F. combined. Suffice it to say that the minutes of the meeting close with the following significant note by the secretary:

"Subsequently to the meeting, the secretary received notice from the manager of Anderton's Hotel that the Society could not be accommodated there for any further meetings."

. . . Outside Socialist circles in London the Society remained unknown. It was still unable to bring up its roll of members to a hundred names; and its funds were so modest that nobody ever thought of proposing that we should keep a banking account or rent an office. In fact, we were literally passing rich on £40 a year. . . . If ever there was a Society which lived by its wits, and by its wits alone, that Society was the Fabian.

By far our most important work at this period was our renewal of that historic and economic equipment of Social Democracy of which Ferdinand Lassalle boasted, and which had been getting rustier and more obsolete ever since his time and that of his contemporary Karl Marx. In the earlier half of this century, when these two leaders were educated, all the Socialists in Europe were pouncing on Ricardo's demonstration of the tendency of wages to fall to bare subsistence, and on his labor theory of value, believing that they constituted a scientific foundation for Socialism; and the truth is that since that bygone time no Socialist (unless we count Ruskin) had done twopennyworth of economic thinking, or made any attempt to keep us up to date in the scientific world. In 1885 we used to prate about Marx's theory of value and Lassalle's Iron Law of Wages as if it were still 1870. In spite of Henry George, no Socialist seemed to have any working knowledge of the theory of economic rent: its application to skilled labor was so unheard of that the expression "rent of ability" was received with laughter when the Fabians first introduced it into their lectures and discussions; and as for the modern theory of value, it was scouted as a blasphemy against Marx, with regard to whom the Social Democratic Federation still maintains a Dogma of Finality and Infallibility which has effectually prevented it from making a single contribution to the economics of Socialism since its foundation. As to history, we had a convenient stock of imposing gen-

eralizations about the evolution from slavery to serfdom and from serfdom to free wage labor. We drew our pictures of society with one broad
line dividing the bourgeoisie from the proletariat, and declared that there
were only two classes really in the country. We gave lightning sketches
of the development of the medieval craftsman into the manufacturer and
finally into the factory hand. We denounced Malthusianism quite as
crudely as the Malthusians advocated it, which is saying a good deal;
and we raged against emigration, National Insurance, Co-operation,
Trade Unionism, old-fashioned Radicalism, and everything else that was
not Socialism; and that, too, without knowing at all clearly what we
meant by Socialism. The mischief was, not that our generalizations were
unsound, but that we had no detailed knowledge of the content of them:
we had borrowed them ready-made as articles of faith; and when opponents like Charles Bradlaugh asked us for details we sneered at the
demand without being in the least able to comply with it. The real
reason why Anarchist and Socialist worked then shoulder to shoulder
as comrades and brothers was that neither one nor the other had any
definite idea of what he wanted or how it was to be got. . . .

 . . . From 1887 to 1889 we were the recognized bullies and swash-
bucklers of advanced economics. . . . Now this, as you may imagine, was
not done without study; and as that study could not possibly be carried
on by the men who were organizing the unemployed agitation in the
streets, the Fabians had a monopoly of it. We had to study where we
could and how we could. I need not repeat the story of the Hampstead
Historic Club, founded by a handful of us to read Marx and Proudhon,
and afterwards turned into a systematic history class in which each student took his turn at being professor. My own experience may be taken
as typical. For some years I attended the Hampstead Historic Club once
a fortnight, and spent a night in the alternate weeks at a private circle
of economists which has since blossomed into the British Economic Association—a circle where the social question was left out, and the work
kept on abstract scientific lines. I made all my acquaintances think me
madder than usual by the pertinacity with which I attended debating
societies and haunted all sorts of hole-and-corner debates and public meetings and made speeches at them. I was President of the Local Government Board at an amateur Parliament where a Fabian ministry had to
put its proposals into black-and-white in the shape of Parliamentary Bills.
Every Sunday I lectured on some subject which I wanted to teach to
myself; and it was not until I had come to the point of being able to

deliver separate lectures, without notes, on Rent, Interest, Profits, Wages, Toryism, Liberalism, Socialism, Communism, Anarchism, Trade Unionism, Co-operation, Democracy, the Division of Society into Classes, and the Suitability of Human Nature to Systems of Just Distribution, that I was able to handle Social Democracy as it must be handled before it can be preached in such a way as to present it to every sort of man from his own particular point of view. In old lecture lists of the Society you will find my name down for twelve different lectures or so. . . .

Now at this time Annie Besant was the greatest orator in England, perhaps the greatest in Europe. . . . I have never heard her excelled; and she was then unapproached. Certainly the combination of Bradlaugh and Annie Besant was one so extraordinary that its dissolution was felt as a calamity, as if someone had blown up Niagara or an earthquake had swallowed a cathedral. Socialism had many colleagues to offer her who were more accomplished than Bradlaugh. One of them, William Morris, was a far greater man. But there was no platform warrior so mighty: no man who could dominate an audience with such an air of dominating his own destiny. Unhappily for him, she was right and he was wrong on the point that divided them; and when they parted, his sun set in a rosy glow of parliamentary acceptance, even by Lord George Hamilton, whilst hers was still stormily rising.

In selecting the Fabian Society for her passage through Socialism Annie Besant made a very sound choice; for it was the only one of the three Socialist societies then competing with one another in which there was anything to be learnt that she did not already know. It was managed by a small group of men who were not only very clever individually, but broken into team work with one another so effectually that they raised the value of the Society's output far above that of the individual output of any one of them. They were not only reducing Socialism to a practical political programme on the ordinary constitutional lines, but devising an administrative machinery for it in the light of a practical knowledge of how Government works (some of them being Government officials of the upper division), in which the other societies were hopelessly deficient. This was exactly what Annie Besant needed at the moment to complete her equipment. But it could not hold her when once she had rapidly learnt what she could from it. To begin with, it was unheroic; and the secret of her collaboration with Bradlaugh had been that she, too, was as essentially heroic in her methods as in her power, courage, and oratorical genius. Now Fabianism was in reaction against the heroics by which Socialism had suffered so much in 1871: its mission was to make Socialism as possible as Liberalism or Conservatism for the pottering suburban voter who desired to go to church because his neighbours did, and to live always on the side of the police. It recognised the truth for political purposes of Mark Twain's saying: "The average man is a coward." And Annie Besant, with her heroic courage and energy, was wasted on work that had not some element of danger and extreme arduousness in it.

Besides, considering the world from Shakespeare's point of view as a stage on which all the men and women are merely players, Annie Besant, a player of genius, was a tragedian. Comedy was not her clue to life: she had a healthy sense of fun; but no truth came to her first as a joke. Injustice, waste, and the defeat of noble aspirations did not revolt her by way of irony and paradox: they stirred her to direct and powerful indignation and to active resistance. Now the Fabian vein was largely the vein of comedy, and its conscience a sense of irony. We laughed at Socialism and laughed at ourselves a good deal. In me especially, as events have proved, there was latent a vocation for the theatre which was to give to tragedy itself the tactics of comedy. It attracted and amused Annie Besant for a time, and I conceived an affection for her in which I have never since wavered; but in the end the apparently heartless levity with which I spoke and acted in matters which seemed deeply serious, before I had achieved enough to show that I had a perspective in which they really lost their importance, and before she had realised that her own destiny was to be one which would also dwarf them, must have made it very hard for her to work with me at times.

There were less subtle difficulties also in the way. The direction of the Fabian Society was done so efficiently by the little group of men already in possession, that Annie Besant must have found, as other women found later on, that as far as what may be called its indoor work was concerned, she was wasting her time as fifth wheel to the coach. The Fabians were never tired of saying that you should do nothing that somebody else was doing well enough already, and Annie Besant had too much practical sense not to have made this rule for herself already. She, therefore, became a sort of expeditionary force, always to the front when there was trouble and danger, carrying away audiences for us when the dissensions in the movement brought our policy into conflict with that of the other societies, founding branches for us throughout the country, dashing into the great strikes and free-speech agitations of that time (the eighteen-eighties), forming on her own initiative such *ad hoc* organisations as were necessary to make them effective, and generally leaving the routine to us and taking the fighting on herself. Her powers of continuous work wre prodigious. Her displays of personal courage and resolution, as when she would march into a police-court, make her way to the witness-stand, and compel the magistrate to listen to her by sheer force of style and character, were trifles compared to the way in which she worked day and night to pull through the strike of the over-exploited matchgirls who had walked into her office one day and asked her to help them somehow, any-how. An attempt to keep pace with her on the part of a mere man gen-erally wrecked the man: those who were unselfish enough to hold out to the end usually collapsed and added the burden of nursing them to her already superhuman labours.

I have somewhere said of Annie Besant that she was an incorrigible benefactor, whereas the Fabians were inclined to regard ill-luck as a crime in the manner of Butler and Maeterlinck. The chief fault of her extraor-dinary qualities was that she was fiercely proud. I tried, by means of elaborate little comedies, to disgust her with beneficence and to make her laugh at her pride; but the treatment was not, as far as I know, very successful. I would complain, fondly, that I wanted something that I could not afford. She would give it to me. I would pretend that my pride was deeply wounded, and ask her how she dared insult me. In a transport of generous indignation she would throw her present away or destroy it. I would then come and ask for it, barefacedly denying that I had ever repudiated it, and exhibiting myself as a monster of frivolous ingratitude and callousness. But though I succeeded sometimes in making her laugh at me, I never succeeded in making her laugh at herself or check her inveterate largesse. I ought to have done much more for her, and she much less for me, than we did. But . . . this was not her path.[11] She had at that time neither lost faith in the idealism which Ibsen handled so pitilessly, nor had she taken her own measure boldly enough to know that she, too, was to be one of the master builders who have to learn that for them at least there are no such small luxuries as "homes for happy people." The only permanent interest the Fabian Society or any other society could have for her personally lay in such advance as it was capable of towards a religious philosophy, and when I led this advance into a channel repugnant to her her spiritual interest in the Society died.

The end came as suddenly as the beginning. The years had been so full and passed so rapidly that it seemed only a short time since I had gone to a meeting of the Dialectical Society to deliver an address advocating Socialism, and had found the members perturbed and excited by the appearance of Annie Besant, who had long ceased to attend the Dialectical meetings, and was still counted as the most redoubtable champion of the old individualist freethought of which Bradlaugh was the exponent. I was warned on all hands that she had come down to destroy me, and that from the moment she rose to speak my cause was lost. I resigned myself to my fate, and pleaded my case as best I could. When the discussion began everyone waited for Annie Besant to lead the opposition. She did not rise; and at last the opposition was undertaken by another member. When he had finished, Annie Besant, to the amazement of the meeting, got up and utterly demolished him. There was nothing left for me to do but gasp and triumph under her shield. At the end she asked me to nominate her for election to the Fabian Society and invited me to dine with her.

The end was equally startling. One day I was speaking to Mr. H. W. Massingham, then editor of the Star, at the office of that paper in Stonecutter Street. I glanced at the proofs which were lying scattered about the table. One of them was headed "Why I became a Theosophist." I immediately looked down to the foot of the slip for the signature, and saw that it was Annie Besant. Staggered by this unprepared blow, which meant to me the loss of a powerful colleague and of a friendship which had become part of my daily life, I rushed round to her office in Fleet Street and there delivered myself of an unbounded denunciation of Theosophy in general, of female inconstancy, and in particular of H. P. Blavatsky, one of whose books—I forget whether it was The Secret Doctrine or Isis Unveiled—had done all the mischief. The worst of it was that I had given her this book myself as one that she might like to review. . . .

What happened was this. I was reviewing books for the Pall Mall Gazette at two guineas a column. William Archer had planted me on that paper by handing over a book he had received from it for review to me, and giving me an opportunity of showing what I could do. In due course the literary editor, with whom Stead, the political editor, never interfered, sent me for review the Secret Doctrine, a huge tome which I contemplated with some dismay, as it meant some weeks of careful reading for three guineas.

Just then Mrs. Besant told me that she was in serious want of money, as her writing for the National Reformer and her lecturing for the National Secular Society had ceased with her conversion to Socialism. Could I get her some reviewing to do for the Pall Mall Gazette? I immediately thought of the Secret Doctrine, and of what Archer had done for me. I gave her the book to review.

Not long after I called at the office of the Star, and saw among the proofs that littered the editor's table an article headed, "How I Became a Theosophist." I turned to the signature. It was Annie Besant. I was utterly confounded. I had done a trick I never intended. I rushed round to the Secular Society's shop in Fleet Street and finding her there in an exasperatingly happy mood, asked her whether she was quite mad, and whether she knew that Madame Blavatsky's shrine at Adyar had just been convincingly shown up as a fraud by an Indian gentleman named Mohini at a meeting of the Psychical [Research] Society at which I was present.

It was no use.[12] . . . I played all the tricks by which I could usually puzzle her, or move her to a wounded indignation which, though it never elicited a reproach from her (her forbearance with me was really beyond description), at least compelled her to put on herself the restraint of silence. But this time I met my match. She listened to me with complete kindness and genuine amusement, and then said that she had become a vegetarian (as I was) and that perhaps it had enfeebled her mind. In short, she was for the first time able to play with me; she was no longer in the grip of her pride; she had after many explorations found her path and come to see the universe and herself in their real perspective.

That was the end of our collaboration. Years later we met at Lady Delawar's, but except on that one occasion we never met again, though my high regard for her never changed. Our separation was entirely her doing.

Like all great public speakers she was a born actress. She was successively a Pusyite Evangelical, an Atheist Bible-smasher, a Darwinian secularist, a Fabian Socialist, a Strike Leader, and finally a Theosophist, exactly as Mrs. Siddons was a Lady Macbeth, Lady Randolph, Beatrice, Rosalind, and Volumnia. She "saw herself" as a priestess above all. That was how Theosophy held her to the end. There was a different leading man every time: Bradlaugh, Robertson, Aveling, Shaw, and Herbert Burrows. That did not matter.

This, as far as I know, is the history of Annie Besant's last unsuccessful exploration in search of her appointed place in the world. It had many striking incidents, chief among them the matchgirls' strike, "Bloody Sunday" in Trafalgar Square and its sequel, and her election to the London School Board after such election meetings as, thanks to her eloquence, are unique and luminous in the squalid record of London electioneering. In such experiences she lost her illusions, if she had any, as to the impudent idolatry of the voter which we call democracy. It has seemed to me, too, that the diplomacy and knowledge of men and affairs in the governing class which characterised the Fabians played its part afterwards in her educational work in India. But here I am only guessing. After the inauguration of her career as a Theosophist, I dropped out of her saga. I have not forgotten my part in it. My affections have two excellent qualities: extreme levity and extreme tenacity. I do not like the proverb "Love me little: love me long"; but whoever invented it had a very narrow escape of finding its true form, which is, "Love me lightly: love me long." And that is how I loved, and still love, Annie Besant.

Morris and Others

AT THE beginning of my career, when I was a nobody reviewing books for the old Pall Mall Gazette . . . I received a book entitled Luck, or Cunning?, and, on reviewing it at some length, was infuriated when some fool of a sub-editor, treated the book and its author as of no importance, and cut a great chunk out of it. I learned later on that this truncated article of mine seemed almost epoch making to the author, an old bachelor living in Clifford's Inn who, though having won a certain select celebrity by a queer Utopia entitled Erewhon (Nowhere backwards) was carrying on a metabiological crusade against Darwinism which was being ignored by the Press and the biologists of the day to such an extent that he had to publish his polemics at his own expense, always at a loss which made marriage an economic impossibility for him.

As I was then under the same disability . . . I was myself a compulsory bachelor and controversialist *contra mundum*, and moreover one of the select few who had read Erewhon and swore by it, I was to that extent in Butler's camp. . . . Among his many oddities, he was a strict monogamist, yet by no means a celibate; for he remained faithful to the French lady whom he visited once a fortnight, and was wholly innocent of polygamy.

He never had any literary ambition, though he was a born writer. . . . He himself put the secret of his greatness into a single sentence of six words, which he addressed to me as we were crossing the courtyard of the British Museum together. He said, with the most intense emphasis, "Darwin banished mind from the universe." He added, "My grandfather quarrelled with Darwin's grandfather; my father quarrelled with Darwin's father; I quarrelled with Darwin; and my regret for having no son is that he cannot quarrel with Darwin's son." As a matter of fact Darwin had converted [Samuel] Butler for six weeks because in those days all we clever people who called ourselves Secularists, Freethinkers, Agnostics, Atheists, Positivists, Rationalists, or what not, and were called Infidels doomed to eternal damnation, were all anti-Clericals snatching at any stick big enough to whack the parsons; and the biggest stick was the Natural Selection of Darwin and Wallace, carried to absurdity. . . . We all, Butler included, grabbed it joyously. Butler alone thought it out deeply and quickly enough to grasp the horror of its banishment of mind from the universe.

The ensuing controversies only obscured this fundamental issue. They did not affect me because I had read the Patmos Evangelist's [1] "In the Beginning was the Thought" and came up against the neo-Darwinist shallowness. . . . (Darwin, by the way, was no more a Darwinist than I am a Shavian.)

. . . I must also warn readers that Butler's guess that the author of the Odyssey was a woman was not an Erewhonian joke, and that it is now impossible to read it again without being at least half convinced that he was as right as Dickens was about George Eliot.

. . . Exactly how and when I made his acquaintance I do not remember. . . . One London group incident should be immortalized. It was in the [Fabian] WC group, which met in Gt. Ormond Street. It consisted of two or three members who used to discuss bi-metallism. I was a member geographically, but never attended. One day I saw on the notice of meetings which I received an announcement that Samuel Butler would address the group on the authorship of the Odyssey. Knowing that the group would have no notion of how great a man they were entertaining, I dashed down to the meeting; took the chair; gave the audience (about five strong, including Butler and myself) to understand that the occasion was a great one; and when we had listened gravely to Samuel's demonstration that the Odyssey was written by Nausicaa, carried a general expression of enthusiastic agreement with Butler, who thanked us with old fashioned gravity and without giving a sign of his feelings at finding so small a meeting of the famous Fabian Society. Considering how extraordinary a man Butler is now seen to have been, there is something tragic in the fact that the greatest genius among the long list of respectable dullards who . . . addressed us, never got beyond this absurd little group.

Our best lecturers . . . spent a certain number of years plodding away at footling little meetings and dull discussions, doggedly placing these before all private engagements, however tempting. A man's Socialistic acquisitiveness must be keen enough to make him actually prefer spending two or three nights a week in speaking and debating, or in picking up social information even in the most dingy and scrappy way, to going to the theatre, or dancing or drinking, or even sweethearting, if he is to become a really competent propagandist—unless, of course, his daily work is of such a nature as to be in itself a training for political life; and that, we know, is the case with very few of us indeed. It is at such lecturing and debating work, and on squalid little committees and ridiculous little delegations to conferences of the three tailors of Tooley Street, with perhaps a deputation to the Mayor thrown in once in a blue moon or so, that the ordinary Fabian workman or clerk must qualify for his future seat on the Town Council, the School Board, or perhaps in the Cabinet. . . .

. . . When, driven in disgrace out of Anderton's Hotel, and subsequently out of a chapel near Wardour Street in which we had taken refuge, we went to Willis's Rooms, the most aristocratic, and also, as it turned out, the cheapest place of meeting in London, our favorite sport was inviting politicians and economists to lecture to us, and then falling on them with all our erudition and debating skill, and making them wish they had never been born. The curious may consult the files of Mr George Standring's extinct journal, called The Radical, for a graphic account, written by an individualist, of the fate of a well-known member of Parliament who was lured into our web on one of these occasions. The article is suggestively entitled Butchered to make a Fabian Holiday. . . .[2]

It was in 1885 that the Fabian Society, amid the jeers of the catastrophists, turned its back on the barricades and made up its mind to turn heroic defeat into prosaic success. We set ourselves two definite tasks: first, to provide a parliamentary program for a Prime Minister converted to Socialism as Peel was converted to Free Trade; and second, to make it as easy and matter-of-course for the ordinary respectable Englishman to be a Socialist as to be a Liberal or a Conservative.

. . . In 1888 we had not been found out. . . . The Liberal party was too much preoccupied over Mr O'Brien's breeches and the Parnell Commission, with its dramatic climax in the suicide of the forger Pigott, to suspect that the liveliness of the extreme left of the Radical wing in

London meant anything but the usual humbug about working-class interests. We now adopted a policy which snapped the last tie between our methods and the sectarianism of the Federation. We urged our members to join the Liberal and Radical Associations of their districts, or, if they preferred it, the Conservative Associations. We told them to become members of the nearest Radical Club and Co-operative Store, and to get delegated to the Metropolitan Radical Federation and the Liberal and Radical Union if possible. On these bodies we made speeches and moved resolutions, or, better still, got the Parliamentary candidate for the constituency to move them, and secured reports and encouraging little articles for him in the Star. We permeated the party organizations and pulled all the wires we could lay our hands on with our utmost adroitness and energy; and we succeeded so far that in 1888 we gained the solid advantage of a Progressive majority, full of ideas that would never have come into their heads had not the Fabian put them there, on the first London County Council. The generalship of this movement was undertaken chiefly by Sidney Webb, who played . . . bewildering conjuring tricks with the Liberal thimbles and the Fabian peas. . . .

. . . It was exciting whilst it lasted, all this "permeation of the Liberal party," as it was called; and no person with the smallest political intelligence is likely to deny that it made a foothold for us in the press and pushed forward Socialism in municipal politics to an extent which can only be appreciated by those who remember how things stood before our campaign. When we published Fabian Essays at the end of 1889, having ventured with great misgivings on a subscription edition of a thousand, it went off like smoke; and our cheap edition brought up the circulation to about twenty thousand. In the meantime we had been cramming the public with information in tracts, on the model of our earliest financial success in that department, namely, Facts for Socialists, the first edition of which actually brought us a profit—the only instance of the kind then known. In short, the years 1888, 1889, 1890 saw a Fabian boom . . . .

The first Fabian Socialist programme on which a General Election was fought and won in 1892 was drafted by Sidney Webb; but it was called the Newcastle Programme and put forward as the programme of the Liberal Party. It was in fact fobbed on it by me at an obscure meeting of an obscure branch of the Liberal Association in a speech of which the reporters and the Liberal Parliamentary candidate who seconded me (the whole audience) did not understand a single sentence. But as the Liberal Party were facing a General Election with nothing to offer the electorate beyond what the most backward Conservatives were offering except Home Rule for Ireland, and the Fabians knew that the dumb masses of the British electorate did not care a dump for Ireland, the Newcastle Programme caught on irresistibly. Candidates in all directions scrapped their Home Rule election literature and sent frantically for Fabian tracts. Gladstone, their aged leader, was humbugged into believing that the programme meant nothing more revolutionary than payment of members of parliament, of which he approved. And the Liberals won the election. This was a triumph for the Fabian principle of permeation, and for Webb . . . as a tactician.

The distinctive mark of the Fabian Society among the rival bodies of Socialists with which it came in conflict in its early days, was its resolute constitutionalism. When the greatest Socialist of that day, the poet and craftsman William Morris, told the workers that there was no hope for them save in revolution, we said that if that were true there was no hope at all for them, and urged them to save themselves through Parliament, the municipalities, and the franchise. Without, perhaps, quite converting Morris, we convinced him that things would probably go our way.

To suppose that this change . . . produced no effect in Morris, is to assume that he still lived in the old circle with books and pictures, looms and dye-vats, instead of in the very rough jostle with real life which followed his step down into the streets to preach Socialism. The turning-point with him was a personal experience: the battle of Trafalgar Square.

There was a trade-depression in the years 1886–7 and the unemployed got out of hand. The Democratic Federation made the most of their opportunity and on a February day in '86 marched with the workless from Trafalgar Square to Hyde Park, passing through Pall Mall whilst the police, through a mistake which cost their chief his place, were waiting for them in the Mall. The rich men gathered in their club windows to see the fun. The unemployed, fancying that they were being mocked, broke the club windows, and went on to the park where they held their meeting. Some of the stragglers looted a shop or two and captured the carriage of a lady by the Achilles Statue. Hyndman, John

Burns and two others were arrested and tried as ringleaders; but by good luck the foreman of the jury was an imposing Christian Socialist in whose hands the rest were like sheep; and the four were acquitted.

This beginning of insurrection grew until it centered on the supposed right to hold meetings in Trafalgar Square. The cry of Free Speech rallied all the workers to the Socialists, and a grand mass meeting there was announced for the 13th November 1887, thereafter to be known as "Bloody Sunday." The police prohibited it. . . .

. . . The papers which declared that the workers had an excellent forum in Hyde Park without obstructing Trafalgar Square, were reminded that in 1866 the convenience of Trafalgar Square for public meetings was made an excuse for the attempt to put down meetings in the Park. Mr Stead, who was then editing the Pall Mall Gazette, and who, with all his enthusiasm, had about as much practical knowledge of how to do the Dod Street trick as a London tram-conductor has of conducting classical concerts, gave the word "To the Square!" To the Square we all went, therefore, with drums beating and banners waving, in our tens of thousands, nominally to protest against the Irish policy of the Government, but really to maintain the right of meeting in the Square. The meeting had been proclaimed; but the authority cited was an Act for the Regulation of Traffic which clearly gave no power to the police to prohibit processions, and which was abandoned by the Government when they had to justify their action in court. However, the new Chief Commissioner of Police, successor to him who had been dismissed for making that mistake in the previous year about Pall Mall, had no notion of sharing his predecessor's fate. He took no half measures in the matter . . . .

Salt went with me . . . to Trafalgar Square on Bloody Sunday. All the Labour Forces marched to hold a meeting there and were broken up in every avenue to it by squads of police, and a detachment of cavalry kept riding round it with a magistrate in front to read the Riot Act. Carpenter was clubbed, as in his fury he wrote "by that crawling thing a policeman." Salt had his watch pickpocketed but he could not appeal to the police! I, with the scattered remnants of the procession, made my way to the Square, and kept "moving on" without moving off. . . . The heroes of it were Burns and Cunninghame Graham, who charged, two strong, at the rampart of policemen round the Square and were overpowered and arrested. The heroine was Mrs Besant, who may be said without the slightest exaggeration to have all but killed herself with overwork in looking after the prisoners, and organizing on their behalf a "Law and Liberty League" with Mr. Stead. Meanwhile the police received the blessing of Mr Gladstone; and Insurrectionism, after a two years' innings, vanished from the field and has not since been much heard of. . . .

. . . Morris joined one of the processions in Clerkenwell Green, where he made a speech, urging the processionists to keep steadily together and press on if they were attacked. It was the speech of a man who still saw in a London trades procession a John Ball fellowship. He then placed himself at the head of the column, and presently witnessed the attack on it by a handful of policemen, who must have been outnumbered fifty to one at least. The frantic stampede that followed made a deep impression on Morris. He understood at once how far his imagination had duped him. The translation of ten Odysseys would only have deepened the illusion that was dispelled in that moment. From that time he paid no more serious attention to the prospects of the Socialist bodies as militant organizations. . . .

. . . These free speech difficulties with the police [were] . . . opportunities for a sense of humor . . . Morris spoke in a street off the Edgware Road, and, refusing to stop at the request of a "mighty civil inspector," was fined a shilling. . . . His working-class friend John Williams . . . repeatedly suffered imprisonment for the same offence. I met Morris on his return from the police-court on the Edgware Road occasion. With Williams in his mind, he described himself as "a funkster" for letting himself get off so easily. He then got one of Dumas' novels (Dumas père, of course), and sat in his garden to air himself morally and physically after the contamination of the police-court, from which he shrank sensitively. On one occasion, when he went there to bail a comrade, his fellow surety was the late Charles Bradlaugh. Morris afterwards described to me his own nervousness among the officials, and his envy of the tremendous *aplomb* of Bradlaugh, who behaved as if the whole place belonged to him, and was deferred to with awe by everybody. . . .

The free speech contests were perhaps the worst worries which Socialism brought on Morris . . . the feeling, whenever a poor man went to prison, that he should have gone instead. On being remonstrated with for proposing to do so at Edgware Road, he betrayed this feeling by replying, "Noblesse oblige": one of the few occasions on which he let slip his consciousness of his noblesse. . . .

. . . In . . . the Dod Street . . . affair (another free speech difficulty) . . . three victims had been selected for sacrifice to the police on the day in question; to wit, Dr Aveling, Mr George Bateman, and myself as representative of the Fabian Society. But on the night before the morning of the meeting the police called on Dr Aveling, and announced the welcome news that they had orders to surrender. The news spread; and next morning, instead of three condemned speakers, the entire oratorical force of the Socialist movement turned up, resolute to assert their right of Free Speech or die on the place. They all wanted to speak first; but Aveling, who had faced the music before the danger was over, claimed first place, and got it. A quarrel ensued, in which nothing was agreed on but a general denunciation of Aveling, although the Dod Street incident was perhaps the most creditable incident in his morally somewhat chequered career. But it must be remembered that the struggle at Dod Street had been going on for months, during which Morris had been kept in continual anxiety, not only as to its upshot, but as to the extent of his own obligation to take his turn with the arrested and imprisoned speakers. Finally, it was arranged that he and Mr Stewart Headlam should speak and be arrested; and he was looking forward to this very disagreeable ordeal when the Home Office capitulated, and the melodrama became a farcical comedy.

Trivial as these particulars now seem, they form the real history of Morris's plunge into politics . . . .

. . . I once urged him to revive the manufacture of musical instruments and rescue us from the vulgar handsomeness of the trade articles with which our orchestras are equipped; and he was by no means averse to the idea, having always, he avowed, thought he should like to make a good fiddle. Only neither in music nor in anything else could you engage him in any sort of intellectual dilettantism: he would not waste his time and energy on the curiosities and fashions of art, but went straight to its highest point in the direct and simple production of beauty. He was ultra-modern—not merely up to date, but far ahead of it: his wall papers, his hangings, his tapestries, and his printed books have the twentieth century in every touch of them; whilst as to his prose word-weaving, our worn-out nineteenth-century Macaulayese is rancid by comparison. He started from the thirteenth century simply because he wished to start from the most advanced point instead of from the most backward one— say 1850 or thereabout. When people called him "archaic," he explained, with the indulgence of perfect knowledge, that they were fools, only they did not know it. In short, the man was a complete artist, who became great by a pre-eminent sense of beauty, and practical ability enough (and to spare) to give effect to it.

And yet—and yet—and yet—! I am sorry to have to say it; but I never could induce him to take the smallest interest in the contemporary theatrical routine of the Strand.

. . . Now, when Morris would not take an interest in anything, and would not talk about it—and his capacity for this sort of resistance, both passive and active, was remarkably obstinate—it generally meant that he had made up his mind, on good grounds, that it was not worth talking about. . . . On the subject of the theatre, an enthusiastic young firstnighter would probably have given Morris up, after the first attempt to gather his opinion of The Second Mrs. Tanqueray, as an ordinary citizen who had never formed the habit of playgoing, and neither knew nor cared anything about the theatre except as a treat for children once a year during the pantomime season. But Morris would have written for the stage if there had been any stage that a poet and artist could write for. When the Socialist League once proposed to raise the wind by a dramatic entertainment, and suggested that he should provide the play, he set to at once and provided it. And what kind of play was it? Was it a miracle play on the lines of those scenes in the Towneley mysteries between the "shepherds abiding in the field," which he used to quote with great relish as his idea of a good bit of comedy? Not at all: it was a topical extravaganza, entitled Nupkins Awakened, the chief "character parts" being Sir Peter Edlin, Tennyson, and an imaginary Archbishop of Canterbury. Sir Peter owed the compliment to his activity at that time in sending Socialists to prison on charges of "obstruction," which was always proved by getting a policeman to swear that if any passerby or vehicle had wished to pass over the particular spot in a thoroughfare on which the speaker or his audience happened to be standing, their presence would have obstructed him. This contention, which was regarded as quite sensible and unanswerable by the newspapers of the day, was put into a nutshell in the course of Sir Peter's summing-up in the play. "In fact, gentlemen, it is a matter of grave doubt whether we are not all of us continually committing this offence from our cradles to our graves." This speech, which the real Sir Peter of course never made, though he certainly would have done so had he had wit enough to see the absurdity of solemnly sending a man to prison for two months because another man could not walk through him—especially when it would have been so easy to lock him up for three on some respectable pretext—will probably keep Sir Peter's memory green when all his actual judicial utterances are forgotten. As to Tennyson, Morris took a Socialist who happened to combine the right sort of beard with a melancholy temperament, and drilled him in a certain portentous incivility of speech which, taken with the quality of his remarks, threw a light on Morris's opinion of Tennyson which was all the more instructive because he delighted in Tennyson's verse as keenly as Wagner delighted in the music of Mendelssohn, whose credit for qualities of larger scope he, nevertheless, wrote down and destroyed. Morris played the ideal Archbishop himself. He made no attempt to make up the part in the ordinary stage fashion. He always contended that no more was necessary for stage illusion than some distinct conventional symbol, such as a halo for a saint, a crook for a bishop, or, if you liked, a cloak and dagger for the villain, and a red wig for the comedian. A pair of clerical bands and black stockings proclaimed the archbishop: the rest he did by obliterating his humor and intelligence, and presenting his own person to the audience like a lantern with the light blown out, with a dull absorption in his own dignity which several minutes of the wildest screaming laughter at him when he entered could not disturb. I laughed immoderately myself; and I can still see quite clearly the long top floor of that warehouse in the Farringdon Road as I saw it in glimpses between my paroxysms with Morris gravely on the stage in his bands at one end; Mrs. Stillman, a tall and beautiful figure, rising like a delicate spire above a skyline of city chimney-pots at the other; and a motley sea of rolling, wallowing, guffawing Socialists between. There has been no other such successful first night within living memory, I believe; but I only remember one dramatic critic who took care to be present—Mr. William Archer. Morris was so interested by his experiment in this sort of composition that he for some time talked of trying his hand at a serious drama, and would no doubt have done it had there been any practical occasion for it, or any means of consummating it by stage representation under proper conditions without spending more time on the job than it was worth. Later, at one of the annual festivities of the Hammersmith Socialist Society, he played the old gentleman in the bath-chair in a short piece called The Duchess of Bayswater (*not* by himself), which once served its turn at the Haymarket as a curtain raiser. It was impossible for such a born teller and devourer of stories as he was to be indifferent to an art which is nothing more than the most vivid and real of all ways of story-telling. . . .

. . . No man was more liberal in his attempts to improve Morris's mind than I was; but I always found that, in so far as I was not making a most horrible idiot of myself out of misknowledge (I could forgive myself for pure ignorance), he could afford to listen to me with the patience of a man who had taught my teachers. There were people whom we tried to run him down with—Tennysons, Swinburnes, and so on; but their opinions about things did not make any difference. Morris's did.

It was as an agitator in the Socialist movement of the eighteen eighties that I came into personal contact with Morris. He was our one acknowledged Great Man; but we knew very little about him. Of William Morris of the Red House, head centre and organizer of a happy Brotherhood of artists who all called him Topsy and thought of him as a young man, we knew nothing. The small minority of us who had any contacts with the newest fashions in literature and art knew that he had become famous as the author of a long series of poems called The Earthly Paradise which few of us had read, though that magic line "the idle singer of an empty day" had caught our ears somehow. We knew that he kept a highly select shop in Oxford Street where he sold furniture of a rum aesthetic sort, and decorated houses with extraordinary wallpapers. I myself had read enough of his work to know that his self-appointed work in poetry was the retelling of all the world's old stories in a tuneful dialect which went back past the pomposities of Dr. Johnson and the rhetoric of Shakespear all the way to Chaucer, and which, though it rescued some good old English from disuse and oblivion, and was agreeable enough to my ear, seemed affected and ridiculous to the Philistines. And that was about all.

It was a curious situation for Morris (I have heard him discuss it). He had escaped middle age, passing quite suddenly from a circle of artistic revolutionists, mostly university men gone Agnostic or Bohemian or both, who knew all about him and saw him as much younger and less important than he really was, into a proletarian movement in which, so far as he was known at all, he was venerated as an Elder. The atmosphere had changed from one of enthusiastic understanding and intimate good fellowship to an ignorant and uncertain reverence, poisoned at first by a class mistrust which he lived down by the irresistible evidence in himself that he was far above classification.

Once or twice, some tactless ghost from his past wandered into the Socialist world and spoke of him and even to him as Topsy. It was soon morally booted out in miserable bewilderment for being silly and impudent. Such momentary incidents did not matter. What did matter was that many of the Socialists, especially the middle class ones who presently organized themselves as Fabians, were arrant Philistines, regarding all poets and artists as undesirable cranks. However, there was no love lost on the other side. Morris heartily disliked the Fabians, not because they undervalued him, but as a species.

. . . As an evangelist of Socialism . . . I became known to the leading Socialists of the moment before we had all quarrelled and divided into rival societies; and so it came about that I found myself one evening at a social gathering of the Democratic Federation (later the Social-Democratic Federation or S.D.F.) with Hyndman and Morris present as colleagues in that body. I have elsewhere described how I was the author of five novels which nobody would publish, and how I had dug them up to make padding for a Socialist magazine called To-day, to which we all had to contribute as best we could. It really had not occurred to me that anyone would read this fifty times rejected stuff of mine: it was offered and accepted solely to bulk out the magazine to saleable size when the supply of articles ran short; but Morris, who read everything that came in his way, and held that nobody could pass a shop window with a picture in it without stopping, had read a chapter of An Unsocial Socialist, and been sufficiently entertained to wish to meet the author.

Here, then, was Morris in his blue suit and bluer shirt, his tossing mane which suggested that his objection to looking-glasses extended to brushes and combs, and his habit, when annoyed by some foolish speaker, of pulling single hairs violently from his moustache and growling "damned fool!" He maintained that his blue suit was aimed at when Andrew Lang wrote of the shock of meeting your favorite poet and finding that he looked like a ship's purser; but Morris did not look like a purser; for pursers always smooth their hair, whereas the disarrangement of Morris's was so effectively leonine that I suspected him of spending at least a quarter of an hour every morning getting it just right.

I was soon in triple conversation with him and Hyndman, as our proletarian friends were a little out of it when we three got going. Hyndman could talk about anything with a fluency that left Morris nowhere. He was a most imposing man, and seemed to have been born in a frock coat and top hat. In old age he looked like God in Blake's illustrations to Job. In the prime of life, as he was then, he was more like the deity in Raphael's Vision of Ezekiel. He was a leading figure in any assembly, and took that view of himself with perfect self-confidence. Altogether an assuming man, quite naturally and unconsciously.

Morris was quite unassuming: he impressed by his obvious weight and quality. On this occasion he disclaimed all capacity for leadership, and said he was ready to do anything he was told, presumably by Hyndman as chairman of the Federation, plus the leader who had called him as a disciple. I smiled grimly to myself at this modest offer of allegiance, measuring at sight how much heavier Morris's armament was; but Hyndman accepted it at once as his due. Had Morris been accompanied by Plato, Aristotle, Gregory the Great, Dante, Thomas Aquinas, Milton and Newton, Hyndman would have taken the chair as their natural leader without the slightest misgiving, and before the end of the month have quarrelled with them all and left himself with no followers but the devoted handful who could not compete with him, and to whom he was a sort of god. But he was always excellent company as a perfect Victorian freethinking gentleman, like Meredith and Dilke, who had known everyone and was never at a loss for anecdotes about them. His talk was a most entertaining performance; and both Morris and I could listen to it without being bored for a moment. There was, however, an important difference between his talk and Morris's. What Morris said he meant, sometimes very vehemently; and it was always worth saying. Of Hyndman's most brilliant conversational performances it was impossible to believe a single word. The people he described so entertainingly were not authentic human beings. The things he told as having happened to them could not possibly have happened to anybody.

After the Morris-Hyndman fission there were in the field four Socialist Societies, the Democratic Federation, which presently threw off that ambiguity and became the Social-Democratic Federation, with Hyndman as its Perpetual Grand; the Socialist League, which was really Morris and nothing else; an admirable group of Christian Socialist clergymen called The Guild of St Matthew captained by Stewart Headlam; and the Fabian Society, which I had picked out as the place for me, and which rapidly drew away from the others as the only one of them that could work as a purveyor of immediately constructive election programs. The explanation of this was very simple. The League and the Federation held their meetings in public halls and invited the working class to join them at a cost of a penny a week, the idea being that when the entire proletariat had been convinced by the speeches, and had joined in irresistible numbers, a revolution would be achieved by the Federation or the League, as the case might be. Each of them, I may add, denounced the other in terms of unmeasured vituperativeness. Both were incapable of real committee work because their councils were not homogeneous: a combination of one exceptionally brilliant gentleman politician and writer (Hyndman) or one man of genius of unique culture and mental power (Morris) with a handful of poor men coming from a different world seemed very democratic and equalitarian; but it made skilled criticism and genuine intellectual co-operation farcically impossible.

Morris was right when he contracted his would-be world league into the little Hammersmith Socialist Society, and told it to go on with its job and make Socialists, *advienne que pourra.*

However, this was in the future when I made Morris's acquaintance at that soirée, and smiled to myself as aforesaid when he offered himself as a humble private to Generalissimo Hyndman. We must have got on fairly well together; for I presently found myself not only lecturing at the little meeting hall into which he had converted his Hammersmith coach house, but appearing with him at the neighboring street corners on Sunday mornings conducting what most of the passers-by took to be prayer meetings. He and I complemented one another admirably; for I had a positive taste for abstract economics, and used my knowledge so effectively against the capitalist enemy that Morris said in the course of one of his addresses "In economics Shaw is my master." The shock this gave me, which I still remember vividly, shews how far I placed him above myself. I was positively scandalized.

The lectures in the little hall on Sunday nights were followed by a supper in the house, to which the lecturer was invited. In this way I penetrated to the Morris interior . . . . Some people, going into Morris's house, and finding it remarkably unlike their own house, would say "What a queer place!" Others, with a more cultivated sense of beauty, would say "How very nice!" But neither of them would necessarily have seen what I saw at once, that there was an extraordinary discrimination at work in this magical house. Nothing in it was there because it was interesting or quaint or rare or hereditary, like grandmother's or uncle's portrait. Everything that was necessary was clean and handsome: everything else was beautiful and beautifully presented. There was an oriental carpet so lovely that it would have been a sin to walk on it; consequently it was not on the floor but on the wall and half way across the ceiling. There was no grand piano: such a horror would have been impossible. On the supper table there was no table cloth: a thing common enough now among people who see that a table should be itself an ornament and not a clothes horse, but then an innovation so staggering that it cost years of domestic conflict to introduce it.

. . . Morris was a very great literary artist: his stories and essays and letters no less than his poems are tissues of words as fine as the carpet on the ceiling; but he was quite often at a loss for a critical word in dealing with some uncongenial modern thing. On such occasions I would hand him the appropriate adjective, and he would grab at it with a gasp of relief. It was like giving a penny to a millionaire who had bought a newspaper and found his pockets empty.

. . . I once told him that the reason I did not write verse was that instead of saying what I wanted to say in it I had to say something that would rhyme, and that to find the rhyme I had to go through the alphabet, so that if my first line ended with my own name I had to follow it up with a caw or a daw, a flaw or a jaw, a paw or a saw, whether these things had anything to do with the subject or not. Morris looked at me exactly as if I had told him I was blind or deaf or impotent, or at best an utter fool. He could not understand anyone finding any difficulty in finding a rhyme or having to force it in any way, just as Elgar could not understand anyone inventing a tune without knowing at the same time what instrument should play it.

. . . Somehow, I found myself frequenting the Morris household instead of merely earning a supper there by lecturing occasionally on Sunday evenings in the ex-coach house. . . . I had no association to bias me; yet I, the most irreverent of mankind, felt its magic instantly and deeply. Mrs Morris made a startling impression on me. It was in the evening; and I had never been upstairs to her drawingroom before. I had time to take in all the lovely things that were in the room before she came in. Rossetti's pictures, of which I had seen a collection at the Burlington Fine Arts Club, had driven her into my consciousness as an imaginary figure. When she came into the room in her strangely beautiful garments, looking at least eight feet high, the effect was as if she had walked out of an Egyptian tomb at Luxor. Not until she had disposed herself very comfortably on the long couch opposite the settle did I compose myself into an acceptance of her as a real woman, and note that the wonderful curtain of hair was touched with grey, and the Rossetti face years older than it was in his pictures.

I always felt apologetic with Mrs Morris. I knew that the sudden eruption into her temple of beauty, with its pre-Raphaelite priests, of the proletarian comrades who began to infest the premises as Morris's fellow-Socialists, must be horribly disagreeable to her (I knew how my mother felt about the more discordant of them); and as one of this ugly rag-tag-and-bobtail of Socialism I could not expect her to do more than bear my presence as best she might. Fortunately she did not take much notice of me. She was not a talker: in fact she was the silentest woman I have ever met. She did not take much notice of anybody, and none whatever of Morris, who talked all the time. When I presently found myself dining at Kelmscott House my position was positively painful; for the Morris meals were works of art almost as much as the furniture. To refuse Morris's wine or Mrs. Morris's viands was like walking on the great carpet with muddy boots.[3]

Now, as it happened, I practise the occidental form of Yoga: I am a vegetarian and teetotaller. Morris did not demur to the vegetarianism: he maintained that a hunk of bread and an onion was a meal for any man; but he insisted on a bottle of wine to wash it down. Mrs. Morris did not care whether I drank wine or water; but abstinence from meat she regarded as a suicidal fad. Between host and hostess I was cornered; and Mrs. Morris did not conceal her contempt for my folly. At last pudding time came; and as the pudding was a particularly nice one, my abstinence vanished and I showed signs of a healthy appetite. Mrs. Morris pressed a second helping on me, which I consumed to her entire satisfaction. Then she said "That will do you good: there is suet in it." And that is the only remark,[4] as far as I can remember, that was ever addressed to me by this beautiful stately and silent woman, whom the Brotherhood and Rossetti had succeeded in consecrating. Happily she had a certain plain good sense which had preserved her sanity perfectly under treatment that would have spoiled most women. . . .

I did not see much of Morris after his health failed. The last meeting I can remember is one at Kelmscott House on a Sunday evening when I lectured there. Morris was in extreme trouble and low spirits; for many things had gone awry with him, and his mother had just died. He could not face the usual supper with a tableful of guests; and I tried to get away without adding to his trouble; but he insisted on my coming in alone to eat something. He found great difficulty in entertaining me; and I was at my wits' end to think of any way of cheering him. We had both given it up as a bad job and all but lapsed into silence when I had a fortunate inspiration. "Why don't you do a Pilgrim's Progress?" I said, meaning on the Kelmscott Press. Instantly he shot up from the depths of misery to the liveliest interest. He was another man in a moment; and it ended in our having quite an eager time together. Nobody has ever described Morris as mercurial; but certainly no man could change more rapidly or through a larger scale.

It was, I think, some time before this that he made a final effort to make the Socialists stop quarrelling. Now it was he himself who had set the first example of fission, and justified it as a necessary division of labor. But instead of each sect going its own way to Socialism they took to vituperating each other's leading personalities. In vain had the Guild of St. Matthew, through the mouth of Stewart Headlam, said "Sirs: ye are brothers: wherefore do ye wrong one to another?" At last Keir Hardie, simpleminded apostle of fraternity, forced the Societies, by a sentimental appeal to the rank and file, to form a committee to amalgamate them. The result was, first, to put a stop to every activity in the Societies except that of arguing fiercely about the resolutions sent in for approval by the amalgamating committee, and, second, Keir Hardie's discovery that the only way to secure unity was to expel the refractory sections one after another by the combined votes of all the rest. The last meeting of the amalgamators took place in the office of the Fabian Society, lent for the occasion. It terminated, amid roars of laughter, in the solemn expulsion of the Fabians from their own premises, leaving poor Hardie with a solidly unanimous few of his own personal followers in the room and all the others outside. Morris, who had taken no part in this comedy, again compelled the leaders to confer about it, but with a view, not to amalgamation, but drawing up and jointly signing a manifesto of Socialist aims, which were becoming obscured and forgotten in the conflicts of the factions.

The conferences were held in Hammersmith at Kelmscott House. They consisted virtually of Hyndman representing the S.D.F., myself representing the Fabian Society, and Morris representing the Hammersmith Socialist Society. The proletariat was represented by a comrade whom we appointed secretary to our Conference. He celebrated the compliment by turning up at the next meeting helplessly drunk, and thereby reducing himself to an attitude purely apologetic during the rest of the proceedings. Morris had drafted the manifesto.

The Conferences began by we three, Hyndman, Shaw, and Morris, gathering up round the fire and having a good talk about everything on earth except the object of our meeting. Hyndman, as I have said, was a very good talker; and I am not afflicted with any sort of dumbness. We kept the ball rolling very pleasantly until after an hour or so the pro-letariat, who mostly slept through our performances, insisted mildly on our getting to business.

In drafting the manifesto Morris had taken care to give some expression to both the Fabian policy and the Social-Democratic Federation policy. Hyndman immediately proposed the omission of the Fabian program of municipal Socialism, and its explicit denunciation as "gas and water Socialism." I was equally determined not to endorse the policy of the S.D.F. Morris soon saw that we were irreconcilable. There was nothing for it but to omit both policies and substitute platitudes that any Church Congress could have signed. Morris's draft, horribly eviscerated and patched, was subsequently sold for a penny as the Joint Manifesto of the Socialists of Great Britain. It was the only document any of the three of us had ever signed and published that was honestly not worth a farthing. Hyndman soon characteristically persuaded himself that it was important and that he had drafted it; and bibliographers like Buxton Forman were presently asking me whether it should be included in their list of Morris's works, finishing in considerable perplexity as to whether Hyndman or I was the greater liar. I submit that the internal evidence irresistibly bears me out.

Then came Morris's long illness and death. My old delicacy about Mrs Morris kept me away when he became bedridden, and even prevented me from attending his funeral, which I vainly regretted when I learnt that enough of the comrades had appeared to make one more or less a matter of indifference.

. . . I feel nothing but elation when I think of Morris. My intercourse with him was so satisfying that I should be the most ungrateful of men if I asked for more. You can lose a man like that by your own death, but not by his.

8

Love Affairs

THERE ARE matters so intimate that one cannot write about them because one cannot talk about them. For instance, some writers have written about their love affairs: in fact, some of them have written about nothing else. In this there is the initial difficulty that as there are necessarily two persons concerned, neither of them has the right to make a unilateral confession to the public. But there is the deeper objection that they include experiences which are in their nature silent: there is no language for them. From the Song of Songs in the Bible to the clinical fictions of . . . D. H. Lawrence and the downright scientific treatises of Havelock Ellis, there is an erotic literature which has its moments of beauty and its masses of documentary evidence; but I have nothing to add to it except what I cannot express because it is inexpressible. I have no patience with the writers who will not recognize this fact of nature. They think it a pity that Dante did not spread Francesca all over the Inferno instead of dismissing her in three or four lines. . . .

Unlike the general reader, I have been in love, like Beethoven, and have written idiotic love letters, many of which, I regret to say, have not been returned; so that instead of turning up among my papers after my death, they will probably be published by my inconsiderate admirers during my lifetime, to my utter confusion. My one comfort is, that whatever they might contain—and no man is more oblivious of their contents than I am—they cannot be more fatuous than Beethoven's. I have a modest confidence that at the worst I shall not fall below the standard of punctuation set by that great man. . . .

The prodigious literary vogue which these tender episodes enjoy is due to the fact that very few people in the world have ever had a love affair. . . . As to personal relations with actresses, the affectionate free-masonry of the profession makes it very difficult to let the public see it without misleading them absurdly. Morals and emotions are not the same on both sides of the footlights. Ellen Terry and I exchanged about two hundred and fifty letters in the nineties. An old fashioned governess would say that many of them were wild love letters; and yet, though we were all the time within a shilling hansom ride of one another's doors, we never saw one another in private; and the only time I ever touched her was on the first night of Brassbound, when I formally kissed her hand. For some time before the war I was on much the same intimate terms with Mrs. Campbell as King Magnus with Orinthia in The Apple Cart. Yet I was as faithful a husband as Magnus; and his phrase "our strangely innocent relations" is true.[1] I may say that from Ellen Terry to Edith Evans all the famous actresses with whom I had any personal contact have given me their unreserved friendship; but only with one, long since dead, and no great actress either. . . . had I any Harrisian adventures.[2] From Lady Colin Campbell onward, I have been familiar with celebrated beauties and with what is by no means the same thing, really beautiful women, without either of us moulting a feather of our integrity. I am, and always have been, an incorrigible philanderer, retaining something of the obsolete gallantry of the Irishmen of my generation; but you may count the women who have left me nothing to desire on less than the fingers of one hand. To these occasions I attach comparatively no importance: it is the others which endure. . . .

. . . I lived on pictures and music, opera and fiction, and thus escaped seduction until I was 29. . . . At last a widow lady[3] . . . , one of my mother's pupils, . . . at whose house I sometimes visited, and of whose sentiments toward me I had not the least suspicion, grew desperate at my stupidity, and one evening threw herself into my arms and confessed her passion for me. The surprise, the flattery, my inexperience, and her pretty distress, overwhelmed me. I was incapable of the brutality of repulsing her; and indeed for nearly a month I enjoyed without scruple the pleasure she gave me, and sought her company whenever I could find nothing better to do. It was my first consummated love affair; and though for nearly two years the lady had no reason to complain of my fidelity, I found the romantic side of our intercourse, which seemed never to pall on her, tedious, unreasonable, and even forced and insincere except at rare moments, when the power of love made her beautiful, body and soul.

Unfortunately, I had no sooner lost my illusions, my timidity, and my boyish curiosity about women, than I began to attract them irresistibly. My amusement at this soon changed to dismay. I became the subject of fierce jealousies. . . . If you want to know what it was like, read The Philanderer, and cast her for the part of Julia, and me for that of Charteris.[4]

I made the acquaintance of Florence Farr in the eighteen eighties, when the Socialist revival of those years, in which I took an active part as one of the Fabian leaders and as an indefatigable platform orator, took me on many Sundays to the house of William Morris on the Mall in Hammersmith to lecture there in the converted coach house which served as a meeting hall for Morris's followers.

Florence was the daughter of Dr. William Farr, famous as a sanitary reformer in the mid-nineteenth century when he and Sir Edwin Chadwick were forcing us to realize that England was dying of dirt.

Florence had been born unexpectedly long after her mother had apparently ceased childbearing: she was possibly indulged as a welcome surprise on that account. Though Dr. Farr survived his wits and lost most of his means by senile speculations before his death in 1883, he left enough to enable Florence to live modestly without having to sell herself in any fashion, or do anything that was distasteful to her.

She went on the stage and married a clever actor who was a member of the wellknown histrionic Emery family. There was some trouble (not domestic) that ended in his emigrating to America and passing out of Florence's life. She attached so little importance to the incident, being apparently quite content to forget him, that I had some difficulty in persuading her to divorce him for desertion by pointing out that as long as their marriage remained undissolved, he might turn up any moment with very serious legal claims on her.

Whatever the trouble was that took him out of the country Florence gave up the stage for the moment, and set herself to learn the art of embroidery under Morris's daughter May. She acted in an entertainment at the house on the Mall; and on this occasion I made her acquaintance, and had no difficulty in considerably improving it. She set no bounds to her relations with men whom she liked, and already had a sort of Leporello list of a dozen adventures, none of which however, had led to anything serious. She was in violent reaction against Victorian morals, especially sexual and domestic morals; and when the impact of Ibsen was felt in this country, and I wrote somewhere that "home is the girl's prison and the woman's workhouse" I became *persona grata* with her; and for some years we saw a great deal of one-another . . . .

She played the heroine in my first play in 1892.[5] In 1894 the late Miss Horniman gave her money to produce modern plays at the old Avenue Theatre, now replaced by The Playhouse. The first production, inadequately cast and acted, failed; and Florence was about to replace it by my first play, when I wrote Arms and the Man for her instead, selecting the cast myself. With Yeats' Land of Heart's Desire as an exquisite curtain raiser it had a startling first night success, and kept the theatre open (average receipts £17) until Miss Horniman's money was exhausted.

Being bound to secrecy to avoid shocking Miss Horniman's Puritan family, Florence could not tell me who was backing her. Years later I had a dream in which I went into a room and found Miss Horniman sitting there, whereupon I exclaimed "YOU were the backer at the Avenue." Next day I wrote to her and asked her whether this revelation had any foundation. . . .

I made desperate efforts to work up Florence's technique and capacity for hard professional work to the point needed for serious stage work; but her early life had been too easy. I failed, and had to give up worrying and discouraging her. She found the friend she really needed in Yeats. What she called "cantilating" for him was within her powers. We detached ourselves from one another naturally and painlessly; and presently I got married.

I heard about her departure for the East, but had no suspicion that her health was impaired in any way until I heard that she had undergone an operation. I telegraphed urgently for full information. My anxiety pleased her; and I learnt from her that the operation had been, so far, "successful." Months later, her sister wrote to me that she was dead.[6]

. . . Among the many beautiful things in Morris's two beautiful houses was a very beautiful daughter, then in the flower of her youth. You can see her in Burne-Jones's picture coming down *The Golden Stair,* the central figure. I was a bachelor then, and likely to remain so; for I not only felt about marriage very much as Jack Tanner does in Man and Superman,[7] but I was so poor that I could hardly have supported Morris's daughter on Morris's scale for a week on my income for a year; and nothing could have induced me to ask any woman to face the fate of my mother, who had been so "well brought up" that, knowing nothing of the value of money, she married an unsuccessful man whose means were quite inadequate to keep up her standard of expenditure. But these material considerations only made the Morris paradise more celestial and my part in it quite irresponsible. For if I could not immediately marry the beautiful daughter I could all the more light-heartedly indulge my sense of her beauty.[8]

One Sunday evening after lecturing and supping, I was on the threshold of the Hammersmith house when I turned to make my farewell, and at this moment she came from the diningroom into the hall. I looked at her, rejoicing in her lovely dress and lovely self; and she looked at me very carefully and quite deliberately made a gesture of assent with her eyes. I was immediately conscious that a Mystic Betrothal was registered in heaven, to be fulfilled when all the material obstacles should melt away, and my own position rescued from the squalors of my poverty and unsuccess; for subconsciously I had no doubt of my rank as a man of genius. Less reasonably I had no doubt that she, too, knew her own value, a knowledge that involved a knowledge of everyone else's. I did not think it necessary to say anything. To engage her in any way—to go to Morris and announce that I was taking advantage of the access granted to me as comrade-Communist to commit his beautiful daughter to a desperately insolvent marriage, did not occur to me as a socially possible proceeding. It did not occur to me even that fidelity to the Mystic Betrothal need interfere with the ordinary course of my relations with other women. I made no sign at all: I had no doubt that the thing was written on the skies for both of us.

So nothing happened except that the round of Socialist agitation went on and brought us together from time to time as before. . . .

Suddenly, to my utter stupefaction, and I suspect to that of Morris also, the beautiful daughter married one of the comrades.[9]

This was perfectly natural, and entirely my own fault for taking the Mystical Betrothal for granted; but I regarded it, and still regard it in spite of all reason, as the most monstrous breach of faith in the history of romance. The comrade was even less eligible than I; for he was no better off financially; and, though he could not be expected to know this, his possibilities of future eminence were more limited. But he was a convinced Socialist and regular speaker for the Cause, and his character was blameless; so there was nothing to be done but accept the situation. Apparently my limitless imagination had deceived me in the matter of the Mystical Betrothal.

But it had not deceived me in the least. For it presently happened that the overwork and irregular habits of the combination of continual propaganda with professional artistic activities, which killed Morris ten years before his time, reduced me to a condition in which I needed rest and change very pressingly; and holidays of the usual sort were beyond my means. The young couple thereupon invited me to stay with them for awhile. I accepted, and so found myself most blessedly resting and content in their house, which had the Morris charm . . . .

. . . Everything went well for a time in that *ménage à trois*. She was glad to have me in the house; and he was glad to have me because I kept her in good humor and produced a cuisine that no mere husband could elicit. It was probably the happiest passage in our three lives.

But the violated Betrothal was avenging itself. It made me from the first the centre of the household; and when I had quite recovered and there was no longer any excuse for staying unless I proposed to do so permanently and parasitically, her legal marriage had dissolved as all illusions do; and the mystic marriage asserted itself irresistibly. I had to consummate it or vanish.

I have in the scraps of autobiography I have written described how my mother was enabled to bear a disappointing marriage by the addition to our household of a musician of genius who gave her a career as a singer, and plenty of occupation as his partner in all his general musical activities, and especially in a technique of singing which was an article of faith with her. I had therefore, to my own great advantage, been brought up in a *ménage à trois,* and knew that it might be a quite innocent and beneficial arrangement. But when it became evident that the Betrothal would not suffer this to be an innocent arrangement the case became complicated. To begin with, the legal husband was a friend whose conduct towards me had always been irreproachable. To be welcomed in his house and then steal his wife was revolting to my sense of honor and socially inexcusable; for though I was as extreme a freethinker on sexual and religious questions as any sane human being could be, I was not the dupe of the Bohemian Anarchism that is very common in socialist and literary circles. I knew that a scandal would damage both of us and damage The Cause as well. It seems easy in view of my later position to have sat down together as three friends and arranged a divorce; but at that time I could not afford to marry and I was by no means sure that he could afford to be divorced. Besides, I hated the idea of a prosaic and even mercenary marriage: that, somehow or other, was not on the plane of the Mystic Betrothal. The more I reasoned about the situation the worse it was doomed to appear. So I did not argue about it. I vanished.

Then the vengeance of the violated Betrothal consummated itself in a transport of tragedy and comedy. For the husband vanished too! The *ménage* which had prospered so pleasantly as a *ménage à trois* proved intolerable as a *ménage à deux*. This marriage which all the mystic powers had forbidden from the first went to pieces when the unlucky parties no longer had me between them. Of the particulars of the rupture I know nothing; but in the upshot he fled to the Continent and eventually submitted chivalrously to being divorced as the guilty party, though the alternative was technically arranged for him. If I recollect aright he married again, this time I hope more suitably, and lived as happily as he might until his death, which came sooner than an actuary would have predicted.

The beautiful one abolished him root and branch, resuming her famous maiden name, and, for all I could prove, abolished me too. . . .

. . . You can learn nothing about . . . biographees from their sex histories. The sex relation is not a personal relation. It can be irresistibly desired and rapturously consummated between persons who could not endure one another for a day in any other relation. If I were to tell you every such adventure I have enjoyed you would be none the wiser as to the sort of man I am. You would know only what you already know: that I am a human being. If you have any doubts as to my normal virility, dismiss them from your mind. I was not impotent; I was not sterile; I was not homosexual; and I was extremely susceptible, though not promiscuously.

Also I was entirely free from the neurosis (as I class it) of Original Sin. I never associated sexual intercourse with delinquency, nor had any scruples or remorses or misgivings of conscience about it. Of course I had scruples, and effectively inhibitive ones too, about getting women "into trouble" or cuckolding my friends; and I held chastity to be a passion just as I hold intellect to be a passion; but St. Paul's case was to me always pathological. Sexual experience seemed a natural appetite, and its satisfaction a completion of human experience necessary for fully qualified authorship. I was not attracted by virgins as such. I preferred fully matured women who knew what they were doing.

. . . I told you that my first adventure did not occur until I was 29. But it would be a prodigious mistake to take that as the date of the beginning of my sexual life. Do not misunderstand this: I had been perfectly continent except for the involuntary incontinences of dreamland, which were very unfrequent. But as between Oscar Wilde who gave 16 as the age at which sex begins, and Rousseau who declared that his blood boiled with it from his birth, my personal experience confirms Rousseau and confutes Wilde. Just as I cannot remember any time when I could not read and write, I cannot remember any time when I did not exercise my imagination in daydreams about women. . . . Some day I will try to found a genuine psychology of fiction by writing down the history of my imagined life: duels, battles, love affairs with queens and all. The difficulty is that so much of it is too crudely erotic to be printable by an author of any delicacy.[10]

. . . I lived, a continent virgin, but an incorrigible philanderer, until I was 29, running away when the handkerchief was thrown to me; for I wanted to love, but not to be appropriated and lose my boundless . . . liberty. During the 14 years before my marriage at 43 there was always some lady in the case; and I tried all the experiments and learned what there was to be learnt from them. The ladies were unpaid; for I had no spare money: I earned only enough to keep me on a second floor, taking the rest out not in money but in freedom to preach Socialism. Prostitutes, who often accosted me, never attracted me.

As soon as I could afford to dress presentably, I became accustomed to women falling in love with me. I did not pursue women: I was pursued by them.

Here again do not jump to conclusions. All my pursuers did not want sexual intercourse. Some were happily married, and appreciated our understanding that sex was barred. They wanted Sunday husbands, and plenty of them. Some were prepared to buy friendship with pleasure, having learnt from a varied experience that men are made that way. Some were enchantresses, quite unbearable as housemates. No two cases were alike. William Morris's dictum "they all taste alike" was not, as Longfellow puts it, "spoken to the soul."

I was never duped by sex as a basis for permanent relations, nor dreamt of marriage in connection with it. I put everything else before it, and never refused or broke an engagement to speak on Socialism to pass a gallant evening. I valued sexual experience because of its power of producing a celestial flood of emotion and exaltation which, however momentary, gave me a sample of the ecstasy that may one day be the normal condition of conscious intellectual activity.

Not until I was past 40 did I earn enough to marry without seeming to marry for money, nor my wife at the same age without suspicion of being driven by sex starvation. As man and wife we found a new relation in which sex had no part.[11] It ended the old gallantries, flirtations, and philanderings for both of us. Even of these it was the ones that were never consummated that left the longest and kindliest memories.

How to Become a
Musical Critic

BEHOLD ME, then, in London in an impossible position. I was a foreigner—
an Irishman—the most foreign of all foreigners when he has not gone
through the British university mill. I was not, as I shall presently shew,
uneducated; but what I knew was what the English university graduates
did not know; and what they knew I either did not know or did not
believe. I was provincial; I was opinionated; I had to change London's
mind to gain any sort of acceptance or toleration.

My ambition was to be a great painter like Michael Angelo (one of my
heroes); but my attempts to obtain instruction in his art at the School of
Design presided over by the South Kensington Department of Science
and Art only prevented me from learning anything except how to earn
five shilling grants for the masters (payment by results) by filling up
ridiculous examination papers in practical geometry and what they called
freehand drawing.

With competent instruction I daresay I could have become a painter
and draughtsman of sorts; but the School of Design convinced me that I
was a hopeless failure in that direction on no better ground than that I
found I could not draw like Michael Angelo or paint like Titian at the
first attempt without knowing how.

It was this equipment that saved me from being starved out of literature. . . . In 1885 William Archer found me in the British Museum
Reading Room, poring over Deville's French version of Karl Marx's

Capital, with the orchestral score of Wagner's Tristan and Isolde beside it. He took my affairs in hand with such success that The Pall Mall Gazette, then still extant, sent me books to review; and the appointment of art critic to The World, which Archer was for the moment doubling with his regular function of dramatic critic, was transferred to me. I suddenly began to make money: £117 in the first year.

When . . . Archer delegated to me a job as a critic of painting which had been pushed on him, and for which he was quite unqualified, I rose like a rocket. My weekly feuilletons on all the fine arts in succession are still readable . . . . All that the exhibitions and performances that London could provide were open freely to me throughout the decade that followed my unanimous rebuffs as novelist. The better my novels the more they revolted the publishers' professional readers; but as a critic I came to the top irresistibly, whilst contemporary well-schooled literary beginners, brought up in artless British homes, could make no such mark.

I was capable of looking at a picture then, and, if it displeased me, immediately considering whether the figures formed a pyramid, so that, if they did not, I could prove the picture defective because the composition was wrong. And if I saw a picture of a man foreshortened at me in such a way that I could see nothing but the soles of his feet and his eyes looking out between his toes, I marveled at it and almost revered the painter, though veneration was at no time one of my strong points. I did not read dramatic or literary criticism much, and therefore I never explained the failure of a play on the ground that the fourth act was longer than the third, or ascribed the superiority of Great Expectations to Dombey and Son to the effect produced on Dickens by the contemplation of Mr Wilkie Collins's plots; but I said things quite as idiotic, and I can only thank my stars that my sense of what was real in works of art somehow did survive my burst of interest in irrelevant critical conventions and the pretensions of this or that technical method to be absolute.

When I was more among pictures than I am at present, certain reforms in painting which I desired were advocated by the Impressionist party, and resisted by the Academic party. Until those reforms had been effectually wrought I fought for the Impressionists—backed up men who could not draw a nose differently from an elbow against Leighton and Bouguereau—did everything I could to make the public conscious of the ugly unreality of studio-lit landscape and the inanity of second-hand classicism. Again, in dealing with the drama, I find that the forces which tend to make the theatre a more satisfactory resort for me are rallied for the moment, not round the so-called French realists, whom I should call simply anti-obscurantists, but around the Scandinavian realists; and accordingly I mount their platform, exhort England to carry their cause on to a glorious victory, and endeavor to surround their opponents with a subtle atmosphere of absurdity.

It is just the same in music. I am always electioneering. At the Opera I desire certain reforms; and, in order to get them, I make every notable performance an example of the want of them, knowing that in the long run these defects will seem as ridiculous as Monet has already made Bouguereau's backgrounds, or Ibsen the "poetical justice" of Tom Taylor. Never in my life have I penned an impartial criticism; and I hope I never may. As long as I have a want, I am necessarily partial to the fulfilment of that want, with a view to which I must strive with all my wit to infect everyone else with it. Thus there arises a deadly enmity between myself and the impresarios; for whereas their aim is to satisfy the public, often at huge risk and expense, I seize on their costliest efforts as the most conspicuous examples of the short-comings which rob me of the fullest satisfaction of my artistic cravings.

They may feel this to be diabolically unfair to them whenever they have done the very utmost that existing circumstances allowed them; but that does not shake me, since I know that the critic who accepts existing circumstances loses from that moment all his dynamic quality. He stops the clock. His real business is to find fault; to ask for more; to knock his head against stone walls, in the full assurance that three or four good heads will batter down any wall that stands across the world's path. He is no dispenser of justice: reputations are to him only the fortresses of the opposing camps; and he helps to build or bombard them according to his side in the conflict. . . .

My own most polemical writings are to be found in the files of The Times, The Morning Post, The Daily Express, The World, and The Saturday Review. I found out early in my career that a Conservative paper may steal a horse when a Radical paper dare not look over a hedge, and that the rich, though very determined that the poor shall read nothing unconventional, are equally determined to be preached at themselves. In short, I found that only for the classes would I be allowed, and indeed tacitly required, to write on revolutionary assumptions. I filled their columns with sedition; and they filled my pockets (not very deep ones then) with money. In the press as in other departments the greatest freedom may be found where there is least talk about it.

In my sixteenth year an emergency made me very precociously cashier-in-chief (there was no other) to a leading estate agent in Dublin. It was part of my duty to pay the metropolitan shopping bills of our country clients. I began by calling at the shops on my way from the bank, and paying them across the counter. To my surprise I was handed a percentage on the amount of the bill. Being then the greenest of innocents, I astonished the shopkeepers by refusing the tip. I did this not in the least because I had any scruple against being paid twice over for the same service. I did not think of it in that way. It was my class snobbery that could not brook the indignity of tips from shopkeepers. I stopped calling on them, and left them to call on me for their money. . . .

When I broke loose from my cashier's desk and with desperate imprudence jumped overboard into the literary market in London only to find that nobody would publish my attempts at writing books, I made my living for some years as a critic of literature, painting, music, and the theatre. My good word was of some value then; but no painter, picture dealer, music seller, composer, actor, or manager ever offered me cash down for a favorable notice. One innocent youth in the provinces sent me a patent tobacco pipe with a letter asking me to be kind to his brother, to whom he was deeply attached, and who had taken to the stage as a profession. He had failed to ascertain that I do not smoke. I was touched by his brotherly devotion, and would certainly have paid a little special attention to the case if I had ever seen the brother acting or remembered his name. The methods of the theatre managers were less crude. They would consult me as an expert on the advisability of producing some foreign play of which they had purchased the performing rights. If I thought well of it, would I translate it and sell the option of performing my translation within six months, for, say, £50? If I had made a translation of some noted foreign play, preferably a French one, I believe I could have made a hundred a year by selling an option on it twice a year. One eminent actor-manager offered to accept an original play of mine, not committing himself to a date for production, but intimating that if at any time I desired an advance on account of royalties it could be arranged. At his theatre on every first night the stage was cleared after the performance for a banquet at which it was a coveted privilege to be a guest. The critics were invited discreetly by the box office chief as they entered. I always accepted the invitation as a courteous tribute to my influence; but I never went.

In the picture market nobody ever offered me hard cash, directly or indirectly, for a favorable notice. The picture dealers had personal contacts with the critics on the days they set apart for the Press before the opening of their exhibitions; and the older hands were experts in the art of personally humbugging reporters who, being only newsmen who could not tell a Greco from a Guido or a Frith from a Burne-Jones at sight, got on by praising the eminent painters and ignoring the beginners unless they were talked by the dealer into believing that his latest speculation in a beginner's work was the discovery of a new genius. At my first appearance at these "Press Views" I was addressed very flatteringly by a famous dealer, now long deceased, who expatiated to me rapturously on the marvellous qualities of half a dozen respectable but quite ordinary sketches in water-color by an unknown painter. I listened gravely and then said "Mr—: how can you talk such nonsense to Me? You know better." Without turning a hair he beckoned me confidentially and said, "Come with me" and led me to a private room in which he kept a few real treasures by old masters: mostly primitives.

His chief contemporary and rival in picture dealing, also long since passed away, had a subtler method. He invited me to see the latest picture by a well-known painter, and received me not very genially, like a man disgusted with the popular taste in art. "Oh!" he said, "Youve come to see this. Here it is. Pish! It is what you people like; and we have to provide it for you. Now here [pointing to a picture quite inconspicuously hung] is a picture to my taste worth ten of it. But it means nothing to you: you wouldnt know the painter's name if I told it to you. Look at his handling! Look at that sky. But you gentlemen of the Press pass it by without a glance." Of course the reporters who did not know chalk from cheese in painting would hasten to shew their connoisseurship by "writing up" the neglected genius for all they were worth. I was not taken in; but I had not the heart to spoil the old man's comedy by telling him so. I was soon recognized as a qualified critic and admitted to the inner fellowship that exists between the genuine critics and the dealers who are real connoisseurs. In that circle the tricks of the trade were dropped, with the result that many of the best critics knew nothing of the humbug and corruption practised on newsmen employed by editors who were ignorant of art and impatient of the convention that obliged their papers to notice it. They sent their worst and wordiest reporters to the galleries, the theatre, and the opera, reserving their best for political meetings and the criminal courts.

However, the relations of critics with dealers do not cover the whole field of possible corruption. I was never bribed by a dealer, and after my first appearances never humbugged. But I once gave up a valuable appointment as picture critic to a prominent weekly journal because I was asked to write flattering notices of the pictures painted by the proprietor's friends regardless of their merits, the argument being that as I was welcome to do the same for my own personal friends, I could not be so churlish as to refuse to do as much for my employer. Later on I obtained an equally desirable appointment, but had to give that up also, because the proprietress of the paper insisted on interpolating over my signature ecstatic little raptures about minor Academy pictures by painters who invited her to tea at their studios.

In the musical world no direct bribes ever came my way, nor did I ever hear of any. All I can say is that at the Opera as in the theatres and all other places of public entertainment it was far easier and pleasanter to praise everything, flatter everybody, and say nothing about shortcomings, than to write the critical truth. At the Opera my easygoing colleagues in the foyer between the acts would expatiate indignantly on the demerits of the new world-famous Italian tenor with the voice of a newspaper crier and the manners of a trooper who was that night proving himself utterly unpresentable in London as an adequate Manrico or Lohengrin. The conductor would have been in his proper place among the second violas; the cuts made in the score were unpardonable Vandalisms; the work was only half rehearsed or perhaps not rehearsed at all; in the love duet the soprano was sharp and the tenor flat all through; the Wagner Leitmotifs were phrased one way by the strings, another by the brass, and yet another by the wood-wind so that no one could recognize them as the same; the leaders of the chorus were in their seventh or eighth decades, almost voiceless and never in the middle of the note, but indispensable because they were "good starters," and so on through the series of impostures and makeshifts which make the Opera a hell for composers and for critics who know. "You must really shew this up," the easygoers would say to me. But they did not shew it up themselves. By their accounts the performances shone with all the brilliancy of the diamonds with which the ladies in the grand tier boxes were decked to advertize the riches of their financier husbands. Complaisant critics were welcomed in the theatre even when all the stalls were sold out and they had to be content as "rovers" without allotted seats, sitting or standing about wherever they could. From the agents and henchmen of the favored prima donna of that day I received hints that not only were unlimited tickets for her concerts at my disposal for the asking, but that invitations to her delightful castle in Wales were not beyond possibility for a critic who could be depended on not to mention that she was no longer sure of her high F and preferred to transpose and make it E flat. I was never a guest at that castle, even after I had asked the lady's accompanist in what key she sang "Ah, non giunge." He took it as a threat of exposure if I were not invited.

Those lazy spectators of the pageant of life who love to reflect on the instability of human greatness have by this time yawned and gone to bed after reading the last of the subsiding rush of paragraphs about the late Sir Augustus Harris. The day after his death one of the greetings addressed to me was, "And so your old enemy is gone." This shocked me at the moment; for, though I had no illusions whatever about his imaginary greatness as an operatic reformer, I did not dislike him personally; and I was naturally in a softer mood after the news of his premature death than I used to be at the time when, as a musical critic, I was making onslaught after onslaught on the spurious artistic prestige of Covent Garden. In those days the relations between us were certainly somewhat strained. There were seasons when I always sat down in my stall at Covent Garden with the virtuous consciousness of having paid hard money for it, instead of being the invited guest of the manager whose scalp it was my business to take. There were times, too, when I was warned that my criticisms were being collated by legal experts for the purpose of proving "prejudice" against me, and crushing me by mulcting my editor in fabulous damages. And, as sure as fate, if the editor had been a skinflint and a coward; if he had corruptly regarded his paper, in its critical relation to the fine arts, solely as a convenient instrument for unlimited sponging on managers, publishers, and picture-dealers for gratuitous boxes, stalls, books, prints, and private-view invitations; if he had been willing to sell his critic for an advertisement or for an invitation to the dinner or garden parties of the smartest partizans of the fashionable tenor or prima donna of the season; or if he had been a hired editor at the mercy of a proprietor of that stamp, then I should have been silenced, as many other critics were silenced. But the late Edmund Yates was not that sort of editor. He had his faults; but he did not run away from his own sword for fear of cutting his fingers with it; he did not beg the tribute he could compel; and he had a strong and loyal *esprit de corps*. The World proved equal to the occasion in the conflict with Covent Garden; and finally my invitations to the Opera were renewed; the impresario made my personal acquaintance, and maintained the pleasantest personal relations with me from that time onward . . . .

. . . There was one gigantic business obligation which was peculiar to Sir Augustus Harris. In ordinary theatrical management nobody proposes a policy of monopoly. It is quite understood that Mr Alexander must count on the competition of Mr Tree, Mr Hare, Sir Henry Irving, and, in fact, as many competitors as there are suitable theatres in London. But the Augustan policy at Covent Garden was one of monopoly at all costs. The impresario well knew what the old system of two competing operas, one at Her Majesty's and the other at Covent Garden, was like behind the scenes. To issue flashy lying prospectuses; to slip into your theatre by back ways so as to avoid the ambuscades of the unpaid chorus; to hold your artists spellbound with flattering conversations until after bank hour lest they should present their cheques before money could be scraped together to meet them: all these shifts and dodges of the bankrupt two-opera system were no part of the Harris *régime,* under which the credit of the Covent Garden treasury became as that of the Bank of England. Sir Augustus Harris paid more money every year to prevent artists from working for anybody else than some of his predecessors paid for work actually done on their stages. The grievance at Covent Garden was, not that you could not get your money, but that you were not allowed to earn it. He not only held Drury Lane and Covent Garden against all comers, but took Her Majesty's and locked it up until it was demolished. Even in smaller theatres tenants found clauses in their agreements barring Italian Opera. Just as he forestalled possible rivals as a pantomime manager by engaging all the stars of the music-hall, whether he had work for them or not, so, as an impresario, he engaged every operatic artist who shewed the slightest promise of becoming a source of strength to a competitor. When Signor Lago discovered Cavaleria, the Ravoglis, and Ancona, they were bought over his head immediately. There was no malice in the matter. The alternative to monopoly was bankruptcy. Sir Augustus Harris's triumph as a business impresario was his acceptance of that big condition and his achievement of the feat of finance and organization involved by it.

. . . Quite the most enthralling memorial of him would be the publication of his accounts, if he kept any. Copies should be appended of the contracts imposed by him on the more dependent classes of artists engaged. The extent to which he succeeded in inducing such people to

place themselves at his disposal when wanted without exacting any reciprocal obligation would considerably astonish those innocent persons
who think of the operatic stage as a specially free and irresponsible profession. You can drive a second-class prima donna to sign an agreement
that a mason, a carpenter, or an engine-fitter, backed by their Trade-
Unions, would tear up and throw in your face.

To discuss the operations of a commercial organization of this extent
as if they were the outcome of the private character of the entrepreneur
is idle. It is like discussing whether the battle of Waterloo was a humane
proceeding on Wellington's part, or a personally courageous one on
Napoleon's. The Reverend Dr Ker Gray, we are told, gave an impressive
address at the funeral on the work of the dead man, "honest, honorable,
straightforward." But one feels a want of real life in this description . . . .

For my own part I confess to liking the man better than I had any
reason to like him. There was a certain pathos about him, with a touch of
humor; and I do not doubt the assurances of his friends that he was very
sensitive to stories of distress. But I know that he was not a great manager; and I am not convinced that he was even a very clever one. Attentive observers of great "captains of industry" know that their success often
comes to them in spite of themselves—that instead of planning and
guiding complicated enterprises with a master-hand, they are simply following the slot of the market with a sort of doglike instinct into the
centre of all sorts of enterprises which are too big to be upset by their
misunderstandings. I am perfectly certain that if Sir Augustus Harris had
managed the Opera according to his own ideas, he would have destroyed
it quite as effectually as Mr Mapleson did. It seems hardly credible now
that I once exhausted myself, in the columns of The World, in apparently
hopeless attempts to shame the de Reszkes out of their perpetual Faust
and Mephistopheles, Romeo and Laurent, and in poohpoohed declara-
tions that there were such works in existence as Die Walküre and Tristan.
It was not Sir Augustus Harris that roused Jean de Reszke from his long
lethargy, but his own artistic conscience and the shock of Vandy's brilliant success in Massenet's Manon. . . .

In short, on this subject, I am, like the gentleman in The Corsican
Brothers, "still implacable." I said it all when he was alive; I say it now
that he is dead; and I shall say it again whenever I see the Press bowing
a little too low before commercial success, and offering it the wreaths
that belong to genius and devotion alone.

These years of criticism advanced my mental education by compelling me to deliver carefully considered judgments, and to discriminate between the brilliant talents and technical accomplishments of the fashionable celebrities whose vogue ended with their deaths or sooner, and the genius that is not for an age but for all time. I heard beginners who, fresh from their teachers' coaching, gave the most promising displays. But not knowing the value of what they had been taught, they collapsed into commonplace when they escaped from tutelage. Only from such experiences can a critic become skilled in analysis, and learn that the critic who cannot analyze is easily duped. . . .

So, as reviewer for the old Pall Mall Gazette and picture critic for Edmund Yates's then fashionable weekly, The World, I carried on until I found an opening which I can explain only by describing the musical side of my childhood, . . . which was of cardinal importance in my education.

Some years ago I came upon a barrel-organ in the streets of Haarlem; and it was so long since I had heard one . . . that I stopped to listen to it for the sake of old times. I did not stop long because I did not know enough of Dutch law to feel sure of a verdict of justifiable homicide in case I impulsively killed the performer; but I could not pass by without dwelling for a moment on the archaic thing that had once been so familiar and so accursed. . . .

When I was a child every respectable house guarded its privacy from the pryings of the people over the way by fitting its parlor window with a perforated wire blind. If you take a magnifying glass and examine the nose of any middle-aged man you will discover a minute roseate ring pattern printed all over the tip. You can see it on my nose, for instance; and it will go with me to my grave. It is the mark of the perforated wire blind through which I used to peer at the barrel-organs when they ground out their tunes at the area railings. When I look back it seems to me that my whole childhood was passed with my nose pressed against that chilling blind and my eyes riveted upon either an organ-grinder or upon a ton of coals being emptied out of grimy bags through the cellar-plate. The spectacle was not exactly a liberal education; but it enables me to tell the children of to-day what they have lost through the disappearance of the barrel-organ.

There were four varieties of the instrument; the upright, or cottage model, with an effeminate tone intended to be birdlike or fairylike, and perhaps a set of dancing dolls with cymbals; the ordinary square, usually covered with green baize on which a monkey sat enthroned; the trombone model, which was simply the square one with a trombone bell mounted on it like a maxim gun; and finally the organ on wheels, with a sort of dickey behind in which sat a baby who never grew up. All these, except the last, hung round the performer's neck by a strap, and were supported, when in action, by a stick hooked on underneath. They did weigh more than half a hundred-weight . . . . As to the tone, I will speak as moderately as I can. There were two stops, one consisting of flue pipes, which produced a sort of bronchial cooing, and the other of reed pipes, which snarled self-assertively. Both had the property of not standing in tune when exposed to the vicissitudes of our climate. . . .

All that is necessary . . . I submit, is to fall back on the old custom of outlawry. Let a short Act of Parliament be passed, placing all street musicians outside the protection of the law, so that any citizen may assail them with stones, sticks, knives, pistols, or bombs without incurring any penalties—except, of course, in the case of the instrument itself being injured; for Heaven forbid that I should advocate any disregard of the sacredness of property, especially in the form of industrial capital!

. . . From my earliest recorded sign of an interest in music when as a small child I encored my mother's singing of the page's song from the first act of Les Huguenots (note that I shared Herbert Spencer's liking for Meyerbeer) music has been an indispensable part of my life. Harley Granville-Barker was not far out when, at a rehearsal of one of my plays, he cried out "Ladies and gentlemen: will you please remember that this is Italian opera." . . . The wildest pirates and highwaymen in fiction did not fascinate me more than the prima donnas in Queens of Song, nor could the pictures of their deeds and the tales of their exploits please me as did Heath's gift books with decorative borders and operatic tableaux, or the anecdotes in that quite inimitable work, Sutherland Edwards's History of the Opera, which I take to be the most readable book of its kind ever written. I have lived to become the colleague, and to all appearances considerably the senior of Mr Sutherland Edwards; and I tired long ago of paying at the Opera doors and then supplying all the charm of the performance from my own imagination, in flat defiance of my eyes and ears.

Yet I still remember the old feeling of the days when the Opera was a world of fable and adventure, and not a great art factory. . . . When I was a small boy I was taken to the opera. I did not then know what an opera was, though I could whistle a good deal of opera music. I had seen in my mother's album photographs of all the great opera singers, mostly in evening dress. In the theatre I found myself before a gilded balcony filled with persons in evening dress whom I took to be the opera singers. I picked out one massive dark lady as Albani, and I wondered how soon she would stand up and sing. I was puzzled by the fact that I was made to sit with my back to the singers instead of facing them. When the curtain went up, my astonishment and delight were unbounded.

. . . I shall have to repeat here some of my father's history, but only so far as is necessary to explain the situation of my mother.

Technically speaking I should say she was the worst mother conceivable, always, however, within the limits of the fact that she was incapable of unkindness to any child, animal, or flower, or indeed to any person or thing whatsoever. But if such a thing as a maternity welfare centre had been established or even imagined in Ireland in her time, and she had been induced to visit it, every precept of it would have been laughably strange to her. Though she had been severely educated up to the highest standard for Irish "carriage ladies" of her time, she was much more like a Trobriand islander as described by Mr Malinowski than like a modern Cambridge lady graduate in respect of accepting all the habits, good or bad, of the Irish society in which she was brought up as part of an uncontrollable order of nature. She went her own way with so complete a disregard and even unconsciousness of convention and scandal and prejudice that it was impossible to doubt her good faith and innocence; but it never occurred to her that other people, especially children, needed guidance or training, or that it mattered in the least what they ate and drank or what they did as long as they were not actively mischievous. She accepted me as a natural and customary phenomenon, and took it for granted that I should go on occurring in that way. In short, living to her was not an art: it was something that happened. But there were unkind parts of it that could be avoided; and among these were the constraints and tyrannies, the scoldings and browbeatings and punishments she had suffered in her childhood as the method of her education. In her righteous reaction against it she reached a negative attitude in which, having no substitute to propose, she carried domestic anarchy as far as in the nature of things it can be carried.

I myself was never on bad terms with my mother: we lived together until I was forty-two years old, absolutely without the smallest friction of any kind; yet when her death set me thinking curiously about our relations, I realized that I knew very little about her. Introduce me to a strange woman who was a child when I was a child, a girl when I was a boy, an adolescent when I was an adolescent; and if we take naturally to one another I will know more of her and she of me at the end of forty days (I had almost said of forty minutes) than I knew of my mother at the end of forty years. A contemporary stranger is a novelty and an enigma, also a possibility; but a mother is like a broomstick or like the sun in the heavens, it does not matter which as far as one's knowledge of her is concerned: the broomstick is there and the sun is there; and whether the child is beaten by it or warmed and enlightened by it, it accepts it as a fact in nature . . . .

She had been tyrannously taught French enough to recite one or two of Lafontaine's fables; to play the piano the wrong way; to harmonize by rule from Logier's Thoroughbass; to sit up straight and speak and dress and behave like a lady, and an Irish lady at that. She knew nothing of the value of money nor of housekeeping nor of hygiene nor of anything that could be left to servants or governesses or parents or solicitors or apothecaries or any other member of the retinue, indoor and outdoor, of a country house. She had great expectations from a humpbacked little aunt, a fairylike creature with a will of iron, who had brought up her motherless niece with a firm determination to make her a paragon of good breeding, to achieve a distinguished marriage for her, and to leave her all her money as a dowry.

My father was a very ineligible suitor for a paragon with great expectations. His family pretensions were enormous; but they were founded on many generations of younger sons, and were purely psychological. He had managed to acquire a gentlemanly post in the law courts. This post had been abolished and its holder pensioned. By selling the pension he was enabled to start in business as a wholesaler in the corn trade (retail trade was beneath his family dignity) of which he knew nothing. He accentuated this deficiency by becoming the partner of a Mr. Clibborn, who had served an apprenticeship to the cloth trade. Their combined ignorances kept the business going, mainly by its own inertia, until they and it died. Many years after this event I paid a visit of curiosity to Jervis St. Dublin; and there, on one of the pillars of a small portico, I found the ancient inscription "Clibborn & Shaw" still decipherable, as it were on the tombs of the Pharaohs. I cannot believe that this business yielded my father at any time more than three or four hundred a year; and it got less as time went on, as that particular kind of business was dying a slow death throughout the latter half of the nineteenth century.

My father was past forty, and no doubt had sanguine illusions as to the future of his newly acquired business when he fell in love with my mother and was emboldened by her expectations and his business hopes to propose to her just at the moment when marriage seemed her only way of escape from an angry father and a stepmother. Immediately all her relatives, who had tolerated this middle-aged gentleman as a perfectly safe acquaintance with an agreeable vein of humor, denounced him as a notorious drunkard. My mother, suspicious of this sudden change of front, put the question directly to my father. His eloquence and sincerity convinced her that he was, as he claimed to be, and as he was in principle, a bigoted teetotaller. She married him; and her disappointed and infuriated aunt disinherited her, not foreseeing that the consequences of the marriage would include so remarkable a phenomenon as myself.

When my mother was disillusioned, and found out what living on a few hundreds a year with three children meant, even in a country where a general servant could be obtained for eight pounds a year, her condition must have been about as unhappy and her prospects as apparently hopeless as her aunt could have desired even in her most vindictive moments.

But there was one trump in her hand. She was fond of music, and had a mezzo-soprano voice of remarkable purity of tone. . . . In order to exercise it seriously, she had to associate with other people who had musical talent. My first doubt as to whether God could really be a good Protestant was suggested by the fact that the best voices available for combination with my mother's in the works of the great composers had been unaccountably vouchsafed to Roman Catholics. Even the Divine gentility was presently called in question; for some of these vocalists were undeniably shopkeepers. If the best tenor, undeniably a Catholic, was at least an accountant, the buffo was a frank stationer.

There was no help for it: if my mother was to do anything but sing silly ballads in drawing rooms, she had to associate herself on an entirely unsectarian footing with people of like artistic gifts without the smallest reference to creed or class. She must actually permit herself to be approached by Roman Catholic priests, and at their invitation to enter that house of Belial, the Roman Catholic chapel, and sing the Masses of Mozart there. If religion is that which binds men to one another, and irreligion that which sunders, then must I testify that I found the religion of my country in its musical genius, and its irreligion in its churches and drawing rooms.

. . . In the next street to ours, Harrington Street, where the houses were bigger and more fashionable than in our little by-street, there was a teacher of singing, lamed by an accident in childhood which had left one of his legs shorter than the other, but a man of mesmeric vitality and force. He was a bachelor living with his brother, whom he supported and adored, and a terrible old woman who was his servant of all work. His name was George John Vandeleur Lee, known in Dublin as Mr G. J. Lee. Singing lessons were cheap in Dublin; and my mother went to Lee to learn how to sing properly. He trained her voice to such purpose that she became indispensable to him as an amateur prima donna. For he was a most magnetic conductor and an indefatigable organizer of concerts, and later on of operas, with such amateur talent, vocal and orchestral, as he could discover and train in Dublin, which, as far as public professional music was concerned, was, outside the churches, practically a vacuum.

Lee soon found his way into our house, first by giving my mother lessons there, and then by using our drawing-room for rehearsals. I can only guess that the inadequacies of old Ellen in the Harrington Street house, and perhaps the incompatibilities of the brother, outweighed the comparative smallness of our house in Synge Street. My mother soon became not only prima donna and chorus leader but general musical factotum in the whirlpool of Lee's activity. Her grounding in Logier's Thoroughbass enabled her to take boundless liberties with composers. When authentic band parts were missing she thought nothing of making up an orchestral accompaniment of her own from the pianoforte score. Lee, as far as I know, had never seen a full orchestral score in his life: he conducted from a first violin part or from the vocal score, and had not, I think, any decided notion of orchestration as an idiosyncratic and characteristic part of a composer's work. He had no scholarship according to modern ideas; but he could do what Wagner said is the whole duty of a conductor: he could give the right time to the band; and he could pull it out of its amateur difficulties in emergencies by sheer mesmerism. Though he could not, or at any rate within my hearing never did sing a note, his taste in singing was classically perfect. In his search for the secret of *bel canto* he had gone to all the teachers within his reach. They told him that there was a voice in the head, a voice in the throat, and a voice in the chest. He dissected birds, and, with the connivance of medical friends, human subjects, in his search for these three organs. He then told the teachers authoritatively that the three voices were fabulous, and that the voice was produced by a single instrument called the larynx. They replied that musical art had nothing to do with anatomy, and that for a musician to practise dissection was unheard-of and disgusting. But as, tested by results, their efforts to teach their pupils to screech like locomotive whistles not only outraged his ear but wrecked the voices and often the health of their victims, their practice was as unacceptable to him as their theory.

Thus Lee became the enemy of every teacher of singing in Dublin; and they reciprocated heartily. In this negative attitude he was left until, at the opera, he heard an Italian baritone named Badeali, who at the age of 80, when he first discovered these islands, had a perfectly preserved voice, and, to Lee's taste, a perfectly produced one. Lee, thanks to his dissections, listened with a clear knowledge of what a larynx is really like. The other vocal organs and their action were obvious and conscious. Guided by this knowledge, and by his fine ear, his fastidious taste, and his instinct, he found out what Badeali was doing when he was singing. The other teachers were interested in Badeali only because one of his accomplishments was to drink a glass of wine and sing a sustained note at the same time. Finally Lee equipped himself with a teaching method which became a religion for him: the only religion, I may add, he ever professed. And my mother, as his pupil, learnt and embraced this musical faith, and rejected all other creeds as uninteresting superstitions. And it did not fail her; for she lived to be Badeali's age and kept her voice without a scrape on it until the end.

I have to dwell on The Method, as we called it in the family, because my mother's association with Lee, and the *ménage à trois* in which it resulted, would be unpleasantly misunderstood without this clue to it. For after the death of Lee's brother, which affected him to the verge of suicide, we left our respective houses and went to live in the same house, number one Hatch Street, which was half in Lower Leeson Street. The arrangement was economical; for we could not afford to live in a fashionable house, and Lee could not afford to give lessons in an unfashionable one, though, being a bachelor, he needed only a music room and a bedroom. We also shared a cottage in Dalkey, high up on Torca Hill, with all Dublin Bay from Dalkey Island to Howth visible from the garden, and all Killiney Bay with the Wicklow mountains in the background from the hall door. Lee bought this cottage and presented it to my mother, though she never had any legal claim to it and did not benefit by its sale later on. It was not conveniently situated for rehearsals or lessons; but there were musical neighbors who allowed me to some extent to run in and out of their houses when there was music going on.

Great as is my debt to famous books, great pictures, and noble music for my education I should be even more ignorant than I am but for my removal at the age of ten from the street in which I was born, half of it faced with a very unpicturesque field which was soon obscured by a hoarding plastered with advertisements, to Torca Cottage, high on Dalkey Hill, commanding views of Dublin Bay from Dalkey Island to Howth Head and of Killiney Bay from the island to Bray Head, with a vast and ever changing expanse of sea and sky far below and far above.

The *ménage à trois,* alternating between Hatch St. and Dalkey, worked in its ramshackle way quite smoothly until I was fifteen or thereabouts, when Lee went to London and our family broke up into fragments that never got pieced together again.

In telling the story so far, I have had to reconstruct the part of it which occurred before I came into it and began, as my nurse put it, to take notice. I can remember the ante-Lee period in Synge St. when my father, as sole chief of the household, read family prayers and formally admitted that we had done those things which we ought not to have done and left undone those things which we ought to have done, which was certainly true as far as I was personally concerned. He added that there was no health in us; and this also was true enough about myself; for Dr Newland, our apothecary, was in almost continual attendance to administer cathartics; and when I had a sore throat I used to hold out for sixpence before submitting to a mustard plaster round my neck. We children (I had two sisters older than myself and no brothers) were abandoned entirely to the servants, who, with the exception of Nurse Williams, who was a good and honest woman, were utterly unfit to be trusted with the charge of three cats, much less three children. I had my meals in the kitchen, mostly of stewed beef, which I loathed, badly cooked potatoes, sound or diseased as the case might be, and much too much tea out of brown delft teapots left to "draw" on the hob until it was pure tannin. Sugar I stole. I was never hungry, because my father, often insufficiently fed in his childhood, had such a horror of child hunger that he insisted on unlimited bread and butter being always within our reach. When I was troublesome a servant thumped me on the head until one day, greatly daring, I rebelled, and, on finding her collapse abjectly, became thenceforth uncontrollable. I hated the servants and liked my mother because, on the one or two rare and delightful occasions when she buttered my bread for me, she buttered it thickly instead of merely wiping a knife on it. Her almost complete neglect of me had the advantage that I could idolize her to the utmost pitch of my imagination and had no sordid or disillusioning contacts with her. It was a privilege to be taken for a walk or a visit with her, or on an excursion.

My ordinary exercise whilst I was still too young to be allowed out by myself was to be taken out by a servant, who was supposed to air me on the banks of the canal or round the fashionable squares where the atmosphere was esteemed salubrious and the surroundings gentlemanly. Actually she took me into the slums to visit her private friends, who dwelt in squalid tenements. When she met a generous male acquaintance who insisted on treating her she took me into the public house bars, where I was regaled with lemonade and gingerbeer; but I did not enjoy these treats, because my father's eloquence on the evil of drink had given me an impression that a public house was a wicked place into which I should not have been taken. Thus were laid the foundations of my lifelong hatred of poverty, and the devotion of all my public life to the task of exterminating the poor and rendering their resurrection for ever impossible.

. . . At the end of my schooling I knew nothing of what the school professed to teach; but I was a highly educated boy all the same. I could sing and whistle from end to end leading works by Handel, Haydn, Mozart, Beethoven, Rossini, Bellini, Donizetti and Verdi. I was saturated with English literature, from Shakespear and Bunyan to Byron and Dickens. And I was so susceptible to natural beauty that, having had some glimpse of the Dalkey scenery on an excursion, I still remember the moment when my mother told me that we were going to live there as the happiest of my life.

And all this I owed to the meteoric impact of Lee, with his music, his method, his impetuous enterprise and his magnetism, upon the little Shaw household where a thoroughly disgusted and disillusioned woman was suffering from a hopelessly disappointing husband and three uninteresting children grown too old to be petted like the animals and birds she was so fond of, to say nothing of the humiliating inadequacy of my father's income. We never felt any affection for Lee; for he was too excessively unlike us, too completely a phenomenon, to rouse any primitive human feeling in us. When my mother introduced him to me, he played with me for the first and last time; but as his notion of play was to decorate my face with moustaches and whiskers in burnt cork in spite of the most furious resistance I could put up, our encounter was not a success; and the defensive attitude in which it left me lasted, though without the least bitterness, until the decay of his energies and the growth of mine put us on more than equal terms. He never read anything except Tyndall on Sound, which he kept in his bedroom for years. He complained that an edition of Shakespear which I lent him was incomplete because it did not contain The School for Scandal, which for some reason he wanted to read; and when I talked of Carlyle he understood me to mean the Viceroy of that name who had graciously attended his concerts in the Antient Concert Rooms. Although he supplanted my father as the dominant factor in the household, and appropriated all the activity and interest of my mother, he was so completely absorbed in his musical affairs that there was no friction and hardly any intimate personal contacts between the two men: certainly no unpleasantness. At first his ideas astonished us. He said that people should sleep with their windows open. The daring of this appealed to me; and I have done so ever since. He ate brown bread instead of white: a startling eccentricity. He had no faith in doctors, and when my mother had a serious illness he took her case in hand unhesitatingly and at the end of a week or so gave my trembling father leave to call in a leading Dublin doctor, who simply said "My work is done" and took his hat. As to the apothecary and his squills, he could not exist in Lee's atmosphere; and I was never attended by a doctor again until I caught the smallpox in the epidemic of 1881. He took no interest in pictures or in any art but his own; and even in music his interest was limited to vocal music: I did not know that such things as string quartets or symphonies existed until I began, at sixteen, to investigate music for myself. Beethoven's sonatas and the classical operatic overtures were all I knew of what Wagner called absolute music. I should be tempted to say that none of us knew of the existence of Bach were it not that my mother sang My Heart Ever Faithful, the banjo like obbligato of which amused me very irreverently.

Lee was like all artists whose knowledge is solely a working knowledge: there were holes in his culture which I had to fill up for myself. Fortunately his richer pupils sometimes presented him with expensive illustrated books. He never opened them; but I did. He was so destitute of any literary bent that when he published a book entitled The Voice, it was written for him by a scamp of a derelict doctor whom he entertained for that purpose, just as in later years his prospectuses and press articles were written by me. He never visited the Dublin National Gallery, one of the finest collections of its size in Europe, with the usual full set of casts from what was called the antique, meaning ancient Greek sculpture. It was by prowling in this gallery that I learnt to recognize the work of the old masters at sight. I learnt French history from the novels of Dumas *père,* and English history from Shakespear and Walter Scott. Good boys were meanwhile learning lessons out of schoolbooks and receiving marks at examinations: a process which left them pious barbarians whilst I was acquiring an equipment which enabled me not only to pose as Corno di Bassetto when the chance arrived, but to add the criticism of pictures to the various strings I had to my bow as a feuilletonist.

Meanwhile nobody ever dreamt of teaching me anything. At fifteen, when the family broke up, I could neither play nor read a note of music.

My father did not die in the workhouse. In his last years he was left alone in Dublin by his wife and children for the very solid reason that he could not support them, and that life with him had absolutely no prospects for them. In doing so, they took off his shoulders a burden he was unable to bear and glad to discard, though he had given up drinking, and was now the most inoffensive of mortals. What he could do for them he did, which was to send them a pound a week until he died. Meanwhile he lived very comfortably in lodgings in the Appian Way (a highly respectable suburban residential quarter), much appreciated by his landlady, and in due time was gathered to his fathers in Mount Jerome Cemetery in the fullest Shavian gentility. I believe it was the happiest time of his life. No more Lee, no more wife, no more grown-up children. Towards the end, one or two newspaper cuttings and reviews convinced him that his son was going to achieve his father's somehow missed destiny and be "a great man."

. . . Lee's end was . . . tragic . . . . I do not know at what moment he began to deteriorate. He was a sober and moderate liver in all respects; and he was never ill until he treated himself to a tour in Italy and caught malaria there. He fought through it without a doctor on cold water, and returned apparently well; but whenever he worked too hard it came back and prostrated him for a day or two. Finally his ambition undid him. Dublin in those days seemed a hopeless place for an artist; for no success counted except a London success. The summit of a provincial conductor's destiny was to preside at a local musical festival modelled on the Three

Choirs or Handel Festivals. Lee declared that he would organize and conduct a Dublin Festival with his own chorus and with all the famous leading singers from the Italian opera in London. This he did in connection with an Exhibition in Dublin. My mother, of course, led the chorus. At a rehearsal the contralto, Madame de Meric Lablache, took exception to something and refused to sing. Lee shrugged his shoulders and asked my mother to carry on, which she did to such purpose that Madame Lablache took care not to give her another such chance.

At the Festivals Lee reached the Dublin limit of eminence. Nothing remained but London. He was assured that London meant a very modest beginning all over again, and perhaps something of an established position after fifteen years or so. Lee said that he would take a house in Park Lane, then the most exclusive and expensive thoroughfare in the west end, sacred to peers and millionaires, and—stupendous on the scale of Irish finance—make his pupils pay him a guinea a lesson. And this he actually did with a success that held out quite brilliantly for several seasons and then destroyed him. For whereas he had succeeded in Dublin by the sheer superiority of his method and talent and character, training his pupils honestly for a couple of years to sing beautifully and classically, he found that the London ladies who took him up so gushingly would have none of his beauty and classicism, and would listen to nothing less than a promise to make them sing "like Patti" in twelve lessons. It was that or starve.

He submitted perforce; but he was no longer the same man, the man to whom all circumstances seemed to give way, and who made his own musical world and reigned in it. He had even to change his name and his aspect. G. J. Lee, with the black whiskers and the clean shaven resolute lip and chin, became Vandeleur Lee, whiskerless, but with a waxed and pointed moustache and an obsequious attitude. It suddenly became evident that he was an elderly man, and, to those who had known him in Dublin, a humbug. Performances of Marchetti's Ruy Blas with my sister as the Queen of Spain, and later on of Sullivan's Patience and scraps of Faust and Il Trovatore were achieved; but musical society in London at last got tired of the damaged Svengali who could manufacture Pattis for twelve guineas; and the guineas ceased to come in. Still, as there were no night clubs in those days, it was possible to let a house in Park Lane for the night to groups of merrymakers; and Lee was holding out there without pupils when he asked me to draft a circular for him announcing that he could cure clergyman's sore throat. He was still at Park Lane when he dropped dead in the act of undressing himself, dying as he had lived, without a doctor. The postmortem and inquest revealed the fact that his brain was diseased and had been so for a long time.[1] I was glad to learn that his decay was pathological as well as ecological, and that the old efficient and honest Lee had been real after all. But I took to heart the lesson in the value of London fashionable successes. To this day I look to the provincial and the amateur for honesty and genuine fecundity in art.

Meanwhile, what had happened to the *ménage à trois?* and how did I turn up in Park Lane playing accompaniments and getting glimpses of that artstruck side of fashionable society which takes refuge in music from the routine of politics and sport which occupies the main Philistine body?

Well, when Lee got his foot in at a country house in Shropshire whither he had been invited to conduct some private performances, he sold the Dalkey cottage and concluded his tenancy of Hatch Street. This left us in a house which we could afford less than ever; for my father's moribund business was by now considerably deader than it had been at the date of my birth. My younger sister was dying of consumption caught from reckless contacts at a time when neither consumption nor pneumonia was regarded as catching. All that could be done was to recommend a change of climate. My elder sister had a beautiful voice. In the last of Lee's Dublin adventures in amateur opera she had appeared as Amina in Bellini's La Sonnambula, on which occasion the tenor lost his place and his head, and Lucy obligingly sang most of his part as well as her own. Unfortunately her musical endowment was so complete that it cost her no effort to sing or play anything she had once heard, or to read any music at sight. She simply could not associate the idea of real work with music; and as in any case she had never received any sort of training, her very facility prevented her from becoming a serious artist, though, as she could sing difficult music without breaking her voice, she got through a considerable share of public singing in her time.

Now neither my mother nor any of us knew how much more is needed for an opera singer than a voice and natural musicianship. It seemed to us that as, after a rehearsal or two, she could walk on to the stage, wave her arms about in the absurd manner then in vogue in opera, and sing not only her own part but everybody else's as well, she was quite qualified to take the place of Christine Nilsson or Adelina Patti if only she could get a proper introduction. And clearly Lee, now in the first flush of his success in Park Lane, would easily be able to secure this for her.

There was another resource. My now elderly mother believed that she could renounce her amateur status and make a living in London by teaching singing. Had she not the infallible Method to impart? So she realized a little of the scrap of settled property of which her long deceased aunt had not been able to deprive her; sold the Hatch Street furniture; settled my father and myself in comfortable lodgings at 61 Harcourt St; and took my sisters to the Isle of Wight, where the younger one died. She then took a semi-detached villa in a *cul-de-sac* off the Fulham Road, and waited there for Lucy's plans and her own to materialize.

The result was almost a worse disillusion than her marriage. That had been cured by Lee's music: besides, my father had at last realized his dream of being a practising teetotaller, and was now as inoffensive an old gentleman as any elderly wife could desire. It was characteristic of the Shavian drink neurosis to vanish suddenly in this way. But that Lee should be unfaithful! unfaithful to The Method! that he, the one genuine teacher among so many quacks, should now stoop to outquack them all and become a moustachioed charlatan with all the virtue gone out of him: this was the end of all things; and she never forgave it. She was not unkind: she tolerated Lee the charlatan as she had tolerated Shaw the dipsomaniac because, as I guess, her early motherless privation of affection and her many disappointments in other people had thrown her back on her own considerable internal resources and developed her self-sufficiency and power of solitude to an extent which kept her up under circumstances that would have crushed or embittered any woman who was the least bit of a clinger. She dropped Lee very gently: at first he came and went at Victoria Grove, Fulham Road; and she went and came at 13 Park Lane, helping with the music there at his At Homes, and even singing the part of Donna Anna for him (elderly prima donnas were then tolerated as matters of course) at an amateur performance of Don Giovanni. But my sister, who had quarrelled with him as a child when he tried to give her piano lessons, and had never liked him, could not bear him at all in his new phase, and, when she found that he could not really advance her prospects of becoming a prima donna, broke with him completely and made it difficult for him to continue his visits.[2] When he died we had not seen him for some years; and my mother did not display the slightest emotion at the news. He had been dead for her ever since he had ceased to be an honest teacher of singing and a mesmeric conductor.

Her plans for herself came almost to nothing for several years. She found that Englishwomen do not wish to be made to sing beautifully and classically: they want to sing erotically; and this my mother thought not only horrible but unladylike. Her love songs were those of Virginia Gabriel and Arthur Sullivan, all about bereaved lovers and ending with a hope for reunion in the next world. She could sing with perfect purity of tone and touching expression

> *Oh, Ruby, my darling, the small white hand*
> *Which gathered the harebell was never my own.*

But if you had been able to anticipate the grand march of human progress and poetic feeling by fifty years, and asked her to sing

> *You made me love you.*
> *I didnt want to do it.*
> *I didnt want to do it,*

she would have asked a policeman to remove you to a third-class carriage.

Besides, though my mother was not consciously a snob, the divinity which hedged an Irish lady of her period was not acceptable to the British suburban parents, all snobs, who were within her reach. They liked to be treated with deference; and it never occurred to my mother that such people could entertain a pretension so monstrous in her case. Her practice with private pupils was negligible until she was asked to become musical instructress at the North London College. Her success was immediate; for not only did her classes leave the other schools nowhere musically, but the divinity aforesaid exactly suited her new rôle as schoolmistress. Other schools soon sought her services; and she remained in request until she insisted on retiring on the ground that her age made her public appearances ridiculous. By that time all the old money troubles were over and forgotten, as my financial position enabled me to make her perfectly comfortable in that respect.

And now, what about myself, the incipient Corno di Bassetto? Well, when my mother sold the Hatch Street furniture, it never occurred to her to sell our piano, though I could not play it, nor could my father. We did not realize, nor did she, that she was never coming back, and that, except for a few days when my father, taking a little holiday for the first time in his life within my experience, came to see us in London, she would never meet him again. Family revolutions would seldom be faced if they did not present themselves at first as temporary makeshifts. Accordingly, having lived since my childhood in a house full of music, I suddenly found myself in a house where there was no music, and could be none unless I made it myself.

. . . I learnt my notes at the age of sixteen or thereabouts; and since that time I have inflicted untold suffering on my neighbors without having on a single occasion given the smallest pleasure to any human being except myself. Then, it will be asked, Why did I begin? Well, the motive arose from my previous knowledge of music. I had been accustomed all my life to hear it in sufficing quantities; and the melodies I heard I could at least sing; so that I neither had nor desired any technical knowledge. But it happened one day that my circumstances changed, so that I heard no more music. It was in vain now to sing: my native woodnotes wild—just then breaking frightfully—could not satisfy my intense craving for the harmony which is the emotional substance of music, and for the rhythmic figures of accompaniment which are its action and movement. I had only a single splintering voice; and I wanted an orchestra. This musical starvation it was that drove me to disregard the rights of my fellow lodgers and go to the piano. I learnt the alphabet of musical notation from a primer, and the keyboard from a diagram. Then, without troubling Czerny or Plaidy, I opened . . . the overture to Don Giovanni, thinking rightly that I had better start with something I knew well enough to hear whether my fingers were on the right notes or not.

. . . It took ten minutes to get my fingers arranged on the chord of D minor with which the overture commences; but when it sounded right at last, it was worth all the trouble it cost. At the end of some months I had acquired a technique of my own . . . .

. . . I soon acquired a terrible power of stumbling through pianoforte arrangements and vocal scores; and my reward was that I gained penetrating experiences of Victor Hugo and Schiller from Donizetti, Verdi, and Beethoven; of the Bible from Handel; of Goethe from Schumann; of Beaumarchais and Molière from Mozart; and of Mérimée from Bizet, besides finding in Berlioz an unconscious interpreter of Edgar Allan Poe. When I was in the schoolboy-adventure vein, I could range from Vincent Wallace to Meyerbeer; and if I felt piously and genteelly sentimental, I, who could not stand the pictures of Ary Scheffer or the genteel suburban sentiment of Tennyson and Longfellow, could become quite maudlin over Mendelssohn and Gounod. And, as I searched all the music I came across for the sake of its poetic or dramatic content, and played the pages in which I found drama or poetry over and over again, whilst I never returned to those in which the music was trying to exist ornamentally for its own sake and had no real content at all, it followed that when I came across the consciously perfect art work in the music dramas of Wagner, I ran no risk of hopelessly misunderstanding it as the academic musicians did. Indeed, I soon found that they equally misunderstood Mozart and Beethoven, though, having come to like their tunes and harmonies, and to understand their mere carpentry, they pointed out what they supposed to be their merits with an erroneousness far more fatal to their unfortunate pupils than the volley of half-bricks with which they greeted Wagner (who, it must be confessed, retaliated with a volley of whole ones fearfully well aimed).

. . . There were plenty of vocal scores of operas and oratorios in our lodging; and although I never acquired any technical skill as a pianist, and cannot to this day play a scale with any certainty of not foozling it, I acquired what I wanted: the power to take a vocal score and learn its contents as if I had heard it rehearsed by my mother and her colleagues. I could manage arrangements of orchestral music much better than piano music proper. At last I could play the old rum-tum accompaniments of those days well enough (knowing how they *should* be played) to be more agreeable to singers than many really competent pianists. I bought more scores, among them one of Lohengrin, through which I made the revolutionary discovery of Wagner. I bought arrangements of Beethoven's symphonies, and discovered the musical regions that lie outside opera and oratorio. Later on, I was forced to learn to play the classical symphonies and overtures in strict time by hammering the bass in piano duets with my sister in London. I played Bach's Inventions and his Art of Fugue. I studied academic textbooks, and actually worked out exercises in harmony and counterpoint under supervision by an organist friend named Crament, avoiding consecutive fifths and octaves, and having not the faintest notion of what the result would sound like. I read pseudo-scientific treatises about the roots of chords which candidates for the degree of Mus.Doc. at the universities had to swallow, and learnt that Stainer's commonsense views would get you plucked at Oxford, and Ouseley's pedantries at Cambridge. I read Mozart's Succinct Thoroughbass (a scrap of paper with some helpful tips on it which he scrawled for his pupil Sussmaier); and this, many years later, Edward Elgar told me was the only document in existence of the smallest use to a student composer. It was, I grieve to say, of no use to me; but then I was not a young composer. . . .

When I look back on all the banging, whistling, roaring, and growling inflicted on nervous neighbors during this process of education, I am consumed with useless remorse. But what else could I have done? . . . When, after my five years office slavery, I joined my mother in London and lived with her for twenty years until my marriage, I used to drive her nearly crazy by my favorite selections from Wagner's Ring, which to her was "all recitative," and horribly discordant at that. She never complained at the time, but confessed it after we separated, and said that she had sometimes gone away to cry. . . . But . . . my business here is to account for my proposal to Tay Pay and my creation of Bassetto.

In 1888, I being then 32 and already a noted critic and political agitator, the Star newspaper was founded under the editorship of the late T. P. O'Connor (nicknamed Tay Pay by Yates), who had for his very much more competent assistant the late H. W. Massingham. . . .

Sometime in the eighteen-eighties I became conscious of H. W. Massingham in the journalistic world. . . . We occasionally made Sunday morning excursions of a kind then in vogue among journalists. They had a double object: first, to walk four miles from home and thus become *bona fide* travellers in the legal sense, entitled to obtain drinks as such, and, second, to buy a copy of The Observer. This was pure tradition; for I was a teetotaller; and Massingham, though convivial enough, was no toper. I only once saw him intoxicated (drunk is hardly the word); and then he was in the wildest high spirits, and had to be restrained from dropping over the bannisters in his soaring disdain for the stairs. But this was at one of those dreadful men's dinner parties at which all the guests get drunk to save themselves from going melancholy mad.

As to The Observer, it was very different then from the Garvinian Observer. . . . It cost fourpence; and its sale was a superstition from the Franco-Prussian war of 1870–71, when, as it happened, some big battles were fought at the end of the week. The Observer had a good foreign news service, and thus made itself indispensable on Sunday to all journalists, and in all the clubs and country houses and rectories where political news still meant diplomatic and military news. The habit thus established persisted; so that long after the Franco-Prussian war had faded into a reminiscence of our boyhood Massingham would solemnly waste fourpence every Sunday morning on The Observer when any of the penny weeklies would have served him better. The revival of The Observer by Mr. Garvin after some rather desperate vicissitudes is one of the great journalistic feats of our time.

During one of these walks Massingham told me the story of his brother's startling end. He regarded this as something that he never spoke of to anybody; and he soon forgot having spoken of it to me. All men have certain sacred subjects which they firmly believe they never mention to a living soul, though as a matter of fact they mention them sooner or later to their more intimate and congenial friends. Some time afterwards I made unscrupulous use of this confidence at a bogus spiritualistic séance to which I treated a friend of ours with whom we were spending a week-end. He had expressed himself so contemptuously about people who believed in such things that I thought it allowable to demonstrate to him that he himself could be taken in with the utmost ease. One of my earliest steps in the demonstration was to call up a spirit who, after admitting that he was a relative of someone present, gradually eliminated, question by question, myself, our host, and every possible relationship except that of brother to Massingham, who was so visibly and unmistakably upset by this communication that I was rather shocked by the success of my own trick. As to our host, it was impossible for him, after seeing Massingham change color as he did, to doubt his entire good faith; and this was his undoing; for when, as usually happens, he made Massingham hold me hand and foot on one side whilst he did the same on the other, the rappings and other phenomena proceeded as impressively as ever. Of course what happened was what always happens on these occasions. I took Massingham into my confidence without a word by working away with the foot he was supposed to be holding down; and he, much relieved and enormously amused, threw himself ecstatically into the game, and was presently treating our host to manifestations on which I should never have ventured. All professional mediums know that if they can only get hold of one of these stories that the teller regards as never told, and his friends nevertheless know by heart, they need not be afraid of the amateur detectives he will set on them, as none of them ever resist the temptation to become confederates. . . .

. . . Tay Pay survived until 1936; but his mind never advanced beyond the year 1865, though his Fenian sympathies and his hearty detestation of the English nation disguised that defect from him. Massingham induced him to invite me to join the political staff of his paper; but as I had already, fourteen years before Lenin, read Karl Marx, and was preaching Socialism at every street corner or other available forum in London and the provinces, the effect of my articles on Tay Pay may be imagined. He refused to print them, and told me that, man alive, it would be five hundred years before such stuff would become practical political journalism. He was too goodnatured to sack me; and I did not want to throw away my job; [3] so I got him out of his difficulty by asking him to let me have two columns a week for a feuilleton on music. He was glad to get rid of my politics on these terms; but he stipulated that—musical criticism being known to him only as unreadable and unintelligible jargon—I should, for God's sake, not write about Bach in B Minor. I was quite alive to that danger: in fact I had made my proposal because I believed I could make musical criticism readable even by the deaf. Besides, my terms were moderate: two guineas a week.

. . . My proposal to turn my attention to musical criticism was hailed with inexpressible relief, the subject being one in which lunacy is privileged. I was given a column to myself precisely as I might have been given a padded room in an asylum; and from that time up to . . . [1894]—a period of nearly seven years—I wrote every week, in that paper or another, an article under the general heading "Music," the first condition of which was, as a matter of good journalism, that it should be as attractive to the general reader, musician or non-musician, as any other section of the paper in which it appeared. Most editors do not believe that this can be done. But then most editors do not know how to edit.

I was strong on the need for signed criticism written in the first person instead of the journalistic "we"; but as I then had no name worth signing, and G.B.S. meant nothing to the public, I had to invent a fantastic personality with something like a foreign title. I thought of Count di Luna (a character in Verdi's Trovatore), but finally changed it for Corno di Bassetto, as it sounded like a foreign title, and nobody knew what a corno di bassetto was.

As a matter of fact the corno di bassetto is not a foreigner with a title but a musical instrument called in English the basset horn. It is a wretched instrument, now completely snuffed out for general use by the bass clarionet. It would be forgotten and unplayed if it were not that Mozart has scored for it in his Requiem, evidently because its peculiar watery melancholy, and the total absence of any richness or passion in its tone, is just the thing for a funeral. Mendelssohn wrote some chamber music for it, presumably to oblige somebody who played it; and it is kept alive by these works and by our Mr Whall. If I had ever heard a note of it in 1888 I should not have selected it for a character which I intended to be sparkling. The devil himself could not make a basset horn sparkle.

10

"Corno di Bassetto"

ON MONDAY the editor of The Star summoned me to a private conference. "The fact is, my dear Corno," he said, throwing himself back in his chair and arranging his moustache with the diamond which sparkles at the end of his pen-handle, "I dont believe that music in London is confined to St James's Hall, Covent Garden, and the Albert Hall. People must sing and play elsewhere. Whenever I go down to speak at the big Town Halls at Shoreditch, Hackney, Stratford, Holborn, Kensington, Battersea, and deuce knows where, I always see bills at the door announcing oratorios, organ recitals, concerts by local Philharmonic and Orpheus societies, and all sorts of musical games. Why not criticise these instead of saying the same thing over and over again about Henschel and Richter and Norman Neruda and the rest?" I replied, as best I could, that my experience as a musical critic had left me entirely unacquainted with these outlandish localities and their barbarous minstrelsy; that I regarded London as bounded on the extreme north-east by Stonecutter Street,[1] on the extreme south-west by Kensington Gore, on the south by the Thames, and on the north by the Strand and Regent-street. He assured me that the places he had mentioned actually existed; but that, as I was evidently hurt by the suggestion that I should condescend to visit them, he would hand the ticket he had just received for a Purcell-Handel performance at Bow, to Musigena.[2] "What!" I exclaimed, "Purcell! the greatest of English composers, left to Musigena! to a man whose abnormal gifts in every other direction have blinded him to his utter ignorance of music!" "Well, the fact is" said the editor "Musigena told me only half an hour ago that he was at a loss to imagine how a writer so profound and accomplished as di Bassetto could be in music a mere superficial amateur." I waited to hear no more. Snatching the tickets from the editor's desk, I hastily ran home to get my revolver as a precaution during my hazardous voyage to the east end. Then I dashed away to Broad-street, and asked the booking-clerk whether he knew of a place called Bow. He was evidently a man of extraordinary nerve, for he handed me a ticket without any sign of surprise, as if a voyage to Bow were the most commonplace event possible. A little later the train was rushing through the strangest places: Shoreditch, of which I had read in historical novels; Old Ford, which I had supposed to be a character in one of Shakespeare's plays; Homerton, which is somehow associated in my mind with pigeons; and Haggerston, a name perfectly new to me. When I got into the concert-room I was perfectly dazzled by the appearance of the orchestra. Nearly all the desks for the second violins were occupied by ladies: beautiful young ladies. Personal beauty is not the strong point of West-end orchestras, and I thought the change an immense improvement until the performance began, when the fair fiddlers rambled from bar to bar with a certain sweet indecision that had a charm of its own, but was not exactly what Purcell and Handel meant. When I say that the performance began, I do not imply that it began punctually. The musicians began to drop in at about ten minutes past eight, and the audience were inclined to remonstrate; but an occasional apology from the conductor, Mr F. A. W. Docker, kept them in good humor. . . . At the end of the concert, a gentleman, to my entire stupefaction, came forward and moved a vote of thanks to the performers. It was passed by acclamation, but without musical honors.

. . . Tuesday, when, turning over my invitations, I found a card addressed to me, not in my ancestral title of Di Bassetto, but in the assumed name under which I conceal my identity in the vulgar business of life. It invited me to repair to a High School for Girls in a healthy south-western suburb, there to celebrate the annual prize-giving with girlish song and recitation. Here was exactly the thing for a critic. "Now is the time," I exclaimed to my astonished colleagues, "to escape from the stale iterations of how Mr Santley sang The Erl King, and Mr Sims Reeves Tom Bowling; of how the same old orchestra played Beethoven in C minor or accompanied Mr Henschel in Pogner's Johannistag song or Wotan's farewell and fire charm. Our business is to look with prophetic eye past these exhausted contemporary subjects into the next generation—to find out how much beauty and artistic feeling is growing up for the time when we shall be obsolete fogies, mumbling anecdotes at the funerals of our favorites." Will it be credited that the sanity of my project and the good taste of my remarks were called in question, and that I was absolutely the only eminent critic who went to the school!

I found the school on the margin of a common, with which I have one ineffaceable association. It is not my custom to confine my critical opinions to the columns of the Press. In my public place I am ever ready to address my fellow-citizens orally until the police interfere. Now it happens that once, on a fine Sunday afternoon, I addressed a crowd on this very common for an hour, at the expiry of which a friend took round a hat, and actually collected 16s. 9d. The opulence and liberality of the inhabitants were thus very forcibly impressed on me; and when, last Tuesday, I made my way through a long corridor into the crowded schoolroom, my first thought as I surveyed the row of parents, was whether any of them had been among the contributors to that memorable hatful of coin. My second was whether the principal of the school would have been pleased to see me had she known about the 16s. 9d.

When the sensation caused by my entrance had subsided somewhat, we settled down to a performance which consisted of music and recitation by the rising generation, and speechification by the risen one. The rising generation had the best of it. Whenever the girls did anything, we were all delighted: whenever an adult began, we were bored to the very verge of possible endurance. The deplorable member of Parliament who gave away the prizes may be eloquent in the House of Commons; but before that eager, keen, bright, frank, unbedevilled, unsophisticated audience he quailed, he maundered, he stumbled, wanted to go on and couldnt, wanted to stop and didnt, and finally collapsed in the assuring us emotionally that he felt proud of himself, which struck me as being the most uncalled-for remark I ever heard, even from an M.P. The chairman was self-possessed, not to say hardened. He quoted statistics about Latin, arithmetic, and other sordid absurdities, specially extolling the aptitude of the female mind since 1868 for botany. I incited a little girl near me to call out "Time" and "Question," but she shook her head shyly and said "Miss — would be angry"; so he had his say out. Let him deliver that speech next Sunday on the common, and he will not collect 16s. 9d. He will be stoned.

. . . We were much entertained . . . but let it suffice to add that when God save the Queen was sung, the substitution of two quavers for the triplet at the beginning of the last line so completely spoiled it that I instantly suspected the headmistress of being a Fenian. She was a slender, elegant lady, who somehow reminded me of Mrs Kendal in Coralie; and there was certainly nothing revolutionary in her aspect. . . . I hurried back by the common, with a fine driving snow dispelling all chance of an impromptu repetition of the sixteen-and-ninepenny experiment . . . .

. . . Wednesday I was told that Siegfried was to be produced that evening at Covent Garden. I was incredulous, and asked my informant whether he did not mean Carmen, with Miss Zélie de Lussan in the title part. He said he thought not. I suggested Faust, Les Huguenots, even Die Meistersinger; but he stuck to his story: Siegfried, he said, was really and truly in the bills, and the house was sold out. Still doubting, I went to the box-office, where they confirmed the intelligence, except that they had just one stall left. I took it, and went away wondering and only half convinced. But when I reached the theatre in the evening a little late, fully expecting to find notices on the seats to the effect that Siegfried was unavoidably postponed, in consequence of the sudden indisposition of the dragon, and Philémon and Cavalleria substituted, I found the lights out and the belated stall-holders wandering like ghosts through the gloom in search of their numbers, helped only by the glimmer from the huge orchestra and some faint daylight from the ventilators.

The darkness was audible as well as visible; for there was no mistaking that cavernous music, with the tubas lowing like Plutonian bullocks, Mime's hammer rapping weirdly, and the drums muttering the subterranean thunder of Nibelheim. And before I left the house—to be exact, it was at half-past twelve next morning—I actually saw Rosa Sucher and Sir Augustus Harris hand in hand before the curtain, looking as if Covent Garden had been the birthplace of her reputation, and as if he had never heard La Favorita in his life. Perhaps it was all a dream; but it seemed real to me, and does so still. Assuming that I was awake, I may claim that at least one of those curtain-calls was not for the manager at all, but for me and for those colleagues of mine who so strongly urged Sir Augustus Harris to try this experiment in the golden years . . . .

I remember once coming to loggerheads [3] with the late Dr Francis Hueffer, about fifteen seconds after the opening of our first conversation, on the subject of musical culture in English society. Whenever the subject arose between us, I declared that English society did not care about music—did not know good music from bad. He replied, with great force, that I knew nothing about it; that nobody had ever seen me in really decent society; that I moved amidst cranks, Bohemians, unbelievers, agitators, and—generally speaking—riff-raff of all sorts; and that I was merely theorising emptily about the people whom I called bloated aristocrats. He described, by way of example, an evening at Lord Derby's house, where he had greatly enjoyed some excellent music; and he asked me whether I knew that such music was, in a quiet way, a constant grace of the best sort of English social life. I suggested that he should give me an opportunity to judge for myself by introducing me to these circles; but this he entirely declined to do; having no confidence whatever in my power of behaving myself in a seemly manner for five consecutive minutes.

On the first occasion it so happened, fortunately for me, that a firm of music publishers, having resolved to venture on the desperate step of publishing six new pianoforte sonatas, had just sent out a circular containing an appeal *ad misericordiam* that at least a few people would, either in public spirit or charity, take the unprecedented step of buying these compositions. I promptly hurled this at Hueffer's head, and asked whether that looked like evidence of a constant and enlightened patronage such as the upper classes accord to racing, millinery, confectionery, and in a minor degree to literature and painting (for, hang it all! even if the sonatas were not as good as Beethoven's, they were at any rate no duller than the average three-volume novel or Academy picture). There the subject dropped, my method of controversy being at that time crudely unscrupulous and extravagant. Hueffer, I fancy, regarded me as an unschooled dangerous character; but once, when I was perched on the gunwale of a wagon in Hyde Park, filling up some ten minutes of a "demonstration" with the insufferable oratorizing which is the only sort feasible on such occasions, I was astonished to see his long golden beard and massive brow well to the front among the millions of "friends and fellow citizens." He never told me what he thought about the contrast between the new musical criticism demonstrating on wagons in the sunlight, and the old, groping in perpetual evening dress from St James's Hall to Covent Garden Opera House and back again.

The other evening, feeling rather in want of a headache, I bethought me that I had not been to a music-hall for a long time. One of the horrors of a critic's life is his almost nightly suffering from lack of ventilation.

Now when to the ordinary products of respiration are added the smoke of hundreds of cigarets and of the hundreds of holes which the discarded ends of them are burning in the rather stale carpets, the effect on a professionally sensitive person who does not smoke is indescribably noxious.

The privilege of smoking and burning the carpets is supposed to make the music-hall more comfortable than the theatre. Also, no doubt, the rousing explosions of cornet, trombone, and sidedrum every twenty seconds or so, help to reassure the audience as to the suspension of all usages based on a recognition of the fact that some superfine people are almost as particular about the sounds they hear and the air they breathe as about the opinion of their next-door neighbors as to their respectability.

I foresee the day when our habit of sitting for two and a half hours at a stretch in St James's Hall or in a theatre, breathing air that is utterly unfit for human consumption, and that becomes steadily worse and worse as the evening wears on, will seem as sluttish—there is really no other adequate expression—as we now consider those habits of the spacious times of great Elizabeth which startle us in Much Ado About Nothing, when Claudio remarks of Benedick, "And when [before he fell in love] was he wont to wash his face?"

Well, I went to a music-hall, where I got a comfortable seat at a reasonable price as compared with theatre accommodation, and where I also got my headache, a thoroughly satisfactory one, which lasted all the next day, and was worth the money by itself alone. For once I resisted the attraction of Cavallazzi and Vincenti at the Empire, and went to the Alhambra instead, curious as to whether that institution still maintained its ancient glories as a temple of the ballet.

I found it much the same as ever. The veteran Jacobi was still there, monarchical as *chef d'orchestre,* bold, ingenious, and amazingly copious as composer of dance music. The danseuses were still trying to give some freshness to the half-dozen *pas* of which every possible combination and permutation has been worn to death any time these hundred years, still calling each hopeless attempt a "variation," and still finishing up with the teetotum spin which is to the dancer what the high note at the end of a dull song is to a second-rate singer. I wonder is there anything on earth as stupid as what I may call, in the Wagnerian terminology, "absolute dancing"! Sisyphus trying to get uphill with the stone that always rolls down again must have a fairly enjoyable life compared with a ballet-master.

On the whole, it might easily have been made much more amusing.

Unfortunately, when you get thoroughly "popular" audiences, you may always expect to have to endure a mass of academic pedantry which no really cultivated audience would tolerate for a moment. Your ordinary Englishman is scandalized by anything that interests or amuses him: his criterion of a firstrate entertainment, after he is satisfied as to the splendor of its appearance, is that he shall not understand it and that it shall bore him. His recompense for the tedium of the artistic or *in*side of it is the intense unreality of its outside. For it must not be supposed that the poets and artists are the romantic people, and their readers and audiences the matter-of-fact people. On the contrary, it is the poets and artists who spend their lives in trying to make the unreal real; whereas the ordinary man's life-struggle is to escape from reality, to avoid all avoidable facts and deceive himself as to the real nature of those which he cannot avoid.

No fact is ever attended to by the average citizen until the neglect of it has killed enough of his neighbors to thoroughly frighten him. He does not believe that happiness exists except in dreams; and when by chance he dreams of his real life, he feels defrauded, as if he had been cheated into night-work by his employer or his clients. Hence the more unnatural, impossible, unreasonable, and morally fraudulent a theatrical entertainment is, the better he likes it. He abhors the play with a purpose, because it says to him, "Here, sir, is a fact which you ought to attend to." This, however, produces the happy result that the great dramatic poets, who are all incorrigible moralists and preachers, are forced to produce plays of extraordinary interest in order to induce our audiences of shirkers and dreamers to swallow the pill.

When I arrived at my door after these dissipations I found Fitzroy Square, in which I live, deserted. It was a clear, dry cold night; and the carriage way round the circular railing presented such a magnificent hippodrome that I could not resist trying to go just once round in Vincenti's fashion. It proved frightfully difficult. After my fourteenth fall I was picked up by a policeman. "What are you doing here?" he said, keeping fast hold of me. "I'bin watching you for the last five minutes." I explained, eloquently and enthusiastically. He hesitated a moment, and then said, "Would you mind holding my helmet while I have a try. It dont look so hard." Next moment his nose was buried in the macadam and his right knee was out through its torn garment. He got up bruised and bleeding, but resolute. "I never was beaten yet" he said; "and I wont be beaten now. It was my coat that tripped me." We both hung our coats on the railings, and went at it again. If each round of the square had been a round in a prize fight, we should have been less damaged and disfigured; but we persevered, and by four o'clock the policeman had just succeeded in getting round twice without a rest or a fall, when an inspector arrived and asked him bitterly whether that was his notion of fixed point duty. "I allow it aint fixed point" said the constable, emboldened by his new accomplishment; "but I'll lay a half sovereign *you* cant do it." The inspector could not resist the temptation to try (I was whirling round before his eyes in the most fascinating manner); and he made rapid progress after half an hour or so. We were subsequently joined by an early postman and by a milkman, who unfortunately broke his leg and had to be carried to hospital by the other three. By that time I was quite exhausted, and could barely crawl into bed. It was perhaps a foolish scene; but nobody who has witnessed Vincenti's performance will feel surprised at it.

. . . During one of my East End expeditions, I discovered the People's Palace, which consists of a board with an inscription to the effect that if I choose to produce £50,000, the palace will be built for me forthwith. This rather took me aback; for I had thought that the palace was an accomplished fact. But no: there was a huge concert-room, a reading-room, and shanties containing a bath, a gymnasium, and a restaurant; also a little clubhouse, but no palace. In the concert-room some unfortunate artists were bawling ballads in the vain hope of fixing the attention of an immense audience. But the thing was impossible: the place was too big. Hundreds of young people loafed and larked, or stared and wandered in and out . . . .

From the People's Palace I went to the Bow and Bromley Institute. There I found a sixpenny and threepenny audience, of discouragingly middle-class aspect, listening to M. Gigout, who was performing on the "kist o' whustles" which is the pride of the Institute. Presently came Madame Belle Cole, a robust lady with an extraordinary voice and an effective adaptation of the style of Madame Antoinette Sterling. She sang Gounod's Entreat me not to Leave Thee to such purpose that the audience, instead of entreating her to leave them, insisted on her singing again, whereupon she gave Home, sweet Home. The next artist that turned up was Henry Seiffert, the Dutch violinist, whose breadth of tone and command of his instrument completely confirmed the very favorable opinion I formed of him when he first played in London. The audience clamored for an encore; but a gentleman came forward in the midst of the hubbub, and when his evident wish to speak had produced a breathless and expectant silence, said he wanted somebody to give a theme for M. Gigout to improvize upon. This simply struck us dumb. Then he smiled reassuringly, and his eye began to travel slowly along the bench where I sat. Ere it reached my vacant chair I was safe on the roof of an Aldgate tram.

On Friday evening . . . I went to the Wind Instrument Society's concert at the Royal Academy of Music in Tenterden-street. Having only just heard of the affair from an acquaintance, I had no ticket. The concert, as usual, had been kept dark from me: Bassetto the Incorruptible knows too much to be welcome to any but the greatest artists. I therefore presented myself at the doors for admission on payment as a casual amateur. Apparently the wildest imaginings of the Wind Instrument Society had not reached to such a contingency as a Londoner offering money at the doors to hear classical chamber music played upon bassoons, clarionets, and horns; for I was told that it was impossible to entertain my application, as the building had no license. I suggested sending out for a license; but this, for some technical reason, could not be done. I offered to dispense with the license; but that, they said, would expose them to penal servitude. Perceiving by this that it was a mere question of breaking the law, I insisted on the secretary accompanying me to the residence of a distinguished Q.C. in the neighbourhood, and ascertaining from him how to do it. The Q.C. said that if I handed the secretary five shillings at the door in consideration of being admitted to the concert, that would be illegal. But if I bought a ticket from him in the street, that would be legal. Or if I presented him with five shillings in remembrance of his last birthday, and he gave me a free admission in celebration of my silver wedding, that would be legal. Or if we broke the law without witnesses and were prepared to perjure ourselves if questioned afterwards (which seemed to me the most natural way), then nothing could happen to us.

I cannot without breach of faith explain which course we adopted: suffice it that I was present at the concert. . . .

On our way back to Victoria, a signal stopped our train in the snow, and when it fell the engine gasped and refused to budge. At last another train overtook us, and butted us into Clapham . . . .

On cold Saturday afternoons in winter, as I sit in the theatrical desert, making my bread with great bitterness by chronicling insignificant plays and criticizing incompetent players, it sometimes comes upon me that I have forgotten something—omitted something—missed some all-important appointment. This is a legacy from my old occupation of musical critic. All my old occupations leave me such legacies. When I was in my teens I had certain official duties to perform, which involved every day the very strict and punctual discharge of certain annual payments, which were set down in a perpetual diary. I sometimes dream now that I am back at those duties again, but with an amazed consciousness of having allowed them to fall into ruinous arrear for a long time past. My Saturday afternoon misgivings are just like that. They mean that for several years I passed those afternoons in that section of the gallery of the Crystal Palace concert-room which is sacred to Sir George Grove[4] and to the Press. There were two people there who never grew older—Beethoven and Sir George. August Manns' hair changed from raven black to swan white as the years passed; young critics grew middle-aged and middle-aged critics grew old; Rossini lost caste and was shouldered into the promenade; the fire-new overture to Tannhäuser began to wear as threadbare as William Tell: Arabella Goddard went and Sophie Menter came; Joachim, Hallé, Norman Neruda, and Santley no longer struck the rising generations with the old sense of belonging to tomorrow, like Ysaye, Paderewski, and Bispham; the men whom I had shocked as an iconoclastic upstart Wagnerian, braying derisively when they observed that "the second subject, appearing in the key of the dominant, contrasts effectively with its predecessor, not only in tonality, but by its suave, melodious character," lived to see me shocked and wounded in my turn by the audacities of J. F. Runciman; new evening papers launched into musical criticism, and were read publicly by Mr Smith, the eminent drummer, whenever he had fifty bars rest; a hundred trifles marked the flight of time; but Sir George Grove fed on Beethoven's symphonies as the gods in Das Rheingold fed on the apples of Freia, and grew no older. Sometimes, when Mendelssohn's Scotch symphony, or Schubert's Ninth in C, were in the program, he got positively younger, clearing ten years backward in as many minutes when Manns and the band were at their best. I remonstrated with him more than once on this unnatural conduct; and he was always extremely apologetic, assuring me that he was getting on as fast as he could. He even succeeded in producing a wrinkle or two under stress of Berlioz and Raff, Liszt and Wagner; but presently some pianist would come along with the concerto in E flat; and then, if I sat next him, strangers would say to me "Your son, sir, appears to be a very enthusiastic musician." And I could not very well explain that the real bond between us was the fact that Beethoven never ceased to grow on us. In my personality, my views, and my style of criticism there was so much to forgive that many highly amiable persons never quite succeeded in doing it. To Sir George I must have been a positively obnoxious person, not in the least because I was on the extreme left in politics and other matters, but because I openly declared that the finale of Schubert's symphony in C could have been done at half the length and with twice the effect by Rossini. But I knew Beethoven's symphonies from the opening bar of the first to the final chord of the ninth, and yet made new discoveries about them at every fresh performance. And I am convinced that "G" regarded this as evidence of a fundamental rectitude in me which would bear any quantity of superficial aberrations. Which is quite my own opinion too.

. . . Saturday evening, feeling the worse for want of change and country air, I happened to voyage in the company of Mr William Archer as far as Greenwich. Hardly had we inhaled the refreshing ozone of that place for ninety seconds when, suddenly finding ourselves opposite a palatial theatre, gorgeous with a million gaslights, we felt that it was idiotic to have been to Wagner's Theatre at Bayreuth and yet be utterly ignorant concerning Morton's Theatre at Greenwich. So we rushed into the struggling crowd at the doors, only to be informed that the theatre was full. Stalls full; dress circle full; pit, standing room only. As Archer, in self-defence, habitually sleeps during performances, and is subject to nightmare when he sleeps standing, the pit was out of the question. Was there room anywhere, we asked. Yes, in a private box or in the gallery. Which was the cheaper? The gallery, decidedly. So up we went to the gallery, where we found two precarious perches vacant at the side. It was rather like trying to see Trafalgar Square from the knifeboard of an omnibus half-way up St Martin's Lane; but by hanging on to a stanchion, and occasionally standing with one foot on the seat and the other on the backs of the people in the front row, we succeeded in seeing as much of the entertainment as we could stand.

The first thing we did was to purchase a bill; which informed us that we were in for "the entirely original pastoral comedy-opera in three acts, by B. C. Stephenson and Alfred Cellier, entitled Dorothy, which has been played to crowded houses at the Lyric Theatre, London, 950 and (still playing) in the provinces 788 times." This playbill, I should add, was thoughtfully decorated with a view of the theatre showing all the exits, for use in the event of the performance proving unbearable. From it we further learnt that we should be regaled by an augmented and powerful orchestra; that the company was "Leslie's No. I"; that C. J. Francis believes he is now the only HATTER in the county of Kent who exists on the profits arising solely from the sale of HATS and CAPS; and so on. Need I add that Archer and I sat bursting with expectation until the overture began.

I cannot truthfully say that the augmented and powerful orchestra proved quite so augmented or so powerful as the composer could have wished; but let that pass: I disdain the cheap sport of breaking a daddy-long-legs on a wheel (butterfly is out of the question, it was such a dingy band). My object is rather to call attention to the condition to which 788 nights of Dorothying have reduced the unfortunate wanderers known as "Leslie's No. I." I submit to Mr Leslie that in his own interest he should take better care of No. I. Here are several young persons doomed to spend the flower of their years in mechanically repeating the silliest libretto in modern theatrical literature, set to music which, pretty as it is, must pall somewhat on the seven hundred and eighty-eighth performance.

As might have been expected, a settled weariness of life, an utter perfunctoriness, an unfathomable inanity pervaded the very souls of "No. I." The tenor, originally, I have no doubt, a fine young man, but now cherubically adipose, was evidently counting the days until death should release him from the part of Wilder. He had a pleasant speaking voice; and his affability and forbearance were highly creditable to him under the circumstances; but Nature rebelled in him against the loathed strains of a seven hundred-times repeated rôle. He omitted the song in the first act, and sang Though Born a Man of High Degree as if with the last rally of an energy decayed and a willing spirit crushed. The G at the end was a vocal earthquake. And yet methought he was not displeased when the inhabitants of Greenwich, coming fresh to the slaughter, encored him.

The baritone had been affected the other way: he was thin and worn; and his clothes had lost their lustre. He sang Queen of My Heart twice in a hardened manner, as one who was prepared to sing it a thousand times in a thousand quarter hours for a sufficient wager. The comic part, being simply that of a circus clown transferred to the lyric stage, is better suited for infinite repetition; and the gentleman who undertook it addressed a comic lady called Priscilla as Sarsaparilla during his interludes between the haute-école acts of the prima donna and tenor, with a delight in the rare aroma of the joke, and in the roars of laughter it elicited, which will probably never pall. But anything that he himself escaped in the way of tedium was added tenfold to his unlucky colleagues, who sat out his buffooneries with an expression of deadly malignity. I trust the gentleman may die in his bed; but he would be unwise to build too much on doing so. There is a point at which tedium becomes homicidal mania.

The ladies fared best. The female of the human species has not yet developed a conscience: she will apparently spend her life in artistic self-murder by induced Dorothitis without a pang of remorse, provided she be praised and paid regularly. Dorothy [5] herself, a beauteous young lady of distinguished mien, with an immense variety of accents ranging from the finest Tunbridge Wells English (for genteel comedy) to the broadest Irish (for repartee and low comedy), sang without the slightest effort and without the slightest point, and was all the more desperately vapid because she suggested artistic gifts wasting in complacent abeyance. Lydia's voice, a hollow and spectral contralto, alone betrayed the desolating effect of perpetual Dorothy: her figure retains a pleasing plumpness akin to that of the tenor; and her spirits were wonderful, all things considered. The chorus, too, seemed happy; but that was obviously because they did not know any better. The pack of hounds darted in at the end of the second act evidently full of the mad hope of finding something new going on; and their depression, when they discovered it was Dorothy again, was pitiable. The S.P.C.A. should interfere. If there is no law to protect men and women from Dorothy, there is at least one that can be strained to protect dogs.

I did not wait for the third act. My companion had several times all but fallen into the pit from sleep and heaviness of spirit combined; and I felt as if I were playing Geoffrey Wilder for the millionth night. As we moped homeward in the moonlight we brooded over what we had seen. Even now I cannot think with composure of the fact that they are playing Dorothy tonight again—will play it tomorrow—next year—next decade—next century. I do not know what the average lifetime of a member of "No. I" may be; but I do not think it can exceed five years from the date of joining; so there is no question here of old men and old women playing it with white hair beneath their wigs and deep furrows underlying their make-up. Doubtless they do not die on the stage: they first become mad and are removed to an asylum, where they incessantly sing, One, two three: one, two, three: one, two, three: one, two, be wi-eyes in, ti-I'm oh, Ph-ill is, mine, etc., until the King of Terrors (who ought to marry Dorothy) mercifully seals their tortured ears for ever.

I have always denounced the old-fashioned stock company, and laughed to scorn the theorists who fancy that they saw in them a training school for actors; but I never bargained for such a thing as this 789th performance of Dorothy. No: it is a criminal waste of young lives and young talents; and though it may for a time make more money for Mr Leslie, yet in the end it leaves him with a worn-out opera and a parcel of untrained novices on his hands when he might have a repertory of at least half a dozen works and a company of fairly-skilled artists able to play them at a day's notice. We exclaim at the dock directors' disregard of laborers' bodies; but what shall we say of the managers' disregard of artists' souls. Ti, rum ti ty, rum ti ty, rum ti ty, rum m m: tiddy tum tiddy tum tiddity, tum! Heavens! what hum I? Be wi-eyes in—Malediction!

Obviously, I have never seen Goethe or Shakespear or Plato: they were before my time. But I have seen Richard Wagner, who was so vehemently specialized by Nature as a man of genius that he was totally incapable of anything ordinary. He fought with the wild beasts all his life; and when you saw him coming through a crowded cage, even when they all felt about him as the lions felt about Daniel, he had an air of having his life in his hand, as it were, and of wandering in search of his right place and his own people, if any such there might be. When he had nothing else to do he would wander away to the walls and corners, apparently in search of some door or stairway or other exit from the world not finding which he would return disconcerted, and either sit down in desperation for a moment before starting off on a fresh exploration, or else—being a most humane man—pet one of the animals with a little conversation.

In 1883 Wagner wandered to Venice, and there at last stumbled upon that long-sought exit, since when he has not been seen by mortal man. You may well believe, then, how ghostly a sensation I had when, at Queen's Hall in London ten years later, I saw, making its guarded way through the crowd on the platform, a phantom Wagner, again, in Bunyan's phrase, "walking through the wilderness of this world." Of course I knew perfectly well that it was really Siegfried Wagner, son of Richard, and grandson of Liszt; for had I not come there expressly to see him? But, for all that, what appeared to me was the father of his habit as he lived, the old face with immortal youth in it, the set expression of endurance, the apprehensive step, and the unmistakable feeling of super-naturalness among the wild beasts.

This illusion did not wear off so soon as I expected: it came back again and again whilst Siegfried was conducting. It only broke up completely when, in response to the applause, he turned round smiling; made a series of boyish bows which had all the pleasant qualities of friendly nods; and became quite a young fellow in his earliest manhood. When he got to work again, the old look came back: there was something of the quaint gravity of an old-fashioned child: one remembered, in trying to account for it, that his father was over fifty when he was born, and his mother, though much younger than that, still a mature woman. His handling of the music, too, was very Wagnerian, more so even than that of Wagner himself; for Wagner had roots in the past which have been pulled up since before Siegfried's time. No man born in 1813, as Richard Wagner was, could have conducted Les Preludes or the Siegfried Idyll with such a complete detachment from the mechanical swing of the old dance and march measures from which their forms are descended. . . .

. . . He gave us the Mephisto Waltzes without a whiff of brimstone, the Flying Dutchman overture without a touch of violence. He treated the overture's atmosphere of curse and storm, its shrieking tempest and scurrying damnation, with scrupulous artistic care and seriousness, albeit with a certain youthful share in the excitement which was perhaps not far remote from amusement; but it was with the theme of love and salvation that he opened the music to its very depths. And this is the clue to him as a conductor, and to those complaints of sentimentality which have been made against him by critics who were in an unregenerate mood and missed the violence and the brimstone—missed the bitterness of death in his beatific version of Isolde's Liebestod—found heaven, in short, rather dull after London. For my part, I was touched, charmed, more than satisfied.

. . . The magic of Siegfried's first concert was not maintained at the second. The orchestra had thrown itself wholeheartedly into making a success of his first appearance; but he must have got on the wrong side of his players after this; for at the second concert they were not helpful; and the evening fell rather flat. Siegfried, it appeared, was the sort of conductor his father most abhorred: a gentleman conductor, meaning a conductor who is a gentleman first and a conductor afterwards, an order of things which ends in his not being a conductor at all. In short, a snob conductor. Our universities produced a succession of them which made the advent in London of Richter with Wagner in 1877 a revelation and a revolution. It was many many years before Siegfried came to London again to conduct a concert at the Albert Hall. He was then an elderly person, still extremely gentlemanly. His conducting was too depressing to be describable as maddening; but it made us all feel as if we were at a garden party in a cathedral town being welcomed by a highly connected curate who failed to find any tea for us. There was in the program a harmless little piece by himself: the elegant diversion of a superior person who dabbled in light composition. The farewell and fire music from Die Walküre was handled as it had never within our experience been handled before, and will, I trust, never be handled again. The trombones echoing Wotan's final *Wer meines Speeres Spitze fürchtet* sounded like an evening hymn, slow and sweet, all but *sotto voce*. The critics, I think (I was no longer one of them) got up and left after this; for the man seemed hopeless; and the politeness of the applause was deadlier than silence.

Then an incredible thing happened. The last item in the program was the overture to Die Meistersinger. The last, and, as it at once promised, the worst. Its slowness, its genteelness, made me doubt whether I was not dreaming. I felt that the overture would certainly peter out and stop from sheer inertia if he did not speed up the final section. Instead, to my amazement, he achieved the apparently impossible feat of slowing it down. And the effect was magical. The music broadened out with an effect that is beyond description. It was immense, magnificent. At the end the audience, which ten minutes before would have murdered him but for the police, was frantically recalling him to the platform again and again and again and yet again. The next we heard of him was that he was dead. It was his swan song.

"We are losing, we are sorry to say, Corno di Bassetto. The larger salary of a weekly organ of the classes has proved too much for the virtue even of a Fabian, and he has abandoned us. We wish him well, and twice even the big salary that is coming to him from the bloated coffers of the organ of the aristocracy. Let us give his adieu to The Star readers, with whom he has been on terms of such pleasant intercourse, in his own words."— T.P. [6]

For two years I sparkled every week in The Star under this ridiculous name, and in a manner so absolutely unlike the conventional musical criticism of the time that all the journalists believed that the affair was a huge joke, the point of which was that I knew nothing whatever about music. . . . The critic whose articles are at all readable by people who only read to be amused is usually suspected by his fellow journalists of being a musical impostor, a suspicion which reaches absolute certainty in the mind of his editor. When my own articles on music first began to attract some attention, the cream of the joke was supposed by many persons to be the fact that I knew nothing whatever about music. Several times it happened to me to be introduced to admirers who, on discovering from my reply to the question, "What put it into your head to write about music?" that I did so because it happened to be the art I knew most about, have turned away cruelly disappointed and disillusioned by this prosaic explanation, which seemed to rob my exploits of all their merit.

In 1890 the late Louis Engel, the best hated musical critic in Europe, and Archer's colleague on The World, got into a scrape, and had to leave the country. Archer instantly assured Edmund Yates, the editor, that Corno di Bassetto was Engel's only possible successor; and I left The Star, and, as G.B.S., wrote a page of The World on music every week. . . . And the success of this page proved that in the hands of a capable writer music is quite as good a subject from the purely journalistic point of view as either painting or the drama, whilst the interest taken in it is much more general than in party politics, the stock exchange, or even the police intelligence. Let me add that Edmund Yates had no more special interest in music than he had in chemistry . . . .

Bassetto's stuff . . . was great fun when it was fresh . . . . I knew all that was necessary about music; but in criticism I was only a beginner. It is easy enough from the first to distinguish between what is pleasant or unpleasant, accurate or inaccurate in a performance; but when great artists have to be dealt with, only keenly analytical observation and comparison of them with artists who, however agreeable, are not great, can enable a critic to distinguish between what everybody can do and what only a very few can do, and to get his valuations right accordingly. All artsmen know what it is to be enthusiastically praised for something so easy that they are half ashamed of it, and to receive not a word of encouragement for their finest strokes.

I cannot deny that Bassetto was occasionally vulgar; but that does not matter if he makes you laugh. Vulgarity is a necessary part of a complete author's equipment; and the clown is sometimes the best part of the circus. The Star, then a hapenny newspaper, was not catering for a

fastidious audience: it was addressed to the bicycle clubs and the poly-
technics, not to the Royal Society of Literature or the Musical Association. I purposely vulgarized musical criticism, which was then refined
and academic to the point of being unreadable and often nonsensical.
Editors, being mostly ignorant of music, would submit to anything from
their musical critics, not pretending to understand it. If I occasionally
carried to the verge of ribaldry my reaction against the pretentious
twaddle and sometimes spiteful cliquishness they tolerated in their ignorance, think of me as heading one of the pioneer columns of what
was then called The New Journalism; and you will wonder at my
politeness.

You may be puzzled, too, to find that the very music I was brought
up on: the pre-Wagner school of formal melody in separate numbers
which seemed laid out to catch the encores that were then fashionable,
was treated by me with contemptuous levity as something to be swept
into the dustbin as soon as possible. The explanation is that these works
were standing in the way of Wagner, who was then the furiously abused
coming man in London. Only his early works were known or tolerated.
Half a dozen bars of Tristan or The Mastersingers made professional
musicians put their fingers in their ears. The Ride of the Valkyries was
played at the Promenade Concerts, and always encored, but only as an
insanely rampagious curiosity. The Daily Telegraph steadily preached
Wagner down as a discordant notoriety-hunting charlatan in six silk
dressing-gowns, who could not write a bar of melody, and made an
abominable noise with the orchestra. In pantomime harlequinades the
clown produced a trombone, played a bit of the pilgrims' march from
Tannhäuser fortissimo as well as he could, and said "The music of the
future!" The wars of religion were not more bloodthirsty than the discussions of the Wagnerites and the Anti-Wagnerites. I was, of course, a
violent Wagnerite; and I had the advantage of knowing the music to
which Wagner grew up, whereas many of the most fanatical Wagnerites
(Ashton Ellis, who translated the Master's prose works, was a conspicuous example) knew no other music than Wagner's, and believed
that the music of Donizetti and Meyerbeer had no dramatic quality whatever. "A few arpeggios" was the description Ellis gave me of his notion
of Les Huguenots.

Nowadays the reaction is all the other way. Our young lions have no
use for Wagner the Liberator. His harmonies, which once seemed monstrous cacophonies, are the commonplaces of the variety theatres. Auda-

cious young critics disparage his grandeurs as tawdry. When the wireless strikes up the Tannhäuser overture I hasten to switch it off, though I can always listen with pleasure to Rossini's overture to William Tell, hackneyed to death in Bassetto's time. The funeral march from Die Götterdämmerung hardly keeps my attention, though Handel's march from Saul is greater than ever. Though I used to scarify the fools who said that Wagner's music was formless, I should not now think the worse of Wagner if, like Bach and Mozart, he had combined the most poignant dramatic expression with the most elaborate decorative design. It was necessary for him to smash the superstition that this was obligatory; to free dramatic melody from the tyranny of arabesques; and to give the orchestra symphonic work instead of rosalias and rum-tum; but now that this and all the other musical superstitions are in the dustbin, and the post-Wagnerian harmonic and contrapuntal anarchy is so complete that it is easier technically to compose another Parsifal than another Bach's Mass in B Minor or Don Giovanni I am no longer a combatant anarchist in music, not to mention that I have learnt that a successful revolution's first task is to shoot all revolutionists. This means that I am no longer Corno di Bassetto. He was pre- and pro-Wagner; unfamiliar with Brahms; and unaware that a young musician named Elgar was chuckling over his irreverent boutades. As to Cyril Scott, Bax, Ireland, Goossens, Bliss, Walton, Schönberg, Hindemith, or even Richard Strauss and Sibelius, their idioms would have been quite outside Bassetto's conception of music, though today they seem natural enough. . . . I very greatly doubt whether poor old Bassetto is worth reading now.

"Corno di Bassetto" . . . was a mixture of triviality, vulgarity, farce and tomfoolery with genuine criticism. Now that I had learnt how to write and to criticise, my old knowledge of music, practically useless to me before, filled my hands with weapons. . . .

I . . . resigned my post as musical critic to The World on the death of its editor . . . on the 19th May 1894. But his successor pleaded that it would seem a personal slight to himself if I did not go on under his editorship until the end of the season; and this, to save appearances, I consented to do. After the autumn recess my vacant place was filled by Mr. Robert Smythe Hichens, who had trained himself as a musician, not knowing that he was destined to be a famous novelist . . . of Green Carnation fame. . . . I never again undertook regular duties as a critic of music.

Saturday Reviewer in
the Theatres

UP TO A CERTAIN point, I have never flinched from martyrdom. By far the heaviest demand ever made upon me by the public weal is that which . . . devoted my nights to the theatres and my days to writing about them. If I had known how exceedingly trying the experience would be, I am not sure that I should not have seen the public weal further before making this supreme sacrifice to it. But I had been so seldom to the theatre in the previous years that I did not realize its horrors. I firmly believe that the trials upon which I then entered . . . injured my brain. At all events matters reached a crisis . . . . I felt that I must have a real experience of some kind, under conditions, especially as regards fresh air, as unlike those of the stalls as possible. After some consideration it occurred to me that if I went into the country, selected a dangerous hill, and rode down it on a bicycle at full speed in the darkest part of the night, some novel and convincing piece of realism might result. It did.

Probably no man has ever misunderstood another so completely as the doctor misunderstood me when he apologized for the sensation produced by the point of his needle as he corrected the excessive openness of my countenance after the adventure. To him who has endured points made by actors for . . . years, the point of a surgeon's darning needle comes as a delicious relief. I did not like to ask him to put in a few more stitches merely to amuse me, as I had already, through pure self-indulgence, cut into his Sunday rest to an extent of which his kindness made me ashamed; but I doubt if I shall ever see a play again without longing for the comparative luxury of that quiet country surgery, with the stillness without broken only by the distant song and throbbing drumbeat of some remote Salvation Army corps, and the needle, with its delicate realism, touching my sensibilities, stitch, stitch, stitch, with absolute sincerity in the hands of an artist who had actually learned his business and knew how to do it.

To complete the comparison it would be necessary to go into the economics of it by measuring the doctor's fee against the price of a stall in a West End theatre. But here I am baffled by the fact that the highest art revolts from an equation between its infinite value and a finite pile of coin. It so happened that my voice, which is an Irish voice, won for me the sympathy of the doctor. This circumstance must appear amazing almost beyond credibility in the light of the fact that he was himself an Irishman; but so it was. He rightly felt that sympathy is beyond price, and declined to make it the subject of a commercial transaction. Thereby he made it impossible for me to mention his name without black ingratitude; for I know no more effectual way of ruining a man in this country than by making public the smallest propensity on his part to adopt a benevolent attitude towards necessitous strangers. Here the West End manager will perhaps whisper reproachfully, "Well; and do *I* ever make you pay for your stall?" To which I cannot but reply, "Is that also due to the sympathy my voice awakens in you when it is raised every Saturday?" I trust I am not ungrateful for my invitations; but to expect me to feel towards the manager who lacerates my nerves, enfeebles my mind, and destroys my character, as I did towards the physician who healed my body, refreshed my soul, and flattered my vocal accomplishments when I was no more to him than an untimely stranger with an unheard-of black eye, is to dethrone justice and repudiate salvation. Besides, he said it was a mercy I was not killed. Would any manager have been of that opinion?

Perhaps the most delightful thing about this village was that its sense of the relative importance of things was so rightly adjusted that it had no theatrical gossip; for this doctor actually did not know who I was. With a cynicism for which his charity afterwards made me blush, I sought to reassure him as to the pecuniary competence of his muddy, torn, ensanguined and facially spoiled visitor by saying "My name is G.B.S.," as who should say "My name is Cecil Rhodes, or Henry Irving, or William of Germany." Without turning a hair, he sweetly humored my egotistic garrulity by replying, in perfect lightness of heart, "Mine's

F——: *what are you?"* Breathing at last an atmosphere in which it mattered so little who and what G.B.S. was, that nobody knew either one or the other, I almost sobbed with relief whilst he threaded his needle with a nice white horsehair, tactfully pretending to listen to my evasive murmur that I was a "sort of writer," an explanation meant to convey to him that I earned a blameless living by inscribing names in letters of gold over shop windows and on perforated wire blinds. To have brought the taint of my factitious little vogue into the unperverted consciousness of his benevolent and sensible life would have been the act of a serpent.

On the whole, the success of my experiment left nothing to be desired; and I recommend it confidently for imitation. My nerves completely recovered their tone and my temper its natural sweetness. . . .

In my boyhood in the 1860s there were two theatres in Dublin. The Royal, in Hawkins-street, was nobly spacious, lofty, beautifully proportioned, and in every architectural way worthy of the arts which were its home. There were four circles: the five-shilling dress circle of courtly splendor, the three-and-sixpenny undress for genteel persons in everyday attire, the eighteenpenny middle gallery for the lower middle class, but frequented by respectable but impecunious ladies who could not afford the circles nor appear in the pit, and the sixpenny top gallery or "gods" for the riffraff.

Stalls not having then been invented, the pit, furnished with hard wood forms, ran right up to the orchestra. Women were not seen there. Admission was two shillings except during the opera season when it was four shillings, and the "gods" sat in their shirt sleeves and tried to keep up a musical entertainment of their own between the acts, mostly very unsuccessfully. I used to come out of the opera-pit crush with all my front buttons down the middle of my back; but I got a front seat at that price. Queues were undreamt of.

The acting was provided by stars on tour who were supported by the stock company, and used the old stock scenery with its wings and flats and drop scenes which were changed in full view of the audience. The old stock scenery was bearable because it dated from the days of Telbin, Stanfield, and de Loutherbourg.

One in particular, with Big Ben as its centre, was quite cosmopolitan and served for all places and periods, figuring impartially as a street in modern London, in Don Giovanni, and in Richard III. What was really intolerable was the stock company. One got tired of them with their one-step dance, one combat (sixes), and their invariable treatment of every part in every play; for each of them had his "line" and, having a new part to swallow every week or so, had no time for studying anything beyond his cues.

The notion that they all became versatile is the wildest of delusions. Versatility was the much-needed quality of which they became quite incapable. There was the leading juvenile and the walking gentleman, the heavy (for villains), the first and second low comedians, and fathers, noble and vulgar, with their feminine counterparts the leading lady, the singing chambermaid, the heavy, the first and second old women, etc. etc. A few of them were favorites, especially the comedians Mrs Huntley and Sam Johnson; and there was one first-rate actor, Peter Granby, whose Kent in King Lear I have never seen approached, nor his Polonius surpassed; but on the whole and in the lump, every trick of the stock lines, every gesture, every tone became so familiar that they could not produce any illusion; and when the new touring London companies with their modern drawing-room sceneries began to arrive, the change was an enormous relief and the stock company perished, unwept, unhonored, and unsung.

The highlights of the season were the Christmas pantomime, the Opera with the pit at four shillings and the titanic unqueued struggle to get in, and the visits of Barry Sullivan, a very great Shakespearean star actor, who always played to full houses, and preferred making £300 a week in the provinces and leaving £100,000 at his death, to playing in London for thirty years as Irving did and having to take to the road penniless at the end.

There was one other theatre, the Queen's in Brunswick-street (it may be there still); but respectable people did not then frequent it, as it served not only as a theatre for crude melodrama but as a market for ladies who lived by selling themselves, and who flaunted their profession in Dublin to a degree that astonished all travelers.

Suddenly all this was upset by a certain Michael Gunn, who kept a music shop at 61 Grafton-street: a handsome man with a tall consumptive brother John. The two built a new theatre in King-street that was as unlike the old Royal as any theatre could well be. The Royal, with its carriage yard, was built as if land could be had in Hawkins-street for a penny an acre. The new theatre, the Gaiety, was built so as to cram into the space it occupied the utmost possible number of saleable seats. It had stalls. It had next to no boxes: rows of cushioned seats took their places.

To compare the new theatre with the old was like comparing a bandbox with the Parthenon. But it held more money per square foot of ground than the classical Royal, and it was decidedly more comfortable. For half a century after, until Herbert Tree ordered the rebuilding of Her Majesty's Theatre in London as His Majesty's, every new theatre built in Britain was a bandbox theatre like the Gaiety; and [C.J.] Phipps was the master theatre architect of the day.

The Gaiety had no stock company, although one remembers as a very frequent performer there Edward Royce, irresistible supernumerary funny man and a wonderful dancer, the only perfect harlequin I have ever seen. I made my first acquaintance with Gilbert and Sullivan at the Gaiety in Trial by Jury, and remember very well how astonishingly "churchy" Sullivan's music sounded after Offenbach.

Conceive me then, a future playwright, with no conscious prevision of that destiny, gathering my practical knowledge of the stage from a company of such actors . . . playing round a star on tour. Of the English speaking stars incomparably the greatest was Barry Sullivan, who was in his prime when I was in my teens, the last of the race of heroic figures which had dominated the stage since the palmy Siddons-Kemble days. Ellen Terry shrank from his acting as from a display of pugilism in which his trembling supporters had no part except to give him his cues and be played off the stage by him. His stage fights in Richard III and Macbeth appealed irresistibly to a boy spectator like myself: I remember one delightful evening when two inches of Macbeth's sword, a special fighting sword carried in that scene only, broke off and whizzed over the heads of the cowering pit (there were no stalls then) to bury itself deep in the front of the dress circle after giving those who sat near its trajectory more of a thrill than they had bargained for. Barry Sullivan was a tall powerful man with a cultivated resonant voice: his stage walk was the perfection of grace and dignity; and his lightning swiftness of action, as when in the last scene of Hamlet he shot up the stage and stabbed the king four times before you could wink, all provided a physical exhibition which attracted audiences quite independently of the play. To John Coleman and T. C. King and other provincial stars with whom he has been sometimes ignorantly classed by London stage historians he was as Hyperion to a very thirdrate satyr. He was as proud as Lucifer, and as imposing; but he was the only actor I ever heard come before the curtain at the end of a play to apologize for having acted badly. He had opened on Monday night in Hamlet (he was at his best in Hamlet and Richelieu) after a very rough passage from Holyhead. Certainly some of the usual charm was lacking; but only very sensitive Barry Sullivan connoisseurs could have noticed it. With an unanswerable dignity he informed the applauding Dublin playgoers that he had done justice neither to them nor to himself, and begged their indulgence. They were awestruck; and then their applause had a note of bewilderment; for most of them had thought it all very splendid.

Yet this great actor—for such of his kind and in his prime he was—had no notion of what we now require as artistic production. He went into a provincial theatre as into a rag and bottle shop; made them drag out the old scenes that the people of the town had seen hundreds of times in all sorts of plays; and, by summary methods that involved a good deal of swearing and bullying, drilled the stock company in a day's rehearsal into giving him his cues and playing up to his strokes of stage business that night. At first he brought with him nothing but his costumes and swords. Later on, he travelled with a fairly good looking young leading lady (possibly in consequence of an experience with a local Ophelia who reduced me to such paroxysms of laughter that I narrowly escaped ejection from the theatre) and an old actor, Cathcart, who had supported Charles Kean, and who, as Richmond or Macduff, got the worst of all the stage fights except the final fatal thrust under the arm, and who relieved the star of the worst drudgery of rehearsal when advancing age compelled him to husband his still mighty forces. In spite of this relief and of his haughty sobriety and irreproachable private life Barry Sullivan died paralysed, exhausted by the impossible task of being superhuman for six nights in every week; for, clever as he was technically, he revelled in his work too keenly to keep within the limits of that passionless science of acting which enabled Salvini to make his audiences imagine him a volcano in eruption when he was in sober fact hardly moving, and Coquelin, without turning a hair, to get through a night's work that would have worn most of our actors to rags or driven them to stimulants to pull them through.

Had I passed my boyhood in London I should have seen nothing of the very important side of stage art represented by Barry Sullivan's acting. He had appeared there with Helen Faucit as Hamlet at the Haymarket Theatre, and been hailed by The Times as the leading legitimate actor of the British stage. But when he found, as Irving found later, that this meant being skinned alive by the London landlords, he shook the dust of London off his feet, and, first in Australia and then in the English provinces and in Ireland and Scotland, set to work with a fixed determination that, however scanty the audience, whoever once saw him act would come again. He soon secured crowded houses every night, and died leaving £100,000 at about the age at which Irving had to abandon his London theatre penniless and fall back on America and the provinces. Had Barry Sullivan produced Shakespear's plays as handsomely as Irving did at the Lyceum they would not have drawn an extra farthing (for a theatre can be no more than full) and he would have had to spend much more money on them.

I certainly learnt nothing from Barry Sullivan's exploits of how far the grand style in acting can be carried by women. Most fortunately for me, however, a visit was paid to Dublin by Adelaide Ristori, who completed my education in this respect, besides convincing me that an Italian stock company, when the novelty of its foreign conventions wears off, can become even more unbearably stale than an English one. The nearest English approach to a tragic actress was Ada Cavendish, whose performance as Wilkie Collins's New Magdalen made an extraordinary impression; but she only flashed across the sky and vanished, leaving no successor until Janet Achurch arrived fifteen years later and inaugurated the Ibsen movement. Both of them, like Edmund Kean, Robson, and many others, called to their aid powers that destroyed them. Ellen Terry did not visit Dublin, and was only a name to me when I came to London in 1876; but everything that the perfection of technical accomplishment could do with youth, cleverness, wit, and irresistible charm in drawing-room drama was demonstrated by Madge Robertson, who came with Buckstone and the entire Haymarket company from London, and struck the first shattering blow at our poor old stock company.

The stock company was hard enough to bear when there was no alternative; but when the London successes began touring through the provinces and the Irish and Scottish capitals, and were performed there not as now by secondrate companies giving a mechanical imitation of the original London production, but by the London cast which had created the success, the stock companies fell dead at their impact. To say that they perished unwept, unhonored, and unsung would be to give only the faintest idea of their death and damnation. When we who had seen them scrambling anyhow through all sorts of plays . . . first saw finished acting, careful production, thorough identification of the performers with parts for which they had been carefully selected as suitable, with new faces, new voices, new clothes, and new scenery, a return to the stock company was impossible.

. . . Among these London successes which brought London productions unchanged to Dublin was a play called The Two Roses, by Albery. One of the characters was a selfish old humbug named Digby Grant. It made the success of the piece by a certain egotistical intensity, sinister and yet dignified in its indignity, which was not in the play but in the actor: an actor with a tall thin figure, which, if it could not be convicted of grotesqueness was certainly indescribably peculiar, and a voice which was dependent so much on the resonance of a cavernous nose that it was, compared to the powerful and musical chest voice of Barry Sullivan, a highly cultivated neigh. His name was Henry Irving. I instinctively felt that a new drama inhered in this man, though I had then no conscious notion that I was destined to write it; and I perceive now that I never forgave him for baffling the plans I made for him (always, be it remembered, unconsciously). His stage disguise was so perfect that I did not even know that he was still a young man: indeed the one effect he never could produce on the stage was a youthful effect: his Romeo was no younger than his Digby Grant. He was utterly unlike anyone else: he could give importance and a noble melancholy to any sort of drivel that was put into his mouth; and it was this melancholy, bound up with an impish humour, which forced the spectator to single him out as a leading figure with an inevitability that I never saw again in any other actor until it rose from Irving's grave in the person of a nameless cinema actor who afterwards became famous as Charlie Chaplin. Here, I felt, is something that leaves the old stage and its superstitions and staleness completely behind, and inaugurates a new epoch in the theatre.

The theatrical system to which the stock company belonged decomposed and broke up; and when I came to London it seemed to recede into a remote provincial past. I hastened to the famous little theatre off Tottenham Court Road, . . . to see the Cup and Saucer drama of Robertson handled by the Bancrofts. The play I hit on was Ours; and in it I saw Ellen Terry for the first time. She left on me an impression of waywardness: of not quite fitting into her part and not wanting to; and she gave no indication of her full power, for which the part afforded no scope. As her portraits had prepared me to find her interesting and singular (I have never been susceptible to mere prettiness) I was less struck than I should have been if she had been quite new to me. It was not until I saw her in New Men and Old Acres, which was made a success by her performance as The Two Roses had been made a success by Irving's, that I was completely conquered and convinced that here was the woman for the new drama which was still in the womb of Time, waiting for Ibsen to impregnate it. If ever there were two artists apparently marked out by Nature to make a clean break with an outworn past and create a new stage world they were Ellen Terry and Henry Irving. Nobody can really understand my correspondence with Ellen Terry twenty years later without grasping this situation.

What actually happened was an anticlimax which in its public aspect was a glorious success for both of them. Irving fascinated London in a play called The Bells under an oldfashioned management. His success was so great and so entirely personal that he was able to lift the theatre out of the hands of his manager and take its professional destiny into his own hands with all shackles cast off from his art, in the position as head of the English stage which he held almost unchallenged for thirty years. The earliest notable use he made of his freedom was to engage Ellen Terry as his leading lady. It was his first and last enlightened stroke of policy. For he immediately turned back to the old Barry Sullivan repertory of mutilated Shakespear and Bulwer Lytton, to which he actually added The Iron Chest of the obsolete Colman. From the public point of view he never looked back: from my point of view he never looked forward. As far as the drama was concerned he was more old-fashioned than the oldest of his predecessors, and apparently more illiterate than the most ignorant of them. The taste and judgment which enabled him to achieve so much beauty and dignity in scenery and costume and to rid his theatre of all the old vulgarities when he had Ellen Terry to reveal such possibilities to him did not extend to literature.

. . . He took no interest in the drama as such: a play was to him a length of stuff necessary to his appearance on the stage, but so entirely subordinate to that consummation that it could be cut to his measure like a roll of cloth. Of the theatre at large he knew almost nothing; for he never left his own stage. I am exaggerating when I say that he regarded an author as a person whose business it was to provide plays at five shillings an act, and, in emergencies, to write the fifth act whilst the fourth was being performed; and yet, in spite of his intercourse with Tennyson, Traill, Wills, and Comyns Carr, I believe that this caricature of his attitude gives a juster impression of it than any statement of the sober facts. He composed his acting with extraordinary industry and minuteness: his Matthias in The Bells and his Charles I were wonderful mosaics of bits of acting thought out touch by touch. His Macaire and Louis XI will hardly be surpassed: they were limit achievements in their *genre*. Even in his Shakespearean impostures (for such they were) there were unforgettable moments. But he composed his parts not only without the least consideration for the play as a whole, or even for the character as portrayed by the author (he always worked out some fancy of his own), but without any for the unfortunate actors whom he employed to support him. A great deal of that absence of vulgarity which I have noted as characteristic of his management was secured by the simple method of not allowing his company to act. He worked hard to make them do what he wanted for his own effects; but if they tried to make independent effects of their own, he did not hesitate to spoil them by tricks of stage management. In this way he threw on himself the enormous burden of attracting the public singlehanded. He achieved the celebrated feat of performing Hamlet with the part of Hamlet omitted and all the other parts as well, substituting for it and for them the fascinating figure of Henry Irving, which for many years did not pall on his audience, and never palled on himself. . . .

. . . Later on I saw him as Macbeth, his first assumption of which had provoked something like a storm of derision from the unconverted. I found it a performance of refined beauty. It was not any conceivable historical Macbeth; but then neither is Shakespear's. And I have not the faintest recollection of any other figure in the play, from which I infer that Ellen Terry cannot have played Lady Macbeth on that occasion, nor of any particular scene except the banquet scene, in which the violence of Macbeth's defiance of Banquo's ghost was rather ridiculously beyond the actor's resources; but still his performance was a fine piece of work within its limits.

To me, however, Irving's thirty years at the Lyceum, though a most imposing episode in the history of the English theatre, were an exasperating waste of the talent of the two artists who had seemed to me peculiarly fitted to lift the theatre out of its old ruts and head it towards unexplored regions of drama. With Lyceum Shakespear I had no patience. Shakespear, even in his integrity, could not satisfy the hungry minds whose spiritual and intellectual appetites had been whetted and even created by Ibsen; and Shakespear in his integrity was then unknown in the theatre, and remained so until William Poel and Harley Granville-Barker rediscovered and revived him. The shreds and patches which

Irving and his predecessors tore out of his plays and tacked crudely together for performances which were interrupted four or five times by intolerable intervals, during which the women in the audience sat in silent boredom whilst the men wandered about the corridors and refreshment bars, were endurable only by people who, knowing no better, thought they were assisting at a very firstrate solemnization, and were helped by that illusion to persuade themselves that they were enjoying the best that a great institution and two great performers could do for them. I knew better. Irving, wasting his possibilities in costly Bardicide, was wasting Ellen Terry's as well. Her only rival as a Shakespearean actress was the great Ada Crehan (who by a printer's error became famous as Ada C. Rehan); and her genius too was being wasted by Augustin Daly, another master-mutilator of the unfortunate playwright whom he professed to adore. But as Daly did not himself act, his hackings and hewings were very largely addressed to the object of taking all the good lines out of the other parts and adding them to Ada Rehan's; and she spoke them so harmoniously that when listening to her it was impossible to care much about anything but the mere music of her voice and Shakespear's, whereas at the Lyceum Irving's peculiarities were the first consideration. To him, professionally, Ellen Terry was only the chief ornament of his theatre. Besides, his method was so slow that it was almost impossible to act with him. She had to stop too often and wait too long to sustain her part continuously when he was on the stage.

All this enraged me. I can keep my temper as well as most people; for my double training as a critic of highly sensitive living persons and a propagandist of seditious, not to say subversive, political views, kept me constantly on my guard against letting my temper get the better of me or my manners the worse of me: in short, against the least indulgence of personal malice. Besides, I am tolerant in matters of morals which provoke most people to censoriousness; for to me a great deal of current morality is unsound and mischievous. But when questions of art are concerned I am really malicious. Retrogressive art and wasted or unworthily used talent (the theatre is full of both) make me aware that I am capable of something as near to hatred as any emotion can be that has no taint of fear of it. . . . Because Irving would not put his peculiar talent at the service of the new and intensely interesting development of the drama which had begun with Ibsen, and because he wasted not only his own talent but Ellen Terry's, I destroyed her belief in him and gave shape and consciousness to her sense of having her possibilities sterilized by him. Then her position became unbearable; and she broke loose from the Ogre's castle, as I called it, only to find that she had waited too long for his sake, and that her withdrawal was rather a last service to him than a first to herself.[1]

The castle did not long survive her departure. . . .

. . . Long and intimate correspondence can occur only between people who never meet one another. Swift's journal to Stella would not have been written if they had met every day as Ellen Terry and Irving did, instead of living in separate islands. Ellen and I lived within twenty minutes of each other's doorstep, and yet lived in different worlds: she in a theatre that was a century behind the times, and I in a political society (the Fabian) a century ahead of them. We were both too busy to have any personal intercourse except with the people we were working with. Our correspondence began when I was a professional critic of music through a move she made to help a young musician in whom she was interested. Now critics, like dentists, are a good deal occupied in hurting sensitive people in sensitive places; and as they have to do it in an entertaining manner, which no doubt gives them an air of enjoying it, they produce an impression of Sadism. And so I, being a critic, and, I hope, an entertaining one, had been classed by Ellen Terry as an unamiable person. This was fortunate for me, because instead of having to live up to an exalted estimate of my merits I had only to be commonly civil and helpful to produce a surprised and pleased reaction in my favor. Finding her delightful as a correspondent, and having some gifts in that way myself, I improved the opportunity to such purpose that we presently became occupied with one another in a paper courtship, which is perhaps the pleasantest, as it is the most enduring, of all courtships. We both felt instinctively that a meeting might spoil it, and would certainly alter it and bring it into conflict with other personal relationships. And so I hardly ever saw her, except across the footlights, until the inevitable moment at last arrived when we had to meet daily at the rehearsals of the play I wrote for her: Captain Brassbound's Conversion. By that time Irving had passed out of her life, and indeed out of his own; and Ellen's heart was for the moment vacant. I could not help speculating as to the possibility of my filling the vacancy. But Providence had other views. At our first serious meeting in the rehearsal room at the Court Theatre, Ellen and I were talking together before business began when the door opened, and a young American actor, James Carew, who had been engaged to play the part of Captain Hamlin Kearney, came in. "Who is that?" said Ellen, looking at him with quick interest. "That's the American captain," I answered. Without an instant's hesitation she sailed across the room; put Mr Carew in her pocket (so to speak); and married him. The lucky captive naturally made no resistance . . . .

After the play was disposed of our meetings were few, and all accidental. One of these chance meetings was on a summer day in the country near Elstree, where I came upon a crowd of people at work on a cinema film. Ellen Terry was there, acting the heroine. She was astonishingly beautiful. She had passed through that middle phase, so trying to handsome women, of matronly amplitude, and was again tall and slender, with a new delicacy and intensity in her saddened expression. She was always a little shy in speaking to me; for talking, hampered by material circumstances, is awkward and unsatisfactory after the perfect freedom of writing between people who *can* write. She asked me why I did not give her some work in the theatre. "I do not expect leading parts," she said: "I am too old. I am quite willing to play a charwoman. I should like to play a charwoman." "What would become of the play?" I said. "Imagine a scene in which the part of a canal barge was played by a battleship! What would happen to my play, or to anyone else's, if whenever the charwoman appeared the audience forgot the hero and heroine, and could think of nothing but the wonderful things the charwoman was going to say and do?" It was unanswerable; and we both, I think, felt rather inclined to cry.

She became a legend in her old age; but of that I have nothing to say; for we did not meet, and, except for a few broken letters, did not write; and she never was old to me.

Let those who may complain that it was all on paper remember that only on paper has humanity yet achieved glory, beauty, truth, knowledge, virtue, and abiding love.

. . . Years ago [in 1889], when Mr. Charrington, with A Doll's House, struck the decisive blow for Ibsen—perhaps the only one that . . . really got home in England . . . —I rejoiced in it, and watched the ruin and havoc it made among the idols and temples of the idealists as a young war correspondent watches the bombardment of the unhealthy quarters of a city. . . .

In the spring of 1890, the Fabian Society, finding itself at a loss for a course of lectures to occupy its summer meetings, was compelled to make

shift with a series of papers put forward under the general heading of
Socialism in Contemporary Literature. The Fabian Essayists, strongly
pressed to do "something or other," for the most part shook their heads;
but in the end Sydney Olivier consented to "take Zola"; I consented to
"take Ibsen"; and Hubert Bland undertook to read all the Socialist novels
of the day, an enterprise the desperate failure of which resulted in the
most amusing paper of the series. William Morris, asked to read a paper
on himself, flatly declined, but gave us one on Gothic Architecture. Stepniak also came to the rescue with a lecture on modern Russian fiction;
and so the Society tided over the summer without having to close its
doors, but also without having added anything whatever to the general
stock of information on Socialism in Contemporary Literature. After this
I cannot claim that my paper on Ibsen, which was duly read at the St
James's Restaurant on the 18th July 1890, under the presidency of Mrs.
Annie Besant, and which was the first form of [*The Quintessence of
Ibsenism*], is an original work in the sense of being the result of a spontaneous internal impulse on my part. Having purposely couched it in the
most provocative terms (of which traces may be found by the curious in
its present state), I did not attach much importance to the somewhat
lively debate that arose upon it; and I had laid it aside as a *pièce d'occasion* which had served its turn, when the production of Rosmersholm at
the Vaudeville Theatre by Florence Farr, the inauguration of the Independent Theatre by Mr J. T. Grein with a performance of Ghosts, and
the sensation created by the experiment of Elizabeth Robins and Marion
Lea with Hedda Gabler, started a frantic newspaper controversy, in which
I could see no sign of any of the disputants having ever been forced by
circumstances, as I had, to make up his mind definitely as to what Ibsen's
plays meant, and to defend his view face to face with some of the keenest
debaters in London. I allow due weight to the fact that Ibsen himself has
not enjoyed this Fabian advantage; but I have also shewn that the existence of a discoverable and perfectly definite thesis in a poet's work by
no means depends on the completeness of his own intellectual consciousness of it. At any rate, the controversialists, whether in the abusive stage,
or the apologetic stage, or the hero-worshipping stage, by no means made
clear what they were abusing, or apologizing for, or going into ecstasies
about; and I came to the conclusion that my explanation might as well
be placed in the field until a better could be found. . . .

. . . As I read the old Quintessence of Ibsenism I may find things that I see now at a different angle, or correlate with so many things then un-noted by me that they take on a different aspect. But though this may be a reason for writing another book, it is not a reason for altering an exist-ing one. . . . Now that Ibsen is no longer frantically abused, and is safe in the Pantheon, his message is in worse danger of being forgotten or ignored than when he was in the pillory. Nobody now dreams of calling me a "muck ferretting dog" because I think Ibsen a great teacher. I will not go so far as to say I wish they did; but I do say that the most effective way of shutting our minds against a great man's ideas is to take them for granted and admit he was great and have done with him. It really matters very little whether Ibsen was a great man or not: what does mat-ter is his message and the need of it.

That people are still interested in the message is proved by the history of this book. It has long been out of print in England; but it has never been out of demand. In spite of the smuggling of unauthorized Amer-ican editions, which I have winked at because the absence of an English reprint was my own fault (if it be a fault not to be able to do more than a dozen things at a time), the average price of copies of the original edi-tion stood at twenty-four shillings some years ago, and is no doubt higher now. But it was not possible to reprint it without additions. When it was issued in 1891 Ibsen was still alive, and had not yet produced The Master Builder, or Little Eyolf, or John Gabriel Borkman, or When We Dead Awaken. Without an account of these four final masterpieces, a book en-titled The Quintessence of Ibsenism would have been a fraud on its purchasers; and it was the difficulty of finding time to write the additional chapters on these plays, and review Ibsen's position from the point of view reached when his work ended with his death and his canonization as an admitted grand master of European literature, that . . . prevented me for twenty years from complying with the demand for a second edi-tion . . . .

[In 1895] I was the Saturday Reviewer in the theatres. D. S. MacColl was the Saturday Reviewer in the picture galleries. Cunninghame Gra-ham was a Saturday Reviewer in the universe, with perhaps a slight specialization towards Spanish South America. Music was reviewed by J. F. Runciman, young, clever, and quite genuine, but, like many middle-class Bohemians, without a notion of public or private manners. He drank, died, and is forgotten; but he held his own among us for a time. The editor was Frank Harris, who had no quality of editorship except the supreme one of knowing good work from bad, and not being afraid of it.

People who did not understand the peculiar structure of English society were puzzled by weeklies like The Saturday Review when they thought about them at all. These weeklies were not Radical. They were snortingly aristocratic; and yet they were staffed (when they were lucky enough to find the right men) by writers . . . with . . . unbounded contempt for the bourgeoisie, . . . uncompromising repudiation of their prejudices, their tastes, and their religion, . . . ruthlessly candid self-criticism, . . . subtle analytical power as a critic, and . . . trenchant skill with the pen. . . .

. . . I was a . . . Socialist; Cunninghame Graham was a Socialist, militant to his spurs; Runciman was a Socialist; Harris was a Socialist. We never asked MacColl what he was: it was enough that he was an artist and a very fine critic and brilliant writer; let it suffice that if he had any conventional weaknesses he knew better than to betray them in the Saturday. No Liberal, Radical, or Labor paper would have dared to employ us; one whiff of our brimstone would have terrified their editors out of their senses. Only in unchallengeably aristocratic papers could we have been let rip as we were.

The explanation of this paradox of aristocratic papers manned (and to some extent womaned) by revolutionaries, is simply that England was governed by an oligarchy of aristocrats and plutocrats; and as Nature obstinately refused to conform to this arrangement by making every aristocratic or plutocratic baby a completely conventional Conservative, there was always a Left and Right in the party of privilege as there is in the party of Labor, except that the aristocratic Right was more prejudiced and the aristocratic Left much more seditious than the Labor Right and Left. The aristocratic Left constituted a nineteenth century Fronde; [2] and the papers which appealed to it were those which, without saying a word against Church or State which could disqualify them for the tables of the most exclusive clubs, country houses, or even rectories, nevertheless criticized everything and everybody without the smallest respect for either. That was the secret of The World under the editorship of Edmund Yates when I was the critic of music; and it was the secret of The Saturday Review also. On both papers I was perfectly at home when the Radical and Socialist papers would have been partly shocked and partly terrified by my audacities . . . .

. . . I never read any dramatic criticism except the proofs of my own articles. People used to accuse me of paradox because when Henry Irving, the leading actor of that day, was quoted as an authority on the theatres, I pointed out that he knew less about the theatres than anyone else in London, because he was on the stage—the same stage—every night. . . .

I know that to students of the British Schimpflexikon which Archer compiled to chronicle the Press reception of Ibsen in this country we must needs appear an obscene rabble throwing mud, screaming foul abuse at every great man who came our way. Our musical colleagues had cut an equally poor figure when confronted with Wagner. And I cannot pretend to consider my own reception as a playwright by my quondam colleagues as, on the whole, a critical success. But critics must be judged by their normal activities, and not by their convulsions when a new departure upsets them. The critics who declared that Wagner's music had no melody; that his harmonies were meaningless discords, his orchestration a hideous uproar, and the man himself a despicable charlatan, were quite good judges of Gounod and Arthur Sullivan. Those who yelled for the prosecution as disorderly houses of theatres in which Ibsen's plays were performed were sane enough about Robertson and Tom Taylor, Sardou and Dumas *fils;* and they could stand the advance led by Pinero, Jones, and Gilbert without losing their heads. Oscar Wilde had no more to complain of than is in the day's worries of any successful playwright.

. . . Thanks to the development of the literary and artistic sides of the daily newspapers, to the gramophone, . . . and wireless, the supply of journalists with a knowledge and love of art, and a cultivated sensibility to refinements in artistic execution, is much greater than it was. Editors are no longer contemptuously ignorant of art; they may still be ignorant, but they are ashamed of their ignorance, and no longer dare to hand over the theatre with a snub to the least cultivated of their casual reporters. When, as a beginner, I got an introduction to Morley (not then Lord Morley), and he asked me what I thought I could do, I threw away the opportunity by saying that I thought I could write about art. In utter disgust he turned away, flinging over his shoulder a muttered "Pooh! ANYBODY can write about art." "O, CAN they???" I retorted, with a contempt equal to his own; and I honestly thought I was showing great self-restraint in not adding "you wretched Philistine second-hand Macaulay." That concluded the interview; and Morley missed his chance of becoming my editor.[3] As to Stead, who succeeded Morley, and under whom I became a contributor to the old Pall Mall Gazette, he was an abyss of ignorance in part; a theatre was to him a sort of *maison tolérée* which God forbid he should ever enter . . . .

As to the theatre itself, it is beginning to educate its critics, whereas in the old days it stultified them. I have no space left in which to describe how completely the theatre used to be divorced from the national life. It was more secluded than any modern convent, and much more prudish. It knew nothing of religion, politics, science, or any art but its own. It had only one subject, which the censorship did not allow it to mention. Janet Achurch was forbidden to produce a little play by Octave Feuillet, about a lady with what we called a past, until she gave the Censor her word of honor to say every night on the stage, "I sinned but in intention," which she accordingly whispered to the conductor most faithfully always on her first entry . . . .

In justice to many well-known public persons who are handled rather recklessly . . . I beg my readers not to mistake my journalistic utterances for final estimates of their worth and achievements as dramatic artists and authors. It is not so much that the utterances are unjust; for I have never claimed for myself the divine attribute of justice. But as some of them are hardly even reasonably fair I must honestly warn the reader that [my theatre criticism] is not a series of judgments aiming at impartiality, but a siege laid to the theatre of the XIXth Century by an author who had to cut his own way into it at the point of the pen, and throw some of its defenders into the moat.

Pray do not conclude from this that the things . . . written were not true, or not the deepest and best things I knew how to say. Only, they must be construed in the light of the fact that all through I was accusing my opponents of failure because they were not doing what I wanted, whereas they were often succeeding very brilliantly in doing what they themselves wanted. I postulated as desirable a certain kind of play in which I was destined ten years later to make my mark (as I very well foreknew in the depth of my own unconsciousness); and I brought everybody: authors, actors, managers and all, to the one test: were they coming my way or staying in the old grooves?

Sometimes I made allowances for the difference in aim, especially in the case of personal friends. But as a rule I set up my own standard of what the drama should be and how it should be presented; and I used all my art to make every deviation in aiming at this standard, every recalcitrance in approaching it, every refusal to accept it seem ridiculous and old-fashioned. In this, however, I only did what all critics do who are worth their salt. The critics who attacked Ibsen and defended Shakespear whilst I was defending Ibsen and attacking Shakespear; or who were acclaiming the reign of Irving at the Lyceum Theatre as the Antonine age of Shakespearean drama whilst I was battering at it in open preparation for its subsequent downfall, were no more impartial than I. And when my own turn came to be criticized, I also was attacked because I produced what I wanted to produce and not what some of my critics wanted me to produce.

... When I criticized I really did know definitely what I wanted. Very few journalistic critics do. When they attack a new man as Ibsen was attacked, they are for the most part only resisting a change which upsets their habits. ...

... Weariness of the theatre is the prevailing note of London criticism. Only the ablest critics believe that the theatre is really important: in my time none of them would claim for it, as I claimed for it, that it is as important as the Church was in the Middle Ages and much more important than the Church was in London in the years under review. A theatre to me is a place "where two or three are gathered together." The apostolic succession from Eschylus to myself is as serious and as continuously inspired as that younger institution, the apostolic succession of the Christian Church.

Unfortunately this Christian Church, founded gaily with a pun, has been so largely corrupted by rank Satanism that it has become the Church where you must not laugh; and so it is giving way to the older and greater Church to which I belong: the Church where the oftener you laugh the better, because by laughter only can you destroy evil without malice, and affirm good fellowship without mawkishness. When I wrote, I was well aware of what an unofficial census of Sunday worshippers presently proved: that churchgoing in London has been largely replaced by playgoing. This would be a very good thing if the theatre took itself seriously as a factory of thought, a prompter of conscience, an elucidator of social conduct, an armory against despair and dullness, and a temple of the Ascent of Man. I took it seriously in that way, and preached about it instead of merely chronicling its news and alternately petting and snubbing it as a licentious but privileged form of public entertainment. This, I believe, is why my sermons gave so little offense, and created so much interest. The artists of the theatre, led by Sir Henry Irving, were winning their struggle to be considered ladies and gentlemen, qualified for official honors. Now for their gentility and knighthoods I cared very little: what lay at the root of my criticism was their deeper claim to be considered, not merely actors and actresses, but men and women, not hired buffoons and posturers, however indulged, but hierophants of a cult as eternal and sacred as any professed religion in the world. And so, consciously or unconsciously, I was forgiven when many of my colleagues, less severe because less in earnest on the subject, gave deadly offence.

. . . If my head had not been full of Ibsen and Wagner in the nineties I should have been kinder and more reasonable in my demands. Also, perhaps, less amusing. . . .

Let me hasten to reassure those who have been terrified by certain striking examples of the destructive force of this column, and who are aghast at such power being wielded by one man. Their fears are vain: I am no more able to make or mar artistic enterprises at will than the executioner has the power of life and death. It is true that to all appearance a fourteen thousand pound pantomime, which the critics declared the best in London, collapsed at a touch of my pen. And the imagination of the public has undoubtedly been strongly seized by the spectacle of the much-written-up Tosca at the height of its prosperity, withering, like Klingsor's garden, at three lines in a postscript to my weekly article. But there is no magic in the matter. Though the east wind seems to kill the consumptive patient, he dies, not of the wind, but of phthisis. On the strong-lunged man it blows in vain. La Tosca died of disease, and not of criticism, which, indeed, did its best to keep it alive.

For my part, I have struck too many blows at the well-made play without immediate effect, to suppose that it is my strength and not its own weakness that has enabled me to double it up this time. When the critics were full of the "construction" of plays, I steadfastly maintained that a work of art is a growth, and not a construction. When the Scribes and Sardous turned out neat and showy cradles, the critics said, "How exquisitely constructed!" I said, "Where's the baby?" Of course, there never was any baby; and when the cradles began to go out of fashion even the critics began to find them as dowdy as last year's bonnets. A *fantoccini* theatre, in which puppets play the parts of men and women, is amusing; but the French theatre, in which men and women play the parts of puppets, is unendurable. Yet there was a time when some persons wrote as if Adrienne Lecouvreur was a superior sort of tragedy, and Dora (alias Diplomacy) a masterpiece of comedy. Even now their artificiality passes for ingenuity. Just as a barrister in England gets an immense reputation as a criminals' advocate when a dozen of his clients have been hanged (the hanging being at once a proof and an advertisement of the importance of the case), so when a dramatist has written five or six plays in which two hours of intrigues and telegrams are wasted in bringing about some situation which the audience would have accepted at once without any contrivance at all, he receives his diploma as a master of play construction!

. . . There was no inquiry into my qualifications. I was never interfered with by an editor. I remember on one occasion I wrote a notice in which I referred to an old melodrama and gave a little description of how it used to be acted. When my notice appeared I found this passage had been cut, and I asked the editor what was wrong with it. He said there was nothing wrong with it, but that the actress whom I had mentioned was his mother.

. . . I remember a critic who was interfered with, not on artistic, but on purely political grounds. Austin Harrison was critic of The Daily Mail, and when I began to make trouble in the theatre Austin Harrison was interested and wrote long notices of my plays. They were either not put in or they were cut extremely short. When Harrison, not understanding why this happened, asked Lord Northcliffe the reason, Northcliffe said, "I am not running my paper to advertise a damned Socialist."

. . . When I felt I must find another editor with the qualities of Yates: one not afraid of everything unusual, and aware how far he might safely venture in the novelty and heterodoxy which make criticism readable . . . I . . . in 1895 accepted the post of theatre critic from Frank Harris, who had just become editor of The Saturday Review.

Harris had emigrated to America, where he had adventures as a cowboy, as a laborer employed in the building of Brooklyn Bridge, as a hotel manager, and as a lawyer. He had returned to England with the morals, manners, and conversation of a buccaneer, combined with a voice and elocution that gave him an imposing personal distinction and secured his acceptance at first sight into English professional and political society. But his love was for literature. He knew good writing from bad; and preferred good to bad. He was afraid of heterodoxy, not indeed knowing that it was dangerous; for he believed himself to be a Christlike saint, and had no suspicion that in London he would have passed more easily as another Captain Kidd.

In short, the very man for me, and I the very man for him. Knowing that he would bully me if I did not first bully him in my own Irish fashion, I established the same footing with him as with Yates. We agreed for £6 a week. Yates had paid me £5. Not bad pay in those days.

Frank Harris [was] everything except a humorist, not, apparently, from stupidity, but because scorn overcomes humor. . . . Nobody ever dreamt of reproaching Milton's Lucifer for not seeing the comic side of his fall. . . .

When [Harris] was editor of the Saturday Review he chose and held together for a while a team of contributors whom no one else had the gumption to choose or the courage to back with a free hand. I think I know pretty well all the grievances his detractors had against him; but if I had to write his epitaph it should run, *"Here lies a man of letters who hated cruelty and injustice and bad art, and never spared them in his own interest. R. I. P."* . . . Like Hedda Gabler he was tormented by a sense of sordidness in the commonplace realities which form so much of the stuff of life, and was not only disappointed in people who did nothing splendid, but savagely contemptuous of people who did not want to have anything splendid done.

He often reminded me of a revolutionist who rose at an obscure meeting held in a cellar near Gower Street shortly after the settlement of the great London dock strike of 1889. In that struggle the champions of the dockers were Mr. John Burns, Mr. Tom Mann, and Cardinal Manning. Mr. Burns shared with the Cardinal the credit of the settlement; and I, being the principal speaker at the meeting, gave him his due.

But this hero had been dreaming of greater things than the miserable sixpence an hour which I was claiming as a great victory for the dockers. He denounced Mr. Burns in unmeasured terms; and he denounced me similarly for supporting him. He was quite beyond argument; so I put the critical question to him, "What would you have done had you been in John Burns's place?"

He was quite equal to the occasion. "Done!" he thundered. "I would have taken the scarlet cardinal by the scruff of his gory neck and chucked him into the incarnadined river."

What else could a man say when, dazzled by millenial visions, he was invited to cheer himself hoarse over sixpence an hour for a job so heavy and dangerous that accidents requiring hospital treatment occurred every twenty minutes? I sympathized with the protest, though I knew very well what an enormous effort it had cost to get the dockers that wretched sixpence, and how utterly incapable my Boanergic denouncer would have been of getting a farthing for them.

Frank, too, was a man of splendid visions, unreasonable expectations, fierce appetites which he was unable to relate to anything except to romantic literature, and especially to the impetuous rhetoric of Shakespear. It is hardly an exaggeration to say that he ultimately quarrelled with everybody but Shakespear . . . . Many of those spirits, who, like Frank, can by no means learn to live in the real world and suffer fools and humbugs gladly, have nobility of soul, though for want of adequate secular facilities—economic faculty, legal faculty, mathematical faculty, business faculty, and objective faculty generally—this nobility cannot always save them from comparatively squalid adventures in the material sphere. Harris seized his opportunities with a confident audacity that carried everything before it. His resonant voice, capable of every accent of scorn, his brilliant eyes, his ready tongue, his bold individual style, imposed him, on men and women alike, as one who was his own best credential. His knowledge and capacity were assumed without evidence at first sight. He believed himself to be a strong man and a man of action; and he was taken by everyone at his own valuation from the moment when his first marriage rescued him from some very dark days of poverty in Germany, whither he had been drawn in pursuit of literary learning, and where the only thing he learnt was that unless he had money the world would have no mercy on him. But though he took the tide in his affairs unhesitatingly at the flood, he was not thick-skinned enough to hold his friendships; and the worst of it was that instead of showing his sensitiveness he made everyone believe that he was as tough as hickory.

I remember my own surprise when the late Julia Frankau (Frank Danby) one day remonstrated with me very earnestly for treating him too roughly. She urged me to remember that he was an exquisitely sensitive man. My own early experience, which included nearly ten years of apparently hopeless failure, had hardened me to such a degree that I had lost all sensitiveness to any criticism but my self-criticism. Is is impossible to acquire this hardness and retain a sympathetic understanding of how something that falls on you with the weight of a fly's foot can sting apparently tougher men like the lash of a whip. So I was somewhat incredulous at first; but I soon saw that Mrs. Frankau was right, and that

Harris could not bear the spurns that patient merit from the unworthy takes with any sort of equanimity. He accumulated quarrels and tired of all his enterprises. It was at last apparent that in any concern which depended on his co-operation with and management of colleagues he would never get anywhere because he always stopped to fight somebody, and imagined every position that occurred instead of studying it. He blazed through London like a comet, leaving a trail of deeply annoyed persons behind him . . . .

He really had not one career but two, simultaneous but on different planes. On the imaginative plane the invariable generosity of his transports of indignation, scorn, pity, chivalry, and defiance of snobberies, powers, and principalities enabled him to retain the regard of people who had the same sympathies. But on the prosaic plane of everyday life he got into difficulties and incurred maledictions from which it was not always possible to defend him.

These difficulties are not worth bothering about now. They were all made worse by his main delusion, which was an enormous one and sometimes highly comic. He was firmly persuaded that the human race consisted entirely of Frank Harris and women of the sort Frank Harris idealized. Any departure from this standard was in his eyes delinquency, cretinism, unforgivable sin, diabolism. As there was only one Frank Harris in the world, and the sort of woman he idealized never completely existed except in his imagination, the effect on his social manners was often disastrous. And the matter was complicated further by his manifold nature; for his scope ranged from depths of materialism to heights of spirituality; and his ideal of womanhood varied accordingly.

As a result his dinner-table conversation was often of the most disconcerting inappropriateness. If he took in a quiet deaconess he would entertain her on the assumption that her personal morals and religious views were those of our post-war night clubs. If, knowing this, you took care to put him beside the most abandoned lady present, he would discourse to her on his favourite subject of the beauty of the character of Jesus, and his intention of writing a great book about it. And as all his conversation was uttered in a resonant and arresting voice that reached the farthest corners of the room, he was apt to produce the situation which was in Oscar Wilde's mind when he said, "Frank Harris has been received in all the great houses—*once.*" . . . The end . . . was inevitable . . . .

I myself was present at a curious meeting between the two, when Harris, on the eve of the Queensberry trial, prophesied to Wilde with miraculous precision exactly what immediately afterwards happened to him, and warned him to leave the country. . . . Wilde, though under no illusion as to the folly of the quite unselfish suit-at-law he had been persuaded to begin, nevertheless so miscalculated the force of the social vengeance he was unloosing on himself that he fancied it could be stayed by putting up the editor of The Saturday Review (as Mr. Harris then was) to declare that he considered Dorian Gray a highly moral book, which it certainly is. . . . Harris foretold him the truth, . . . something like this: "For God's sake, man, put everything on that plane out of your head. You don't realize what is going to happen to you. It is not going to be a matter of clever talk about your books. They are going to bring up a string of witnesses that will put art and literature out of the question. Clarke will throw up his brief. He will carry the case to a certain point; and then, when he sees the avalanche coming, he will back out and leave you in the dock. What you have to do is to cross to France tonight. Leave a letter saying that you cannot face the squalor and horror of a law case; that you are an artist and unfitted for such things. Don't stay here clutching at straws like testimonials to Dorian Gray. *I tell you I know.* I know what is going to happen. I know Clarke's sort. I know what evidence they have got. You must go."

It was no use. Wilde was in a curious double temper. He made no pretence either of innocence or of questioning the folly of his proceedings against Queensberry. But he had an infatuate haughtiness as to the impossibility of his retreating. . . . Oscar finally rose with a mixture of impatience and his grand air, and walked out with the remark that he had now found out who were his real friends.

. . . I am sure Oscar has not found the gates of heaven shut against him: he is too good company to be excluded; but he can hardly have been greeted as "Thou good and faithful servant."

Lady Wilde was nice to me in London during the desperate days between my arrival in 1876 and my first earning of an income by my pen in 1885, or rather until, a few years earlier, I threw myself into Socialism and cut myself contemptuously loose from everything of which her at-homes—themselves desperate affairs enough . . . —were part. I was at two or three of them; and I once dined with her in company with an ex-tragedy queen named Miss Glynn, who, having no visible external ears, reared a head like a turnip. Lady Wilde talked about Schopenhauer; and Miss Glynn told me that Gladstone formed his oratorical style on Charles Kean.

I ask myself where and how I came across Lady Wilde; for we had no social relations in the Dublin days. The explanation must be that my sister, then a very attractive girl who sang beautifully, had met and made some sort of innocent conquest of both Oscar and Willie. I met Oscar once at one of the at-homes; and he came and spoke to me with an evident intention of being specially kind to me. We put each other out frightfully; and this odd difficulty persisted between us to the very last, even when we were no longer mere boyish novices and had become men of the world with plenty of skill in social intercourse. I saw him very seldom, as I avoided literary and artistic coteries like the plague, and refused the few invitations I received to go into society with burlesque ferocity, so as to keep out of it without offending people past their willingness to indulge me as a privileged lunatic.

The last time I saw him was at that tragic luncheon . . . at the Café Royal; and I am quite sure our total of meetings from first to last did not exceed twelve, and may not have exceeded six.

I definitely recollect six: (1) At the at-home aforesaid. (2) At Mackmurdo's house in Fitzroy Street in the days of the Century Guild and its paper The Hobby Horse. (3) At a meeting somewhere in Westminister at which I delivered an address on Socialism, and at which Oscar turned up and spoke. Robert Ross surprised me greatly by telling me, long after Oscar's death, that it was this address of mine that moved Oscar to try his hand at a similar feat by writing The Soul of Man Under Socialism.[4] (4) A chance meeting near the stage door of the Haymarket Theatre, at which our queer shyness of one another made our resolutely cordial and appreciative conversation so difficult that our final laugh and shakehands was almost a reciprocal confession. (5) A really pleasant afternoon we spent together on catching one another in a place where our presence was an absurdity. It was some exhibition in Chelsea: a naval commemoration, where there was a replica of Nelson's Victory and a set of P. & O. cabins which made one seasick by mere association of ideas. I don't know why I went or why Wilde went; but we did; and the question what the devil we were doing in that galley tickled us both. It was my sole experience of Oscar's wonderful gift as a raconteur. I remember particularly an amazingly elaborate story . . . an example of the cumulation of a single effect, as in Mark Twain's story of the man who was persuaded to put lightning conductor after lightning conductor at every possible point on his roof until a thunderstorm came and all the lightning in the heavens went for his house and wiped it out.

Oscar's much more carefully and elegantly worked out story was of a young man who invented a theatre stall which economized space by ingenious contrivances which were all described. A friend of his invited twenty millionaires to meet him at dinner so that he might interest them in the invention. The young man convinced them completely by his demonstration of the saving in a theatre holding, in ordinary seats, six hundred people, leaving them eager and ready to make his fortune. Unfortunately he went on to calculate the annual savings in all the theatres of the world; then in all the churches of the world; then in all the legislatures; estimating finally the incidental and moral and religious effects of the invention until at the end of an hour he had estimated a profit of several thousand millions: the climax of course being that the millionaires folded their tents and silently stole away, leaving the ruined inventor a marked man for life.

Wilde and I got on extraordinarily well on this occasion. I had not to talk myself, but to listen to a man telling me stories better than I could have told them. We did not refer to Art, about which, excluding literature from the definition, he knew only what could be picked up by reading about it. He was in a tweed suit and low hat like myself, and had been detected and had detected me in the act of clandestinely spending a happy day at Rosherville Gardens instead of pontificating in his frock-coat and so forth. And he had an audience on whom not one of his subtlest effects was lost. And so for once our meeting was a success; and I understood why Morris, when he was dying slowly, enjoyed a visit from Wilde more than from anybody else . . . . I understand . . . even though he was incapable of friendship, though not of the most touching kindness on occasion.

Our sixth meeting, the only other one I can remember, was the one at the Café Royal. On that occasion he was not too preoccupied with his danger to be disgusted with me because I, who had praised his first plays, handsomely, had turned traitor over The Importance of Being Earnest. Clever as it was, it was his first really heartless play.[5] In the others the chivalry of the eighteenth-century Irishman and the romance of the disciple of Théophile Gautier (Oscar was old-fashioned in the Irish way, except as a critic of morals) not only gave a certain kindness and gallantry to the serious passages and to the handling of the women, but provided that proximity of emotion without which laughter, however irresistible, is destructive and sinister. In The Importance of Being Earnest this had vanished; and the play, though extremely funny, was essentially hateful. I had no idea that Oscar was going to the dogs, and that this represented a real degeneracy produced by his debaucheries. I thought he was still developing; and I hazarded the unhappy guess that The Importance of Being Earnest was in idea a young work written or projected long before under the influence of Gilbert and furbished up for Alexander as a potboiler. At the Café Royal that day I calmly asked him whether I was not right. He indignantly repudiated my guess, and said loftily (the only time he ever tried on me the attitude he took to John Gray and his more abject disciples) that he was disappointed in me. I suppose I said, "Then what on earth has happened to you?" but I recollect nothing more on that subject except that we did not quarrel over it.

When he was sentenced I spent a railway journey on a Socialist lecturing excursion to the North drafting a petition for his release. After that I met Willie Wilde at a theatre which I think must have been the Duke of York's, because I connect it vaguely with St Martin's Lane. I spoke to him about the petition, asking him whether anything of the sort was being done, and warning him that though I and Stewart Headlam would sign it, that would be no use, as we were two notorious cranks, and our names would by themselves reduce the petition to absurdity and do Oscar more harm than good. Willie cordially agreed, and added, with maudlin pathos and an inconceivable want of tact: "Oscar was NOT a man of bad character: you could have trusted him with a woman anywhere." He convinced me . . . that signatures would not be obtainable; so the petition project dropped; and I don't know what became of my draft.

When Wilde was in Paris during his last phase I made a point of sending him inscribed copies of all my books as they came out; and he did the same to me.[6]

In writing about Wilde and Whistler, in the days when they were treated as witty triflers, and called Oscar and Jimmy in print, I always made a point of taking them seriously and with scrupulous good manners. Wilde on his part also made a point of recognizing me as a man of distinction by his manner, and repudiating the current estimate of me as a mere jester. This was not the usual reciprocal-admiration trick: I believe he was sincere, and felt indignant at what he thought was a vulgar underestimate of me; and I had the same feeling about him. My impulse to rally to him in his misfortune, and my disgust at "the man Wilde" scurrilities of the newspapers, was irresistible: I don't quite know why; for my charity to his perversion, and my recognition of the fact that it does not imply any general depravity or coarseness of character, came to me through reading and observation, not through sympathy. I have all the normal violent repugnance to homosexuality—if it be really normal, which nowadays one is sometimes provoked to doubt.

Also, I was in no way predisposed to like him: he was my fellow-townsman, and a very prime specimen of the sort of fellow-townsman I most loathed: to wit, the Dublin snob. His Irish charm, potent with Englishmen, did not exist for me; and on the whole it may be claimed for him that he got no regard from me that he did not earn.

What first established a friendly feeling in me was, unexpectedly enough, the affair of the Chicago anarchists . . . . I tried to get some literary men in London, all heroic rebels and sceptics on paper, to sign a memorial asking for the reprieve of these unfortunate men. The only signature I got was Oscar's. It was a completely disinterested act on his part; and it secured my distinguished consideration for him for the rest of his life.

To return for a moment to Lady Wilde. You know that there is a disease called giantism, caused by "a certain morbid process in the sphenoid bone of the skull—viz., an excessive development of the anterior lobe of the pituitary body" (this is from the nearest encyclopedia). "When this condition does not become active until after the age of twenty-five, by which time the long bones are consolidated, the result is acromegaly, which chiefly manifests itself in an enlargement of the hands and feet." I never saw Lady Wilde's feet; but her hands were enormous, and never went straight to their aim when they grasped anything, but minced about, feeling for it. And the gigantic splaying of her palm was reproduced in her lumbar region.

Now Oscar was an overgrown man, with something not quite normal about his bigness: something that made Lady Colin Campbell, who hated him, describe him as "that great white caterpillar." . . . I have always maintained that Oscar was a giant in the pathological sense, and that this explains a good deal of his weakness.

. . . I think [friends] . . . have affectionately underrated his snobbery, mentioning only the pardonable and indeed justifiable side of it; the love of fine names and distinguished associations and luxury and good manners. . . . *On certain planes,* truly . . . he was not bitter and did not use his tongue to wound people. But this is not true on the snobbish plane. On one occasion he wrote about T. P. O'Connor with deliberate, studied, wounding insolence, with his Merrion Square Protestant pretentiousness in full cry against the Catholic. He repeatedly declaimed against the vulgarity of the British journalist, not as . . . I might, but as an expression of the odious class feeling that is itself the vilest vulgarity. He made the mistake of not knowing his place. He objected to be addressed as Wilde, declaring that he was Oscar to his intimates and Mr Wilde to others, quite unconscious of the fact that he was imposing on the men with whom, as a critic and journalist, he had to live and work, the alternative of granting him an intimacy he had no right to ask or a deference to which he had no claim. The vulgar hated him for snubbing them; and the valiant men damned his impudence and cut him. Thus he was left with a band of devoted satellites on the one hand, and a dining-out connection on the other, with here and there a man of talent and personality enough to command his respect, but utterly without that fortifying body of acquaintance among plain men in which a man must move as himself a plain man, and be Smith and Jones and Wilde and Shaw and Harris instead of Bosie and Robbie and Oscar and Mister. This is the sort of folly that does not last forever in a man of Wilde's ability; but it lasted long enough to prevent Oscar laying any solid social foundations.

Another difficulty I have already hinted at. Wilde started as an apostle of Art; and in that capacity he was a humbug. . . . Now it was quite evident to me, as it was to Whistler and Beardsley, that Oscar knew no more about pictures than anyone of his general culture and with his opportunities can pick up as he goes along. He could be witty about Art, as I could be witty about engineering; but that is no use when you have to seize and hold the attention and interest of people who really love music and painting. Therefore, Oscar was handicapped by a false start, and got a reputation for shallowness and insincerity which he never retrieved until too late.

Comedy: the criticism of morals and manners *viva voce,* was his real forte. When he settled down to that he was great. But . . . his initial mistake had produced that "rather low opinion of Wilde's capacities," that "deep-rooted contempt for the showman in him," which persisted as a first impression and will persist until the last man who remembers his æsthetic period has perished. The world has been in some ways so unjust to him that one must be careful not to be unjust to the world.

In the preface on education, called Parents and Children, to my volume of plays beginning with Misalliance, there is a section headed Artist Idolatry, which is really about Wilde. Dealing with "the powers enjoyed by brilliant persons who are also connoisseurs in art," I say, "the influence they can exercise on young people who have been brought up in the darkness and wretchedness of a home without art, and in whom a natural bent towards art has always been baffled and snubbed, is incredible to those who have not witnessed and understood it. He (or she) who reveals the world of art to them opens heaven to them. They become satellites, disciples, worshippers of the apostle. Now the apostle may be a voluptuary without much conscience. Nature may have given him enough virtue to suffice in a reasonable environment. But this allowance may not be enough to defend him against the temptation and demoralization of finding himself a little god on the strength of what ought to be a quite ordinary culture. He may find adorers in all directions in our uncultivated society among people of stronger character than himself, not one of whom, if they had been artistically educated, would have had anything to learn from him, or regarded him as in any way extraordinary apart from his actual achievements as an artist. Tartufe is not always a priest.

12

Widowers' Houses

THERE IS an old saying that if a man has not fallen in love before forty, he had better not fall in love after. I long ago perceived that this rule applied to many other matters as well: for example, to the writing of plays; and I made a rough memorandum for my own guidance that unless I could produce at least half a dozen plays before I was forty, I had better let playwriting alone. It was not so easy to comply with this provision as might be supposed. Not that I lacked the dramatist's gift. As far as that is concerned, I have encountered no limit but my own laziness to my power of conjuring up imaginary people in imaginary places, and finding pretexts for theatrical scenes between them. But to obtain a livelihood by this insane gift, I must have conjured so as to interest not only my own imagination, but that of at least some seventy or a hundred thousand contemporary London playgoers. To fulfil this condition was hopelessly out of my power. I had no taste for what is called popular art, no respect for popular morality, no belief in popular religion, no admiration for popular heroics. As an Irishman I could pretend to patriotism neither for the country I had abandoned nor the country that had ruined it. As a humane person I detested violence and slaughter, whether in war, sport, or the butcher's yard. I was a Socialist, detesting our anarchical scramble for money, and believing in equality as the only possible permanent basis of social organization, discipline, subordination, good manners, and selection of fit persons for high functions. Fashionable life, open on indulgent terms to unencumbered "brilliant" persons, I could not endure, even if I had not feared its demoralizing effect on a character which required looking after as much as my own. I was neither a sceptic nor a cynic in these matters: I simply understood life differently from the average respectable man; and as I certainly enjoyed myself more—mostly in ways which would have made him unbearably miserable—I was not splenetic over our variance.

. . . I got a clue to my real condition from a friend of mine, a physician who had devoted himself specially to ophthalmic surgery. He tested my eyesight one evening, and informed me that it was quite uninteresting to him because it was normal. I naturally took this to mean that it was like everybody else's; but he rejected this construction as paradoxical, and hastened to explain to me that I was an exceptional and highly fortunate person optically, normal sight conferring the power of seeing things accurately, and being enjoyed by only about ten per cent of the population, the remaining ninety per cent being abnormal. I immediately perceived the explanation of my want of success in fiction. My mind's eye, like my body's, was "normal": it saw things differently from other people's eyes, and saw them better.

This revelation produced a considerable effect on me. At first it struck me that I might live by selling my works to the ten per cent who were like myself; but a moment's reflection shewed me that these must all be as penniless as I, and that we could not live by taking in oneanother's literary washing. How to earn daily bread by my pen was then the problem. Had I been a practical commonsense money-loving Englishman, the matter would have been easy enough: I should have put on a pair of abnormal spectacles and aberred my vision to the liking of the ninety per cent of potential book-buyers. But I was so prodigiously self-satisfied with my superiority, so flattered by my abnormal normality, that the resource of hypocrisy never occurred to me. Better see rightly on a pound a week than squint on a million. The question was, how to get the pound a week. The matter, once I gave up writing novels, was not so very difficult. Every despot must have one disloyal subject to keep him sane. Even Louis the Eleventh had to tolerate his confessor, standing for the eternal against the temporal throne. Democracy has now handed the sceptre of the despot to the sovereign people; but they, too, must have their confessor, whom they call Critic. Criticism is not only medicinally salutary: it has positive popular attractions in its cruelty, its gladiatorship, and the gratification given to envy by its attacks on the great, and to enthusiasm by its praises. It may say things which many would like to say, but dare not, and indeed for want of skill could not even if they durst. Its iconoclasms, seditions, and blasphemies, if well turned, tickle those whom they shock; so that the critic adds the privileges of the court jester to those of the confessor. Garrick, had he called Dr Johnson Punch, would have spoken profoundly and wittily; whereas Dr Johnson, in hurling that epithet at him, was but picking up the cheapest sneer an actor is subject to.

It was as Punch, then, that I emerged from obscurity. All I had to do was to open my normal eyes, and with my utmost literary skill put the case exactly as it struck me, or describe the thing exactly as I saw it, to be applauded as the most humorously extravagant paradoxer in London. The only reproach with which I became familiar was the everlasting "Why can you not be serious?" Soon my privileges were enormous and my wealth immense. I had a prominent place reserved for me on a prominent journal every week to say my say as if I were the most important person in the kingdom. My pleasing toil was to report upon all the works of fine art the capital of the world can attract to its exhibitions, its opera house, its concerts and its theatres. The classes eagerly read my essays: the masses patiently listened to my harangues. I enjoyed the immunities of impecuniosity with the opportunities of a millionaire. If ever there was a man without a grievance, I was that man.

But alas! the world grew younger as I grew older: its vision cleared as mine dimmed: it began to read with the naked eye the writing on the wall which now began to remind me that the age of spectacles was at hand. My opportunities were still there: nay, they multiplied tenfold; but the strength and youth to cope with them began to fail, and to need eking out with the shifty cunning of experience. I had to shirk the platform; to economize my health; even to take holidays. In my weekly columns, which I once filled full from a magic well that never ran dry or lost its sparkle provided I pumped hard enough, I began to repeat myself; to fall into a style which, to my great peril, was recognized as at least partly serious; to find the pump tiring me and the water lower in the well; and, worst symptom of all, to reflect with little tremors on the fact that my mystic wealth could not, like the money for which other men threw it away, be stored up against my second childhood. The younger generation, reared in an enlightenment unknown to my schooldays, came knocking at the door too: I glanced back at my old columns and realized that I had timidly botched at thirty what newer men do now with gay confidence in their cradles. I listened to their vigorous knocks with exultation for the race, with penurious alarm for my own old age. When I talked to this generation, it called me Mister, and, with its frank, charming humanity, respected me as one who had done good work in my time. A famous playwright wrote a long play to shew that people of my age were on the shelf; and I laughed at him with the wrong side of my mouth.

It was at this bitter moment that my fellow citizens, who had previously repudiated all my offers of political service, contemptuously allowed me to become a vestryman: *me,* the author of Widowers' Houses!

At the end of the nineteenth century the borough of St. Pancras contained a quarter of a million of the population of London. The culture of that quarter million may be inferred from the fact that there was not a single bookshop in the entire borough. It contained clusters of houses of ill-fame. It was cheerfully corrupt politically: a cheque for £1,000, placed in the right quarter, would have secured the return of a baby in arms to Parliament or the County Council for the southern division, where I resided. When cheques were not forthcoming, as at the vestry elections, the little groups of politically-minded local shopkeepers and men of business elected one another for no particular reason except that they seemed likely to keep the rates down to the extreme possible minimum. In fact they kept them below it, and were in debt to the bank £17,000 deep when they were found out by the Local Government Board auditor on the promotion of the Vestry to the rank of Borough Council by Act of Parliament.

When I was a Member of this Municipality,[1] I never once had to vote on the merits of a question otherwise than on its merits and not in the least because I belonged to this Party or that Party. If I voted one way or the other there was not a fresh election, it put me to no expense. Now . . . that was why fifty years ago, instead of going into Parliament I went into the Municipality of St. Pancras. It was not that I was not pressed to go into Parliament. The Government offered me a choice collection of seats, which I couldn't possibly win and which they couldn't possibly win; the number of times I was offered the Strand Constituency—I can't really remember how many. However, I went into municipal life and there I found that things could be done.

When I . . . became a member of the Health Committee[2] . . . the question of providing accommodation for women, which was part of our business, was one which I conceived to be pressingly important. And you can have no idea of the difficulty I had in getting that notion, to a limited extent, into the heads of the gentlemen who were working with me on the Committee. At that time women were not on those public bodies; and women's special needs were therefore not thought of. I well remember one of my earliest experiences on the Health Committee. A doctor rose to call attention to a case in which a woman was concerned. He happened to mention that she had been in his hands because she was expecting her confinement. . . .

. . . No sooner had the doctor uttered this revelation than the whole Committee burst into a roar of laughter. You see, there was not only the angel conception: there was also the inevitable reaction against it. If anyone betrayed the secret or gave it away, half the world was shocked, and the other half roared with laughter.

There was a noteworthy feature in the pantomimes of my early days. No part of the harlequinade was complete unless one of the scenes shewed an old woman dropping from a top window or climbing over a wall, the joke being that in the course of these gymnastics she thrust her leg from under her skirt, in a white stocking, and allowed the audience to see almost up to her knee, eliciting a shriek of laughter. Propriety was saved by the fact that the old woman was obviously a man dressed up as a woman. You can tell from the old comic pictures of those days that to see even a woman's ankle was considered half a shocking thing and half an obscene joke!

I have taken up . . . time . . . with all this because . . . this thing remains still with us as a superstition even now, when we think we have completely freed ourselves of it. . . .

It is the real reason why, when on that public body I talked and talked to get proper, common, sanitary accommodation for women, I found it impossible for a long time to get over the opposition to it as an indecency. A lavatory for women was described as an abomination.

Into this stagnant bywater an energetic Methodist, Hugh Price Hughes and his wife, launched a devoted West London Mission which soon found that it must make its way into local politics and stir them up in the interest of the poor. I found earnest Methodist women calling on me as election canvassers. I told them that they had not the least notion of how to get votes, and explained to them how to vary their attack according to the class and interests of the voter. At first they said they would rather see their candidates dead than achieve their return by such ungodly duplicity; but as the day of election came nearer and nearer they usually returned in a completely demoralized condition to consult me as to how to get round some specially obdurate elector. Anyhow, they soon proved that vestrydom could do nothing where Methodism was really alive; when by some intrigue or other I became a vestryman, I was not surprised to find myself sitting beside a young Methodist minister named Ensor Walters at what was supposed to be the Progressive end of the long table on the Mayor's left. His figure, and a certain boyishly unconscious authority about him, reminded me of Pope Pius IX; and I at once set him down as likely to end as head of his Church,[3] whatever that headship might be. All the more as he was quite natural and unassuming. The vestry, as far as it knew anything about me, classed me as a Socialist and therefore an atheist, sure to differ with the Methodist minister on every question. What actually happened was that he and I immediately formed a party two strong all to ourselves. And we troubled ourselves about no other party. There was a hopelessly outnumbered little section of the vestry which called itself the Progressive Party, and held party meetings under the presidency of an Irish doctor who occasionally rose up at the council meetings and began his speech by the formula, 'This is one of the most stinking scandals that has ever disgraced the annals of St. Pancras.' Nobody took offence at this: it was accepted as the rather amusing duty of a party leader. Naturally neither Ensor nor I had any use for that sort of thing. He was out to make a little corner for the Kingdom of God in St. Pancras; and nothing could have suited me better.

As well as I remember, I did most of the talking. Ensor never wanted to hear himself talk; but when he let himself go the effect was startling. He would bear the follies of the old vestry gang in silence until they were going to do something unconsciously wicked or unintentionally cruel; and then he would explode, in righteous wrath, and, without wasting a word of argument on them, declare that he was not going to stand it and the thing was not to be done. And his word was like a fire: they cowered like naughty children caught at their tricks. Most men make fools of themselves when they lose their tempers. Ensor could lose his in a perfectly selfless way and be all the more effective for it.

In due time we two faded out of vestrydom, having more important work on our hands which took us out of one another's orbit . . . .

I never read Archer's one novel, a youthful exploit called The Doom of the Destroyed, which had been published serially in a Scottish newspaper, and was one of his favorite jokes. I gathered that in point of romance it left George Moore's . . . *quasi* autobiographical tales of adventure nowhere; but it is certain that Archer's adult taste in novels was for merciless realism. Therefore when one day he proposed that we two should collaborate in writing a play, he to supply the constructional scaffolding or scenario, and I to fill in the dialogue, I assumed that I might be as realistic as Zola or De Maupassant with his entire sympathy. But he was always upsetting my assumptions as to his sympathies; and he did so signally on this occasion.

It happened in this way. Archer had planned for two heroines, a rich one and a poor one. The hero was to prefer the poor one to the rich one; and in the end his disinterestedness was to be rewarded by the lucrative discovery that the poor one was really the rich one. When I came to fill in this scheme I compressed the two heroines into one; but I made up the one out of two models, whom I will now describe.

Once, when I was walking homewards at midnight through Wigmore Street, taking advantage of its stillness and loneliness at that hour to contemplate, like Kant, the starry heaven above me, the solitude was harshly broken by the voices of two young women who came out of Mandeville Place on the other side of the street a couple of hundred yards behind me. The dominant one of the pair was in a black rage: the other was feebly trying to quiet her. The strained strong voice and the whimpering remonstrant one went on for some time. Then came the explosion. The angry one fell on the other, buffeting her, tearing at her hair, grasping at her neck. The victim, evidently used to it, cowered against the railings, covering herself as best she could, and imploring and remonstrating in a carefully subdued tone, dreading a police rescue more than the other's violence. Presently the fit passed, and the two came on their way, the lioness silent, and the lamb reproachful and rather emboldened by her sense of injury. The scene stuck in my memory, to be used in due time.

Also I had about this time a friendship with a young independent professional woman,[4] who enjoyed, as such, an exceptional freedom of social intercourse in artistic circles in London. As she was clever, goodnatured, and very goodlooking, all her men friends fell in love with her. This had occurred so often that she had lost all patience with the hesitating preliminaries of her less practised adorers. Accordingly, when they clearly longed to kiss her, and she did not dislike them sufficiently to make their gratification too great a strain on her excessive goodnature, she would seize the stammering suitor firmly by the wrists, bring him into her arms by a smart pull, and saying "Let's get it over," allow the startled gentleman to have his kiss, and then proceed to converse with him at her ease on subjects of more general interest.

I provided Archer with a heroine by inventing a young woman who developed from my obliging but impatient friend in the first act to the fury of Wigmore Street in the second: such a heroine as had not been seen on the London stage since Shakespear's Taming of the Shrew. And my shrew was never tamed.

Now Archer was not such a simpleton as to be unaware that some women are vulgar, violent, and immodest according to Victorian conceptions of modesty. He would probably have assented to the proposition that as vulgarity, violence, and immodesty are elements in human nature, it is absurd to think of them as unwomanly, unmanly, or unnatural. But he also knew that a character practically free from these three vices could be put on the stage without any departure from nature, for the excellent reason that his own character was most unusually free from them, even his strong Scottish sense of humor being, like his conversation, entirely clean. Why, then, impose them wantonly on his charming and refined heroine? He repudiated all complicity in such an outrage. He reproached me for my apparent obsession with abominably ill-tempered characters, over-sexed to saturation. My way in the theatre was evidently not his way; and it was not until, at my third attempt as a playwright, I achieved a play (Mrs Warren's Profession) which appealed to his sense of Zolaistic naturalism, that he ceased to dissuade me from pursuing the occupation into which he had innocently tempted me.

I must mention that his decisive and indignant retirement from the collaboration occurred whilst the play was still in shorthand, and therefore quite illegible by him, and not legible enough by myself to admit of my reading it aloud to him tolerably. But I had made demands on him which betrayed my deliberate and unconscionable disregard of his rules of the art of play construction. His scenario had been communicated to me *viva voce;* and when I told him I had finished the first act, and had not yet come to his plot, asking him to refresh my memory about it, he felt as the architect of a cathedral might if the builder had remarked one day that he had finished the nave and transepts according to his own fancy, and, having lost the architect's plans, would like to have another copy of them before he tackled the tower, the choir, and the lady chapel. I managed to appease my architect by arguing that it was not until the second act that a well-made play came to business seriously, and that meanwhile I had fulfilled his design by making the river Rhine the scene of the meeting of the lovers in the first act. But when, having written some pages of the second act, I said I had used up all his plot and wanted some more to go on with, he retired peremptorily from the firm. He was of course quite right: I was transmogrifying not only his design but the whole British drama of that day so recklessly that my privilege as a paradoxical lunatic broke down under the strain; and he could no longer with any self-respect allow me to play the fool with his scenario. For it was not a question of this particular scenario only. He did not agree with me that the form of drama which had been perfected in the middle of the nineteenth century in the French theatre was essentially mechanistic and therefore incapable of producing vital drama. That it was exhausted and, for the moment, sterile, was too obvious to escape an observer of his intelligence; but he saw nothing fundamentally wrong with it, and to the end of his life maintained that it was indispensable as a form for sound theatrical work, needing only to be brought into contact with life by having new ideas poured into it. I held, on the contrary, that a play is a vital growth and not a mechanical construction; that a plot is the ruin of a story and therefore of a play, which is essentially a story; that Shakespear's plays and Dickens's novels, though redeemed by their authors' genius, were as ridiculous in their plots as Goldsmith's hopelessly spoilt Goodnatured Man: in short, that a play should never have a plot, because, if it has any natural life in it, it will construct itself, like a flowering plant, far more wonderfully than its author can consciously construct it.

On such terms collaboration between us was impossible: indeed my view practically excludes collaboration. . . .

The early history of the play . . . has been given by [William] Archer in The World of the 14th December 1892, in the following terms:—

Partly to facilitate the labours of Mr. George Bernard Shaw's biographers, and partly by way of relieving my own conscience, I think I ought to give a short history of the genesis of Widowers' Houses. Far away back in the olden days [1885], while as yet the Independent Theatre slumbered in the womb of Time, together with the New Drama, the New Criticism, the New Humour, and all the other glories of our renovated world, I used to be a daily frequenter of the British Museum Reading Room. Even more assiduous in his attendance was a young man of tawny complexion and attire, beside whom I used frequently to find myself seated. My curiosity was piqued by the odd conjunction of his subjects of research. Day after day for weeks he had before him two books, which he studied alternately, if not simultaneously—Karl Marx's Das Kapital (in French), and an orchestral score of Tristan und Isolde. I did not know then how exactly this quaint juxtaposition symbolised the main interests of his life. Presently I met him at the house of a common acquaintance, and we conversed for the first time. I learned from himself that he was the author of several unpublished master-pieces of fiction. Construction, he owned with engaging modesty, was not his strong point, but his dialogue was incomparable. Now, in those days, I had still a certain hankering after the rewards, if not the glories, of the playwright. With a modesty in no way inferior to Mr Shaw's, I had realised that I could not write dialogue a bit; but I still considered myself a born constructor. So I proposed, and Mr Shaw agreed to, a collaboration. I was to provide him with one of the numerous plots I kept in stock, and he was to write the dialogue. So said, so done. I drew out, scene by scene, the scheme of a twaddling cup-and-saucer comedy vaguely suggested by Augier's Ceinture Dorée. The details I forget, but I know it was to be called Rhinegold, was to open, as Widowers' Houses actually does, in a hotel-garden on the Rhine, and was to have two heroines, a senti-mental and a comic one, according to the accepted Robertson-Byron-Carton formula. I fancy the hero was to propose to the sentimental heroine, believing her to be the poor niece instead of the rich daugh-ter of the sweater, or slum-landlord, or whatever he may have been; and I know he was to carry on in the most heroic fashion, and was ultimately to succeed in throwing the tainted treasure of his father-in-law, metaphorically speaking, into the Rhine. All this I gravely propounded to Mr Shaw, who listened with no less admirable gravity. Then I thought the matter had dropped, for I heard no more of it for many weeks. I used to see Mr Shaw at the Museum, la-boriously writing page after page of the most exquisitely neat short-hand at the rate of about three words a minute; but it did not occur to me that this was our play. After about six weeks he said to me, 'Look here, I've written half the first act of that comedy, and I've used up all your plot. Now I want some more to go on with.' I told him that my plot was a rounded and perfect organic whole, and that I could no more eke out in this fashion than I could provide him or myself with a set of supplementary arms and legs. I begged him to extend his shorthand and let me see what he had done; but this would have taken him far too long. He tried to decipher some of it orally, but the process was too lingering and painful for endurance. So he simply gave me an outline in narrative of what he had done; and I saw that, so far from having used up my plot, he had not even touched it. There the matter rested for months and years. Mr Shaw would now and then hold out vague threats of finishing 'our play,' but I felt no serious alarm. I thought (judging from my own experience in other cases) that when he came to read over in cold blood what he had written, he would see what impossible stuff it was. Perhaps my free utterance of this view piqued him; perhaps he felt impelled to remove from the Independent Theatre the reproach of dealing solely in foreign products. The fire of his genius, at all events, was not to be quenched by my persistent applications of the wet-blanket. He finished his play; Mr Grein, as in duty bound, accepted it; and the result was the performance of Friday last [9th Dec. 1892] at the Independent Theatre.

To this history I have little to add. The circumstances occurred, in the main, as Mr Archer states them. But I most strenuously deny that there is any such great difference between his Rhinegold and Widowers' Houses as he supposes. I appeal to the impartial public, which has now both my play and Mr Archer's story before it, to judge whether I did not deal faithfully with him. The Rhine hotel garden, the hero proposing to the heroine in ignorance of the source of her father's wealth, the "tainted treasure of the father-in-law," the renunciation of it by the lover: all these will be found as prominently in the pages of the play as in Mr Archer's description of the fable which he persists in saying I did "not even touch." As a matter of fact the dissolution of partnership between us came when I told him that I had finished up the renunciation and wanted some more story to go on with, as I was only in the middle of the second act. He said that according to his calculation the renunciation ought to have landed me at the end of the play. I could only reply that his calculation did not work out, and that he must supply further material. This he most unreasonably refused to do; and I had eventually to fish up the tainted treasure out of the Rhine, so to speak, and make it last out another act and a half, which I had to invent all by myself. Clearly, then, he was the defaulter; and I am the victim.

It will have been noted by the attentive reader that what I have called a story, Mr. Archer calls a plot; and that he mentions two heroines, introduced for the sole purpose of being mistaken for one another. Now, I confess to discarding the second daughter. She was admittedly a mere joist in the plot; and I had then, have now, and have always had, an utter contempt for "constructed" works of art. How any man in his senses can deliberately take as his model the sterile artifice of Wilkie Collins or Scribe, and repudiate the natural artistic activity of Fielding, Goldsmith, Defoe and Dickens, not to mention Æschylus and Shakespear, is beyond argument with me: those who entertain such preferences are obviously incapable people, who prefer a "well made play" to King Lear exactly as they prefer acrostics to sonnets. As a fictionist, my natural way is to imagine characters and spin out a story about them, whether I am writing a novel or a play; and I please myself by reflecting that this has been the way of all great masters of fiction. At the same time I am quite aware that a writer with the necessary constructive ingenuity, and the itch for exercising it for its own sake, can entertain audiences or readers very agreeably by carefully constructing and unravelling mysteries and misunderstandings; and that this ingenuity may be associated with sufficient creative imagination to give a considerable show of humanity and some interest of character to the puppets contrived for the purpose of furthering the plot. The line between the authors who place their imagination at the service of their ingenuity and those who place their ingenuity at the service of their imagination may be hard to draw with precise justice (to Edgar Allan Poe, for instance!); but it is clear that if we draw it as an equator, Scribe and the plot constructors will be at the south pole, and Æschylus and the dramatic poets at the north. Now, Archer's Rhinegold, in the absence of any convincing evidence that I was an Æschylus, was designed for the southern hemisphere; and Widowers' Houses was built for the north. I told the story, but discarded the plot; and Archer at once perceived that this step made the enterprise entirely on my own, since the resultant play, whether good or bad, must on my method be a *growth* out of the stimulated imagination of the actual writer, and not a manufactured article constructed by an artisan according to plans and specifications supplied by an inventor. The collaboration was therefore dropped, and after finishing the second act, so as to avoid leaving a loose end, and noting such beginnings of the third as had already sprouted, I left the work aside for seven years and thought no more of it. [One] . . . August, having been rather overworked by the occurrence of a General Election at the busiest part of the journalistic season in London, I could do nothing for a while but potter aimlessly over my old papers, among which I came across the manuscript of the play; and it so tickled me that I there and then sat down and finished it. But for Mr Grein and the Independent Theatre Society it would probably have gone back to its drawer and lain there for another seven years, if not for ever.

Ibsen . . . was the hero of the new departure. It was in 1889 that the first really effective blow was struck by the production of A Doll's House by Charles Charrington and Janet Achurch. Whilst they were taking that epoch making play round the world, Mr Grein followed up the campaign in London with his Independent Theatre. It got on its feet by producing Ibsen's Ghosts; but its search for unacted native dramatic masterpieces was so complete a failure that in the autumn of 1892 it had not yet produced a single original piece of any magnitude by an English author. In this humiliating national emergency, I proposed to Mr Grein that he should boldly announce a play by me. Being an extraordinarily sanguine and enterprising man, he took this step without hesitation. . . . I saw that the very qualities which had made it impossible for ordinary commercial purposes in 1885 might be exactly those needed by the Independent Theatre in 1892. So I completed it by a third act; gave it the farfetched Scriptural title of Widowers' Houses; and handed it over to Mr Grein, who launched it at the public in the Royalty Theatre with all its original tomfooleries on its head. It made a sensation out of all proportion to its merits or even its demerits; and I at once became infamous as a playwright. . . .

The horrible artificiality of that impudent sham the Victorian womanly woman, a sham manufactured by men for men, and duly provided by the same for the same with a bulbously overclothed "modesty" more lascivious than any frank sensuality, had become more and more irksome to the best of the actresses who had to lend their bodies and souls to it— and by the best of the actresses I mean those who had awakeningly truthful minds as well as engaging personalities. I had so little taste for the Victorian womanly woman that in my first play I made my heroine throttle the parlor maid. The scandal of that outrage shook the London theatre and its Press to their foundations: an easy feat; for their foundations were only an inch deep and very sandy at that; and I was soon shaking more serious impostures, including that of the whole rotten convention as to women's place and worth in human society which had made the Victorian sham possible. But for that I needed the vigorous artificiality of the executive art of the Elizabethan stage to expose and bring back to nature the vapid artificiality of the Victorian play. . . . Take Widowers' Houses; cut out the passages which convict the audience of being just as responsible for the slums as the landlord is; make the hero a ranting Socialist instead of a perfectly commonplace young gentleman; make the heroine an angel instead of her father's daughter only one generation removed from the wash-tub; and you have the successful melodrama of tomorrow. . . . My plays are no more economic treatises than Shakespear's.

It is true that neither Widowers' Houses nor Major Barbara could have been written by an economic ignoramus, and that Mrs Warren's Profession is an economic exposure of the White Slave traffic as well as a melodrama. There is an economic link between Cashel Byron, Sartorius, Mrs Warren, and Undershaft: all of them prospering in questionable activities.

. . . The first performance was sufficiently exciting: the Socialists and Independents applauded me furiously on principle; the ordinary play-going first-nighters hooted me frantically on the same ground; I, being at that time in some practice as what is impolitely called a mob orator, made a speech before the curtain,[5] the newspapers discussed the play for a whole fortnight not only in the ordinary theatrical notices and criticisms, but in leading articles and letters,[6] and finally the text of the play was published with an introduction by Mr Grein, an amusing account by Archer of the original collaboration, and a long preface and several elaborate controversial appendices in my most energetically egotistic fighting style. . . . Widowers' Houses is entirely unreadable, except for the preface and appendices. . . .

The following extracts from letters addressed by the author to the press after the performance of Widowers' Houses are reprinted here to give the reading public some idea of the commotion which can be made in a theatre by a work which, if published as a novel, would surprise no one. First, as to the extent of the commotion, hear The Era of the 24th December, 1892:—

Hardly any recent play has provoked so much newspaper and other controversy as Mr Bernard Shaw's Widowers' Houses. At least

two of the daily papers, on the day after its production, devoted leading articles to its consideration, besides special criticisms of almost
unprecedented length. We should be afraid to say how many journals gave two long columns to it. Then all last week a controversy
on its merits and demerits raged in a morning paper; and it was held
up as an example of the kind of play the Lord Chamberlain did *not*
object to by Mrs Aveling[7] in her lecture to the Playgoers; and,
finally, it was one of the subjects of an interesting lecture delivered
last Sunday night to the Socialists of Hammersmith. The last fact,
however, becomes less surprising when we find that the lecturer was
Mr Bernard Shaw.

This account is not exaggerated. The play occupied the press for weeks
after its production to an extent which, in a really healthy and active
phase of dramatic art, would have been absurd. The discussion raged
chiefly round matters of fact, most of the writers seeming to have no
definite idea of the sources of the revenues enjoyed by the propertied
classes under our industrial system. In replying to these criticisms the
author carefully abstained from confusing issues of fact with . . . artistic
issues . . . . To the editor of The Star the author is indebted for the
publication, on the 19th December, 1892, of a letter of which the following
is an abridgment:—

> SIR,—
> The critics of my play Widowers' Houses have now had their say.
> Will you be so good as to let the author have a turn? I have gone
> through every criticism I could get hold of; and I think it is now
> clear that 'the new drama' has no malice to fear from the serious
> critics. The care with which every possible admission in my favor
> has been made, even in the notices of those who found the play in-
> tolerably disagreeable and the author intolerably undramatic, shews
> that the loss of critical balance produced by the first shock of Ibsen's
> Ghosts was only momentary, and that the most unconventional and
> obnoxious agitator-dramatist, even when he has gone out of his way
> to attack his critics, need not fear a Press vendetta.
> However, the fairness of criticism is one thing, its adequacy quite
> another. I do not hesitate to say that many of my critics have been
> completely beaten by the play simply because they are ignorant of
> society. Do not let me be misunderstood: I do not mean that they
> eat with their knives, drink the contents of their finger-bowls, or sit

down to dinner in ulsters and green neckties. What I mean is that they do not know life well enough to recognize it in the glare of the footlights. They denounce Sartorius, my house-knacking widower, as a monstrous libel on the middle and upper class, because he grinds his money remorselessly out of the poor. But they do not (and cannot) answer his argument as to the impossibility of his acting otherwise under our social system; nor do they notice the fact that though he is a bad landlord he is not in the least a bad man as men go. Even in his economic capacity I have made him a rather favorable specimen of his class. I might have made him a shareholder in a match factory where avoidable 'phossy jaw' is not avoided, or in a tram company working its men seventeen and a half hours a day, or in a railway company with a terrible death-roll of mangled shunters, or in a whitelead factory or chemical works—in short, I might have piled on the agony beyond the endurance of my audience, and yet not made him one whit worse than thousands of personally amiable and respected men who have invested in the most lucrative way the savings they have earned or inherited. I will not ask those critics who are so indignant with my 'distorted and myopic outlook on society' what they will do with the little money their profession may enable them to save. I will simply tell them what they *must* do with it, and that is follow the advice of their stockbroker as to the safest and most remunerative investment, reserving their moral scruples for the expenditure of the interest, and their sympathies for the treatment of the members of their own families. Even in spending the interest they will have no alternative but to get the best value they can for their money without regard to the conditions under which the articles they buy are produced. They will take a domestic pride in their comfortable homes, full of furniture made by 'slaughtered' (*i.e.* extra-sweated) cabinet makers, and go to church on Sunday in shirts sewn by women who can only bring their wages up to subsistence point by prostitution. What will they say to Sartorius then? What, indeed, can they say to him now?—these 'guilty creatures sitting at a play,' who, instead of being struck to the soul and presently proclaiming their malefactions, are naïvely astonished and revolted at the spectacle of a man on the stage acting as we are all acting perforce every day. The notion that the people in Widowers' Houses are abnormally vicious or odious could only prevail in a community in which Sartorius is absolutely typical in his unconscious villainy. Like my critics, he lacks conviction of sin. Now, the didactic object of my play is to bring conviction of sin—to make the Pharisee who repudiates Sartorius as either a Harpagon or a diseased dream of mine, and thanks God that such persons do not represent his class, recognize that Sartorius is his own photograph. In vain will the virtuous critic tell me that he does not own slum property: all I want to see is the label on his matchbox, or his last week's washing-bill, to judge for myself whether he really ever gives a second thought to Sartorius's tenants, who make his matchboxes and wash his stockings so cheaply.

As to the highly connected young gentleman, naturally straightforward and easygoing, who bursts into genuine indignation at the sufferings of the poor, and, on being shewn that he cannot help them, becomes honestly cynical and throws off all responsibility whatever, that is nothing but the reality of the everyday process known as disillusion. His allowing the two business men to get his legs under their mahogany, and to persuade him to 'stand in' with a speculation of which he understands nothing except that he is promised some money out of it, will surprise no one who knows the City, and has seen the exploitation of aristocratic names by City promoters spread from needy guinea-pig colonels, and lords with courtesy titles, to eldest sons of the noblest families. If I had even represented Harry Trench as letting himself in for eighteen months' hard labor for no greater crime than that of being gambler enough to be the too willing dupe of a swindler, the incident would be perfectly true to life. As to the compensation speculation in the third act being a fraud which no gentleman would have countenanced, that opinion is too innocent to be discussed. I can only say that as the object of the scheme is to make a haul at the expense of the rate-payers collectively, it is much less cruel and treacherous in its incidence than the sort of speculation which made the late Mr Jay Gould universally respected during his lifetime. I shall be told next that Panama is a dream of mine.

There is a curious idea in the minds of some of my critics that I have given away my case by representing the poor man, Lickcheese, as behaving, when he gets the chance, exactly as the rich man does. These gentlemen believe that, according to me, what is wrong with society is that the rich, who are all wicked, oppress the poor, who are all virtuous. I will not waste the space of The Star by dealing with

such a misconception further than to curtly but good-humoredly inform those who entertain it that they are fools. I administer the
remark, not as an insult, but as a tonic.

Now comes the question, How far does all this touch the merits
of the play as a work of art? Obviously not at all; but it has most
decidedly touched the value of the opinions of my critics on that
point. The evidence of the notices (I have sheaves of them before
me) is irresistible. With hardly an exception the men who find my
sociology wrong are also the men who find my dramatic work-
manship bad; and *vice versa*. Even the criticism of the acting is
biassed in the same way. The effect on me, of course, is to reassure
me completely as to my own competence as a playwright. The very
success with which I have brought all the Philistines and sentimental
idealists down on me proves the velocity and penetration with which
my realism got across the footlights. I am well accustomed to judge
of the execution I have done by the cries of the wounded.

On one point, however, I heartily thank my critics for their unanimous forbearance. Not one of them has betrayed the licenses I have
taken in the political and commercial details of the play. Considering
that I have made a resident in Surbiton eligible as a St Giles' vestryman; that I have made the London County Council contemporary
with the 1885 Royal Commission on the Housing of the Working
Classes; that I have represented an experienced man of business as
paying 7 per cent on a first mortgage—considering, in short, that I
have recklessly sacrificed realism to dramatic effect in the machinery
of the play, I feel, as may be well imagined, deeply moved by the
compliments which have been paid me on my perfect knowledge of
economics and business.

Before giving the rest of the letter, it is convenient to refer here to a
very funny discussion which arose over the scene in the second act in
which Blanche assaults the servant. Although nothing is commoner on
the stage than bodily violence threatened or executed by indignant heroes,
heroines have hitherto been excluded by convention from this method of
displaying their prowess. The author resolved to redress this injustice to
Woman by making his heroine attack her servant much as Othello attacks his ancient. The resultant sensation testified to the hardihood of the
experiment. The critics were highly scandalized; and their view of the

incident was expressed in the following passage from a notice which appeared the day after the performance.—

"What a ludicrous incident! How we all shrieked with laughter! What has such a scene to do with the play? Why did Mr Shaw introduce it? I will tell you why. Because Mr Shaw wishes to present Blanche as a *type,* a type of the modern middle-class Englishwoman (as he sees her), the woman who will not hear about the poor wretches in their tenement houses because it is so unpleasant, and who, in her own drawing-room, can, in a fit of temper, use brutal violence to her own dependants."

It was not possible for the author to seriously discuss the notion that he regarded temper and violence as class characteristics. He was only able to say, in a letter to The Speaker, "Some people think that ladies with tempers are never personally violent. I happen to know that they are; and so I leave the matter." It is true that the ideal lady—the "typical" lady if that term be preferred—never strikes, never swears, never smokes, never gambles, never drinks, never nags, never makes advances to inept wooers, never, in short, does anything "unladylike," whether "in her own drawing-room" or elsewhere. Just so the ideal clergyman never hunts, never goes to the theatre, and regards the poorest laborer as his equal and his brother by their common Father, God. The author confesses to having jilted *the* ideal lady for *a* real one. He did it intentionally; and he will probably do it again, and yet again, even at the risk of having the real ones mistaken for counter-ideals. Why Blanche should be held to indicate any belief on his part that all ladies are hot-tempered, any more than Hamlet is held to indicate a belief on Shakespear's part that all princes are philosophers, is not apparent to him.

Here is a final extract from the letter to The Star on the subject of Blanche:—

On another point in her conduct one critic makes an objection which, I confess, amazed me. Sartorius, as the son of a very poor woman, knows that the poor are human beings exactly like himself. But his daughter, brought up as a lady, conceives them as a different and inferior species. 'I hate the poor,' she says—'at least, I hate those dirty, drunken, disreputable people who live like pigs.' The critic in question, whose bias towards myself is altogether friendly, cannot conceive that a young lady would avow such inhuman sentiments: hypocrisy, he contends, would prevent her if her heart did not. I can only refer him, if he has really never heard such sentiments boasted of by ladies, to the comments of The Times and the St James's Gazette (to name no other papers written by gentlemen for gentlemen) on the unemployed, on the starving Irish peasants whose rents have since been reduced wholesale in the Irish land courts, or on the most heavily sweated classes of workers whose miserable plight has been exposed before Parliamentary Committees and Royal Commissions, to prove that the thinkers and writers of Blanche Sartorius's party vie with each other in unconscious—nay, conscientious—brutality, callousness, and class prejudice when they speak of the proletariat. Hypocrisy with them takes the shape of dissembling sympathy with the working class when they really feel it, not of affecting it when they do not feel it. My friend and critic must remember the savage caricatures of William Morris, John Burns, Miss Helen Taylor, Mrs. Besant, etc., in which Punch once indulged, as well as the outrageous calumnies which were heaped on the late Charles Bradlaugh during his struggle to enter Parliament, not to mention the cases of unsocial conduct by country gentlemen and magistrates exposed every week in the 'Pillory' columns of Truth. Am I to be told that the young ladies who read these papers in our suburban villas are less narrow and better able to see across the frontiers of their own class than the writers whom their fathers support? The fact is that Blanche's class prejudices, like those of the other characters in the play, are watered down instead of exaggerated. The whole truth is too monstrous to be told otherwise than by degrees.

To this a writer in The Lady's Pictorial (24th December, 1892) retorts:—

"So it comes to this, that Mr. Shaw's defence for drawing a middle-class English girl as a virago who batters her maid and vilifies the starving poor, is that in professedly political papers (written by men for men—women not entering into the question at all), the other side is held up to ridicule by mud being flung upon their humble allies! as though the political game played by political journals has anything whatever to do with the attributes of humanity common to the average woman and the average man!"

. . . The only other utterance of the author's which need be quoted is from a letter to The Speaker (31st December, 1892). It is not a defence of the artistic value of the play, which cannot be established or disestablished by argument, but a renewal of the author's insistence on the impossibility of appreciating a work of art without adequate knowledge of its subject-matter:—

"I now approach the question which is really the most interesting from the critical point of view. Is it possible to treat the artistic quality of a play altogether independently of its scientific quality? For example, is it possible for a critic to be perfectly appreciative and perfectly incredulous and half insensible at the same time? I do not believe it for a moment. No point in a drama can produce any effect at all unless the spectator perceives it and accepts it as a real point; and this primary condition being satisfied, the force of the effect will depend on the extent to which the point interests the spectator—that is, seems momentous to him. The spectacle of Hamlet fencing with an opponent whose foil is 'unbated' produces its effect because the audience knows the danger; but there are risks just as thrilling to those who understand them, risks of cutting arteries in surgical operations, risks of losing large sums by a momentary loss of nerve in the money market, risks of destroying one's whole character by an apparently trifling step, perils of all sorts which may give the most terrible intensity to a scene in the eyes of those who have the requisite technical knowledge or experience of life to fathom the full significance of what they are witnessing, but which would produce as little effect on others as the wheeling forward of a machine gun would on a hostile tribe of savages unacquainted with the 'resources of civilization.'

"It has long been clear to me that nothing will be done for the theatre until the most able dramatists refuse to write down to the level of that imaginary monster the British Public. We want a theatre for people who have lived, thought, and felt, and who have some real sense that women are human beings just like men, only worse brought up, and consequently worse behaved. In such a theatre the merely literary man who has read and written instead of living until he has come to feel fiction as experience and to resent experience as fiction, would be as much out of place as the ideal British Public itself. Well, let him sit out his first mistaken visit quietly and not come again; for it is clear that only by holding the mirror up to literature can the dramatist please him, whereas it is by holding it up to nature that good work is produced. In such a theatre Widowers' Houses would rank as a trumpery farcical comedy; whereas today it is excitedly discussed as a daringly original sermon, political essay, satire, Drapier letter or what not, even by those who will not accept it as a play on any terms because its hero did not, when he learnt that his income came from slum property, at once relinquish it (*i.e.* make it a present to Sartorius without benefiting the tenants) and go to the goldfields to dig out nuggets with his strong right arm, so that he might return to wed his Blanche after a shipwreck (witnessed by her in a vision), just in time to rescue her from beggary, brought upon her by the discovery that Lickcheese was the rightful heir to the property of Sartorius, who had dispossessed and enslaved him by a series of forgeries unmasked by the faithful Cokane. Was it really lack of capacity that led me to forego all this 'drama' by making my hero do exactly what he would have done in real life—that is, apologize like a gentleman (in the favorable sense) for accusing another man of his own unconscious rascality, and admit his inability to change a world that will not take the trouble to change itself?"

The reader will now be in a position to understand the sort of controversy which . . . so magnified the importance of Widowers' Houses.

13

Plays: Pleasant and Unpleasant

... IT WAS the existence of the Independent Theatre that made me finish that play, and by giving me the experience of its rehearsal and performance, revealed the fact (to myself among others) that I possessed the gift of "fingering" the stage. That old play now seems as remote and old-fashioned as Still Waters Run Deep or London Assurance; but the newspapers of 1892 raged over it for a whole fortnight. Everything followed from that: the production of Arms and the Man by Miss Horniman and Florence Farr at the Avenue Theatre, Miss Horniman's establishment of Repertory Theatres in Dublin and Manchester, the Stage Society, H. Granville-Barker's tentative matinées of Candida at the Court Theatre, the full-blown management of Vedrenne and Barker, Edie Craig's Pioneers, and the final relegation of the Nineteenth Century London theatre to the dust-bin . . . .

I had not achieved a success; but I had provoked an uproar; and the sensation was so agreeable that I resolved to try again. In the following year, 1893, when the discussion about Ibsenism, "the New Woman," and the like, was at its height, I wrote for the Independent Theatre the topical comedy called The Philanderer. But even before I finished it, it was apparent that its demands on the most expert and delicate sort of high comedy acting went beyond the resources then at the disposal of Mr Grein. I had written a part which nobody but Charles Wyndham could act, in a play which was impossible at his theatre: a feat comparable to the building of Robinson Crusoe's first boat. I immediately threw it aside, and returning to the vein I had worked in Widowers' Houses, wrote a third play, Mrs Warren's Profession, on a social subject of tremendous

[277]

force. That force justified itself in spite of the inexperience of the play-wright. The play was everything that the Independent Theatre could desire: rather more, if anything, than it bargained for. But at this point I came upon the obstacle that makes dramatic authorship intolerable in England to writers accustomed to the freedom of the Press. I mean, of course, the Censorship.

. . . The terror of the Censor's power gave us trouble enough to break up any ordinary commercial enterprise. Managers promised and even engaged their theatres to us after the most explicit warnings that the play was unlicensed, and at the last moment suddenly realized that Mr. Redford had their livelihoods in the hollow of his hand, and backed out. Over and over again the date and place were fixed and the tickets printed, only to be canceled, until at last the desperate and overworked manager of the Stage Society could only laugh, as criminals broken on the wheel used to laugh at the second stroke. We rehearsed under great difficulties. Christmas pieces and plays for the new year were being pre-pared in all directions; and my six actor colleagues were busy people, with engagements in these pieces in addition to their current professional work every night. On several raw winter days stages for rehearsal were unattainable even by the most distinguished applicants; and we shared corridors and saloons with them whilst the stage was given over to children in training for Boxing night. At last we had to rehearse at an hour at which no actor or actress has been out of bed within the memory of man; and we sardonically congratulated one another every morning on our rosy matutinal looks and the improvement wrought by early rising in our healths and characters. And all this, please observe, for a society without treasury or commercial prestige, for a play which was being denounced in advance as unmentionable, for an author without influence at the fashionable theatres! I victoriously challenge the West End managers to get as much done for interested motives, if they can.

Three causes made the [1902] production the most notable that has fallen to my lot. First, the veto of the Censor, which put the supporters of the play on their mettle. Second, the chivalry of the Stage Society, which, in spite of my urgent advice to the contrary, and my demonstration of the difficulties, dangers, and expenses the enterprise would cost, put my dis-couragements to shame and resolved to give battle at all costs to the attempt of the Censorship to suppress the play. Third, the artistic spirit of the actors, who made the play their own and carried it through triumphantly in spite of a series of disappointments and annoyances much more trying to the dramatic temperament than mere difficulties.

The acting, too, required courage and character as well as skill and intelligence. The veto of the Censor introduced a quite novel element of moral responsibility into the undertaking. And the characters were very unusual in the English stage. The young heroine is, like her mother, an Englishwoman to the backbone, and not, like the heroines of our fashionable drama, a prima donna of Italian origin. Consequently she was sure to be denounced as unnatural and undramatic by the critics. The most vicious man in the play is not in the least a stage villain: indeed, he regards his own moral character with the sincere complacency of a hero of melodrama. The amiable devotee of romance and beauty is shown at an age which brings out the futilization which these worships are apt to produce if they are made the staple of life instead of the sauce. The attitude of the clever young people to their elders is faithfully presented as one of pitiless ridicule and unsympathetic criticism, and forms a spectacle incredible to those who, when young, were not cleverer than their nearest elders, and painful to those sentimental parents who shrink from the cruelty of youth, which pardons nothing because it knows nothing. In short, the characters and their relations are of a kind that the routineer critic has not learned to place; so that their misunderstanding was a foregone conclusion. Nevertheless, there was no hesitation behind the curtain. When it went up at last, a stage much too small for the company was revealed to an audience much too small for the audience. But the players, though it was impossible for them to forget their own discomfort, at once made the spectators forget theirs. It certainly was a model audience, responsible from the first line to the last; and it got no less than it deserved in return.

. . . I was myself officially classed for many years as a pernicious blackguard, and injured in reputation and pocket, because I used my art to expose the real roots of prostitution, and, later on, shewed how a prostitute and a thief, both of them professed enemies of morality and scoffers at religion, got caught and converted by their consciences—theologically speaking, by the Holy Ghost—and "saved." [1]

I was not the only victim. Shelley, Ibsen, Tolstoy, Maeterlinck, and Brieux shared my fate whilst playwrights whose plays did not rise above the level of reports of the proceedings in the police and divorce courts were effectively protected by certificates of propriety from the censor costing only two guineas per play. This absurdity was produced by the fact that when the problem of moralizing the aesthete arises, the first expedient that suggests itself—I resist the temptation to say the first thought that comes into a fool's head—is to appoint a censor to examine all works of art and decide whether they shall be made public or even permitted to exist. The arguments for a censorship are irresistible: it is plain to silly people that all that need be done is to find a censor who combines all the wisdom, learning, and concern for human welfare of the Vatican, the Judicial Committee of the Privy Council, the episcopates of all the Churches, with the omniscience of the Holy Trinity, and put fine art under his thumb. The statesman, unable to find such a paragon, and educated to class artists, especially theatre artists, as Bohemian undesirables, satisfies the demand by giving the job to a petty official with a salary of two or three hundred a year or less. The petty official, finding his mental powers unequal to his judicial duties, makes a list of words that must not be used, and subjects that, being controversial, must not be discussed by frivolous persons such as all artists are assumed to be. Obvious subjects are religion, sex, and politics. Thus an unofficial American Roman Catholic censor, much dreaded in Hollywood, being confronted with a certain play written by myself and entitled St Joan, found the word halo in it and ordered its excision as religious. The heroine happening to remark that soldiers are often fond of babies, that, too, had to come out, because babies are sex. And so on, until there was nothing intelligible left of the play, which, though sexless, is full of religion and politics . . . .[2]

The first play that got me into trouble called attention to the fact that prostitution, supposed to be the fault of the vicious propensities of sexually abandoned women and their male clients, was really an economic phenomenon produced by an underpayment of honest women so degrading, and an overpayment of whores so luxurious, that a poor woman of any attractiveness actually owed it to her self-respect to sell herself in the streets rather than toil miserably in a sweater's den sixteen hours a day for twopence an hour, or risk phosphorus poisoning in a match factory for five shillings a week, or the like. How badly this revelation was needed was proved years after when the international organization of prostitution by capitalist exploiters, known as the White Slavery, became such a tyranny that the Government was forced to take some action. And all it could think of was an Act to have male brothel keepers flogged, with the result that a valuable monopoly was conferred on procuresses: in fact on my Mrs. Warren. If my play had not been suppressed by the censorship the matter might have been better understood, and the remedy not so mischievously futile.

As I knew very well that is it useless to denounce a wrong remedy without finding the right one, and that the only remedy for priviledged slander is to live it down, I did not howl vainly about my personal grievance. I pointed out that the London music halls, which had been sinks of silly smut, had been cleaned up and changed into decent variety theatres by compelling the managers to obtain a licence from the London Country Council from year to year to carry on their operations, leaving them free to perform what they pleased for twelve months at the risk of being driven out of their business at the end if their proceedings had been scandalous enough to convince the majority of a numerous and sufficiently representative public authority that they were not good enough for their job. As usual, I might have saved my breath to cool my porridge . . . .

I could not have done anything more injurious to my prospects at the outset of my career. . . . . . . Besides, in 1894 the ordinary commercial theatres would have nothing to say to me, Lord Chamberlain or no Lord Chamberlain. . . . I turned my . . . hand to play-writing when a great deal of talk about "the New Drama," followed by the actual establishment of a "New Theatre" (the Independent), threatened to end in the humiliating discovery that the New Drama, in England at least, was a figment of the revolutionary imagination. This was not to be endured. I had rashly taken up the case; and rather than let it collapse I manufactured the evidence.

Man is a creature of habit. You cannot write three plays and then stop. Besides, the New movement did not stop. In 1894, Florence Farr, who had already produced Ibsen's Rosmersholm, was placed in command of the Avenue Theatre in London for a season on the new lines by Miss A. E. F. Horniman, who had family reasons for not yet appearing openly as a pioneer-manageress. There were, as available New Dramatists, myself, discovered by the Independent Theatre (at my own suggestion); Dr John Todhunter, who had been discovered before (his play The Black Cat had been one of the Independent's successes); and Mr W. B. Yeats, a genuine discovery. Dr Todhunter supplied A Comedy of Sighs: Mr Yeats, The Land of Heart's Desire. I, having nothing but unpleasant plays in my desk, hastily completed a first attempt at a pleasant one, and

[281]

called it Arms and The Man, taking the title from the first line of Dryden's Virgil. It passed for a success, the applause on the first night being as promising as could be wished; and it ran from the 21st of April to the 7th of July. To witness it the public paid £1777:5:6, an average of £23:2:5 per representation (including nine matinées). . . . The others [had] . . . absurd hole-and-corner performances which took place, for copyrighting purposes, in obscure theatres at unholy hours, before an audience consisting of a single confederate who had gone through the form of paying a guinea for his seat. . . .

In the autumn of 1894 I spent a few weeks in Florence, where I occupied myself with the religious art of the Middle Ages and its destruction by the Renascence. From a former visit to Italy on the same business I had hurried back to Birmingham to discharge my duties as musical critic at the Festival there. On that occasion a very remarkable collection of the works of our British "pre-Raphaelite" painters was on view. I looked at these, and then went into the Birmingham churches to see the windows of William Morris and Burne-Jones. On the whole, Birmingham was more hopeful than the Italian cities; for the art it had to shew me was the work of living men, whereas modern Italy had, as far as I could see, no more connection with Giotto than Port Said has with Ptolemy. Now I am no believer in the worth of any mere taste for art that cannot produce what it professes to appreciate. When my subsequent visit to Italy found me practising the playwright's craft, the time was ripe for a modern pre-Raphaelite play.[3] Religion was alive again, coming back upon men, even upon clergymen, with such power that not the Church of England itself could keep it out. Here my activity as a Socialist had placed me on sure and familiar ground. To me the members of the Guild of St Matthew were no more "High Church clergymen," Dr Clifford no more "an eminent Nonconformist divine," than I was to them "an infidel." There is only one religion, though there are a hundred versions of it. We all had the same thing to say; and though some of us cleared our throats to say it by singing revolutionary lyrics and republican hymns, we thought nothing of singing them to the music of Sullivan's Onward Christian Soldiers or Haydn's God Preserve the Emperor.

Now unity, however desirable in political agitation, is fatal to drama; for every drama must present a conflict. The end may be reconciliation or destruction; or, as in life itself, there may be no end; but the conflict is indispensable: no conflict, no drama. Certainly it is easy to dramatize the prosaic conflict of Christian Socialism with vulgar Unsocialism: for instance, in Widowers' Houses, the clergyman, who does not appear on the stage at all, is the real antagonist of the slum landlord. But the obvious conflicts of unmistakeable good with unmistakeable evil can only supply the crude drama of villain and hero, in which some absolute point of view is taken, and the dissentients are treated by the dramatist as enemies to be piously glorified or indignantly vilified. In such cheap wares I do not deal. Even in my unpleasant propagandist plays I have allowed every person his or her own point of view, and have, I hope, to the full extent of my understanding of him, been . . . sympathetic . . . .

Let Ibsen explain,[4] if he can, why the building of churches and happy homes is not the ultimate destiny of Man, and why, to thrill the unsatisfied younger generations, he must mount beyond it to heights that now seem unspeakably giddy and dreadful to him, and from which the first climbers must fall and dash themselves to pieces. He cannot explain it: he can only shew it to you as a vision in the magic glass of his artwork; so that you may catch his presentiment and make what you can of it. And this is the function that raises dramatic art above imposture and pleasure hunting, and enables the playwright to be something more than a skilled liar and pandar.

Here, then, was the higher but vaguer and timider vision, the incoherent, mischievous, and even ridiculous unpracticalness, which offered me a dramatic antagonist for the clear, bold, sure, sensible, benevolent, salutarily shortsighted Christian Socialist idealism. I availed myself of it in Candida, the drunken scene in which has been much appreciated, I am told, in Aberdeen. I purposely contrived the play in such a way as to make the expenses of representation insignificant; so that, without pretending that I could appeal to a very wide circle of playgoers, I could reasonably sound a few of our more enlightened managers as to an experiment with half a dozen afternoon performances. They admired the play generously: indeed I think that if any of them had been young enough to play the poet, my proposal might have been acceded to, in spite of many incidental difficulties. Nay, if only I had made the poet a cripple, or at least blind, so as to combine an easier disguise with a larger claim for sympathy, something might have been done. Richard Mansfield, who had, with apparent ease, made me quite famous in America by his productions of my plays, went so far as to put the play actually into rehearsal before he would confess himself beaten by the physical difficulties of the part. But they did beat him; and Candida did not see the footlights until my old ally the Independent Theatre, making a propa-gandist tour through the provinces with A Doll's House, added Candida to its repertory, to the great astonishment of its audiences.

Behind the scenes, too, I had my difficulties. In a generation which knew nothing of any sort of acting but drawing-room acting, and which considered a speech of more than twenty words impossibly long, I went back to the classical style and wrote long rhetorical speeches like operatic solos, regarding my plays as musical performances precisely as Shake-spear did. As a producer I went back to the forgotten heroic stage business and the exciting or impressive declamation I had learnt from oldtimers like Ristori, Salvini, and Barry Sullivan. Yet so novel was my post-Marx post-Ibsen outlook on life that nobody suspected that my methods were as old as the stage itself. They would have seemed the merest routine to Kemble or Mrs. Siddons; but to the Victorian leading ladies they seemed to be unleadingladylike barnstorming. When Kate Rorke played Candida I seized the opportunity to pay her a long deferred tribute to her beauti-ful performance of Helena in A Midsummer Night's Dream, which she had treated as a piece of music from beginning to end. To my amaze-ment she changed color, and reproached me for making heartless fun of her only failure. When I convinced her that I was in earnest she told me how her musical rendering of that most musical part had brought on her such a torrent of critical abuse and misunderstanding that she had never ventured to attempt anything of the sort again!

No wonder I often found actors and actresses nervously taking the ut-most care to avoid acting, the climax being reached by an actor engaged for the broadly comic part of Burgess in Candida, who, after rehearsing the first act in subdued tones like a funeral mute, solemnly put up his hand as I vengefully approached him, and said: "Mr. Shaw: I know what you are going to say. But you may depend on me. In the intellectual drama I never clown." And it was some time before I could persuade him that I was in earnest when I exhorted him to clown for all he was worth. I was continually struggling with the conscientious efforts of our players to underdo their parts lest they should be considered stagey. Much as if Titian had worked in black and grey lest he should be considered painty. It took a European war to cure them of wanting to be ladies and gentle-men first and actresses and actors after.

In an idle moment in 1895 I began the little scene called The Man of Destiny, . . . a one act play in which Napoleon is the chief figure;

. . . hardly more than a bravura piece to display the virtuosity of the two principal performers. In the meantime I had devoted the spare moments of 1896 to the composition of two more plays . . . . You Never Can Tell was an attempt to comply with many requests for a play in which the much paragraphed "brilliancy" of Arms and The Man should be tempered by some consideration for the requirements of managers in search of fashionable comedies for West End theatres. I had no difficulty in complying, as I have always cast my plays in the ordinary practical comedy form in use at all the theatres; and far from taking an unsympathetic view of the popular preference for fun, fashionable dresses, a little music, and even an exhibition of eating and drinking by people with an expensive air, attended by an if-possible-comic waiter, I was more than willing to shew that the drama can humanize these things as easily as they, in the wrong hands, can dehumanize the drama. But as often happens it was easier to do this than to persuade those who had asked for it that they had indeed got it.

When the play, after its production by a private society, was announced at the Haymarket Theatre, which was then at the height of its vogue as a popular comedy house under the management of Cyril Maude and Frederick Harrison, it was as if Picasso and Matisse had been chosen to paint a couple of the frescoes in the Panthéon or the Palais de Bourbon. No one was surprised when the announcements were presently withdrawn. No public explanation was given at the time; but some years afterwards, when Cyril Maude . . . published his History of the Haymarket Theatre, it contained a whole chapter giving a startlingly and even scandalously frank account of the breakdown of the rehearsals. . . . In France an author thus held up to public ridicule must have sent his seconds to Mr. Maude and met him formally on the field of honour. In England . . . the explanation was plain enough for readers with a flair for literary style; and it was soon a secret de polichinelle [5] that Mr. Shaw had written the chapter himself. . . .[6]

The production of Arms and the Man at the Avenue Theatre . . . brought the misunderstanding between my real world and the stage world of the critics to a climax, because the misunderstanding was itself, in a sense, the subject of the play. I need not describe the action of the piece in any detail: suffice it to say that the scene is laid in Bulgaria in 1885–86, at a moment when the need for repelling the onslaught of the

Servians made the Bulgarians for six months a nation of heroes. But as they had only just been redeemed from centuries of miserable bondage to the Turks, and were, therefore, but beginning to work out their own redemption from barbarism—or, if you prefer it, beginning to contract the disease of civilization—they were very ignorant heroes, with boundless courage and patriotic enthusiasm, but with so little military skill that they had to place themselves under the command of Russian officers. And their attempts at Western civilization were much the same as their attempts at war—instructive, romantic, ignorant. They were a nation of plucky beginners in every department. Into their country comes, in the play, a professional officer from the high democratic civilization of Switzerland—a man completely acquainted by long, practical experience with the realities of war. The comedy arises, of course, from the collision of the knowledge of the Swiss with the illusions of the Bulgarians . . . .

The extent to which the method brought me into conflict with the martial imaginings of the critics is hardly to be conveyed by language. The notion that there could be any limit to a soldier's courage, or any preference on his part for life and a whole skin over a glorious death in the service of his country, was inexpressibly revolting to them. Their view was simple, manly, and straightforward, like most impracticable views. A man is either a coward or he is not. . . .

In Arms and the Man, this very simple and intelligible picture is dramatized by the contrast between the experienced Swiss officer, with a high record for distinguished services, and the Bulgarian hero who wins the battle by an insanely courageous charge for which the Swiss thinks he ought to be court-martialled.

I shall perhaps here be reminded by some of my critics that the charge in Arms and the Man was a cavalry charge; and that I am suppressing the damning sneer at military courage implied by Captain Bluntschli's reply to Raïna Petkoff's demand to have a cavalry charge described to her:

> BLUNTSCHLI: You never saw a cavalry charge, did you?
>
> RAINA: No; how could I?
>
> BLUNTSCHLI: Of course not. Well, it's a funny sight. It's like slinging a handful of peas against a window pane—first one comes, then two or three close behind them, and then all the rest in a lump.
>
> RAINA: (*Thinking of her lover, who has just covered himself with glory in a cavalry charge.*) Yes; first One, the bravest of the brave!

BLUNTSCHLI: Hm! you should see the poor devil pulling at his horse.

RAINA: Why should he pull at his horse?

BLUNTSCHLI: It's running away with him, of course; do you suppose the fellow wants to get there before the others and be killed?

Imagine the feelings of the critics—countrymen of the heroes of Bala-clava, and trained in warfare by repeated contemplation of the reproduction of Miss Elizabeth Thompson's pictures in the Regent Street shop windows, not to mention the recitations of Tennyson's "Charge of the Light Brigade," which they have criticised—on hearing this speech from a mere Swiss!

It may be urged against me here that in my play I have represented a soldier as shying like a nervous horse, not at bullets, but at such trifles as a young lady snatching a box of sweets from him and throwing it away. But my soldier explains that he has been three days under fire; and though that would, of course, make no difference to the ideal soldier, it makes a considerable difference to the real one . . . .

. . . I am quite aware that the much criticized Swiss officer in Arms and The Man is not a conventional stage soldier. He suffers from want of food and sleep; his nerves go to pieces after three days under fire, ending in the horrors of a rout and pursuit; he has found by experience that it is more important to have a few bits of chocolate to eat in the field than cartridges for his revolver. . . .

. . . What struck my critics as topsy-turvy extravaganza, having no more relation to real soldiering than Mr. Gilbert's "Pinafore" has to real sailoring, is the plainest matter-of-fact. There is no burlesque: I have stuck to the routine of war, as described by real warriors, and avoided such farcial incidents as Sir William Gordon defending his battery by throwing stones, or General Porter's story of the two generals who, though brave and capable men, always got sick under fire, to their own great mortification. I claim that the dramatic effect produced by the shock which these realities give to the notions of romantic young ladies and fierce civilians is not burlesque, but legitimate comedy, none the less pungent because, on the first night at least, the romantic young lady was on the stage and the fierce civilians in the stalls. And since my authorities, who record many acts almost too brave to make pleasant reading, are beyond suspicion of that cynical disbelief in courage which has been freely attributed to me, I would ask whether it is not plain that the difference between my authenticated conception of real warfare and the stage conception lies in the fact that in real warfare there is real personal danger, the sense of which is constantly present to the mind of the soldier, whereas in stage warfare there is nothing but glory? Hence Captain Bluntschli, who thinks of a battlefield as a very busy and very dangerous place, is incredible to the critic who thinks of it only as a theatre in which to enjoy the luxurious excitements of patriotism, victory, and bloodshed without risk or retribution. . . .

I have been much lectured for my vulgarity in introducing certain references to soap and water in Bulgaria. I did so as the shortest and most effective way of bringing home to the audience the stage of civilisation in which the Bulgarians were in 1885, when, having clean air and clean clothes, which made them much cleaner than any frequency of ablution can make us in the dirty air of London, they were adopting the washing habits of big western cities as pure ceremonies of culture and civilisation, and not on hygienic grounds. I had not the slightest intention of suggesting that my Bulgarian major, who submits to a good wash for the sake of his social position, or his father, who never had a bath in his life, are uncleanly people, though a cockney, who by simple exposure to the atmosphere becomes more unpresentable in three hours than a Balkan mountaineer in three years, may feel bound to pretend to be shocked at them, and to shrink with disgust from even a single omission of the daily bath which, as he knows very well, the majority of English, Irish, and Scotch people do not take, and which the majority of the inhabitants of the world do not even tell lies about.

. . . Historical facts are not a bit more sacred than any other class of facts. In making a play out of them you must adapt them to the stage, and that alters them at once, more or less. Why, you cannot even write a history without adapting the facts to the conditions of literary narrative, which are in some respects much more distorting than the dramatic conditions of representation on the stage. Things do not happen in the form of stories or dramas; and since they must be told in some such form, all stories, all dramatic representations, are only attempts to arrange the facts in a thinkable, intelligible, interesting form—that is, when they are not more or less intentional efforts to hide the truth, as they very often are. But my play is not an historical play in your sense at all. It was written without the slightest reference to Bulgaria. In the original MS. the names of the places were blank, and the characters were called simply The Father, The Daughter, The Stranger, The Heroic Lover, and so on. The incident of the machine-gun bound me to a recent war; that was all. My own historical information being rather confused, I asked Mr. Sidney Webb to find out a good war for my purpose. He spent about two minutes in a rapid survey of every war that has ever been waged, and then told me that the Servo-Bulgarian was what I wanted. I then read the account of the war in the Annual Register, with a modern railway map of the Balkan Peninsula before me, and filled in my blanks, making all the action take place in Servia, in the house of a Servian family. I then read the play to Stepniak, and to the Admiral who commanded the Bulgarian Fleet during the war. . . . He made me change the scene from Servia to Bulgaria, and the characters from Servians to Bulgarians, and gave me descriptions of Bulgarian life and ideas, which enabled to fit my play exactly with local colour and character. I followed the facts he gave me as closely as I could, because invented facts are the same stale stuff in all plays, one man's imagination being much the same an another's in such matters, whilst real facts are fresh and varied. So you can judge exactly how far my historical conscience goes. . . .

. . . When many of my critics rejected these circumstances as fantastically improbable and cynically unnatural, it was not necessary to argue them into common sense: all I had to do was to brain them, so to speak, with the first half dozen military authorities at hand, beginning with the present Commander in Chief. But when it proved that such unromantic (but all the more dramatic) facts implied to them a denial of the existence of courage, patriotism, faith, hope, and charity, I saw that it was not really mere matter of fact that was at issue between us. One strongly Liberal critic, who had received my first play with the most generous encouragement, declared, when Arms and the Man was produced, that I had struck a wanton blow at the cause of liberty in the Balkan Peninsula by mentioning that it was not a matter of course for a Bulgarian in 1885 to wash his hands every day. My Liberal critic no doubt saw soon afterwards the squabble, reported all through Europe, between Stambouiloff and an eminent lady of the Bulgarian court who took exception to his neglect of his fingernails. . . .

. . . Idealism, which is only a flattering name for romance in politics and morals, is as obnoxious to me as romance in ethics or religion. In spite of a Liberal Revolution or two, I can no longer be satisfied with fictitious morals and fictitious good conduct, shedding fictitious glory on overcrowding, disease, crime, drink, war, cruelty, infant mortality, and all

[289]

the other commonplaces of civilization which drive men to the theatre to make foolish pretences that these things are progress, science, morals, religion, patriotism, imperial supremacy, national greatness and all the other names the newspapers call them. On the other hand, I see plenty of good in the world working itself out as fast as the idealist will allow it; and if they would only let it alone and learn to respect reality, which would include the beneficial exercise of respecting themselves, and incidentally respecting me, we should all get along much better and faster. At all events, I do not see moral chaos and anarchy as the alternative to romantic convention; and I am not going to pretend I do merely to please the people who are convinced that the world is held together only by the force of unanimous, strenuous, eloquent, trumpet-tongued lying. To me the tragedy and comedy of life lie in the consequences, sometimes terrible, sometimes ludicrous, of our persistent attempts to found our institutions on the ideals suggested to our imaginations by our half-satisfied passions, instead of on a genuinely scientific natural history. And with that hint as to what I am driving at, I withdraw and ring up the curtain.

Appendix: Why Cyril Maude Did Not
Produce "You Never Can Tell"

I NOW come to an episode in the history of the theatre which might have wrecked our enterprise had not Providence, which has never yet disappointed our humble trust in it, caused the danger into which we had stumbled to withdraw itself at the eleventh hour.

I think it must have been in the year 1895 that the devil put it into the mind of a friend of mine to tempt me with news of a play called "Candida" by a writer named Bernard Shaw, of whom until then I had never heard. I wrote to him suggesting that he should let me see the play. He instantly undertook the management of our theatre to the extent of informing me that "Candida" would not suit us, but that he would write a new play for us—which I protest I never asked him to do. As I learnt subsequently, he then took a chair in Regent's Park for the whole season, and sat there in the public eye writing the threatened play.

In the winter of 1897 this play, which was called "You Never Can Tell," came to hand. Some of our friends thought well of the author, and Harrison [1] (who, as my readers have doubtless already gathered, is a perfect ignoramus in all matters connected with plays and acting) liked the play. In short, I allowed myself to be overpersuaded, and we actually put the play into rehearsal.

From the first the author showed the perversity of his disposition and his utter want of practical knowledge of the stage. He proposed impossible casts. He forced us into incomprehensible agreements by torturing us with endless talk until we were ready to sign anything rather than argue for another hour. Had I been properly supported by my colleagues I should not have tolerated his proceedings for a moment. I do not wish to complain of anybody, but as a matter of fact I was not so supported. I expected nothing better from Harrison, because with all his excellent qualities he is too vain—I say it though he is my best friend—to be trusted in so delicate an undertaking as the management of a theatre. The truth is, Shaw flattered him, and thus detached him from me by playing on his one fatal weakness.

The world knows, I think, that whatever my faults may be, I am an affectionate and devoted husband. But I have never pretended that my wife is perfect. No woman is, and but few men. Still, I do think she might have supported me better than she did through our greatest trial. This man from the first exercised a malign influence over her. With my full consent and approval she selected for herself a certain part in his play. He had privately resolved—out of mere love of contradiction—that she should play another. When he read the play he contrived to balance the parts in such a way that my unfortunate and misguided wife actually there and then gave up her part and accepted the one he had determined to throw upon her. I then recognized for the first time that I had to deal with a veritable Svengali.

Our mistake in admitting an author of this type to our theatre soon become apparent. At the reading, that excellent actor, Jack Barnes, whose very name calls up the idea of sound judgment, withdrew, overpowered by fatigue and disgust, at the end of the first act, and presently threw up the part with which we proposed to insult him—and I now publicly apologise to him for that outrage. Miss Coleman soon followed his example, with a very natural protest against a part in which, as she rightly said, there were "no laughs and no exits." Any author with the slightest decency of feeling would have withdrawn in the face of rebuffs so pointed as these. But Mr. Shaw—encouraged, I must say, by Harrison—persisted in what had now become an intolerable intrusion.

I can hardly describe the rehearsals that followed. It may well be that my recollection of them is confused; for my nerves soon gave way; sleep became a stranger to me; and there were moments at which I was hardly in possession of my faculties. I had to stage-manage as well as act—to stage-manage with that demon sitting beside me casting an evil spell on all our efforts!

On one occasion Mr. Shaw insulted the entire profession by wanting a large table on the stage, on the ground that the company would fall over it unless they behaved as if they were coming into a real room instead of, as he coarsely observed, rushing to the float to pick up the band at the beginning of a comic song. This was a personal attack on me, as my vivacity of character and *diable au corps* make me specially impatient of obstacles.

Mr. Shaw was one of those persons who use a certain superficial reasonableness and dexterity of manner to cover an invincible obstinacy in their own opinion. We are engaged for the leading part (I myself having accepted an insignificant part as a mere waiter) no less an artist than Mr. Allan Aynesworth, whose reputation and subsequent achievements make it unnecessary for me to justify our choice. Mr. Shaw had from the first contended that one of the scenes lay outside Mr. Aynesworth's peculiar province. There can be no doubt now that Mr. Shaw deliberately used his hypnotic power at rehearsal to compel Mr. Aynesworth to fulfil his prediction. In every other scene Mr. Aynesworth surpassed himself. In this he became conscious and confused; his high spirits were suddenly extinguished; even his good-humour left him. He was like a man under a spell—as no doubt he actually was—and his embarrassment communicated itself most painfully to my dear wife, who had to sit on the stage whilst Svengali deliberately tortured his victim.

At the same time I must say that Mrs. Maude's conduct was not all I could have desired. I greatly dreaded an open rupture between her and the author; and the fiend somehow divined this, and used it as a means of annoying me. Sometimes, when he had cynically watched one of her scenes without any symptom of pleasure, I would venture to ask him his opinion of it. On such occasions he invariably rose with every appearance of angry disapproval, informed me that he would give his opinion to Miss Emery [2] herself, and stalked up the stage to her in a threatening manner, leaving me in a state of apprehension that my overstrained nerves were ill able to bear. Not until afterwards did I learn that on these occasions he flattered my wife disgracefully, and actually made her a party to his systematic attempt to drive me out of my senses. I have never reproached her with this, and I never shall. I mention it here only because it is the truth; and truth has always been with me the first consideration.

At last Aynesworth broke down under the torture. Mr. Shaw, with that perfidious air of making the best of everything which never deserted him, hypnotised him into complaining of the number of speeches he had to deliver, whereupon Mr. Shaw cut out no less than seventeen of them. This naturally disabled the artist totally. On the question of cutting, Mr.

Shaw's attitude was nothing less than Satanic. When I suggested cutting he handed me the play, begged me to cut it freely, and then hypnotised me so that I could not collect my thoughts sufficiently to cut a single line. On the other hand, if I showed the least pleasure in a scene at rehearsal he at once cut it out on the ground that the play was too long. What I suffered from that man at that time will never be fully known. The heart alone knoweth its own bitterness.

The end came suddenly and unexpectedly. We had made a special effort to fulfil our unfortunate contract, of which even Harrison was now beginning to have his doubts. We had brought back Miss Kate Bishop from Australia to replace Miss Coleman. Mr. Valentine had taken the part repudiated by Mr. Barnes. The scenery had been modelled, and a real dentist's chair obtained for the first act. Harrison, whose folly was responsible for the whole wretched business, came down to the rehearsal. We were honestly anxious to retrieve the situation by a great effort, and save our dear little theatre from the disgrace of failure.

Suddenly the author entered, *in a new suit of clothes ! !*

I have little more to say. Nobody who had not seen Mr. Shaw sitting there day after day in a costume which the least self-respecting carpenter would have discarded months before, could possibly have understood the devastating effect of the new suit on our minds. That this was a calculated *coup de théâtre* I have not the slightest doubt. That it fulfilled its purpose I cannot deny. With distracted attentions, demented imaginations, and enfeebled reasons we made a bewildered effort to go through the first two acts. I saw with inexpressible aggravation that Harrison's face grew longer and longer as he contemplated our company blundering through a rehearsal like disconcerted amateurs (as if it were anybody's fault but his own). Talma himself would have broken down before the famous pit of kings if that new suit had been in the house.

I neither know nor care how it all ended. I remember Svengali privately informing Harrison and myself that he felt that our ruin and disgrace could only be averted by a heroic sacrifice on his part. If Harrison had had a spark of manhood he would have kicked him then and there into the Haymarket. But Harrison's deplorable weakness of character again allowed our enemy to pose as our benevolent rescuer. As for me, the man was in some sort my guest; besides, I was too unspeakably relieved by the prospect of being rid of him and his absurd play to make any difficulties.

In concluding this sickening record of a disastrous experience I desire to say that I have the greatest admiration for Mr. Shaw's talents and the sincerest esteem for his personal character. In any other walk of life than that of a dramatic author I should expect him to achieve a high measure of success. I understand that he has made considerable mark as a vestry-man, collecting dust with punctuality and supervising drainage with public-spirited keenness. I do not blame him for imposing on Harrison, for Harrison's credulity simply invites imposture. I wish him well in every way, and I am glad to hear from time to time that he is prospering. I met him in Garrick Street not long ago, and noticed that he still wore the suit which he purchased in 1897 in anticipation of the royalties on "You Never Can Tell."

His name is never mentioned in my household.

NOTES

Chapter 1

[1] Shaw was born in Dublin on 26 July 1856. His father is apparently reporting a birthday party held the previous day.

Chapter 2

[1] Agnes Shaw died of tuberculosis in a rest home on the Isle of Wight on 27 March 1876, less than two weeks before her brother left Dublin.

[2] Although G.B.S. was partly of Scottish ancestry, his claim that the Shaws were descended from Shaigh, MacDuff's third son, cannot be sustained.

[3] *Maxims for Revolutionists* is one of the appendices to *Man and Superman,* purportedly written by the play's hero, John Tanner.

[4] G.B.S. here stretched his joke too far, for his father had a beard even more substantial than the later—and more familiar—Shavian one.

[5] See Note 13, Chapter 5.

Chapter 3

[1] The quotation is from Canto III of Byron's *Childe Harold's Pilgrimage.*

[2] One such Dublin cathedral was Christ Church, restored in the 1870s by Henry Roe, a distiller. The expenditure of nearly £250,000 on the project left him improverished by beer-baron standards, and his distillery was absorbed into the Guinness firm after his death. Unlike Benjamin Lee Guinness, at whom Shaw's barbs more likely were meant, Roe declined titles and

political preferment offered him as a result of his philanthropies. Guinness, acting as his own architect, invested £150,000 in the restoration of the six hundred year old St. Patrick's Cathedral, near Shaw's home in Dublin, in the mid-1860s, and was created a baronet in recognition of his benefaction. A former Lord Mayor of Dublin, he also became an M.P. in 1865, the year of the grand reopening of the cathedral. (See Sidney P. Albert, "Letters of Fire against the Sky: Bodger's Soul and Shaw's Pub," *Shaw Review,* September, 1968.)

³ Trinity College Dublin.

Chapter 4

¹ From Verdi's *Il Trovatore,* a G.B.S. favorite.

² The bullied, despised clerk in Dickens' *Nicholas Nickleby.*

³ Shaw's story leaves out several significant facts about his motivations for leaving the Townshend firm. His letter of resignation (29 February 1876) giving a month's notice offers as reason "that I object to receive a salary for which I give no adequate value. Not having enough to do, it follows that the little I have is not well done. When I ceased to act as Cashier I anticipated this, and have since become satisfied that I was right." What had happened was that Townshend wanted to place a relative at the cash desk and "kicked Shaw upstairs" to make the place available. But although the new position brought an increased salary, the clerk-at-large duties were minimal and carried few responsibilities. Apparently the letter of resignation inspired fears in Townshend of the possible displeasure of Shaw's influential Uncle Frederick, who had recommended him for the job, and Shaw was offered reinstatement as Cashier. Determined by then to leave Ireland, he spurned the new opportunity to remain in the firm on his own terms.

Chapter 5

¹ Shaw's letter appeared on 3 April 1875, when he was eighteen.

² The medical friend was Dr. James Kingston Barton (1854–1941), who lived then in a lodging-house in the Gloster Road, had a medical practice in Kensington, and was affiliated (as he would be the rest of his life) with St. Bartholomew's Hospital.

³ The watch trick was an old one, attributed to many unbelievers before, to his great discomfort it became attached to Charles Bradlaugh. Bradlaugh's repeated denials were so ineffective that he finally resorted to a libel suit

(against the *British Empire,* a Tory sheet) in 1880 to quash the story. "In their zeal to prove their case," Arthur Nethercot has written, "the officers of the paper produced so many witnesses who swore they had been present at the watch episode at so many diverse places and times that the justice was dazed by their contradictions and held the defendants for trial. . . . (*The First Five Lives of Annie Besant* [1960]).

⁴ Father William Edward Addis (1844–1917) left the Oratory in 1878. A convert to Catholicism in 1866, he had become a priest in 1872; but in 1886 he renounced Roman Catholicism and became minister of the nondenominational Australian Church in Melbourne. In 1901, by this time back in England, he returned to the Anglican faith. From 1898 to 1910 he was Professor of Old Testament at Manchester College, Oxford.

⁵ The member of Father Addis's flock eager to effect Shaw's conversion may have been E. A. Collier, a lady who urged upon Shaw early in 1878 a religious medal of the Virgin. G.B.S. agreed to wear it for six months. Having experienced no striking spiritual alteration during the period of the experiment, he discarded it that September, but utilized the episode in his first novel, *Immaturity,* begun in March 1879. There Shaw's hero and *alter ego* meets Isabella Woodward, a young Catholic convert, while he is out walking early one morning. He is persuaded by her to attend Mass at the Oratory. The rites conducted by Father Ignatius make no favorable impression upon Smith, and his unappreciative comments about superstition and hypocrisy offend Isabella.

⁶ In a 1922 interview published in the *St. Martin's-in-the-Fields Review,* G.B.S. was asked whether he believed "that there must be somebody behind the something," and responded, "No: I believe that there is something behind the somebody. . . ." When asked whether he believed in a First Cause he answered, "A First Cause is a contradiction in terms. . . . There can no more be a First Cause than a first inch in a circle. . . ."

⁷ G.B.S. ghosted for Vandeleur Lee for about a year, beginning in November 1878. The set of cuttings of his reviews Shaw preserved is in the British Museum. Extracts from them were published in *How to Become a Musical Critic* (1961).

⁸ *The Hornet* ceased publication in February 1880. Whether one of the causes of its demise was the lingering effect of G.B.S.'s ghost-criticism is unknown, but Shaw very likely magnified his negative impact.

⁹ Forty-nine pages of blank verse dialogue survive in the British Museum. In the abandoned play, Mary is a shrew while Joseph is a shiftless carpenter. Judas, who contains traces of the young Shaw, declares:

The fittest study for a feeling man
Is ceaseless observation of his fellows
Whereby he comes to know himself by them
Having first learnt their nature from his own.

[10] The article was "Christian Names," published in the 11 October 1879 issue of *One and All*. Shaw's thesis, stated with adolescent pomposity, was that the name with which one is endowed has a direct, and often baneful, influence on the person, particularly when the name is eccentric or historic. Thus Shaw offered parents "the following simple rule. Never confer an uncommon name, or peculiar combination of common names, which has been borne by any personage known to history. A person so christened resembles a jackdaw with a peacock's tail, which he has not himself assumed. . . ."

[11] G.B.S. began working for the Edison Telephone Company in the autumn of 1879 and left its employ on 5 July 1880.

[12] Shaw's first experiment with vegetarianism lasted from January until June (1881). While a victim of smallpox during the summer, 1881 epidemic in London, he was put on a diet over which he had no control; but abandoned meat-eating for good that October, when he had recovered.

[13] Shaw's claim, made to his biographers and in his autobiographical writings, that after the telephone episode he never again "sinned against his nature" by seeking the regular commercial employment he despised, is unsupported by the evidence. He strove mightily for several years to find a job, surviving letters (and copies he retained) identifying some of them as clerk, travelling salesman, tutor, and companion. He apparently answered many classified advertisements in *The Times* for jobs of a literary nature or in journalism, and at least once while writing *The Irrational Knot* confessed while inquiring about a clerkship that he was prepared "to undertake any work in which there is any valuable experience to be gained, or, failing that, a sufficient remuneration to compensate for its absence." To Hubert Bland (18 November 1889), however, he confided that he had no intention of taking many jobs he went after, but made the applications to counter reproaches at home that he was "an idle, lazy, heartless, selfish scoundrel."

[14] The "silly novel" was *Cashel Byron's Profession,* reviewed in *Our Corner* in May, 1886. But George Carr Shaw had died a year earlier, on 19 April 1885, in his seventy-fifth year. What the elder Shaw may have seen, to his dubious gratification, were serial parts of *An Unsocial Socialist,* which appeared in the Socialist monthly *To-Day* from March through December, 1884 (and earned G.B.S. nothing). Only *Immaturity* failed to reach publication in this fashion, waiting to reach print until Shaw's Collected Edition of 1930.

¹⁵ The "young and romantic lady" was Alice Lockett, a young nursing student. Shaw's letters to her make it clear that he was very much in love (as was she at first with him); but she grew weary of his unsalable novels and unpromising future. After yet another of his novels failed to find a publisher, she wrote him that it was all over between them because he was a "machine . . . incapable of feeling" and likely to persist in futile fiction-writing while living off his mother. "Why on earth don't you work?" she appealed. "I wonder how you will account for your life one day. . . ." In 1890 she married a former resident physician at St. Mary's, Paddington, the hospital where she was a nurse.

¹⁶ The reading actually took place on 15 January 1886, at Eleanor Marx's house in Great Russell Street. Her unofficial husband Edward Aveling was Helmer, and May Morris played Mrs. Linde. Urging G.B.S. to play the blackmailer, Krogstad, she wrote him, "It is not in the least necessary that you should be sane to do that. Au contraire. The madder the better. . . ."

¹⁷ At the time English authors had no copyright protection in the United States.

¹⁸ Henley also wrote to Archer about *Cashel Byron,* asking "Who the deuce is Bernard Shaw? And where these many years has he been dissembling his talent? I like his book immensely; it has vigour, humour, originality & wit; it makes me hopeful of fiction." In a postscript he added, "I read the book with astonishment and delight." ("W. E. H." to Archer, 18/3/86; from a.l.s. in the Pattee Library, Pennsylvania State Univ.)

¹⁹ *An Unfinished Novel* was finally published (ed. Stanley Weintraub) in 1958. No one has accepted Shaw's challenge to finish it.

Chapter 6

¹ In *Sixteen Self Sketches* Shaw gave the date as 1879, here corrected by a year. His notebooks record his first appearance at the Zetetical Society as occurring on 28 October 1880, a date confirmed by his letters. Rather than being "dragged" to the meeting, as he recalls, he had actually applied in advance through James Lecky, who formally nominated him for membership.

² Not all the ladies at Browning Society meetings were "pious and old." Katharine Tynan (in *Reminiscences* [1913]) recalled that her first glimpse of G.B.S. was there, when a friend pointed him out and whispered "that he was very brilliant and had a great future. I can only remember that he discussed 'Caliban upon Setebos,' and his remarking that if Caliban was now alive he would belong to the Philharmonic Society."

[3] Shaw incorrectly put the date as 1884 in *Sixteen Self Sketches*. It was actually 5 September 1882.

[4] See also "Tuesday," in the "Corno di Bassetto" chapter.

[5] Shaw then put his ideas into print in H. M. Hyndman's socialist magazine *Justice*. "Who is the Thief?" appeared as a letter signed "G. B. S. Larking," Shaw later confessing that he used the facetious approach because he was worried that more skilled Marxists would cut his arguments down. None did.

[6] A public house which gave its name to the intersection at which it was located.

[7] Joseph Conrad used the 1894 incident as the basis for his novel of subterranean London revolutionary life, *The Secret Agent* (1907), writing in his preface of "the already old story of the attempt to blow up the Greenwich Observatory; a blood-stained inanity of so fatuous a kind that it was impossible to fathom its origin by any reasonable or even unreasonable process of thought. For perverse unreason has its own logical processes . . . so that one remained faced by the fact of a man blown to bits for nothing even most remotely resembling an idea, anarchistic or other. As to the outer wall of the Observatory it did not show as much as the faintest crack."

[8] The debate took place on the evenings of 14 and 15 January, 1891 and was reported upon at considerable length in the *Daily Chronicle,* on the morning following each debate.

[9] Shaw refers here to a controversy which threatened to split the Fabian Society during 1906. Wells attacked the Fabian old guard, led by Webb and Shaw, for its middle-class socialism-via-permeation methods, and impatiently advocated instead more militancy and increased proselytizing among the working classes. In December 1906 Wells's reform movement collapsed under Shaw's wit and parliamentary skill, and Wells turned to purposeful fiction as medium for attacking the bourgeois, benevolent, bureaucratic middle-class society that he conceived to be the wrongheaded Fabian ideal. Among his novels of ideas which followed was *The New Machiavelli* (1910–11), a thinly disguised attack upon Edwardian politics and, in particular, upon the easily recognizable Fabians who engineered his defeat.

[10] The article appeared in the *Pall Mall Gazette* for 25 April 1888, and was reprinted in the Standard Edition of Shaw in *The Black Girl in Search of God and Some Lesser Tales*.

[11] At the close of 1886, Shaw summed up his relationship with Annie Besant in his diary as "intimacy [of] . . . a very close and personal sort, without, however, going further than friendship." But Annie—nine years older than

Shaw—wanted more of him than that, although he was already becoming involved with other women, while she was tied legally to a husband who would not divorce her. Melodramatically, she returned all his letters early in 1887, and contemplated suicide. "Bloody Sunday" in Trafalgar Square (see Chapter 7), and other causes she took up, provided new outlets for her restlessness; but by the end of her inconclusive affair with Shaw her hair had turned gray.

[12] Arthur Nethercot in his definitive two-volume biography of Mrs. Besant (1960, 1963) notes that "in the version of the story told by Annie herself as well as by Stead and his biographers, the review episode was Shawless." Yet Stead's reported words to her on handing Mrs. Besant the two-volume tome suggest G.B.S.'s having declined the assignment in her favor: "My young men all fight shy of them, but you are quite mad enough on these subjects to make something of them."

Chapter 7

[1] St. John (*Revelation,* 1:9) speaks of being exiled to the Dodecanese island of Patmos "because I had preached God's word."

[2] On 16 March 1888, R. B. Haldane, M. P., later Secretary of State for War and Lord Chancellor, addressed the Fabians on "Radical Remedies for Economic Evils." In the discussion that followed, Mrs. Besant, Sidney Webb, and Shaw apparently demolished Haldane, intellectually and emotionally. Under the by-line of "An Individualist," George Standring published his report of the meeting in his own journal, *The Radical,* March, 1888.

[3] Jane Burden Morris had been a groom's daughter elevated by Dante Gabriel Rossetti into chief model for his frescoes. Morris fell in love with her and persuaded her to marry him, although her remote and reticent beauty left others of Rossetti's friends somewhat wary of her. "The idea of his marrying her is insane," Swinburne said in horror. "To kiss her feet is the utmost man should think of doing." It was one of Swinburne's rare wise remarks about women, for Mrs. Morris retreated from her husband's bewildering variety of interests and masked her poor education via the cultivation of brooding, enigmatic distance from everyone and everything, including Morris.

[4] Earlier, Shaw described the dialogue to Hall Caine:
    SHE.   Have some pudding?
    G.B.S.   Thank you. I will. I can't resist it.
    (Then, when he had finished.)
    SHE.   That will do you good: there is suet in it.

Pay" to contribute free-lance pieces, feeling that the loss of regular work was not tragic as long as he could also count upon writing for the *Pall Mall Gazette* and *The World* (primarily book reviews in the former and art criticism in the latter). In June he began filling in occasionally for E. Belfort Bax, music critic of *The Star,* when Bax—who wrote as "Musigena"—was otherwise occupied. His reviews then were unsigned, prompting one London conductor (August Manns) to write curiously to "The Musical Critic of *The Star,*" asking him to identify himself. Shaw answered then that he was "a person of no consequence whatever . . . [of] no position or reputation which entitle him to the smallest consideration as a writer on music. Musical critics, as you know, are of two sorts, musicians who are no writers and writers who are no musicians. The *Star* adventurer belongs to the second class . . . ." But two months later, with the column of 15 February 1889, G.B.S. became the regular music critic in place of Bax, and needed a pseudonym to replace that of "Musigena." Until May, 1890 it was "Corno di Bassetto."

Chapter 10

1 *The Star's* address was Stonecutter Street.

2 "Musigena" was E. Belfort Bax. See Note 3 to Chapter 9.

3 The argument had concerned Shaw's article "Music for the People," which he had written at Hueffer's invitation for the *Musical Review.* Hueffer finally accepted the piece and published it in two parts on 10 and 17 March 1883. (See Shaw's letter to Hueffer dated 19 January 1883 in the *Collected Letters.*)

4 Grove (1820–1900) was best known for his editing of the four-volume *Dictionary of Music and Musicians* (1878–79).

5 The actress who sang the role of Dorothy was Shaw's sister Lucy. The tenor singing opposite her was her husband, Charles Butterfield.

6 "Tay Pay" was not merely being jocular about losing "Corno di Bassetto" to a higher-paying newspaper. "If this column is to cover all the concerts," Shaw wrote H. W. Massingham, the assistant editor, "it is worth five guineas." He was receiving two. A few days later, on 4 March 1890, he insisted to O'Connor, "I am damned if I will go on after this month for two guineas. You know as well as I do that work at once so conscientious and brilliant cannot be kept up at such rates." The editor showed no interest in retaining Shaw at a higher salary, and the Bassetto column concluded in May.

Chapter 11

1 Shaw over-credited his own role in breaking up the Irving-Terry partnership. Ellen Terry apparently remained satisfied that by setting her opposite

him at the Lyceum, Irving was giving her the pre-eminent position in the most prestigious theatre in England. But her private relationship with Irving was fading by 1895, when Shaw had renewed his epistolary assault; and her partnership on the stage was becoming affected by her personal life as well as by the development of the new realistic drama for which the joint Irving-Terry talents were unsuitable.

[2] The Fronde were groups of revolutionaries who fought vainly against the government of Cardinal Mazarin during the minority of Louis XIV (1648–53).

[3] In June 1880 Morley returned two manuscripts to Shaw with the note, "They are not quite suitable for this paper . . . . I cannot hesitate to say, that in my opinion you would do well to get out of journalism. It is a most precarious, dependent, and unsatisfactory profession, excepting for a very few who happen to have the knack, or manage to persuade people that they have it." (See the first volume of the *Collected Letters*.)

[4] The meeting which apparently led to Wilde's writing *The Soul of Man Under Socialism* (1891) was a Fabian lecture by artist Walter Crane on "The Prospects of Art under Socialism," at Willis's Rooms on July 6, 1888. According to *The Star* the next day, "Mr. Crane believed that art would revive under these new socialistic conditions. Mr. Oscar Wilde, whose fashionable coat differed widely from the picturesque bottle-green garb in which he appeared in earlier days, thought that the art of the future would clothe itself not in works of form and color but in literature. . . . Mr. Herbert Burrows contended that the masses loved good art, a fact which Mr. George Bernard Shaw deplored, as he said it proved that the lower classes were following the insincere cant of the middle classes. Mr. Shaw agreed with Mr. Wilde that literature was the form which art would take, pronounced Bunyan the tinker a supreme genius, and voted Beethoven rather vulgar, saying that if a middle-class audience were told that 'Pop goes the Weasel' was a movement from Beethoven's Ninth Symphony they would go into ecstasies over it." Afterwards (according to Shaw's diary) Wilde walked back part of the way with Sidney Webb, Herbert Wildon Carr and Shaw, taking his leave at St. James's Square.

Wilde may have learned of the lecture the week before, at a meeting with Shaw which G.B.S. afterwards had forgotten—an at-home on July 1, 1888 at the house of artist Felix Moscheles near Sloane Square.

[5] Shaw reviewed *The Importance of Being Earnest* in *The Saturday Review* on 23 February 1895 (reprinted in *Our Theatres*, I).

[6] Shaw's first presentation copy to Wilde was acknowledged as "Op. 2 of the great Celtic School" by Oscar (9 May 1893). He had sent G.B.S. a copy of his

Lady Windermere's Fan inscribed "Op. 1 of the Hibernian School . . . ." Thus the letter paid G.B.S. a compliment by linking his successful comedy with Shaw's badly received play. (See *The Letters of Oscar Wilde,* ed. Rupert Hart-Davis [1962].)

Chapter 12

1 Shaw served on the St. Pancras Borough Council as vestryman and councillor from 1897 to 1904, being elected, as he puts it later, "by some intrigue or other." (He had no opposition in return for the unopposed election of another candidate.)

2 He served in a businesslike fashion (this to the surprise of his fellow vestrymen) on the Public Health, Parliamentary, Electricity, Housing, and Drainage Committees.

3 Shaw could hazard such prophecies after the fact. At the time he wrote his memoir of Ensor Walters, his old colleague on the vestry had become a Methodist Bishop.

4 Very likely Florence Farr.

5 Rather than the usual curtain speech, Shaw delivered an impromptu lecture on socialism, inspired by reaction to the message of his "blue book" play. One London paper reported that Shaw had delivered a lecture on socialism, then added, "The lecture was preceded by a play entitled *Widowers' Houses."*

6 Within a fortnight Shaw's own collection of articles and reviews provoked by the production ran to more than 130 press cuttings.

7 Eleanor Marx.

Chapter 13

1 Shaw refers not only to the banned *Mrs. Warren's Profession* (1893), which could not be performed "publicly" in England until 1925, but to the later *The Shewing-up of Blanco Posnet* (1909), a melodrama about the conversion of a horse thief in the American "Wild West." It was refused a license by the censor and received its first production at the Abbey Theatre in Dublin, where the Lord Chamberlain had no jurisdiction.

2 Shaw's own adaptation of *Saint Joan* for the screen ran into objections from Roman Catholic groups in the United States and was scrapped. Shaw's reaction is detailed in a letter to the *New York Times,* 14 September 1936 (also in the *London Mercury,* October 1936). The play, in a lame version scripted by Graham Greene, was finally filmed in 1957.

Notes

[3] A reference to Shaw's *Candida*, written in 1894.

[4] In *The Master Builder* (1892).

[5] *Secret de polichinelle:* open secret.

[6] The chapter follows as an Appendix.

Appendix

[1] Frederick Harrison co-managed the Haymarket Theatre with Maude.

[2] Miss Winifred Emery was Mrs. Maude.

SOURCES

Autobiographical intention (rather than private confession) was the sole criterion for admissibility of material. Chapter headings are the editor's, but the words themselves—as everywhere else in the *Autobiography*—are Shaw's own, adapted from his nonfiction and nondramatic prose.

Some editorial license has been taken in matters of paragraphing and capitalization, and here and there a date or a name has been corrected where Shaw or his printer was clearly in error; however normal autobiographical inconsistencies have been retained.

Although the material comprising the *Autobiography* was written over a period of sixty years, and for a variety of audiences, and has here been utilized in lengths ranging from a single phrase to several thousand unaltered words, in no case is the rearrangement for reasons other than fuller narrative continuity. Ellipses indicate editorial cuts, and square brackets enclose the few bridging words supplied by the editor. Punctuation and spelling are Shaw's own; variations in them through the text are due to the vagaries of original publication.

Where the original texts are not accessible in print, fuller citations to the published or unpublished sources are supplied.

Preface

page 1
All autobiographies . . . contradict him. *Sixteen Self Sketches*, VIII (1949); based upon "In the Days of My Youth," in T. P. O'Connor's magazine *M.A.P.* (*Mainly About People*), 17 September 1898.

pages 1-4
People keep asking me . . . humanly possible. *Sixteen Self Sketches*, II (1949); written originally for *Shaw Gives Himself Away* in January 1939, revised in 1947.

Chapter 1

pages 5-8

"My First Biographer" was also Part I of *Sixteen Self Sketches* (1949).

Chapter 2

pages 9-11

The scene . . . to its grave! Preface to *Immaturity* (1930); written 1921.

page 11

My father . . . of a downstart. Preface to *Immaturity*.

pages 11-12

One of my grandfathers . . . his pawnbroking. *Everybody's Political What's What* (1944).

pages 12-14

This social . . . the elder branch. Preface to *Immaturity*.

page 14

I was born . . . sense of history was formed. "Provocations," *G. K.'s Weekly*, 21 March 1935, p. 8.

page 14

The fact that I . . . intelligible to them.) Review of Dixon Scott's posthumous essays, *New Republic*, 17 February 1917, p. 79.

pages 14-15

I believe Ireland . . . as we did. *Sixteen Self Sketches*, VIII.

page 15

To sit motionless . . . away from church. *London Music in 1888–89;* from a review in *The Star*, 8 November 1889.

page 15

I suffered . . . never resumed it. *Sixteen Self Sketches*, VIII.

pages 15-16

My uncles . . . prodigies of black pomp). Preface to *Immaturity*.

pages 16-17

The fact is . . . saw it performed. *Music in London*, III; from *The World*, 17 January 1894.

pages 17-19

I well remember . . . eradicate that impression. "Woman—Man in Petticoats," in *Platform and Pulpit*, ed. Dan H. Laurence (1961); originally a speech delivered on behalf of the Cecil Houses Fund, London, 20 May 1927, and first published in *New York Times Magazine*, 19 June 1927.

pages 19-20

If my father . . . house had caught fire. Preface to *Immaturity*.

pages 20-24
My mother was . . . of the lot. *Sixteen Self Sketches*, III.

pages 24-25
My parents . . . model father. "Rungs of the Ladder," *The Listener*, 20 July 1932, pp. 74–75.

page 25
Let me tell . . . comedic methods. *Sixteen Self Sketches*, IX.

pages 25-26
Then there was . . . fifteen shillings a week. *Sixteen Self Sketches*, III.

pages 26-27
When I was . . . that I would take it." "Socialism and Medicine," in *Platform and Pulpit*; originally a paper read before the Medico-Legal Society in London, 16 February 1909.

page 27
The change ruined . . . inherited his estate. *Sixteen Self Sketches*, III.

pages 27-28
I discovered . . . waste-paper basket. *Everybody's Political What's What?*

page 28
His father had . . . follow my example. *Sixteen Self Sketches*, III.

pages 28-30
How my mother . . . I was ten years old. Preface to *Immaturity*.

page 30
The first book . . . nobody else had done. *Our Theatres in the Nineties*, III; from *The Saturday Review*, 6 February 1897.

page 30
In my childhood . . . holy water occasionally. Preface to *Immaturity*.

page 30
My own nursemaid . . . diety. *Everybody's Political What's What*.

pages 30-31
But her asceticism . . . repeating it. Preface to *Immaturity*.

page 31
In my infancy . . . as a passion. *Everybody's Political What's What*.

pages 31-34
When I was . . . Catholic Church. "On Going to Church," *The Savoy*, No. 1 (January, 1896).

pages 34-35
I continued . . . my boyhood. Preface to *Immaturity*.

pages 35-36
When I was . . . empty buckets. *Our Theatres in the Nineties*, III; from *The Saturday Review*, 3 April 1897.

page 36
My father . . . of this kind. Preface to *Immaturity*.

page 36
I know how . . . the Higher Criticism. *Everybody's Political What's What.*

pages 36-38
With such a father . . . most irreverent absurdity. Preface to *Immaturity*.

page 38
Try to imagine me . . . genuine religious value. *Religious Speeches of Bernard Shaw*, ed. Warren S. Smith (1963); originally a speech, "The Ideal of Citizenship," delivered in London 11 October 1909.

pages 38-39
It would be . . . called sacred things. Preface to *Immaturity*.

page 39
I remember when . . . an elderly gentleman. *Religious Speeches;* originally "Modern Religion II," delivered in London 13 November 1919, and reprinted in the *New Commonwealth,* 2 January 1920.

pages 39-44
Yet Mark Twain . . . Trinity College, Dublin. Preface to *Immaturity*.

Chapter 3

page 45
May I . . . own schooling? *Everybody's Political What's What.*

page 45
My parents fed . . . nature of division. "Rungs of the Ladder," *Listener,* 20 July 1932.

page 45
because she kept . . . learnt at school. Preface to *London Music in 1888–89 As Heard by Corno di Bassetto* (1937).

page 45
My own . . . three halfpence. "Bernard Shaw's Works of Fiction: Reviewed by Himself," *The Novel Review,* London, February, 1892.

page 45
She tried . . . derisive humor. Preface to *London Music.*

pages 45-46
and as to . . . still wondering. "Rungs of the Ladder."

page 46
She punished me . . . be substantiated. Preface to *London Music.*

page 46
I believe . . . even at the universities. "Rungs of the Ladder."

page 46
I have no . . . in my way.   Shaw on his childhood reading in *T. P.'s Weekly*, 19 December 1902.

page 46
When I was . . . a new idea.   *London Music in 1888–89; from The Star*, 17 January 1890.

pages 46-47
The two literary . . . Cassell's Family Shakespear.   *T. P.'s Weekly*, 19 December 1902.

page 47
I pity the man . . . one in particular.   *Our Theatres in the Nineties*, II; from *The Saturday Review*, 26 September 1896.

page 47
A musician only . . . to *whistle* it.   *London Music; from The Star*, 23 March 1889.

pages 47-48
My first . . . uncle-in-law.   *Sixteen Self Sketches*, IV.

page 48
William George . . . sent to school.   Preface to *London Music*.

page 48
at what is . . . Latin and Greek.   *Sixteen Self Sketches*, IV.

page 48
if asking . . . teaching him Latin.   Preface to *London Music*.

page 48
with a pretence . . . Wesleyan ministers.   *Sixteen Self Sketches*, IV.

page 48
When the time . ... gave only their.   Preface to *Farfetched Fables* (1948–49).

page 48
numbers in the book.   *Sixteen Self Sketches*, IV.

page 48
of which I . . . in Colenso's schoolbook.   Preface to *Farfetched Fables*.

page 48
in *a, b,* and *x* . . . pence and shillings.   *Sixteen Self Sketches*, IV.

pages 48-49
Now an uninstructed . . . their enormous importance.   Preface to *Farfetched Fables*.

page 49
Only in literature . . . but Latin.   *Sixteen Self Sketches*, IV.

pages 49-50
It would be . . . utterly baffles me. *Our Theatres in the Nineties*, I; from *The Saturday Review*, 22 June 1895.

pages 50-51
My school . . . of relaxation. *Everybody's Political What's What.*

page 51
There was only . . . to Dublin. *Sixteen Self Sketches*, IV.

page 51
I must add . . . found out. *Everybody's Political What's What.*

pages 51-52
The day boys . . . as an adult. *Everybody's Political What's What.*

pages 52-54
Then came . . . myself ever since. *Sixteen Self Sketches*, IV.

pages 54-55
I remember thinking . . . for a fortnight. *The Intelligent Woman's Guide* (1928).

pages 55-56
My father's tailor . . . thefts are negligible. *Sixteen Self Sketches*, IV.

pages 56-58
Now that so many . . . such as they were. *Sixteen Self Sketches*, IV.

pages 58-60
I am no doubt . . . home by myself. *Everybody's Political What's What.*

page 60
It is evident . . . public importance is. *Everybody's Political What's What.*

pages 60-63
an unpatriotic habit . . . Stendhalian atmosphere. Preface to *Major Barbara.*

page 63
I was in school . . . had no place. *Everybody's Political What's What.*

page 63
There is in Dublin . . . I prowled. *Nine Answers* (an 1896 interview recast into a pamphlet privately printed for Jerome Kern in 1923); rewritten and abbreviated for *Sixteen Self Sketches*, VII.

page 63
Let me add . . . of the drink trade. *Sixteen Self Sketches*, VIII.

page 63
A well-known . . . and Dalkey Hill. *Nine Answers.*

pages 63-65
What was the . . . illusion and transfiguration. *Our Theatres in the Nineties*, III; from *The Saturday Review*, 26 June 1897.

page 65
I somehow knew . . . a grown-up man.   Preface to *Immaturity*.

Chapter 4

pages 67-68
There was . . . business spirit.   Preface to *Immaturity*.

pages 68-71
In a Gilbert . . . into strange hands.   *Sixteen Self Sketches*, V.

page 71
I vaguely . . . literary energy.   *Sixteen Self Sketches*, IX.

pages 71-72
I also made . . . converted me.   *Sixteen Self Sketches*, V.

page 72
I sometimes dream . . . of considerable responsibility.   *Sixteen Self Sketches*, VI.

pages 72-73
When, later . . . induced her to sell it.   *Sixteen Self Sketches*, VI.

pages 73-74
Forty years after . . . happened every day.   Introduction to *Trade Unionism for Clerks* (n.d.).

pages 74-76
I did not . . . fare for the journey.   Preface to *Immaturity*.

Chapter 5

page 77
I was driven . . . without any wanting.   *Nine Answers*.

page 77
At 20 . . . ripe for me.   *Nine Answers*.

page 77
Statement on "my first appearance in print,"   Intended for an unknown publication, *ca.* late 1940s; from typescript copy of shorthand text at the University of Texas.

pages 77-78
One evening . . . such a blasphemy.   Preface to *Back to Methuselah* (1921).

page 78
The gentleman who . . . eat those children.   *Religious Speeches*; originally "The New Theology," delivered in London 16 May 1907.

pages 78-79
This exquisite confusion . . . supernatural deity.   Preface to *Back to Methuselah*.

page 79
I said . . . out of my pocket. *Religious Speeches;* originally "Modern Religion II."

page 79
The effect . . . were no sceptics. Preface to *Back to Methuselah.*

page 79
One of the . . . in my life. "The New Theology."

page 79
Our host . . . was still calm. Preface to *Back to Methuselah.*

pages 79-81
In those days . . . could get over that. Preface to *Back to Methuselah.*

page 81
For the first . . . and with them. Preface to *Immaturity.*

page 81
I wrote . . . how to criticize. "How to Become a Musical Critic," *Scottish Musical Monthly,* December 1894; reprinted in *How to Become a Musical Critic,* ed. Dan H. Laurence (1961).

pages 81-82
Even now . . . at mine. Preface to *Immaturity.*

page 82
I began . . . sheets of notepaper. *Sixteen Self Sketches,* IX.

page 82
I had one . . . in nine years. *Nine Answers.*

pages 82-38
Then my cousin . . . renewal of it. Preface to *Immaturity.*

pages 83-87
The telephone episode . . . first novel of mine. Preface to *Immaturity.*

pages 87-88
There is nothing . . . ending the book. "Bernard Shaw's Works of Fiction: Reviewed by Himself," *The Novel Review,* London, February 1892.

pages 88-92
Of course . . . comfortable circumstances. Preface to *The Irrational Knot* (1905).

pages 92-93
I became . . . is capable. *Nine Answers.*

pages 93-96
Another reminiscence . . . writer aged 24. Preface to *The Irrational Knot.*

pages 96-97
It is interesting . . . I have not traced. "66 Years Later," typescript preface

added March-April 1946 to the manuscript of *The Irrational Knot,* on presentation to the National Library of Ireland.

page 97
I can recall . . . novel breaks off. Preface to the first American edition of *Love Among the Artists* (1900).

page 97
"Love Among . . . to amuse myself. *The Novel Review.*

pages 97-98
An intimate acquaintance . . . as an outsider. "64 Years Later," typescript preface added March-April 1946 to the manuscript of *Cashel Byron's Profession,* on presentation to the National Library of Ireland.

pages 98-102
I never think . . . to finish it. Preface to *Cashel Byron's Profession* (1901).

pages 102-103
"Cashel Byron's . . . the drawing-room. *The Novel Review.*

pages 103-104
On a previous . . . is finely polyglot)." Preface to *Cashel Byron's Profession.*

page 104
But long before . . . dependent on fiction. *The Novel Review.*

pages 104-105
One day . . . to my imagination. Preface to *Immaturity.*

pages 105-106
I remember once . . . demoralized by it. "Socialism for Millionaires," *Contemporary Review*, London, February 1896.

pages 106-108
Throughout the eighties . . . of his work. Preface to *The Dark Lady of the Sonnets* (1910).

page 108
[My last] novel . . . Too bad. "63 Years Later," typescript preface added March-April 1946 to the manuscript of *An Unsocial Socialist,* on presentation to the National Library of Ireland.

pages 108-109
Eventually the two . . . the year 1891. *The Novel Review.*

page 109
Of [*An Unfinished* . . . another thought. "61 Years Later" [Shaw's error—it was actually 58 years later], typescript preface added March-April 1946 to the manuscript of *An Unfinished Novel,* on presentation to the National Library of Ireland; published in *An Unfinished Novel,* ed. Stanley Weintraub (1958).

pages 109-110
Thus, after five . . . pay my way. Preface to *Immaturity.*

Chapter 6

pages 111-113
In the winter . . . fight in Gethesmane. *Sixteen Self Sketches*, X.

page 113
I was a . . . on the spot. "Notes by George Bernard Shaw," published as Appendix I to *Thomas J. Wise in the Original Cloth*, by Wilfred Partington (1946). Shaw's notes are dated 16 July 1940.

page 113
I joined . . . to economics. *Sixteen Self Sketches*, X.

pages 113-115
I knew he . . . of the world. "George Bernard Shaw's Tribute to the Work of Henry George," *The Single Tax Review*, IV (15 April 1905). Huntington Library.

page 115
I read his . . . always extemporized. *Sixteen Self Sketches*, X.

pages 115-116
Once you are . . . not the drunken sort. Cut from the version of "Who I Am and What I Think" between the appearance of *Shaw Gives Himself Away* and *Sixteen Self Sketches*. The original essay was an interview in Frank Harris's magazine *The Candid Friend*, 11 and 18 May 1901. LaFayette Butler Collection.

pages 116-117
This went on . . . a public speaker. *Sixteen Self Sketches*, XIV.

page 117
I suppose . . . very decisive way. "The Ideal of Citizenship," an address at the City Temple, London, 11 October 1909; published as an appendix to the "popular edition" of the Rev. R. J. Campbell's *The New Theology* (1909) and reprinted in *The Religious Speeches of Bernard Shaw* and *Platform and Pulpit*.

pages 117-121
I never took . . . eightyfifth year. *Sixteen Self Sketches*, XIV.

pages 121-123
A few weeks . . . visits to them. *Sixteen Self Sketches*, X.

page 123
I remember basking . . . meaning *me*. Preface to Stephen Winsten's *Salt and His Circle* (1951).

page 123
Intimate in . . . bleeding feet. *Sixteen Self Sketches*, XI.

pages 123-125
I was always . . . written a lot. Preface to *Salt and His Circle*.

page 125
I met him . . . as Shakespear puts it. "Notes" to *Thomas J. Wise in the Original Cloth.*

pages 125-126
As to Meredith . . . brightly blue eyed. Preface to *Salt and His Circle.*

page 126
Like Morris . . . cottage Walden. Preface to *Salt and His Circle.*

page 126
In this circle . . . Whitman and Thoreau. *Sixteen Self Sketches,* XI.

pages 126-128
I first met . . . in those days. "Some Impressions," a preface to *Sydney Oliver: Letters & Selected Writings* (1948).

pages 128-129
Olivier . . . in its management. *Sixteen Self Sketches,* XI.

pages 129-130
If any . . . organizations. *The Fabian Society. What It Has Done and How It Has Done It* (1892), a paper read at a conference of the London and provincial Fabian Societies on 6 February 1892 and afterwards printed as Tract No. 41; reprinted in *Essays in Fabian Socialism* (1932).

pages 130-131
When Fabianism was . . . of superior persons. "Sixty Years of Fabianism," postscript to Jubilee Edition of *Fabian Essays* (1948).

pages 131-137
Differences . . . lectures or so. The Fabian Society. *What It Has Done . . .* (1892).

pages 137-140
Now at this time . . . like to review. "Mrs. Besant as a Fabian Socialist," *The Theosophist,* October 1917; afterwards in *Dr. Annie Besant. Fifty Years in Public Work* (1924), as "Mrs. Besant's Passage through Fabian Socialism."

pages 140-142
What happened . . . was no use. "Annie Besant and the 'Secret Doctrine,'" corrected galley proof intended for *The Freethinker;* University of Texas Library.

page 142
I played . . . real perspective. "Mrs. Besant as a Fabian Socialist."

page 142
That was . . . did not matter. "Annie Besant and the 'Secret Doctrine.'"

pages 142-143
This, as far . . . Annie Besant. "Mrs. Besant as a Fabian Socialist."

Chapter 7

pages 145-146

At the beginning . . . do not remember. "Old Bachelor Butler," written 23 February 1950 for *The Observer* (London) and quoted from Shaw's original typescript at the University of Texas; published version also (as "Butler When I Was a Nobody") in *Saturday Review of Literature* (New York), 29 April 1950.

page 146

One London group . . . absurd little group. Holograph page, pencil, undated and untitled, but in Shaw's hand; University of Texas Library.

pages 147-148

Our best lecturers . . . a Fabian boom. *The Fabian Society. What It Has Done . . . .*

pages 148-149

The first . . . a tactician. "Sixty Years of Fabian Socialism."

page 149

The distinctive mark . . . go our way. "The Fabian Society. Forty Years Later," in *Essays in Fabian Socialism.*

page 149

To suppose that . . . Trafalgar Square. "William Morris," in *The Daily Chronicle* (London), 20 April 1899; reprinted in *Pen Portraits and Reviews* (1931).

page 149-150

There was . . . police prohibited it. "Bloody Sunday in Trafalgar Square," Shaw's typed (with holograph changes) addition to a chapter in Hesketh Pearson's biography *G.B.S.* (1942), 1 p. *ca.* 1940; somewhat altered from this text by Pearson for the published version. University of Texas.

page 150

The papers which . . . in the matter. *The Fabian Society. What It Has Done . . . .*

page 150

Salt went with . . . without moving off. Preface to *Salt and His Circle.*

pages 150-151

The heroes . . . much heard of. *The Fabian Society. What It Has Done . . . .*

pages 151-152

Morris joined one . . . plunge into politics. "William Morris," *The Daily Chronicle.*

pages 152-155

I once urged . . . Morris's did. "William Morris as Actor and Dramatist," *The Saturday Review,* 10 October 1896; reprinted in *Our Theatres in the Nineties,* II (1932).

pages 155-162

It was as . . . a matter of indifference. *William Morris As I Knew Him* (1936).

page 162

I feel nothing . . . not by his. "William Morris as Actor and Dramatist."

Chapter 8

page 163

There are matters . . . or four lines. *Shaw Gives Himself Away;* from Shaw's personal copy in the Butler Collection.

pages 163-164

Unlike the . . . a love affair. Review in *The World*, 1 November 1893; reprinted in *Music in London*, III.

page 164

As to personal . . . I was 29. Shaw to Frank Harris, 18 September 1930, in a letter intended for—and published in—*Bernard Shaw*, by Frank Harris (1931).

page 164

At last a widow lady. "Don Giovanni Explains" (dated 1 August 1887 but not published until 1932 in the Limited Collected Edition), *The Black Girl in Search of God and Some Lesser Tales*, Standard Edition (1934), p. 177.

page 164

one of my mother's pupils. Shaw to Frank Harris, 18 September 1930.

pages 164-165

at whose house . . . of fierce jealousies. "Don Giovanni Explains."

page 165

If you want . . . that of Charteris. Shaw to Frank Harris, 18 September 1930.

pages 165-166

I made the . . . she was dead. "An Explanatory Word from Shaw," introduction to *Florence Farr, Bernard Shaw, W. B. Yeats*, ed. Clifford Bax (1942).

pages 166-169

Among the . . . me too. *William Morris As I Knew Him.*

pages 169-170

You can learn . . . day dreams about women. Shaw to Harris, 24 June 1930, in a letter intended for—and published in—Harris's *Bernard Shaw;* later revised freely by Shaw for *Sixteen Self Sketches*, XVI.

page 170

Some day I . . . of any delicacy. "Who I Am, and What I Think," reprinted in *Sixteen Self Sketches*, IX.

pages 170-171

I lived . . . kindliest memories. Shaw to Harris, 24 June 1930, as revised for *Sixteen Self Sketches*, XVI.

Chapter 9

page 173

Behold me, then . . . acceptance or toleration. *Sixteen Self Sketches,* VII.

page 173

My ambition . . . without knowing how. Preface to *London Music.*

page 173

It was this . . . out of literature. *Sixteen Self Sketches,* XII.

pages 173-174

In 1885 . . . the first year. *Sixteen Self Sketches,* VII.

page 174

When . . . no such mark. *Sixteen Self Sketches,* XII.

page 174

I was capable . . . to be absolute. "Acting, by One Who Does Not Believe in It," a paper read to the Church and Stage Guild, London, 5 February 1889, in *Platform and Pulpit.*

pages 174-175

When I was . . . in the conflict. Musical review in *The World,* 6 July 1892; reprinted in *Music in London,* II.

page 175

My own most . . . talk about it. "How Free is the Press?," *The Nation,* 9 February 1918; reprinted in *Pen Portraits.*

pages 176-179

In my sixteenth . . . were not invited. *Everybody's Political What's What?*

pages 179-181

Those lazy spectators . . . and devotion alone. "De Mortuis," *The Saturday Review,* 4 July 1896; reprinted *Our Theatres in the Nineties,* II.

pages 181-182

These years . . . is easily duped. *Sixteen Self Sketches,* VII.

page 182

So, as reviewer . . . in my education. Preface to *London Music.*

pages 182-183

Some years ago . . . industrial capital! "The Barrel-Organ Question," London *Morning Leader,* 27 November 1893.

page 183

From my earliest . . . Italian opera. Preface to *London Music. Music.*

page 183

The wildest pirates . . . great art factory. Musical review in *The World,* 26 October 1892; reprinted in *London Music,* II.

pages 183-184

When I was . . . delight were unbounded. Preface to *Heartbreak House* (1919).

Sources

page 184
I shall have . . . can be carried. Preface to *London Music*.

pages 184-185
I myself was . . . fact in nature. "Parents and Children," the preface to *Misalliance* (1910).

pages 185-186
She had been . . . purity of tone. Preface to *London Music*.

pages 186-187
In order to . . . and drawing rooms. *Sixteen Self Sketches*, VIII.

pages 187-189
In the next . . . music going on. Preface to *London Music*.

page 189
Great as is . . . and far above. *Sixteen Self Sketches*, XII.

pages 189-192
The *ménage* . . . note of music. Preface to *London Music*.

page 192
My father did . . . "a great man." Shaw to T. D. O'Bolger, 7 August 1919, as silently revised for publication in *Sixteen Self Sketches*, XIV ("Biographers' Blunders Corrected").

pages 192-197
Lee's end was . . . made it myself. Preface to *London Music*.

page 197
I learnt my . . . I opened. *How to Become a Musical Critic*.

page 197
the overture to . . . notes or not. Preface to *London Music*.

pages 197-198
It took ten . . . fearfully well aimed). *How to Become a Musical Critic*.

pages 198-199
There were plenty . . . creation of Bassetto. Preface to *London Music*.

page 199
In 1888 . . . H. W. Massingham. Preface to *London Music*.

pages 199-200
Sometime in the . . . to become confederates. "H. W. Massingham," in *H. W. M.* (1925), a collection of memoirs of, and essays by, Massingham.

pages 200-201
Tay Pay survived . . . guineas a week. Preface to *London Music*.

page 201
My proposal . . . to edit. *How to Become a Musical Critic*.

pages 201-202
I was strong . . . basset horn sparkle. Preface to *London Music*.

Chapter 10

pages 203-204

On Monday . . . without musical honors. Musical review in *The Star*, 21 February 1889; reprinted in *London Music*.

pages 204-206

Tuesday, when . . . ninepenny experiment. Musical review in *The Star*, 1 March 1889; reprinted in *London Music*.

page 206

Wednesday I was . . . the golden years. Musical review in *The World*, 15 June 1892; reprinted in *Music in London*, II.

pages 206-207

I remember once . . . and back again. Musical review in *The Star*, 6 December 1889; reprinted in *London Music*.

pages 207-209

The other evening . . . swallow the pill. Musical review in *The World*, 24 January 1894; reprinted in *Music in London*, III.

pages 209-210

When I arrived . . . surprised at it. Musical review in *The Star*, 21 February 1890; reprinted in *London Music*.

pages 210-211

During one of . . . an Aldgate tram. Musical review in *The Star*, 13 May 1889; reprinted in *London Music*.

page 211

On Friday evening . . . into Clapham. Musical review in *The Star*, 3 March 1890; reprinted in *How to Become a Musical Critic*.

pages 211-213

On cold Saturday afternoons . . . own opinion too. "Sir George Grove," *The Saturday Review*, 14 November 1896; reprinted in *Pen Portraits and Reviews*.

pages 213-216

Saturday evening . . . in—Malediction! Musical review in *The Star*, 13 September 1889; reprinted in *Music in London*.

pages 216-217

Obviously, I have . . . than satisfied. Musical review in *The Pall Mall Budget*, 15 November 1894; reprinted in *London Music*.

pages 217-218

The magic of . . . his swan song. "Postscript. 1937" to *London Music*.

page 218

"*We are losing . . . words.*"—*T.P.* Announcement by editor T. P. O'Connor prefacing Corno di Bassetto's column in *The Star*, 16 May 1889; quoted by Shaw in *London Music*.

pages 218-219
For two years . . . whatever about music. Preface to *London Music*.

page 219
The critic whose . . . all their merit. *How to Become a Musical Critic*.

page 219
In 1890 . . . music every week. *Sixteen Self Sketches*, VII.

page 219
And the success . . . had in chemistry. *How to Become a Musical Critic*.

pages 219-221
Bassetto's stuff . . . worth reading now. Preface to *London Music*.

page 221
"Corno di Bassetto . . . hands with weapons. *Nine Answers*.

page 221
I . . . a famous novelist. *Music in London*, postscript.

page 221
of Green Carnation fame. *Nine Answers*.

page 221
I never again . . . of music. *Music in London*, postscript.

Chapter 11

pages 223-225
Up to a . . . its natural sweetness. "On Pleasure Bent," *The Saturday Review*, 20 November 1897; reprinted in *Our Theatres in the Nineties*, III.

pages 225-227
In my boyhood . . . after Offenbach. From the Bristol *Evening Post*, 3 December 1946; reprinted in *The Matter with Ireland*, ed. Dan H. Laurence and David H. Greene (1962).

pages 227-235
Conceive me then . . . and abiding love. Preface to *Ellen Terry and Bernard Shaw. A Correspondence* (1932).

page 235
Years ago . . . of a city. "A Doll's House Again," *The Saturday Review*, 15 May 1897; reprinted in *Our Theatres*, III.

pages 235-236
In the spring . . . could be found. Preface to the first edition of *The Quintessence of Ibsenism* (1891).

pages 236-237
As I read . . . a second edition. Preface to the second edition of *The Quintessence of Ibsenism* (1913).

pages 237-240
I was the . . . her first entry. "Theatres and Reviews Then and Now," reprinted in *Shaw on Theatre*, ed. E. J. West (1958).

pages 240-242
In justice to . . . gave deadly offense. "The Author's Apology" to *Dramatic Opinions and Essays*, ed. James Huneker (1906); reprinted by Shaw as preface to *Our Theatres in the Nineties*, I (1931).

page 242
If my head . . . less amusing. "Postscript, 1931" to "The Author's Apology."

pages 242-243
Let me hasten . . . play construction! Musical review in *The Star*, 7 March 1890; reprinted in *London Music*.

page 243
There was no injury . . . damned Socialist." "Shaw Tells Critics They're Never Good," *New York Times*, 12 October 1929, quoting Shaw's speech as guest of honor at the London Critics Circle Annual Luncheon the previous day; reprinted in *Shaw on Theatre*.

pages 243-244
When I felt . . . in those days. *Sixteen Self Sketches*, VII.

page 244
Frank Harris . . . of his fall. Preface to *The Dark Lady of the Sonnets* (1910).

pages 244-246
When [Harris] was editor . . . The end was inevitable. "Postscript by the Subject of this Memoir," to *Bernard Shaw* by Frank Harris (1931).

page 247
I myself was . . . him the truth. Preface to *The Dark Lady of the Sonnets*.

page 247
something like this . . . his real friends. "Oscar Wilde," first a letter authorized for publication in Frank Harris's *Oscar Wilde* (1918); afterwards altered for republication in *Pen Portraits and Reviews* (the version used here).

page 247
I am sure . . . and faithful servant. "Oscar Wilde."

pages 247-253
Lady Wilde was . . . always a priest. "Oscar Wilde."

Chapter 12

pages 255-258
There is an . . . Widowers' Houses! "Mainly about Myself," preface to *Plays Unpleasant* (1898).

page 258
At the end . . . Act of Parliament. "Memories of Early Years," in *Ensor Walters and the London He Loves*, by E. W. Walters (1937). G.B.S.'s preface is dated 17 February 1937.

page 258

When I was . . . could be done. B.B.C. broadcast, 9 October 1946, accepting the Honorary Freedom of the Borough of St. Pancras. Past ninety, he felt too feeble for a public ceremony, and made his acknowledgment by radio.

pages 258-259

When I . . . as an abomination. "Woman—Man in Petticoats" (1927).

pages 259-260

Into this stagnant . . . one another's orbit. "Memories of Early Years."

pages 260-263

I never read . . . practically excludes collaboration. "How William Archer Impressed Bernard Shaw," first a preface to Archer's *Three Plays* (1927); afterwards reprinted in *Pen Portraits*.

pages 263-267

The early history . . . not for ever. Preface to *Widowers' Houses* (1893).

page 267

Ibsen . . . as a playwright. Preface to *Plays Unpleasant*.

pages 267-268

The horrible artificiality . . . the Victorian play. "An Aside," preface to Lillah McCarthy's *Myself and My Friends* (1933).

page 268

Take Widowers' Houses . . . melodrama of tomorrow. "Daly Undaunted," *The Saturday Review*, 18 July 1896; reprinted in *Our Theatres*, II.

page 268

My plays are . . . questionable activities. *Sixteen Self Sketches*, XIV.

page 268

The first performance . . . egotistic fighting style. Preface to *Plays Unpleasant*.

page 268

Widowers' Houses . . . the preface & appendices. *Nine Answers*.

pages 268-276

The following extracts . . . of Widowers' Houses. Preface to *Widowers' Houses*, Appendix II.

Chapter 13

page 277

It was the . . . to the dust-bin. "Introductory" to J. T. Grein's *The World of the Theatre: Impression and Memoirs, March 1920–21* (1921); reprinted in *Shaw on Theatre*.

pages 277-278

I had not . . . the Censorship. Preface to *Plays Unpleasant*.

pages 278-279

The terror of . . . deserved in return. The Author's Apology to *Mrs. Warren's Profession* (1902).

pages 279-281
I was myself . . . cool my porridge. *Everybody's Political What's What.*

page 281
I could not . . . no Lord Chamberlain. Preface (1902) to *Mrs. Warren's Profession.*

pages 281-282
I turned my . . . nine matinées). Preface to *Plays Pleasant* (1898).

page 282
The others . . . for his seat. *Nine Answers.*

pages 282-284
In the autumn . . . of its audiences. Preface to *Plays Pleasant.*

page 284
Behind the scenes . . . and actors after. "An Aside" to *Myself and My Friends.*

page 284
In an idle . . . Man of Destiny. Preface to *Plays Pleasant.*

page 284
a one act . . . the chief figure. *Nine Answers.*

page 285
hardly more than . . . indeed got it. Preface to *Plays Pleasant.*

page 285
When the play . . . the chapter himself. Preface written for Augustin Hamon's French translation of *You Never Can Tell* (January, 1913); reproduced from Shaw's typescript at the University of Texas.

pages 285-287
The production of . . . the real one. "A Dramatic Realist to His Critics," *The New Review*, XI, July 1894; reprinted in *Shaw on Theatre*, and other collections.

page 287
I am quite . . . for his revolver. Preface to *Plays Pleasant.*

pages 287-288
What struck my . . . tell lies about. "A Dramatic Realist to His Critics."

pages 288-289
Historical facts are . . . historical conscience goes. "Ten Minutes with Mr. Bernard Shaw," an interview in *To-Day*, London, 28 April 1894.

pages 289-290
When many of . . . up the curtain. Preface to *Plays Pleasant.*

Appendix

pages 291-295
Chapter XVI of *The Haymarket Theatre*, by Cyril Maude (1903).

INDEX